DEVELOPMENTS IN ASIA

BEITRÄGE ZUR SÜDASIENFORSCHUNG
SÜDASIEN-INSTITUT
UNIVERSITÄT HEIDELBERG

BAND 112

STEINER VERLAG WIESBADEN GMBH
STUTTGART
1987

DEVELOPMENTS IN ASIA:

ECONOMIC, POLITICAL AND CULTURAL ASPECTS

edited by

CHRISTINE EFFENBERG

STEINER VERLAG WIESBADEN GMBH
STUTTGART
1987

CIP-Kurztitelaufnahme der Deutschen Bibliothek

Developments in Asia: economic, political and cultural aspects / Christine Effenberg. - Stuttgart: Steiner-Verlag-Wiesbaden-GmbH, 1987
(Beiträge zur Südasienforschung; Bd. 112)
ISBN 3-515-05049-3

NE: Effenberg, Christine (Hrsg.); GT

 Herstellung: Strauss Offsetdruck GmbH, 6945 Hirschberg 2.
Printed in Germany

Contents

Contents

Contents

P r e f a c e

All contributions of this book are written by thirteen young scholars of the South Asia Institute, University of Heidelberg/FRG. With this collection of contributions the so-called "new generation" of the above mentioned institute intends to provide a survey of their current research interests. Coming from five disciplines, economics, history, political science, anthropology and geography, they present different topics of economic, political and cultural developments in Asia to the reader interested in. The economic contributions deal with models of regional south-south cooperation and indicators of economic development. The historical contributions point out the problem of minorities as well as the problem of "sub-nationalism" in a modern national state like India. The political science contribution inform about the Darul-Islam-Movement and the trade-union movement in Indonesia. The remaining contributions contain special regional case studies of Nepal, Sri Lanka and the Maldives, a comparative study of Swat in Pakistan and Kandy in Sri Lanka and a critical review of different anthropological approaches to the tribe-caste question.

I am thankful to Prof. Dietmar Rothermund, South Asia Institute, Department of History, Prof. Bruno Knall, South Asia Insitute, Department of Economics and Dr. Dieter Halcour, executive secretary of the South Asia Institute, for their support. Thanks also to Mr. Edgar Fenzlein for the computer lay-out.

June 1987, Christine Effenberg

Development in Asia? An Empirical Approach [1a]

by Martin Kaiser

1. Introduction

The problem of grouping or even forming a hierarchy of a number of countries is a well-known, unpopular, but nevertheless a necessary evil. For example, as far as cooperation in the field of development policy is concerned, it is of major importance to the developing countries, which stage of development they are assigned to, since this is the factor that determines the credit conditions and special aid programmes. Additionally, for a continuous assessment of the national and international development policy it is imperative to reveal the success and the failures of the development path applied. The central point during the first period of independent development policy in the developing countries, being the growth of GNP, has changed, due to the knowledge that growth alone is not the measure of all things. Hence, it is indispensable for measuring development or determining the degree of development to employ a more sensitive set of indicators that the indicator GNP per capita represents, which was used and still is used, for example by the World Bank.

If development is understood not only in economic terms, but also in terms of political, cultural and social change, a whole network of relations results, which can hardly be surveyed. An empirical analysis, however, can only cover parts of the whole development process. In addition, there is often a lack of indicators which can be compared on a quantitative and on international level, and are able to satisfy scientific standards. Above all, this is the case with cultural aspects of development, since these cover more changes in its contents than those which can be quantitatively measured. Ultimately, this is also true for aspects that are often (and also in this study) analysed in detail, i.e. economic and social aspects. In a quantitative analysis of the economic development, it is, for example, impossible to determine the "foreign hand" or the "degree of exploitation". The more one tries to advance into the field of social or political development, the more apparent the lack of comparable data becomes.

The attempt made in this study, to measure the economic and social development of Asian countries, certainly cannot be free from the above-mentioned shortcomings. Nevertheless, the set for measuring development will not only cover economic basic data, but also data of other criteria. Moreover, the classification and grouping of the countries will make possible a comparison that is of importance to the evaluation of development

2. Measuring the Physical Quality of Life

Of all the different attempts to measure development separate from economic indicators the most attention on international level was given to the Physical Quality of Life Index (PQLI), presented by the Overseas Council in 1977. In its modified form [1] it comprises three indicators:

- life expectancy at age one
- infant mortality rate
- adult literacy rate.

According to Morris, these indicators have more advantages than other indicators. In addition to general prerequisites, for example that of being available and comparable, these indicators measure outputs, which represent the results of a process, and not the inputs. The aim of such a process is set up by any form of society. Life expectancy and infant mortality rate are generally considered to be valid indicators for various components of the level of living. They reflect different aspects of health, nutrition, income, and conditions of the environment. The adult literacy rate is seen, for example, as an indicator for the people`s participation in economic and social development.

In order to aggregate the various indicators to a total index, they first have to be standardized. The empirical values of each country are transformed to the interval { 0,100 }, with the highest value for the most favourable development. Hence, the country with the highest value gets 100 points, the one with the lowest value 0 points. If high values of the original indicator (X) represent positive results (life expectancy, adult literacy rate), the formula of transformation reads as follows:

$$x_{Trans} = \frac{(x_i - x_{min})}{(x_{max} - x_{min})} * 100$$

If the indicators are to be minimized (infant mortality rate), the corresponding formula is applied:

$$x_{Trans} = \frac{(x_i - x_{max})}{(x_{min} - x_{max})} * 100$$

The values (XTrans) obtained by this process, are put together to the PQLI of a country without weight as simple arithmetic mean.

The PQLI is used as a standard of comparison for a country`s level of development. Measuring the difference of the PQLI between two points of time, the development success can be illustrated. The so-called Disparity Reduction Rate (DRR) is determined by a process similar to that of the annual average growth rate, given indicators that increase unlimitedly. Considering the maximal value of 100, the formula reads as follows:

$$DRR_t^{t+n} = -100 \left\{ \left[\frac{100 - PQLI_{t+n}}{100 - PQLI_t} \right]^{\frac{1}{n}} - 1 \right\}$$

Most problems arise at the stage of evaluating development, Using the DRR, an increase from 50 to 55 is equivalent to that from 90 to 91. Using a single annual average growth rate, an increase

Diagram 1: Physical Quality of Life Index

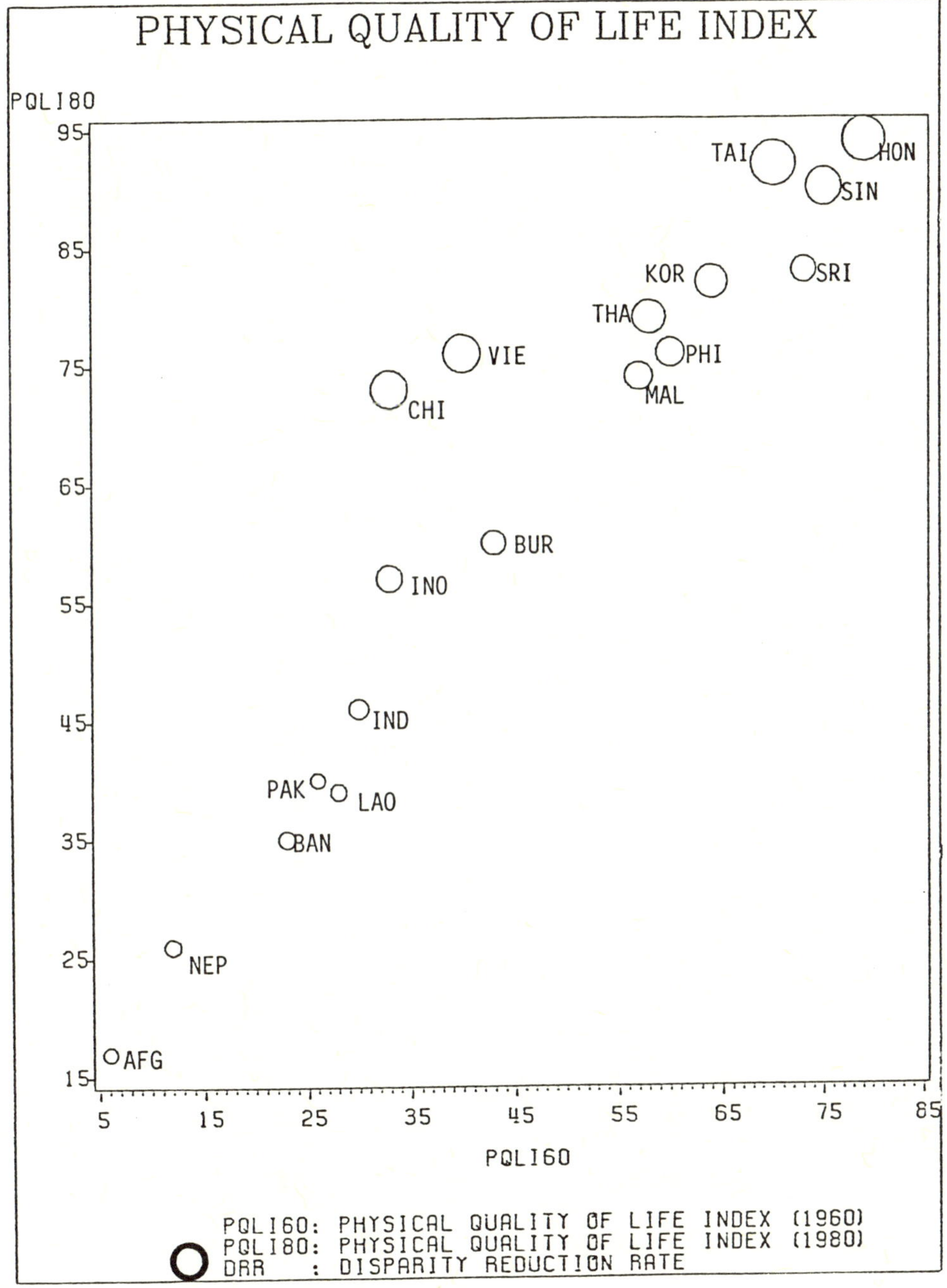

from 50 to 55 would correspond to that from 90 to 99, although apparently more progress becomes the more difficult the closer one gets to the saturation-point.

The analysis made for the PQLI of the Asian countries is illustrated by diagram 1. On the axes the PQLI for the years 1960 and 1980 are indicated, the DRR is illustrated by the size of the point in the system of co-ordinates.

Given the available data the following 18 countries were taken into consideration in the analysis:

(1) Afghanistan (AFG)

(2) Bangladesh (BAN)

(3) Burma (BUR)

(4) China (CHI)

(5) Hong Kong (HON)

(6) India (IND)

(7) Indonesia (INO)

(8) Korea, Rep. (KOR)

(9) Laos (LAO)

(10) Malaysia (MAL)

(11) Nepal (NEP)

(12) Pakistan (PAK)

(13) Philipines (PHI)

(14) Singapore (SIN)

(15) Sri Lanka (SRI)

(16) Taiwan (TAI)

(17) Thailand (THA)

(18) Viet Nam (Vie)

In general, it can be said that in every country the physical quality of life changed positively during the period under consideration. This is important in so far as exactly the indicators represented in the PQLI also reflect the situation of the poor in a society and the fringe groups. Moreover, the success, being decisive for statistics, can be obtained most easily in this sector. However, in many countries the change of the quality of life does not take place by far to the desired extent. Many of those countries with a relatively low index in 1960 (< 35) still have a low PQLI in 1980, generally below 45.[2] What does surprise in this group is the situation of Indonesia and especially China, which have reached a DRR above the average. In the medium group Burma, Malaysia, the Philippines, Thailand, and Sri Lanka have succeeded in improving their PQLI, but not to a remarkable extent. What is astonishing, however, is the DRR of Korea and, above all, that of Viet Nam.[3] Measured in terms of the DRR the newly industrializing countries Taiwan, Hong Kong, and Singapore have reached the best results.

Using the PQLI as an indicator for the fulfillment of basic needs, the statement that economic growth and fulfillment of basic needs do not take place parallely, seems to be questionable. Each of the so-called least developed countries (LLDC) is ranging at the lower end of the PQLI-scale, on the other hand, every Asian new industrializing country is ranging at the upper part of the scale. The above-average improvement of Indonesia, China, Viet Nam, Thailand, and Korea also go hand in hand with a marked increase in economic power.

In addition, it has to be seen that - except Taiwan and Viet Nam - every country has maintained its position on the scale or only changed by one position. In the case of Taiwan and Viet Nam a change of two positions took place.

Measured in terms of the PQLI,[4] there was some kind of development in Asia. All countries participated in this development of quality of life. The economically weak countries, which are also classified as LLDC as a result of other indicators, succeeded less in developing than those Asian developing countries that are classified as more powerful in economic terms. Sri Lanka, being classified as highly developed in terms of quality of life and having ranged in 1960 (with a PQLI of 73) just behind Singapore and before Taiwan, could further increase its social development during the last twenty years (although not to the same extent) and is still ranging among the countries on the top.

3. Classification by mathematical-statistical methods

3.1 The Choice of Indicators

The World Bank`s simple methods of classification or the slightly more differenciated methods of the United Nations [5] and the PQLI show marked differences, above all in their choice of indicators. The pool of indicators to choose from is large. The UN Research Institute for Social Development (UNRISD) [6] processes in its data bank approximately 100 indicators, and the list of the UN Statistical Office is even longer. In its World Development Report of 1985, the World Bank named around 80 indicators. Common source of these list are always the more or less useful lists of the various countries, with all their errors and manipulation. This factor of uncertainty can, however, be minimized by including as much opposing indicators as possible. By doing so in an analysis of the level of development, it becomes a must to reduce the great number of indicators to one dimension or on factor, taking into consideration that the information represented by every single indicator is not lost.

The methods of classification that are employed in this study require a complete data-set, i.e. there must not be any missing values. This restriction reduces the number of possible indicators to a small set. After having used various methods of selection, the final set now comprises twelve indicators, with those having an (*) which include values for 1970 and 1980.

A) Social indicators

LIFEXP * = Life expectancy at birth, in years

INFMOR * = Infant mortality per 1000 live births

CACCAP * = Per capita Calorie Supply in calories

SAFWAT * = Access to safe water in % of households

LITRAT * = Adult literacy rate in %

MEDRAT * = Physicians per 1000 inhabitants

B) Economic indicators

GDPCAP * = Per capita gross national product in US-Dollar

INVRAT = Investment rate in % three year average

MERGOO * = Share of manufactured goods in GDP in %

ENERGY * = Production of electricity per capita in kwh

EXPRAT = Export rate (Export/GNP)

DEPGDP = Official debt/GDP

When choosing the indicators, two things become apparent. First, there is a relation between certain indicators, something which may be helpful rather than being obstructive, since the different components of the level of living also influence each other.[7] Secondly, the indicators are expressed by different units, such as years, calories, percent, inhabitants, dollars, or kilowatt. Hence, the values will be standardized on a mean of 0 and a unit variance. A weighting was not carried out, since this could be done only subjectively and would not contain considerably more information.

3.2 The Cluster Analysis

The cluster analysis is based on the idea of forming significant groups out of a multitude of observations of different objects. In this study, the cluster analysis will be used to compare the various indicators that represent a country`s socio-economic development on a national and international level. Hence, differences (distances) and similarities will be measured. Since all countries will first be analysed on national level and then put together step by step according to their similarities, agglomerative hierarchical algorithms, such as the centroid method, the average linkage or WARD`s method [8] seems to be most appropriate. The result of forming groups agglomeratively can be illustrated graphically by a hierarchical tree or dendregram.

The three methods mentioned above are usually part of the statistics software packages. In this study WARD`s method will be used. [9]

First step of WARD`s method is the definition in which case two clusters are more similar than two others. For this purpose, the centroid, a fictitious object in the centre of the cluster is determined.[10] In a second step the degree of distance is determined. "In Ward`s method the distance between two clusters is the sum of squares between the two clusters added up over all the variables. At each generation, the within-cluster sum of squares is minimized over all partitions (an exhaustive set of disjoint clusters) obtainable by merging two clusters from the previous generation." [11]

The results of the cluster analysis made with nine key-indicators for 14 Asian countries, are illustrated by diagrams 2 and 3. Both the analysis for 1970 and for 1980 show a clear distinction between two groups. On the one hand there are those countries that can be classified as more developed (A), [12] and on the other hand those countries [13] that have to be classified as less developed (B). [14] In addition, group B is already formed at a level of K=5 (1970) and K=4 (1980), whereas in group A (1970) Hong Kong and Singapore act as outsiders, China and Korea form a "medium group", and the Philipines, Malaysia, Sri Lanka, and Thailand form the "lower basis". In 1980 almost the same situation occurs, only Malaysia does reach the "medium group". Hong Kong and Singapore remain outsiders, and the "lower basis" is now represented by the Philipines, Sri Lanka, and Thailand.

If one tries to classify the Asian countries according to different levels of development, it becomes clear that the groups have been stable during the last decade, and that - except Malaysia - no country has changed its group.

Calling into mind the introductory remarks about the importance of membership to a group, further consideration about the credit granting policy of the Asian Development Bank seems to be appropriate. The ADB distributes so-called loans with 100% grant element and soft credits via its Asian Development Fund. Some of its members are not eligible to these grants or soft credits, some of

Diagram 2: Cluster Analysis, WARD 1970

```
WARD'S MINIMUM VARIANCE CLUSTER ANALYSIS

                                        COUNTRY

        I   A   N   B   I   P   H   S   C   K   P   M   S   T
        N   F   E   A   N   A   O   I   H   O   H   A   R   H
        O   G   P   N   D   K   N   N   I   R   I   L   I   A
     1 +XXXXXXXXXXXXXXXXXXXXXXXXXXXXXXXXXXXXXXXXXXXXXXXXXXXXX
       |XXXXXXXXXXXXXXXXXXXXX   XXXXXXXXXXXXXXXXXXXXXXXXXXXXX
       |XXXXXXXXXXXXXXXXXXXXX   XXXXXXXXXXXXXXXXXXXXXXXXXXXXX
     2 +XXXXXXXXXXXXXXXXXXXXX   XXXXXXXXXXXXXXXXXXXXXXXXXXXXX
       |XXXXXXXXXXXXXXXXXXXXX   XXXXX   XXXXXXXXXXXXXXXXXXXXX
       |XXXXXXXXXXXXXXXXXXXXX   XXXXX   XXXXXXXXXXXXXXXXXXXXX
     3 +XXXXXXXXXXXXXXXXXXXXX   XXXXX   XXXXXXXXXXXXXXXXXXXXX
       |XXXXXXXXXXXXXXXXXXXXX   XXXXX   XXXXX   XXXXXXXXXXXXX
       |XXXXXXXXXXXXXXXXXXXXX   XXXXX   XXXXX   XXXXXXXXXXXXX
     4 +XXXXXXXXXXXXXXXXXXXXX   XXXXX   XXXXX   XXXXXXXXXXXXX
       |XXXXXXXXXXXXXXXXXXXXX   XXXXX   XXXXX   .   XXXXXXXXX
N      |XXXXXXXXXXXXXXXXXXXXX   XXXXX   XXXXX   .   XXXXXXXXX
U    5 +XXXXXXXXXXXXXXXXXXXXX   XXXXX   XXXXX   .   XXXXXXXXX
M      |XXXXXXXXX   XXXXXXXXX   XXXXX   XXXXX   .   XXXXXXXXX
B      |XXXXXXXXX   XXXXXXXXX   XXXXX   XXXXX   .   XXXXXXXXX
E    6 +XXXXXXXXX   XXXXXXXXX   XXXXX   XXXXX   .   XXXXXXXXX
R      |XXXXXXXXX   XXXXXXXXX   .   .   XXXXX   .   XXXXXXXXX
       |XXXXXXXXX   XXXXXXXXX   .   .   XXXXX   .   XXXXXXXXX
O    7 +XXXXXXXXX   XXXXXXXXX   .   .   XXXXX   .   XXXXXXXXX
F      |XXXXXXXXX   .   XXXXX   .   .   XXXXX   .   XXXXXXXXX
       |XXXXXXXXX   .   XXXXX   .   .   XXXXX   .   XXXXXXXXX
C    8 +XXXXXXXXX   .   XXXXX   .   .   XXXXX   .   XXXXXXXXX
L      |XXXXXXXXX   .   XXXXX   .   .   XXXXX   .   .   XXXXX
U      |XXXXXXXXX   .   XXXXX   .   .   XXXXX   .   .   XXXXX
S    9 +XXXXXXXXX   .   XXXXX   .   .   XXXXX   .   .   XXXXX
T      |XXXXXXXXX   .   XXXXX   .   .   .   .   .   .   XXXXX
E      |XXXXXXXXX   .   XXXXX   .   .   .   .   .   .   XXXXX
R   10 +XXXXXXXXX   .   XXXXX   .   .   .   .   .   .   XXXXX
S      |.   XXXXX   .   XXXXX   .   .   .   .   .   .   XXXXX
       |.   XXXXX   .   XXXXX   .   .   .   .   .   .   XXXXX
    11 +.   XXXXX   .   XXXXX   .   .   .   .   .   .   XXXXX
       |.   XXXXX   .   .   .   .   .   .   .   .   .   XXXXX
       |.   XXXXX   .   .   .   .   .   .   .   .   .   XXXXX
    12 +.   XXXXX   .   .   .   .   .   .   .   .   .   XXXXX
       |.   XXXXX   .   .   .   .   .   .   .   .   .   .   .
       |.   XXXXX   .   .   .   .   .   .   .   .   .   .   .
    13 +.   XXXXX   .   .   .   .   .   .   .   .   .   .   .
       |.   .   .   .   .   .   .   .   .   .   .   .   .   .
       |.   .   .   .   .   .   .   .   .   .   .   .   .   .
    14 +.   .   .   .   .   .   .   .   .   .   .   .   .   .
```

Diagram 3: Cluster Analysis, WARD 1980

```
WARD'S MINIMUM VARIANCE CLUSTER ANALYSIS

                                  COUNTRY

            A   N   I   B   I   P   H   S   P   S   T   C   K   M
            F   E   N   A   N   A   O   I   H   R   H   H   O   A
            G   P   D   N   O   K   N   N   I   I   A   I   R   L
         1 +XXXXXXXXXXXXXXXXXXXXXXXXXXXXXXXXXXXXXXXXXXXXXXXXXXXXX
           |XXXXXXXXXXXXXXXXXXXXX   XXXXXXXXXXXXXXXXXXXXXXXXXXXXX
           |XXXXXXXXXXXXXXXXXXXXX   XXXXXXXXXXXXXXXXXXXXXXXXXXXXX
         2 +XXXXXXXXXXXXXXXXXXXXX   XXXXXXXXXXXXXXXXXXXXXXXXXXXXX
           |XXXXXXXXXXXXXXXXXXXXX   XXXXX   XXXXXXXXXXXXXXXXXXXXX
           |XXXXXXXXXXXXXXXXXXXXX   XXXXX   XXXXXXXXXXXXXXXXXXXXX
         3 +XXXXXXXXXXXXXXXXXXXXX   XXXXX   XXXXXXXXXXXXXXXXXXXXX
           |XXXXXXXXXXXXXXXXXXXXX   XXXXX   XXXXXXXXX   XXXXXXXXX
           |XXXXXXXXXXXXXXXXXXXXX   XXXXX   XXXXXXXXX   XXXXXXXXX
         4 +XXXXXXXXXXXXXXXXXXXXX   XXXXX   XXXXXXXXX   XXXXXXXXX
           |XXXXX   XXXXXXXXXXXXX   XXXXX   XXXXXXXXX   XXXXXXXXX
N          |XXXXX   XXXXXXXXXXXXX   XXXXX   XXXXXXXXX   XXXXXXXXX
U        5 +XXXXX   XXXXXXXXXXXXX   XXXXX   XXXXXXXXX   XXXXXXXXX
M          |XXXXX   XXXXXXXXXXXXX   XXXXX   XXXXXXXXX   .   XXXXX
B          |XXXXX   XXXXXXXXXXXXX   XXXXX   XXXXXXXXX   .   XXXXX
E        6 +XXXXX   XXXXXXXXXXXXX   XXXXX   XXXXXXXXX   .   XXXXX
R          |XXXXX   .   XXXXXXXXX   XXXXX   XXXXXXXXX   .   XXXXX
           |XXXXX   .   XXXXXXXXX   XXXXX   XXXXXXXXX   .   XXXXX
O        7 +XXXXX   .   XXXXXXXXX   XXXXX   XXXXXXXXX   .   XXXXX
F          |XXXXX   .   XXXXXXXXX   XXXXX   XXXXXXXXX   .   .   .
           |XXXXX   .   XXXXXXXXX   XXXXX   XXXXXXXXX   .   .   .
C        8 +XXXXX   .   XXXXXXXXX   XXXXX   XXXXXXXXX   .   .   .
L          |XXXXX   .   .   XXXXX   XXXXX   XXXXXXXXX   .   .   .
U          |XXXXX   .   .   XXXXX   XXXXX   XXXXXXXXX   .   .   .
S        9 +XXXXX   .   .   XXXXX   XXXXX   XXXXXXXXX   .   .   .
T          |XXXXX   .   .   XXXXX   XXXXX   .   XXXXX   .   .   .
E          |XXXXX   .   .   XXXXX   XXXXX   .   XXXXX   .   .   .
R       10 +XXXXX   .   .   XXXXX   XXXXX   .   XXXXX   .   .   .
S          |.   .   .   .   XXXXX   XXXXX   .   XXXXX   .   .   .
           |.   .   .   .   XXXXX   XXXXX   .   XXXXX   .   .   .
        11 +.   .   .   .   XXXXX   XXXXX   .   XXXXX   .   .   .
           |.   .   .   .   XXXXX   .   .   .   XXXXX   .   .   .
           |.   .   .   .   XXXXX   .   .   .   XXXXX   .   .   .
        12 +.   .   .   .   XXXXX   .   .   .   XXXXX   .   .   .
           |.   .   .   .   .   .   .   .   .   XXXXX   .   .   .
           |.   .   .   .   .   .   .   .   .   XXXXX   .   .   .
        13 +.   .   .   .   .   .   .   .   .   XXXXX   .   .   .
           |.   .   .   .   .   .   .   .   .   .   .   .   .   .
           |.   .   .   .   .   .   .   .   .   .   .   .   .   .
        14 +.   .   .   .   .   .   .   .   .   .   .   .   .   .
```

them have only limited and most of them have full access to these credits. For example, Singapore, Hong Kong, Korea, Malaysia, and China are not eligible. According to the cluster analysis, these countries belong to the two upper groups (at a level of K=4) and are classified as more developed. Thus, they are classified correctly following the analysis of this study.

There are, however, differences between those countries which have limited access to ADF-credits, for example Indonesia, the Philipines, and Thailand. Indonesia had to change with Sri Lanka, which belongs to the group of countries with full access to ADF-credits.

It has to be noticed that the ADB-classification of its members is relatively exact, although its criterium for classification is represented by GNP per capita, together with another economic indicator, the debt repayment capacity,[15] which more or less confirms the first indicator. The fact that the classification as "social" seems to be right - not taking into consideration Sri Lanka and the Philipines - may be the result of the special considerations which also take into account unquantifiable facts, such as "landlocked country", etc.

3.3 Principal Component Analysis (PCA)

The main idea of the principal component analysis (PCA) or factor analysis is relatively simple: groups of indicators that are highly correlated to each other are to be determined out of a number of available indicators. On this basis the variable that cannot directly be determined (and which is indicated by these indicators) is singled out. Such a somewhat synthetic variable is called a factor (Z). The procedure can be different as a result of different facts. The PCA [16] employed in this study does not make an estimation of communalities but starts from the correlation matrix and uses the values indicated on the main diagonal. Thus, the study follows the hypothesis that no specific variance of errors contains any relevance, but that the total variance is to be explained by the common factors.

In contrast to the cluster analysis, where the results bear no information about the comparative level of development, the PCA can illustrate the distances between the countries by the factor scores.

The coefficients of the first principal component are given in Table 1. Since the indicator "infant mortality" was redefined as "number of children not died per 1000 live births", the correlations are positive for both 1970 and 1980. Both principal components cover 74% and 78% respectively, of the total variance. This value can be regarded as being satisfactory, so that the first principal components reflect the most important characteristics of the multivariate system.

Table 1: Coefficients of the First Principal Component

	1970 (Z1)	1980 (Z2)
LIFEXP	0,89	0,92
INFMOR	0,92	0,92
CACCAP	0,88	0,93
SAFWAT	0,78	0,87
MEDRAT	0,77	0,88
GDPCAP	0,92	0,79
MERGOO	0,85	0,91
ENERGY	0,90	0,90
Cum.Variance	74,2%	78,7%

The coefficients are almost the same for 1970 and 1980 and have the same mathematical sign. Hence, in this case the first principal component can be regarded as an appropriate means for measuring the average level of development of a country.

Diagram 4:

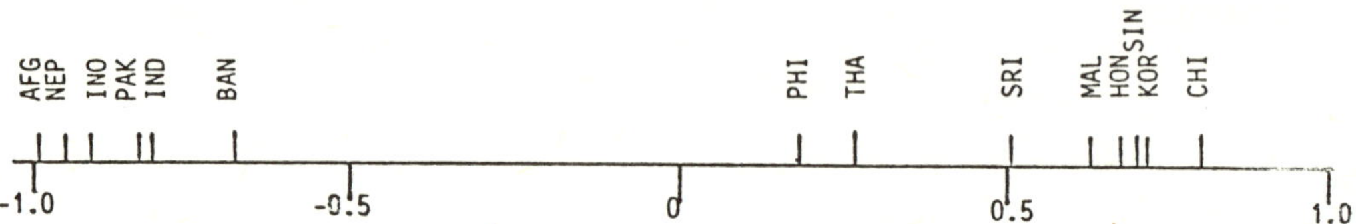

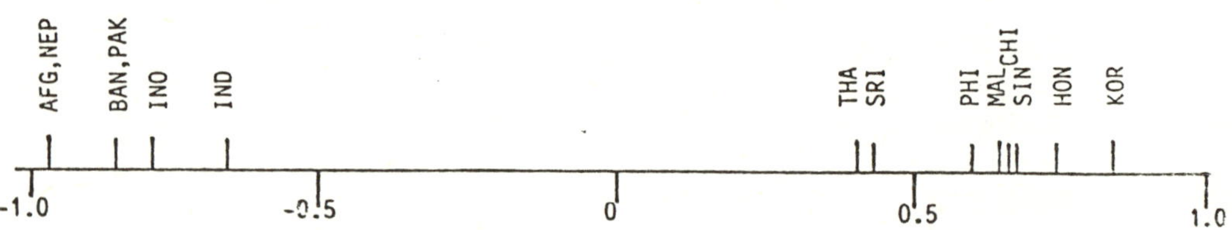

If the factor scores of all countries are drawn on a line, the result will be similar to that of the previously mentioned cluster analysis. The less developed countries can be found on the left side of the line, the more developed ones on the right hand side. Within these groups the positions have changed, and the gap between the different groups seems to have become insurmountable. It is surprising that Hong Kong and Singapore do not appear as leaders but delimitate the upper part of the scale together with China and Korea. For Nepal and Afghanistan the situation becomes increasingly alarming, if not even hopeless. As has been shown by the two preceding analyses, there could neither be reached an absolute development success nor a relative one.

The interpretation of the principal component analysis made in this study illustrates only a small part of the possible spectrum of such a method. A great number of analyses, using this method, were made in the last few years, which led to a new classification of the countries or to an analysis of the fulfillment of regional basic needs. The interpretation of artificial factors remains difficult and requires a great amount of sensitivity. The simple representation in this study is to give an idea of how development can be measured multidimensional, using complex statistical methods.

4. Graphic Representation of multidimensional measurement of development

Those who are not used to statistical representations do not only have difficulties to understand formulas or artificial factors, but also dislike and disapprove of "mathematical playing". Nevertheless, the GNP per capita as the only indicator to measure development has been criticized and better methods of quantitative and qualitative measurement are demanded. These methods, however, cannot be separated from basic knowledge of statistics, and thus, the "vicious circle" is closed. For some time it has been tried to represent statistical results graphically in order to give the necessary information at first or perhaps at second sight. A rather impressive method to represent multivariate data is that of Chernoff. [17] Every object, in our case every country, is represented by a symbol (face). The face changes its facial expression by its mouth, the size of its ears, eyes, and nose, the number of hairs, etc. . Knowing the indicators that influence the different parts of the face, it is easy to realize the situation of a country.

Another method to represent n-dimensional analyses

are the so-called star-charts. Within a circle the transformed data is drawn, starting from the central point. The final points of each indicator can be connected, so that an n-sided polygon results.

The data used in this study were transformed in a way that makes the representation in a circle meaningful. The following transformation were made:

1. LIFE EXPECT = LIFEXP/80
2. INFANT MORT = 1-(INFMOR/220)
3. CALORIES = CACCAP/3000
4. WATER = SAFWAT/100
5. LITERACY = LITRAT/100
6. PHYSICIANS = MEDRAT/100
7. GDP CAPITA = GDPCAP/3000
8. MERCH.GOODS = MERGOO/30
9. ENERGY = ENERGY/3000

Each value is drawn counter-clockwise in alphabetical order, corresponding to the indicators-labels, starting with the three o`clock-position.

Diagram 5 shows the star-charts [18] for 1980, given according to the factor scores. In the case of Afghanistan and Nepal almost no "star" can be drawn, because some values can hardly be represented. In the case of the two lower rows, however, the stars are well-formed. In this method of representation, the radius was orientated by the maximum value of a variable of each country. Other methods would be possible, so that the development over a period of time - via so-called overlays - or the development of the countries in comparison [19] could be demonstrated.

Since these diagrams need much space in order to be useful, a representation of them will not be given in this study.

Graphic representations are very popular because they are impressive. They represent given information, but do not analyse them, so that an analytic interpretation is made more difficult rather than made easier.

5. Conclusion

The comparative analysis of the Asian developing countries illustrated clearly that the socio-economic situation has improved. Both categories of indicators have changed positively: the social indicators that illustrate above all the fulfillment of basic needs, and the economic indicators that make possible to assess the future potential of development. However, among the countries there have been changes concerning their ranking. Taking into consideration the PQLI, the cluster analysis, the factor analysis and the changes over a period of time, Afghanistan, Nepal, Bangladesh, Pakistan, and India not only represent the lower end of the scale of development, but also expanded only to a small degree their economic potential in order to get out of their miserable situation. Indonesia, having reached an above-average growth of GDP, could not transfer its development into social development in such a short period of time, some-

Star Charts of Selected Countries, 1980

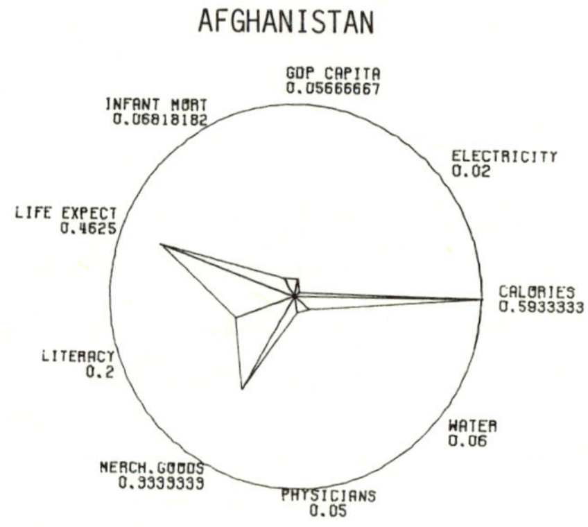

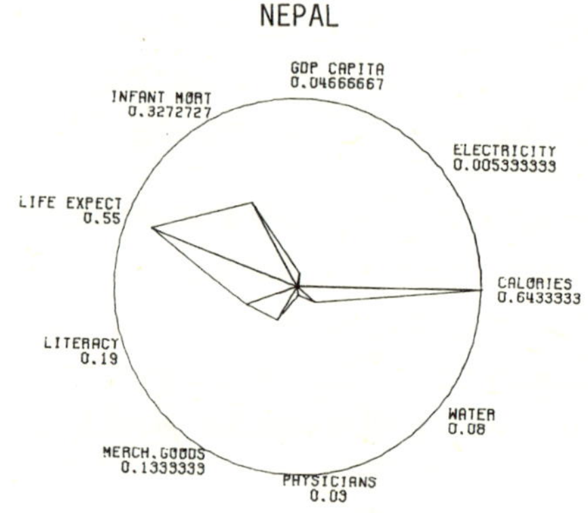

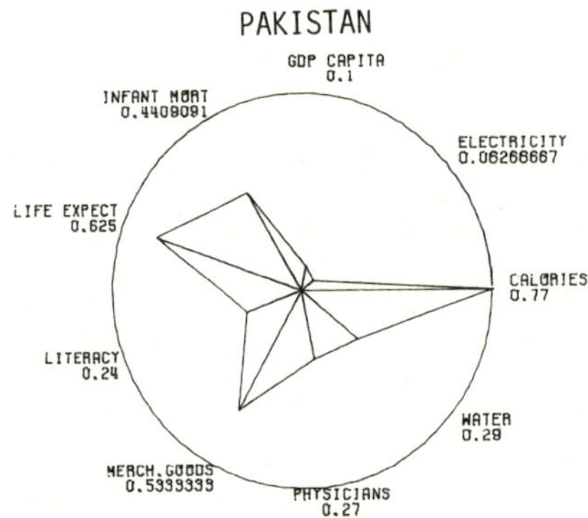

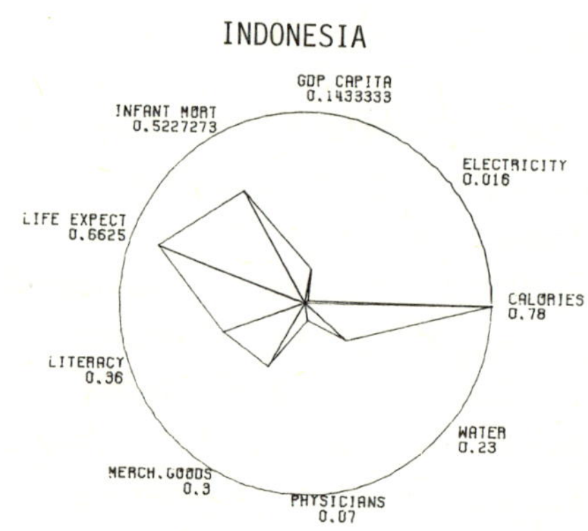

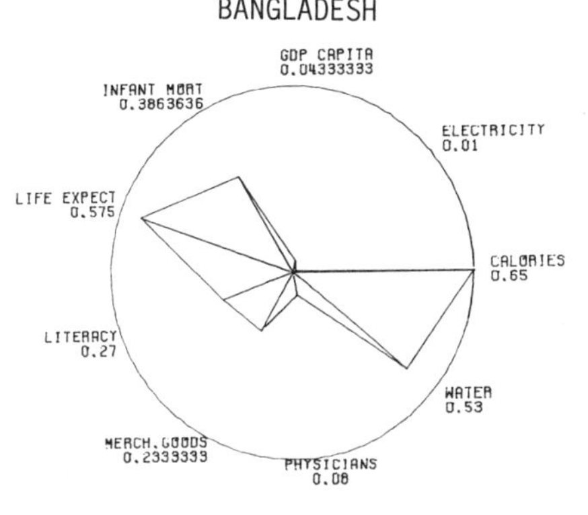
BANGLADESH
GDP CAPITA
0.04333333
ELECTRICITY
0.01
CALORIES
0.65
WATER
0.53
PHYSICIANS
0.08
MERCH.GOODS
0.2333333
LITERACY
0.27
LIFE EXPECT
0.575
INFANT MORT
0.3863636

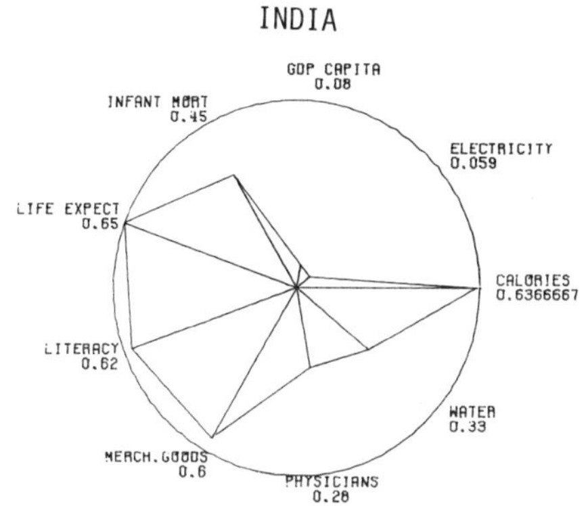
INDIA
GDP CAPITA
0.08
ELECTRICITY
0.059
CALORIES
0.6366667
WATER
0.33
PHYSICIANS
0.28
MERCH.GOODS
0.6
LITERACY
0.62
LIFE EXPECT
0.65
INFANT MORT
0.45

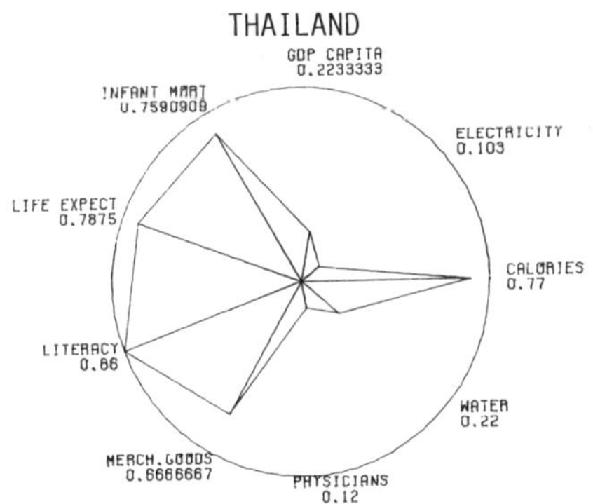
THAILAND
GDP CAPITA
0.2233333
ELECTRICITY
0.103
CALORIES
0.77
WATER
0.22
PHYSICIANS
0.12
MERCH.GOODS
0.6666667
LITERACY
0.86
LIFE EXPECT
0.7875
INFANT MORT
0.7590909

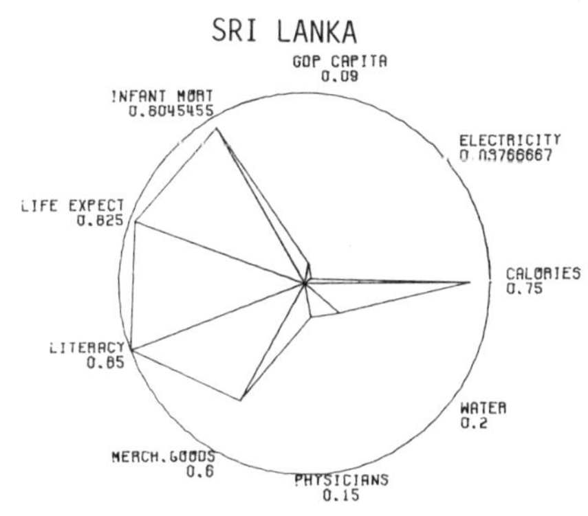
SRI LANKA
GDP CAPITA
0.09
ELECTRICITY
0.03766667
CALORIES
0.75
WATER
0.2
PHYSICIANS
0.15
MERCH.GOODS
0.6
LITERACY
0.85
LIFE EXPECT
0.825
INFANT MORT
0.6045455

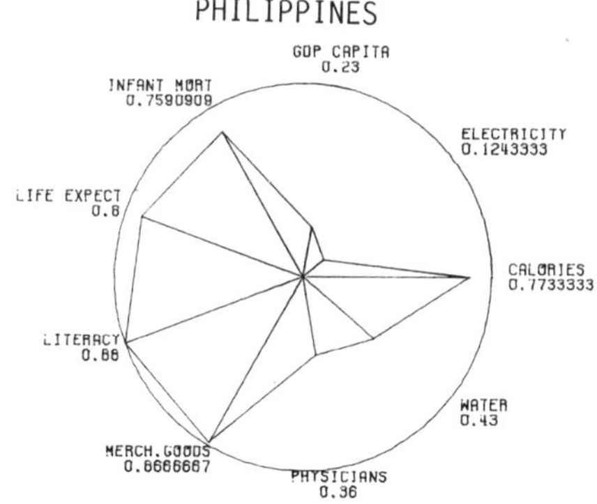
PHILIPPINES
GDP CAPITA
0.23
ELECTRICITY
0.1243333
CALORIES
0.7733333
WATER
0.43
PHYSICIANS
0.36
MERCH.GOODS
0.6666667
LITERACY
0.88
LIFE EXPECT
0.8
INFANT MORT
0.7590909

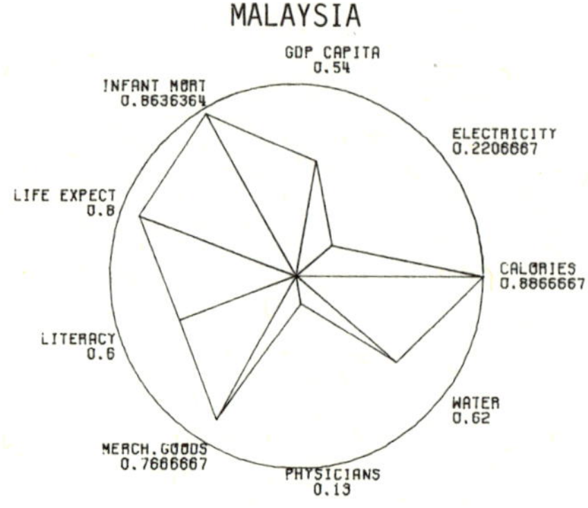
MALAYSIA
GDP CAPITA
0.54
INFANT MORT
0.8636364
ELECTRICITY
0.2206667
LIFE EXPECT
0.8
CALORIES
0.8866667
LITERACY
0.6
WATER
0.62
MERCH.GOODS
0.7666667
PHYSICIANS
0.13

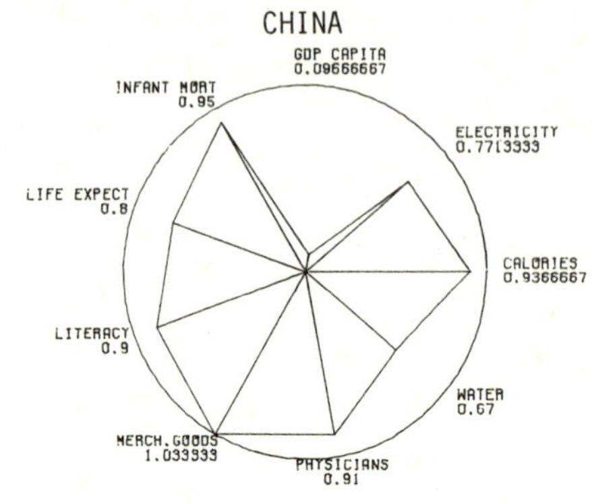
CHINA
GDP CAPITA
0.09666667
INFANT MORT
0.95
ELECTRICITY
0.7713333
LIFE EXPECT
0.8
CALORIES
0.9366667
LITERACY
0.9
WATER
0.67
MERCH.GOODS
1.033333
PHYSICIANS
0.91

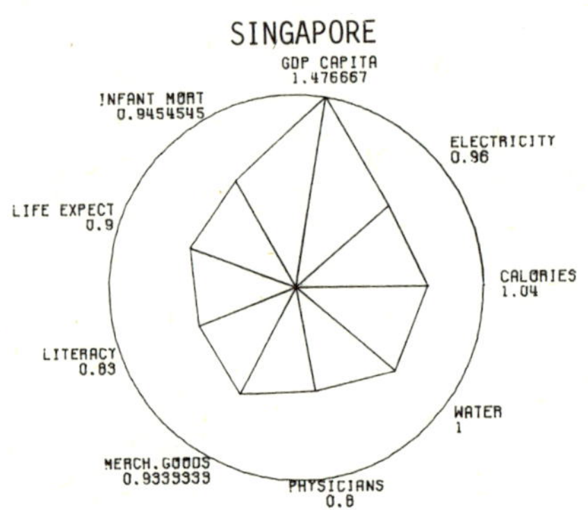
SINGAPORE
GDP CAPITA
1.476667
INFANT MORT
0.9454545
ELECTRICITY
0.96
LIFE EXPECT
0.9
CALORIES
1.04
LITERACY
0.83
WATER
1
MERCH.GOODS
0.9333333
PHYSICIANS
0.8

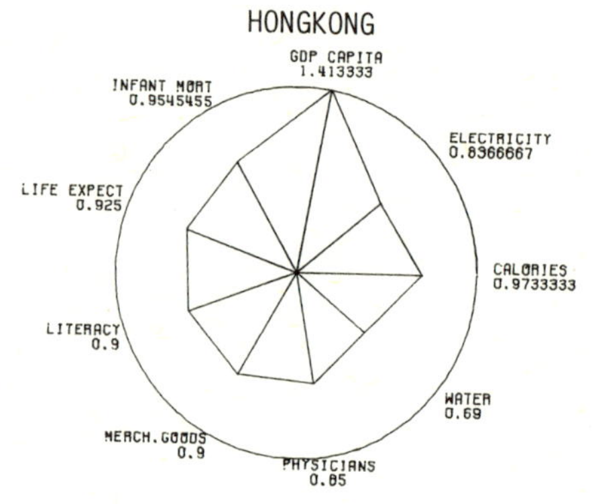
HONGKONG
GDP CAPITA
1.413333
INFANT MORT
0.9545455
ELECTRICITY
0.8366667
LIFE EXPECT
0.925
CALORIES
0.9733333
LITERACY
0.9
WATER
0.69
MERCH.GOODS
0.9
PHYSICIANS
0.85

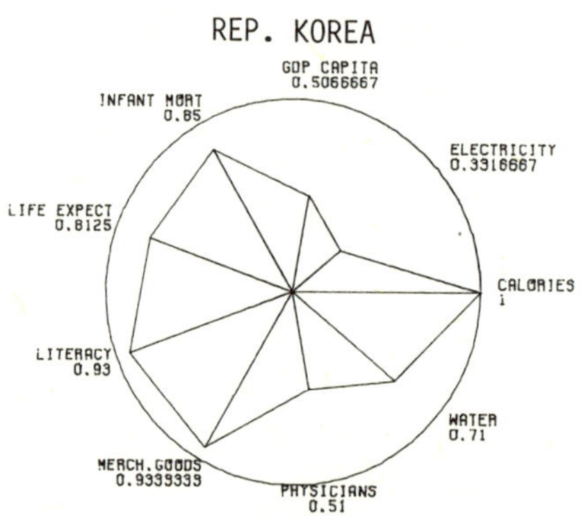
REP. KOREA
GDP CAPITA
0.5066667
INFANT MORT
0.85
ELECTRICITY
0.3316667
LIFE EXPECT
0.8125
CALORIES
1
LITERACY
0.93
WATER
0.71
MERCH.GOODS
0.9333333
PHYSICIANS
0.51

thing which is also due to the shortages of the social indicators, which react to changes only in the long run. Singapore, Hong Kong, and recently also Korea and China are the most developed countries. They established their lead in the Asian area and have even strengthened it. China has caught up with Singapore and Hong Kong. The growth rates of GDP add to the earlier started social development. Sri Lanka, the often-cited example for social development although having small economic growth, has slowed down its growth of social infrastructure. The economic data indicates only small progress.

The empirical analysis on this study gives an impression of the socio-economic development of development in selected countries. However, also the limits of such an approach become apparent. They are less represented by available statistical methods or mathematical problems, but still by the availability and comparability of data.

References

[1] Mooris D. Morris, Measuring the Condition of the World`s Poor - The Physical Quality of Life Index, New York 1979

[2] Afghanistan, Nepal, Bangladesh, Laos, Pakistan, and India.

[3] The figures of Viet Nam should be considered with reservation.

[4] 1980 the mean was 63,5 against 1970 with a mean

of 45,1.

[5] The UN classifies countries in various ways for different purposes. For example, least developed countries (LLDC) status means the weakest in terms of certain economic and social criteria: low income (per capita GNP average of three years at current prices). low literacy rate and low share of manufacturing of total output.

[6] UNRISD Research Data Bank of Development Indicators, 1960 and 1970, Vols. I, II, III, IV. Geneva, and D.Mc Granahan et al., Measurement and analysis of socio-economic Development, Geneva 1985.

[7] EXPRAT and DEPRAT, having GNP in their denominators, are certainly dependent on GDPCAP.

[8] The three algorithms are different only in their definition of distance between and similarities of the clusters.

[9] For the calculations the programmes "CLUSTER" and "TREE" of the Statistical Analysis System, SAS, were used.

[10] The value of the centroid corresponds to the arithmetic mean of all values of the observation.

[11] SAS, User`s Guide: Statistics 1982 Edition, Cary 1982, p. 423.

[12] Hong Kong, Singapore, China, Korea, Philipines, Malaysia, Sri Lanka, and Thailand.

[13] Indonesien, Afghanistan, Nepal, Bangladesh, Indien and Pakistan.

[14] Note: The classification is based on six social and three economic indicators.

[15] Dept repayment capacity represents a hardly quantifiable conglomerate of investment and saving rate, foreign currency, debt, etc.

[16] A special kind of the "classical factor analysis".

[17] H. Chernoff, The use of facts to represent points in k-dimensional space graphically, in Journal of the Americal Statistical Association, No. 67, p. 361-368.

[18] For the representation GCHART/STAR of the SAS/GRAPH programme was used.

[19] It would be possible to orientate the radius by the maximum value of all countries.

Bibliography

Adelman, I/C.T. Morris, A Factor Analysis of the Interrelationship and per capita gross national product, in, The Quarterly Journal of Economics, Vol. 79, 1965

Asian Development Bank, Key Indicators of Developing Member Countries of ADB, Vol. XIV, Manila 1983

David, I.P./D.S. Maligalig, Multivariate statistical and graphical classification techniques applied to the problem of grouping countries, Asian Development Bank, Statistical Report Series, No. 2, Manila 1985

Deichsel, G/H.J. Trampisch, Clusteranalyse und Diskriminanzanalyse, Stuttgart, New York 1985

Flury, B./H. Riedwyl, Angewandte multivariate Statistik. Computergestützte Analyse mehrdimensionale Daten.
Stuttgart, New York 1983.

Morris, M.D., Measuring the Condition of the World`s Poor-The Physical Quality of life Index, New York 1979.

SAS, User`s Guide: Statistics, Version 5 Edition, Cary 1985

SAS, Graph, User`s Guide Version 5 Edition, Cary 1985

Scholing, E., Zur mehrdimensionalen Messung des wirtschaftlichen Entwicklungsstandes, Sozialökonomisches Seminar der Universität Hamburg. Beiträge zur Wirtschaftsforschung, No. 44, Hamburg 1981

Wilkens, Het et al., Wirtschaftliche, soziale und politische Bedingungen der Entwicklung, Köln 1985

Regional Economic Cooperation in South Asia ASEAN: A Model for SAARC?[1]

by Norbert Wagner

1. Introduction

In December 1985 the South Asian Association for Regional Cooperation (SAARC) was set up by the heads of state or Prime Ministers of seven South Asian states (India, Pakistan, Bangladesh, Sri Lanka, Nepal, Bhutan, and the Maledives). The association is supposed to improve the cooperation regarding the economic, social, and technical problems of the region. However, the success of this cooperation will be determined rather by political and economic factors. The European Communities and the Association of Southeast Asian Nations (ASEAN) may have set an example for SAARC.

The attempt to intensify regional cooperation in South Asia goes hand in hand with numerous similar attempts in other regions of the Third World and increased importance of the different forms of cooperation on the part of the developing countries. Therefore, the first section of this paper will deal with the objectives and policies for increased economic cooperation among developing countries in general. A section analysing the aims of regional cooperation among South Asian countries and discussing the prospects of intensified cooperation will be added, studying in particular the possible cooperation at intra-regional projects and the possible expansion of intra-regional trade. In a last section the attempt will be made to draw conclusions from the experience made with regional cooperation among the Association of Southeast Asian Nations for future potential and limits of intensified regional cooperation between SAARC-members.

2. Economic cooperation among developing countries.

Attempts to increase economic cooperation between developing countries date back to the 1950s. In the 1960s and 1970s numerous forms of cooperation between developing countries were established, ranging from cooperation at single projects (e.g. exploitation of resources) over regional banks to regional and inter-regional integration associations. A new impetus to intensified cooperation among developing countries was given by the increasing criticism of the developing countries\` integration into the world market, the discussion about a New International Economic Order, and the success of OPEC at increasing the price of crude oil. By acting solidly the developing countries hoped to wrest further trade advantages from the industrial countries. At a meeting of the Group 77 in Mexico in 1976 the principles of increased cooperation between the developing countries were worked out. In 1979 these principles were passed by the Group 77 in Arusha.[2] This "Arusha-Programme" was introduced in the United Nations Conference on Trade and Development in Manila (UNCTAD V). Since then the South-South-cooperation has been a major point in the international development debate, and in the International Strategy for the United Nations` 3rd decade of development (1981-1990) much importance was attached to South-South-cooperation. Moreover, a programme for cooperation among developing countries was put down in the Caracas Programme of Action adopted by the High-Level Conference on Economic Cooperation Among Developing Countries held at Caracas in 1981.

The aim of such cooperation is to strengthen collective self-reliance. The position of the developing countries towards the industrial countries in terms of negotiation are to be improved and thus increase the expectations of a reformed International Economic Order as envisaged by the developing countries. The most important measures envisaged, concerning the strategy of economic cooperation among developing comprise:[3]

- the creation of a Global System of Trade Preferences among developing countries (GTSP);
- the establishment of a Trade Information System (TIS)
- the cooperation between State-Trading Organisations (STD);
- the promotion of Multinational Marketing Enterprises in developing countries (MME);
- the promotion of Multinational Production Enterprises (MPE);
- the support of economic cooperation and integration agreementsbetween developing countrieson subregional, regional,and inter-regional level;

- the promotion of monetary cooperation and cooperation concerning fiscal policy;
- the foundation of multilateral development banks of the developing countries;
- the promotion of cooperation in the field of Technical Cooperation among Developing Countries (TCDC);
- special aid for least developed countries and island and landlocked countries.

The realization of the measures mentioned in the list above has, however, been only partly successful. Yet, it is just in the developing countries that trade barriers are particularly high or numerous.[4] The mutual granting of tariff preferences [5] would probably cause only a small increase in South-South-trade. [6] Moreover, the reduction of the great number of non-tariff trade barriers of developing countries would be imperative. [7] It is the task of the Trade Information System (TIS) to register all these trade barriers. On the one hand it gives more information to exporters about the possible exports to other developing countries, and on the other hand it is the prerequisite for negotiations on the creation of a system of preferences among the developing countries.

3. Regional Cooperation in South Asia

3.1 Aims of Cooperation

After more than two years of negotiation, in August 1983 the foreign secretaries of seven South Asian states (India, Pakistan, Bangladesh, Sri Lanka, Bhutan, Nepal, and the Maledives) signed the documents of "South Asian Regional Cooperation (SARC)". After this agreement, a parallel was drawn rather precipitately to the European Economic Community and the Association of Southeast Asian Nations (ASEAN). In addition, it was stressed that around one billion people were living in SARC-member states, thus including more than one fifth of global population. While this figure was euphorically regarded as the evidence of the association`s economic importance, it may rather be an indicator for the dimensions of social and economic problems the seven SARC-members will be confronted with.

It was only in December 1985 that the first summit conference of the South Asian Nations was held in Dhaka, at which the heads of state or the prime ministers of the seven member states formed the South Asian Association for Regional Cooperation (SAARC).[8]

Although the aims and possible measures for regional cooperation have been discussed in study groups and committees for more than four years, at present the aims of SAARC do not seem to be very concrete.[9] Neither can it be recognized whether the aims connected with Saarc are primarily political or economic.

On the occasion of the meeting of foreign secretaries in 1983, the Indian Prime Minister Indira Gandhi said she hoped that the member states would in future be able to stand the foreign pressure in a better way. At that time, measures to ease intra-regional trade were still excluded from the agenda in order not to doom the cooperation efforts to failure from the very beginning.[10]

Since then possible fields of cooperation have been discussed in various study groups and committees. For example, proposals for the extension of infrastructure in the field of air and maritime traffic and telecommunication were worked out. An exchange of experience is planned about the cooperation in those areas, where a direct relation to hunger and ignorance in the region exists. Also problems of intra-regional trade no longer seem to be excluded completely from the agenda. A common trade policy is to be formulated, which will take into account the special agricultural situation of each member state. Behind this rather vague statement there is apparently the aim to coordinate the agricultural production of the member states to a larger degree in order to intensify intra-regional trade and make possible additional exports to other countries. Additionally, common research programmes were proposed in the field of agriculture, programmes concerning solar energy and the production of biogas.

Cooperation is also planned in the area of health and population policy, for example via programmes for birth control, coordination of medical education, fighting dangerous diseases and further development of traditional medicine. Additionally, there are plans for common improvement of education, particularly vocational training.

Besides these economic and social objectives of cooperation among SAARC-members, recently, the political effects of this cooperation are stressed again. The SAARC was set up to create a forum in which global decisions can be influenced, it is said. A few years ago, Indira Gandhi had already mentioned that South Asia was threatened by outside forces - in particular by the super powers. She said that they could resist this danger only in common. It is also possible that the seven member states hope to gain more importance out of their cooperation when decisions about global economic problems are to be taken.[11]

3.2 Prospects of Cooperation in South Asia

Thus, the envisaged cooperation in South Asia is based on two principal aims. Externally the cooperation is to strengthen the political influence of the member states; internally the aims are more on the economic and social level. It seems as if the Indian government lays more stress on the effects on inter-national level, whereas the governments of the other states seem to be interested rather in intra-regional cooperation on economic and social issues.

Apart from possibly different aims that are connected with regional cooperation, the prospects for cooperation in South Asia are determined by some other factors:

The dominating role of India both politically and economically, makes trusting cooperation with the neighbouring "smaller" partners difficult. In addition, there are cases of strained bilateral relations between SAARC-members, partly even grave ones. For years there has been a conflict between India and Pakistan because of border disputes in Kashmir and the alleged threat to India of Pakistan`s military armament, particularly its development of nuclear weapons.[12] There are disputes between India and Bangladesh because of the use of water resources. In addition, India plans or has already begun to build a fence at the border to Bangladesh in order to reduce the rapidly increased number of immigrants.

Recently, the tensions between India and Sri Lanka concerning the Tamil separatists, have been growing again. Nepal makes great efforts to reduce its (as it says) one-sided dependence from India. In total, the bilateral political relations between the SAARC-members do not seem to represent favourable conditions for an intensified regional cooperation. If nevertheless the cooperation among South Asian countries is to work and to succeed, two important preconditions have to be fulfilled.

1. A measure for cooperation can only be carried out when every member can expect more advantages than disadvantages and concessions.[13]

2. The advantages of a measure for cooperation have to be distributed among the members in a way that is regarded as just by all the member states.

It seems hardly possible to fulfill both preconditions when a single measure for cooperation is to be passed. Hence, it is necessary to work out whole packages of measures, which meet the requirements as a total. What is also possible is a system of compensation payments, which could compensate for undesirable distributions of net advantages of measures for cooperation. This, however, has probably not been discussed by the SAARC.

As far as inward-oriented intensified cooperation among the seven South Asian countries is concerned, common regional measures in social and economic infrastructure and the expansion of intra-regional trade seem to be in particular appropriate. The prospects for intensified regional cooperation among the SAARC-countries will probably be best in the case of projects improving the economic and social infrastructure, since costs and expected benefits of each country can be calculated most exactly for these projects. In addition, it will be comparably easy to assess the probable advantages for the other member states. Taking into account the serious economic and social problems of these countries, there is a great variety of possible starting points for such common regional measures, ranging from the improvement of telecommunication facilities and coordinated fighting against certain diseases to cooperation in the field of environmental protection. The utilization of the Himalayan water resources is also very often cited as fruitful field for regional cooperation.[14] The member states would probably be particularly prepared to regional cooperation, if some industrial countries and international organisations provided some

Table 1 Foreign Trade of SAARC-Member Countries, 1984 (in US $ million and in %)

Exports/Imports of to/from	Bangladesh exports	Bangladesh imports	India exports	India imports	Maldives exports	Maldives imports
	(in US $ million)					
World	931	2825	10257	17 502	13	70
	(in % of total exports/imports)					
Industrial countries	50,0	45,9	59,1	46,5	23,1	24,3
Developing countries	43,6	35,6	26,1	45,5	76,9	75,7
Developing Asia	19,3	24,9	12,5	15,8	69,2	74,3
SAARC	11,5	3,3	2,5	0,5	21,5	13,0
Bangladesh	–	–	0,5	0,2	.	.
India	3,0	2,0	–	–	.	4,1
Maldives	.	.	0,0	.	–	–
Nepal	1,6	0,0	0,8	0,1	.	.
Pakistan	6,8	1,1	0,1	0,2	9,2	2,4
Sri Lanka	0,0	0,1	1,0	0,1	12,3	6,4

. = no data available.

Source: International Monetary Fund, Direction of Trade Statistics, Yearbook 1985, Washington 1985; author's calculations.

Nepal exports	Nepal imports	Pakistan exports	Pakistan imports	Sri Lanka exports	Sri Lanka imports	SAARC exports	SAARC imports
(in US $ million)							
67	256	2566	5852	1436	1846	15 270	28 351
(in % of total exports/imports)							
62,7	40,2	46,5	51,3	43,9	46,2	55,0	47,3
37,3	59,4	49,6	47,o	42,6	5o,4	32,8	45,4
34,3	59,4	11,6	15,6	9,7	24,o	12,7	17,8
26,9	42,9	3,3	2,1	4,5	7,1	3,4	2,0
0,7	6,3	1,5	1,2	1,0	0,0	0,7	0,4
25,5	36,6	1,0	0,2	0,9	6,0	0,5	1,0
.	.	0,1	0,0	0,2	0,1	0,1	0,0
–	–	0,0	0,0	.	.	0,7	0,1
0,6	0,0	–	–	2,4	0,9	0,7	0,3
.	.	0,8	0,6	–	–	0,8	0,2

capital, especially to finance projects concerning the regional cooperation of the SAARC-countries.[15]

The prospects for the expansion of intra-regional trade, on the other hand, seem less auspicious.

Table 1 illustrates the regional structure of foreign trade of six SAARC-countries.[16] In 1984, Bangladesh`s foreign trade (exports plus imports) with the other SAARC-countries amounted to mere 5.4 percent of its total trade, India`s only to 1.2 percent, that of the Maledives to 14.3 percent, Nepal`s to 39,6 percent, Pakistan`s to 2.5 percent, and that of Sri Lanka to 6.0 percent. The total intra-regional trade among the SAARC-countries runs to only 2.5 percent of their total foreign trade.

Thus, at present intra-regional trade in South Asia has almost no significance. Considerably more important SAARC-trade partners are the industrial countries and the other developing countries. Even the SAARC`s foreign trade with the non-SAARC Asian developing countries is greater than intra-regional trade. 13.5 percent of foreign trade transactions is carried out with non-SAARC-members in (developing) Asia against a percentage of 2.5 percent within the SAARC-region. Foreign trade relations to other SAARC-countries are important only for Nepal and the Maledives and to a smaller degree for Bangladesh and Sri Lanka. For Pakistan and particularly for India, foreign trade with their South Asian neighbours is no factor of importance.

Viewed optimistically, the small intra-regional trade offers the chance of future expansion of the trade among SAARC-countries. Viewed realistically, on the other hand, it shows evidence of the fact that at present the expansion of intra-regional trade flows is hindered by various factors. In this connection high tariffs and non-tariff trade barriers of the South Asian countries are of major importance.

In 1982, the unweighted average of nominal import duties[17] of Bangladesh came to 76,0 percent, that of India to 72,0 percent, and that of Sri Lanka to 38,8 percent.18 Pakistan and Nepal have high import duties, too, which restrict total imports and consequently also those from neighbour countries. In all SAARC-countries also non-tariff trade barriers are used to restrict imports. Of major importance are fiscal levies, consumption taxes, restrictive allowance of import licenses, total import bans, distribution of foreign currency for national (central) development planning, and import monopolies by the state for certain goods.

The actual restriction of intra-regional trade by tariffs and non-tariff trade barriers depends, however, on the structure of import duties and the other trade barriers concerning the goods imported. Usually, the trade barriers for consumer goods are higher on average than those for capital goods. Since the SAARC-countries produce mainly consumer goods besides agricultural products and only to a small extent capital goods, the trade barriers of these countries will probably be important factors for restricting intra-regional trade.19

Thus, the prospects for intensified intra-regional trade largely depend on the preparedness to reduce such trade barriers or even remove them completely. This, however, is not sufficient. In addition, each country must possess comparative advantages for certain goods that can be used in intra-regional trade. These advantages can be static, i.e. a country may have a competitive advantage as against the other member states or third countries as a result of certain factors. Such factors comprise geographic or climatic conditions, the amount of fixed capital and skilled and unskilled workers or the level of technological and entrepreneurial know-how. Differences among the SAARC-countries concerning these factors can be the reason for comparative advantages. However, comparative advantages can shift during a period of time from one country to another in the case that a country`s provision with certain factors compared to another country has changed.

As far as their provision with these factors is concerned, there are considerable differences between the SAARC-countries. Regarding fixed capital and skilled workers and the state of technology, India ranges first, followed by Pakistan and Sri Lanka. At some distance apart Bangladesh, Nepal, Bhutan, and the Maledives follow, which dispose of a comparably low amount of these factors.

The structure of comparative advantages can be illustrated far more detailed by the exports of SAARC-countries than by these very general remarks. Among many other indicators, the "Export Performance Ratio" gives a good idea of the comparative advantage of a country. This indicator represents the relation between a country`s share of exports of a certain product in total exports

Table 2 Products with high Export Performance, India and Pakistan, 1976 - 1978

SITC-code	Commodity description	export performance ratio India	Pakistan
032	fish preparations		3,24
0422	rice, glazed or polished	2,49	92,72
061, 062	sugar, sugar prep., honey	5,45	
074	tea and mate	76,14	
081	tobacco manufactures		2,69
122	feeding-stuff for animals	5,51	
2219	flour and meal of oil seeds		60,90
2312, 2313	synthetic and reclaimed rubber	3,47	
531	synthetic organic dyestuffs	2,02	
611	leather	22,98	19,82

612	manufactures of leather	5,44	
651	textile yarn		9,94
652	cotton fabrics, woven	10,94	24,08
653	textile fabrics, woven other than cotton	3,73	
656	made up articles	16,04	19,64
657	floor coverings	7,95	28,57
661	lime, cement	2,28	
671	pig iron	5,99	
673	iron and steel bars	2,34	
676	rails and railway track constr. mats.	9,60	
693	wire products	2,02	
695	tools	2,00	
697	household equipment	2,59	
733	road vehicles other than motor vehicles	2,13	
841	clothing	3,60	
894	preambulators, toys, games, sporting, goods		3,67

Source: UNIDO, Changing Patterns of Trade in World

Industry: An Empirical Study on Revealed Comparative Advantage, United Nations, New York 1982.

and the share of world exports of this product in total world exports. Thus, the indicator illustrates whether a country exports a certain product with above-average success (compared to the structure of world exports) or only on below-average level. Table 2 gives a list of those export products (on the basis of the three digit level of the Standard International Trade Classification, SITC), where India and Pakistan are particularly successful exporters. India possesses high Performance Ratios for considerably more products than Pakistan. It is further to be noted that India is exporting relatively successfully a great number of manufactured goods (SITC 5-8).

For 50 percent of the products exported by Pakistan with above-average success the Export Performance Ratio for India is high, too. Hence, in the case of rice, leather, cotton fabrics, made-up articles, and floor coverings the two countries are competitors on the export markets. In 1983, these five product groups covered 42 percent of Pakistan`s total exports. Therefore, an intensified Indian-Pakistani trade concerning these products is rather improbable. This becomes even more apparent if one takes into consideration that in 1983 almost two thirds of Pakistan`s exports were made up of cotton (SITC 263), textile fibres (SITC 65), and clothing (SITC 84), products that are also exported by India to a large degree.

An even less favourable position concerning the expansion of intra-regional trade is given by the export structures of the other SAARC-countries. Nearly 75 percent of Bangladesh`s export earnings result from the export of only six products (textiles, jute, fish, leather, and tea, see Table 3).

Table 3 Major Export Products of Bangladesh,1982, share of total exports in percent

SITC	group	of country total in percent
656	Textile etc. products nes	24.3
653	Woven textiles non-cotton	18.6
264	Jute	14.9
031	Fish fresh simply presvd.	9.9
611	Leather	8.4
074	Tea and mate	7.5
Remainder		16.4

Source: UNCTAD, Handbook of International Trade and Development Statistics, 1985 Supplement, United Nations, New York 1985.

Table 4 Major Export Products of Sri Lanka, 1982, share of total exports in percent

SITC	group	of country total in percent
074	Tea and mate	30.7
841	Clothing not of fur	16.6
332	Petroleumprod.	13.1
231	Rubber crude	11.2
051	Fruit fresh	4.4
Remainder		24.0

Source: see table 3

Table 5 Major Export Products of Nepal, 1982, share of total exports in percent

SITC	group	of country total in percent
611	Leather	18.9
657	Floor coverings	16.2
042	Rice	11.0
653	Woven textiles	7.8
291	Crude animal matter	7.4
054	Vegetbl. fresh simply prsvd.	7.3
Remainder		31.4

Source: see table 3

Table 6 Major Export Products of Bhutan, 1982, share of total exports in percent

SITC	group	of country total in percent
075	Spices	50.9
243	Wood shaped	11.9
599	Chemicals	6.1
Remainder		31.1

Source: see table 3

Table 7 Major Export Products of Maledives, 1982, share of total exports in percent

SITC	group	of country total in percent
031	Fish fresh	54.5
032	Fish tinned	25.7
074	Tea and mate	5.4
Remainder		14.4

Source: see table 3

Sri Lanka`s main export product is tea, followed by clothing, rubber and fruit (see Table 4). These four products cover almost two thirds of the country`s total exports. 60 percent of Nepal`s export earnings result from the exports of leather hides, floor coverings, rice and textiles (see Table 5). The major export product of Bhutan are spices (see Table 6); the exports of the Maledives even consist to more than 80 percent of only one product - fish (see Table 7).

Seen as a whole the preconditions for an expansion of intra-regional trade in regard of the pattern of exports of the South Asian countries are not very favourable.[20] Only India and to a smaller degree also Pakistan export a wide range of products. The other SAARC-member states cover most of their exports with only a few products. Very often these are products that are of great importance to other SAARC-countries, too, for example fish, tea, leather, textiles, clothing.

Nevertheless, there is a great number of products that would be suited for intensified intra-regional trade. The best position concerning exports to neighbouring countries is probably held by India, which produces and exports a great variety of those manufactured goods which could be imported by other South Asian countries only from non-SAARC-members, above all from newly industrializing countries and industrial countries. It is doubtful, however, whether India`s neighbours are willing to increase their imports of Indian goods markedly, when on the other hand there is no hope to a substantial increase in their exports to India. The same two preconditions that all participating countries must have more net benefits than costs and that the distribution of the advantages gained by the cooperation must be regarded as just, can be applied to intensified regional trade cooperation. If the smaller SAARC-countries feared, that India gets most advantages of intensified intra-regional trade, and that they had to expect only small advantages or even disadvantages, there would hardly be a basis for regional trade cooperation. Therefore, the measures aimed at intensifying intra-regional trade had to take into consideration the economic and overall situation of each SAARC-member state. Global measures, such as the granting of preferences on tariffs to the amount of 10 or 15 percent are therefore out of question. On the contrary, special measures to ease intra-regional trade had to be taken in individual cases. Possible incentives for intra-regional trade by special measures exist in many branches, for example, by improving transport or by creating joint ventures with the participation of two or more member states. Measures regarding trade policy are also possible, for example the granting of the "most favoured nation status" in the case of Nepal`s and Bhutan`s trade with the other SAARC-countries [21] or the reduction of non-tariff trade barriers which are deliberately discriminating the other SAARC-members. However, no prompt success is to be expected as far as the expansion of intra-regional trade is concerned. And it has to be asked whether it is not more profitable for all SAARC-countries to concentrate on the increase in exports to the world market, above all to industrial countries. This question, however, cannot be discussed in this paper.[22]

4. The Association of Southeast Asian Nations: A Model for SAARC?

The Association of Southeast Asian Nations (ASEAN), which consists of Brunei, Indonesia, Malaysia, the Philippines, Singapore, and Thailand, is often cited as a particularly successful example of economic cooperation among developing countries and as a model for similar attempts of cooperation in other regions. Therefore, the process of economic cooperation of ASEAN will be considered briefly so as to throw some light upon the question whether ASEAN could function as a model for SAARC.

The objectives of ASEAN go beyond economic integration and include cooperation in the fields of politics, technology, social and cultural affairs, science, and administration. Yet, successes of the cooperation are most evident in foreign policy because the member states have managed to present a united front to third countries, particularly with regard to those foreign policy problems which affect the interests of the Association as a whole. Examples for this are the negotiations with Japan, the United States, Australia, and the European Community, as well as the relations with the Communist governments in Indo-China. Very often it is stressed that it was more the political threat from outside than the felt necessity for economic cooperation which gave the cooperation process momentum. This may also explain why till the Bali-Summit in 1976 no concrete cooperation measures had been pursued, even though the Association was already founded in 1967.

From the Bali-Summit the major measures evolved to foster regional cooperation are:

1. Trade liberalization through Preferential Trading Arrangements(PTA) aimed at promoting intra-ASEAN trade and greater specia-lization between the member states.

2. ASEAN Industrial Projects (AIP); the allocation of large-scale industrial projects on a package deal approach.

3. ASEAN Industrial Complementation (AIC), mainly undertaken by the private sector and aimed at rationalizing existing in-dustries by intro-ducing complementary in production.

4.1 Preferential Trading Arrangements (PTA)

ASEAN is a preferential trading zone and no customs union. Initially, trade liberalization among the ASEAN-members followed a product-by-product approach. Since 1981 trade negotiations have been held at half-yearly intervals at which each country submits a list of 400 products for which it is prepared to grant tariff concessions in order to obtain counter-concessions for other products.[23] The preference granted was first 10 percent and then raised to a percentage between 20 and 25 percent after 1981. This product-by-product approach in the liberalization negotiations has suffered some major drawbacks which reduced its practical values in forms of trade creation. The member states tended to offer those products for tariff concessions, which were of only minor importance in their import bundle and thus would have only a limited impact on their national economies. Some countries even offered products that were not produced or traded in the region at all; for instance, Indonesia offered a tariff cut on nuclear reactors, and the Philippines on snow ploughs. Furthermore, the individual countries were more ready to grant tariff concessions for those products whose tariffs were already comparatively low. Moreover, constantly changing lists of tariffs tend to cause confusion among the trading partners, thus making it more difficult to exploit fully the tariff concessions granted.

To ensure that the intra-regional trade liberalization was not entirely depending upon the wearisome product-by-product approach, in 1980 the economic ministers agreed upon across-the-board reductions of tariffs for "lightly traded items", that is to say products whose import value was less than 50,000 US dollar in 1978. This threshold was raised to 10 million US dollar at the end of 1982. Across-the-board tariff cuts range from 20 to 25 percent. However, this approach is hampered by national exclusion lists on "sensitive products". Therefore, the effectiveness of across-the-board tariff cuts depends upon the extent to which individual countries do not exclude sensitive products from tariff concessions.

IN 1984 the total number of products for which preferences under the product-by-product approach and across-the-board tariff cuts were agreed nearly reached 20,000. Despite this rather impressive number of items and although the PTA came into operation already in 1978, its effect on intra-regional trade has been fairly negligible. In 1982 the total value of exports of PTA-products in all member states was 31.3 million US dollar, whereas total intra-regional trade amounted to 11.5 billion US dollar.[24] The poor trade-creating effect of PTA can largely be explained by the small export value of those products for which preferences were granted and by the ceiling on tariff reduction of 25 percent. This may be one reason why presently the question arises whether the tariff cuts have been "deep" enough to restructure the flow of ASEAN`s trade [25] and whether ASEAN should proceed from a preferential trading zone to a free trade area. Considering the different trade policies pursued by the individual ASEAN members, it might be rather unrealistic that ASEAN could proceed to form a custom union.[26]

4.2 ASEAN Industrial Projects (AIP)

The Declaration of ASEAN concord states inter alia that member states "shall cooperate to establish large-scale ASEAN industrial plants particularly to meet regional requirements of essential commodities and that the expansion of trade among member states shall be facilitated through cooperation in ASEAN industrial projects." The criteria for selecting these projects were to be whether a project showed "economies of scale" which could be realized within the ASEAN market; whether the country`s own materials were used; whether it improved internal supplies of food and saved foreign exchange and whether it created industrial jobs. In March 1976 the first package of ASEAN Industrial Projects (AIP) was identified: Urea projects for Indonesia and Malaysia, a diesel engine project for Singapore, a superphosphate project for the Philippines and a soda-ash project for Thailand.

In 1985, about eight years after the inception of AIP, only the urea project in Indonesia had come into production, the urea project in Malaysia was under construction. The other projects are still in the planning stage. Due to the results of feasibility studies the Philippines abandoned the superphosphate project and proposed an ammonium sulphate fertilizer project in 1978. This project was again withdrawn and a copper project was agreed for the Philippines in 1982.

The Singapore project was most hotly disputed because when selecting the project, the fact that diesel engines were already being produced in the member states was overlooked or given too little importance. Indonesia and the Philippines in particular opposed the production of diesel engines with less than 500 HP in Singapore. Moreover, all other member states planned to expand their existing production capacity or to start with the production of diesel engines. Since those countries were not willing to give up their plans in favour of the Singapore project, Singapore withdrew the ASEAN diesel engine project. In May 1984, a vaccine project was approved for Singapore.

The disagreement on the diesel engine project is a graphic example for the difficulties faced by every attempt for regional cooperation. The hoped-for benefits of cooperation can only be achieved if the countries concerned are willing to accept vertical and horizontal specialization. The example also shows that regional cooperation can be successful only if all partner countries are convinced of its potential advantages and of the just distribution of these advantages among the partner countries. Obviously, this was not the case for the diesel engine project. On the one hand, Singapore could not be considered to be a customer for the projects of the other four ASEAN members,[27] on the other hand, it would have been dependent upon those countries as its customers for diesel engines. Consequently, the other countries quite naturally feared that the benefits of such a specialization would be unequally distributed to their disadvantage.

The overall assessment of the attempts at cooperation in Southeast Asia is somewhat ambiguous. Greatest progress has been achieved by the ASEAN states with regard to political cooperation, such as the agreement on a common policy towards the nations of Indo-China or in representing their common interests in relations with third countries (e.g. the EC, the USA, and Japan). In the field of economic cooperation, however, there is an obvious shortfall between the official objectives and the actual results. Yet, the ASEAN members do at least have an unmistakable political desire for integration. Progress towards integration depends, however, to a large extent upon a solution being found to the problem of equitable distribution of the advantages and disadvantages of cooperation. This question of distribution has played a predominant and breaking role in the past process of ASEAN cooperation.

Thus the example of ASEAN once more demonstrates the vital condition for any successful regional cooperation: a balance must be found between the regional and the national interests.

5. Conclusions

The individual member states of SAARC attribute as well political as economic objectives with regional cooperation. The most promising field for regional cooperation might be the improvement of social and physical infrastructure. Intra-regional trade in South Asia is negligible. This opens the chance for an intensified division of labour among the member states. However, it is to be doubted that all SAARC-countries can exploit this chance. Especially the smaller countries might fear that the advantages of increased intra-regional trade may not be equally distributed among the members of the association.

Thus, ASEAN is far from being a model for SAARC, for it would be unrealistic that the just begun cooperation in South Asia could make comparable progress in the near future. However, the SAARC-members could draw some lessons from the experience made in the process of cooperation among the ASEAN member states.

The core problem of any form of regional cooperation between developing countries is the distribution of benefits and costs of intensified cooperation among the partner countries.

1. It is a prerequisite for successful cooperation that for all countries the hoped-for advantages exceed the expected disadvantages of

cooperation. The net advantages of cooperation must be distributed among the partner countries in a manner which is judged as just and fair by all members.

2. In practice the first precondition may be met first in those fields of cooperation which promise benefits but do not involve any or only negligible costs for all member states. This may explain why the success of ASEAN cooperating in those areas of foreign policy where these countries share common interests and where the region is affected as a whole.

3. Cooperation is more difficult when there are positive and negative effects involved. Under those circumstances cooperation should concentrate upon measures where the benefits and costs can easily and safely be calculated.

Therefore, cooperation in certain specific projects to improve the regional infrastructure is more likely to find consensus than a substantial reduction of trade barriers to intensify the intra-regional division of labour.

Even if SAARC aimed at liberalizing intra-regional trade, the trade creating effect would be negligible. First, the South Asian countries would preferably grant concessions which involve only a minor sacrifice. Secondly, the export potential of some SAARC-countries is very limited, so that no major effect of labour division could be expected.

4. Since the SAARC-members have agreed upon unanimity, cooperation measures which cause a net disadvantage in only one single country will not find any consensus.

5. The equitable distribution of net benefits is the second prerequisite for successful cooperation. This precondition has been fulfilled only partly in the ASEAN context, since some ASEAN-members feared that other members would gain more in certain fields of cooperation.

It is to be assumed that the distribution of net benefits will also play a braking role in the South Asian process of cooperation.

6. Seen in political terms, it must be noted that there is an important difference between ASEAN and SAARC. It was only by external political factors that the process of integration of ASEAN got its decisive impetus; only the necessity for cooperation in the field of foreign policy increased the willingness to cooperate in other areas, too. In the case of SAARC, such political pressure from outside cannot be seen. On the contrary, it seems as if internal political problems even hinder the process of cooperation.

References

1 This paper is the abridged version of a paper presented at the 9th European Conference on Modern South Asian Studies held atHeidelberg, July 9-12, 1986.I am very grateful to Mrs. Gabriele Voigt for her assistancein translating this paper.

2 Cf. UNCTAD, Arusha- Programme for Collective Self-Reliance and Framework for Negotiations. Note by the Secretary-Generalof UNCTAD, TD/236, 28 February 1979.

[3] List taken from R.J. Langhammer, D. Spinanger, Wirtschaftliche Zusammenarbeit zwischen Entwicklungsländern, Chancen und Risiken, Tübingen 1984, p. 31.

[4] Tariffs and non-tariff trade barriers are generally higher in developing countries than in industrial countries. About 70 percent of the goods imported in developing countries are subject to controls of quantity and price. Cf. UNCTAD,Protectionism, Trade Relations and Structural Adjustment, Geneva 1983.

[5] Linear tariff reductions of 10 to 15 percent are recommended, for example, for all products, and a reduction of 5 percent for least developed countries.

[6] Langhammer and Spinanger estimate the trade-creating effect of tariff preferences among developing countries, ranging from 10 to 15 percent, up to 6 percent compared to the initial level of trade. Cf. op.cit., p. 40.

[7] Cf. United Nations, Recent Experience in Economic Cooperation Among Developing Countries and Possibilities for Progress inthe 1980s. Supplement to World Economic Survey 1983, New York 1983, pp. 8.

[8] A description of the evolution of SAARC is given in I.H. Bokhari, South Asian Regional Cooperation, Progress, Problems, Potential and Prospects, in: Asian Survey, Vol. 25 (1985), pp. 371-390.

[9] The Integrated Programme of Action approved by the foreign ministers at their August 1983 meeting

contains as prospective fields for cooperation: agriculture, rural development, meteorology, telecommunication, scientific and technological cooperation, health and population, transport, postal services, sports, arts and culture.

10 "Without belittling the efforts and achievements, it can be said that the unanimity reflected comes more from agreement on what not to talk about and not to do to keep the process alive than what to discuss and what to do to make it succeed." I.H. Bokhari, op.cit., p. 379.

11 For instance, at their Male meeting in July 1984 the foreign ministers gave a statement on the London summit of June 1984.

12 Cf. I.H. Bokhari, op.cit., pp. 381-382.

13 The SAARC-members agreed to pass their resolutions unanimously. Cf. Declaration on South Asian Regional Cooperation, August 1983.

14 Cf. I.H. Bokhari, op.cit., pp. 386-388.

15 So far financial assistance to SAARC programmes has been accepted only from international institutions. Particularly India resisted foreign aid to SAARC from individual countries because of fear of foreign influence. Cf. S.D. Muni, Building Regionalism from Below, in: Asian Survey, Vol. 25 (1985), p. 402.

16 The corresponding figures for Bhutan are not available. Cf. IMF, Direction of Trade Statistics, Yearbook 1985, Washington 1985.

[17] That is, the import duties rates are not put into rela-tion to the shares of imports for the products concerned in total imports.

[18] Cf. R.J. Langhammer, D. Spinanger, op.cit., p. 36.

[19] A detailed list of tariffs and non-tariff trade barriers of the SAARC-countries is not available. Hence, a more precise evalua-tion of their effects on intra-regional trade cannot be carried out.

[20] Cf. also S. Rahman, Issues and Agenda for South Asia Regional Cooperation, A Bangladeshi Perspective, in: Asian Survey, Vol. 25 (1985), pp. 415-416.

[21] Nepal and Bhutan are not GATT-members.

[22] This question is discussed in detail in: O. Havrylyshyn (ed.), South-South or South-North Trade: Does the Direction of Developing Country Exports Matter? World Bank Conference Volume, Washington 1985. See also R.J. Langhammer, Märkte in Entwicklungsländern für Entwicklungsländer: Neue Schubkraft für Wachstumsprozesse "von unten"? in: Probleme und Perspek- tiven der weltwirtschaftlichen Entwicklung, ed. by H. Giersch, Berlin 1985, pp. 113-128.

[23] Non-tariff trade barriers are also to be removed. However, so far no perceptible success has been made along these lines.

[24] M.K. Chug, N. Siagian, The ASEAN Experience in Trade Liberalization with Special Reference to Agricultural Trade, ASEAN Secretariat 1983.

[25] Cf. J. Wong, ASEAN`s Experience in Regional Economic Cooperation, in: Asian Development Review, Vol. 3 (1985), p. 88.

[26] Cf. H.C. Rieger, ASEAN: A Free Trade Area Or A Customs Union, in: Far Eastern Economic Review, Vol. 132, No. 18 (1986), p. 58-60.

[27] Brunei became a member of ASEAN in February 1984.

Bibliography

Asian Development Bank, Key Indicators of Developing Member Countries of ADB, Vol. XIV, Bangkok 1983

Bokhari, I.H., South Asian Regional Cooperation: Progress, Problems, Potential and Prospects, in Asian Survey, Vol. 25 (1985), pp. 371-390

Chug, M.K., Siagian, N., The ASEAN Experience in Trade Liberalization with Special Reference to Agricultural Trade, ASEAN Secretariat 1983

Havrylyshyn, O., Wolf, M., Trade Among Developing Countries: Theory, Policy Issues, and Principal Trends, World Bank Staff Working Paper No. 479. Washington 1981

Havrylyshyn, O., (ed.), South-South or South-North Trade: Does the Direction of Developing Countries Exports Matter? World Bank Conference Volume, Washington 1985

International Monetary Fund, Direction of Trade Statistics, Yearbook 1985, Washington 1985

Langhammer, R.J., Märkte in Entwicklungsländern für Entwicklungsländer: Neue Schubkraft für Wachstumsprozesse "von unten"?, in Probleme und Perspektiven der weltwirtschaftlichen Entwicklung, hrsg. v. H. Giersch, Berlin 1985, pp. 113-128

Langhammer, R.J., Spinanger, D., Wirtschaftliche Zusammenarbeit zwischen den Entwicklungsländern, Chancen und Risiken. Tübingen 1984

Maas, C.D., Indien - Nepal - Sri Lanka: Süd-Süd-Beziehungen zwischen Symmetrie und Dependenz,

Wiesbaden 1982

Muni, S.D., Building Regionalism from Below, in Asian Survey, Vol. 25 (1985), pp. 391-404

Rahman, S., Issues and Agenda for South Asia Regional Cooperation, A Bangladeshi Perspective, in Asian Survey, Vol. 25 (1985), pp. 405-425

Rieger, H.C., ASEAN: A Free Trade Area Or A Customs Union, in Far Eastern Economic Review, Vol. 132, No. 18 (1986), pp. 58-60

Rieger, H.C., ASEAN Co-operation and Intra-ASEAN Trade. Institute of Southeast Asian Studies. Singapore 1985

UNCTAD, Arusha-Programme for Collective Self-Reliance and Framework for Negotiations. Note by the Secretary-General of UNCTAD, TD/236, 28 February 1979

UNCTAD, Protectionism, Trade Relations and Structural Adjustment. Geneva 1983

UNCTAD, Handbook on International Trade and Development Statistics Supplement 1985, United Nations, New York 1985

UNIDO, Changing Patterns of Trade and World Industry: An Empirical Study on Revealed Comparative Advantage, United Nations, New York 1985

UNIDO, Industry and Development, Global Report 1985. United Nations, New York 1985

United Nations, Supplement to World Economic Survey 1983, New York 1983

United Nations, 1983 International Trade Statistics Yearbook, vol. I, New York 1985

Wagner, N., Regional Integration between Developing Countries, The Example of South and Southeast Asia, in Intereconomics, No. 6 (1983), pp. 270-277

Wong, J., ASEAN`s Experience in Regional Economic Cooperation, in Asian Development Review, Vol. 3 (1985), pp. 79-98

Improving Capital Supply to Asian Developing Countries:

South-South Cooperation and Financial Integration

by Wolfgang Veit

1. Introduction

This article is to cover a subject often subsumed under the heading of South-South-Cooperation (SSC). Concentrating on the Asian region [1] means to leave aside the global approach of SSC. However, the idea of SSC has its origin here, in Bandung in 1955.

Advocates of SSC divide it into two broad fields: economic and technical cooperation. These areas can again be subdivided into attempts of [2]

- regional economic integration
- cooperation in trade
- cooperation in the field of funds
- scientific and technological exchange

- cooperation towards the raising of the level of self-sufficiency
- technical cooperation in the foodstuff and agricultural sectors
- cooperation in industrial production

Most of these proposals imply the intervention on world markets by developing countries' multilateral institutions.

Despite the current discussion on development aid it is a generally accepted fact that developing countries have a deficit in capital endowment.

The much criticized international financial markets, during the past decades, handled the bulk of capital transfers to developing countries. [3] As this had to be done under market conditions, the redemption of international debt now becomes imminent, at the same time being impossible, though.

Thus, future increase of capital in developing countries should take on different forms. Among them, capital mobilization within and among developing countries becomes increasingly important. This is where we return to South-South-Cooperation. Two basic approaches can be determined:

First, there is a view of SSC as formulated by those organizations representing the developing countries. They favour a change in the conditions of capital transfers to their members. This is to be achieved by a different set of rules governing this transfer. Suggestions have been made at the

'High-Level Conference on Economic Cooperation among Developing Countries` in Caracas in 1981 and the expert group meeting of the Group of 77 in Jamaica in 1982. [4] Both conferences have called for a closing of so-called financial gaps, i.e. a deficiency in the supply of finance for the purpose of programme lending, commodity stabilization, export promotion and improvement of developing countries' cooperation.[5]

It is in particular the following actions, which are to be taken within the framework of financial SSC:[6]

a) Longterm joint ventures of surplus and deficit developing countries should be conducted by a publicly owned and run holding company

b) Energy investment is to be accelerated by a specific institution (for example the proposed Energy Affiliate of the World Bank)

c) Export credit financing, re-finance guarantees and insurance facilities in order to increase South-South trade

d) Commodity Finance to intervene on world markets or at the producers level.

Common to all proposals is the installation of some kind of public organizations which intervene on the financial markets. "Given the size of the funds required..., presumably such a proposal would be open to membership by the developed countries." This notion of Avramovic, originally applied to the financing of energy investment, can be generalized and is another way of saying that developed countries have to finance operations which run counter to their own attitudes.

It can be said that the solution to the financial gaps relies on unrealistic assumptions as far as the help of OPEC and developed countries is concerned.

Second, financial South-South Cooperation can be conceived as being an attempt to increase both the size and the efficiency of the existing financial relations. This finally results in the mobilization of developing countries' resources (capital), which reduces the dependence on developed countries' funds and strengthens the yet relatively weak intra-South economic ties.

The chances of this second conception of SSC are supposed to be better because they do not face the above mentioned obstacles.

The state of financial development in Asian will be covered first in this article.

It has to be pointed out that the important question of financial institutions is excluded from the analysis. This, however, does not deny its relevance to financial integration.

After this basic evaluation, specific opportunities for financial cooperation within the wider framework of regional integration are shown for those countries belonging to either SAARC or ASEAN.

In part 3 and 4 there is given broad attention to the concept of economic regional integration, because the discussion, as far as Asia is concerned, has rather been concentrated on political aspects.

In part 5 and 6 this leads to the application of alternative approaches of monetary integration to Asian financial development.

2. Some Indicators of Financial Development in Asia

Theory considers the proceeding of an economy from the system of subsistence-production via barter-trade to the use of money as a medium of exchange as being a sign of development.

It has already been said that regional integration is relying on the assumption that the countries concerned be not too diverse in their development level. This is particularly true for monetary integration.

A first way to find out about a country`s monetary development is to measure the use of money as a means of payment, store of value and medium of exchange.

For this purpose the common definition of money in an economy is very useful:

> M1: the amount of national currency held by non-banks as cash or deposits is called M1. It represents financial assets of the highest liquidity.
>
> M2: When time-deposits, savings-deposits and financial assets of a maturity of less than

four years (called "quasi-money" because of its lower degree of liquidity) are added to M1 we arrive at M2.

To provide comparable data M1 and M2 usually are related to Gross Domestic Product and population. Instead of M2 here the use of "quasi-money" is preferred, because this aggregate singles out best the "accumulation and diversification of financial wealth" [7] when related to the population. In relation to GDP it approximates the ratio of financial stocks to national income, another important indicator.

Besides measuring its size the way of channeling liquidity from surplus-units to deficit-units (see page 11) hints at the development of the financial sector.

The role of financial intermediaries, reflecting the know-how of the techniques in this field, can be demonstrated by data related to financial activity. For this purpose two different indicators are employed:

first, the claims of the financial sector on other domestic private sectors is related to gross national product (=CPS/GDP). This ratio reflects "the proportions of national wealth held through financial intermediaries" [8]

second, the importance of the financial intermediaries relative to the economy can be approximated by its contribution to national income (=GDP<FS>/GDP). [9]

2.1 The State of Financial Development in ASEAN and SAARC

Table 4 shows that, on the average, in both ASEAN and SAARC there exist regional subgroups. With respect to financial development in its above mentioned sense, Singapore and, to a smaller extent, Malaysia take the lead in ASEAN. Although so such clear distinction can be made as far as SAARC is concerned, India and Pakistan appear to be most advanced there.

Subsistence economy is of importance in Nepal and Bangladesh and Sri Lanka, where the M1-ratios are lowest. On the other hand, diversification of financial assets (M2-ratios) is highest in Sri Lanka and India suggesting that money has taken over the store-of-value functions there.

Turning to ASEAN, this is especially true for Singapore, Malaysia and to a lesser extent Thailand.

As to this particular point, Indonesia and the Philippines do not compare very favorably to SAARC, which is generally thought to be far above the ASEAN-level. This too holds for the activity of the financial intermediaries. Again Singapore, Malaysia and Thailand take the lead in ASEAN while Indonesia and the Philippines remain on the level of the leading SAARC countries India, Pakistan and Sri Lanka.

It becomes evident, that in both regions there exist strong differences in financial deepening. However, the data for the advanced ASEAN countries show too high a development, because they are affected by the existence of off-shore-markets.

Still, before a freeing of monetary markets from government monopoly (as proposed in the following chapters) can be undertaken, a further development in this sector has to be achieved.

2.2 Indicators of Financial Development in Remaining Asia

Obviously Japan is the leading country with respect to financial development. This is no surprise and therefore special attention ought to be paid to the less developed economies of the region.

The smallest countries Fiji, Maldives, Papua New Guinea, Solomon Islands, Tonga, Vanuatu and Western Samoa do not perform in a common way and sometimes even quite well. This partly reflects the bad state of national accounting and statistical information on these countries. On the other hand they have recently been trying to attract foreign financial institutions by offering them off-shore conditions. This essentially means tax-exemptions. The smaller an economy, the more any new financial activity will influence the statistical data.

Burma, compared to Bangladesh, shows a higher ratio of money per capita but lower figures for all other indicators. Obviously there exist no popular financial assets besides money, which is used as a means of payment rather than a store of value. A transfer of funds from surplus to deficit units seems to be less working in Burma. With respect to this transfer of funds China seems to be performing better. There, quasi-money is of substantial importance when related to national income. This seems to be supported by a high CPS/GDP-ratio, reflecting an extended use of credit facilities.

By these standards bank loans are a widely used instrument of finance in Korea and Taiwan, too. The formation of financial wealth measured by the quasi-money indicators is only next to that of Japan. This is especially true for Taiwan.

Obviously financial development so far has not been affected by regional integration: strong discrepancies exist throughout Asia. Of course, this could be expected from ASEAN only, because SAARC has been established only recently and without specific measures in the field of finance. Therefore it seems to be worthwhile to look at the specific opportunities that regional integration offers to financial development.

Before this will be done, attention should be paid to the relative importance of some potential sources (these sources need not necessarily contribute to GCCF because in the case of direct investment and portfolio investment, they can mean a change of ownership of existing fixed capital) of Gross Fixed Capital Formation (GFCF) in Asia (table 5).

The first three columns show the amount of capital formation. Again the so-called newly industrializing countries take the lead, behind Japan, of course. Differences become more evident when capital formation is related to the population, because it is (more) closely related to the level of GDP.

Private flows of capital (Direct Investment DI and Portfolio investment PI) seem to play a role only in Malaysia and Singapore, although this evidence is weak because of missing data for some other countries. However, other long term capital (OLC) flows to the region; including development aid, can not be considered as a complete substitute. Still they are highest in the best known aid recipient of the region, Bangladesh.

As a general conclusion it can be said, that private capital flows are of less importance for the majority of Asian countries. This can be explained by the conditions for private investment in some Asian countries as given in table 6.

However, the fact has to be stressed, that all sources of GCFC are possible ones only. Whether of not this financial capital is converted into fixed capital, can not be seen from these data. Besides the fact that among all foreign sources the private ones are of less importance, it should be noted, that for every country (with the exception of Papua New Guinea) the domestic capital supply (Quasi Money 'Q-M) is dominating all other capital sources.

Because of this it is financial integration of the Asian economies that is of special importance to the domestic 'South-South-financing` of the region`s development.

The next chapters will pay special attention to financial development within the context of regional integration.

3. Aspects of Regional Integration in Asia

The quarrels about regional integration in Europe left strong doubts as to its application in developing countries. However, the author believes that closer cooperation is needed and can be successful under certain conditions. This will be demonstrated in the following.

The South Asian Association for Regional Cooperation (SAARC) and the Association of South East Asian Nations have many predecessors in other parts of the world. Not only have there emerged, since the end of World War II, numerous institutions with the purpose of international cooperation in the fields of jurisdiction, economics and politics, but these elements of integration were typical for many attempts of nationbuilding during the past twenty centuries.

Before integration was made a subject of social scientists, the Romans had put it into practice in founding the 'Römische Reich Deutscher Nation', perhaps the most successful integrational attempt. It showed all the static ingredients of integration, i.e. the geographical, political and economic dimensions. The fact that it broke down in 1815 indicates that an additional dimension of integration is needed in order to gasp it in full scope: time, measured by the term of viability.

Although detailed research on the reasons for the rise and the fall of the Roman Empire must be left to historians, the statement of Johann Jacob Moser, a German professor of political law, in 1745 shows the way to the present problems of regional integration:

"Das Römische Reich wäre ohnstreitig noch jezo die formidabelste Potenz von ganz Europa, wenn dessen Stände, führnehmlich aber die mächtigsten, einig wären und mehr auf das gemeine Beste als auf ihr Privat-Interesse sähen". [10] His notion, that those who are in power and responsible for a community not necessarily pursuit the policies leading to an increase in the common welfare but rather take an overriding interest in their own political fate, seems to be applicable for the quarrels about regional integration in South and Southeast Asia.

So, under the heading of optimality, what we require a politician to be like, is: to exclude personal interest from public decision-making and to know about the means that lead to rational decisions. Given these 'prerequisites`, the question whether or not some kind of integration is advantageous for a group of countries should be decided in terms of costs and benefits (this method is not, or at least should not be, a domain of economics but of social sciences in general).

In order to set a general framework, before dealing with the costs and benefits brought about by economic integration, the neighbouring areas will be covered briefly.

a) The Legal System

If we accept Jean Jaques Rousseau`s thesis, that a 'contrat social` implying a transfer of rights from individuals to a supraindividual institution leads to a net increase in social welfare, we can assume, that a social contract between homogeneous social groupings was what Rousseau would mean on a larger scale. So the benefits of legal integration can roughly be identified as a reduction of frictions between social groups. (Obviously this has positive effects on the areas of politics and economics). The costs are represented by the condition of homogeneity: Forcing heterogeneous social groups to agree to a common social contract can increase frictions when the new common legal system does not meet or even violates the fundamental requirements of all groups.

Applied to the South-Asian scenario this means that optimum legal integration is characterized by a set of legal systems. Whether the present set already is optimal cannot be judged by the author. (Research on the question in how far British Colonial Rule represented a feasible degree of legal integration is, in this context, of more than historical interest).

b) The Political System

Legal regional integration can be achieved, too, by multilateral and stepwise adjustment of different sub-systems which belong to different political systems. This is not possible the other way round, as (at least from a democratic point of view) a political system bases on specific legal regulations. An integration of several political institutions then requires to be covered by a corresponding common legal basis. This, for example, is the characteristic of a federal system. Then the decision to let legal integration be followed by political integration is, again, subject to measuring the net costs or benefits. Leaving aside the positive effects of political integration on the economic system, disadvantages resulting from decreased representation of minorities have to be weighed against advantages resulting from increased power to carry through national conceptions in the field of external relations. Since Roussueau`s model of a 'contrat social` originally referred to the formation of a political and legal integration is nothing but two sides of the same coin. In the presence of political scientists any further examination of this subject does not seem appropriate.

c) The Economic System

Traditionally economic integration has been considered to be a matter of removal of trade-barriers. The basic idea is that trade increases when tariffs and other impediments to trade are reduced or abandoned mutually. By making use of comparative advantages in the production of different goods international specialization will take place and thus lead to higher welfare levels of the participating countries.

At this point the method of measuring costs and benefits can be applied in its pure, economic meaning: increased competition will lead to higher efficiency of production, i.e. a saving of resources (trade creation).

This benefit will come into effect only if a new common external tariff of the integrated countries does not substitute less efficient resources from inside the trade area for the more efficient ones from outside (trade diversion).

The same method, of course, can be applied to the international transfer of financial assets. Comparative advantages in supplying financial capital and converting it into real capital mean increased efficiency of investment for all participating parties. As with trade-integration, there can be observed effects creating or diverting financial flows.

Obviously, the net effect of economic integration depends largely on the composition of the newly formed economic area. Welfare increases will be highest where countries, in spite of a competitive production pattern before integration, have the potential to switch over to complementary production after integration has been established. This differenciation is necessary because of different degrees of homogeneity of the traded goods. This does not hold for the financial sector. "Production" and trade of financial capital means

- a transformation of the term-structure of capital supply into that of capital-demand
- a transfer of funds from surplus units to deficit units

Figure 1: Financial Intermediation

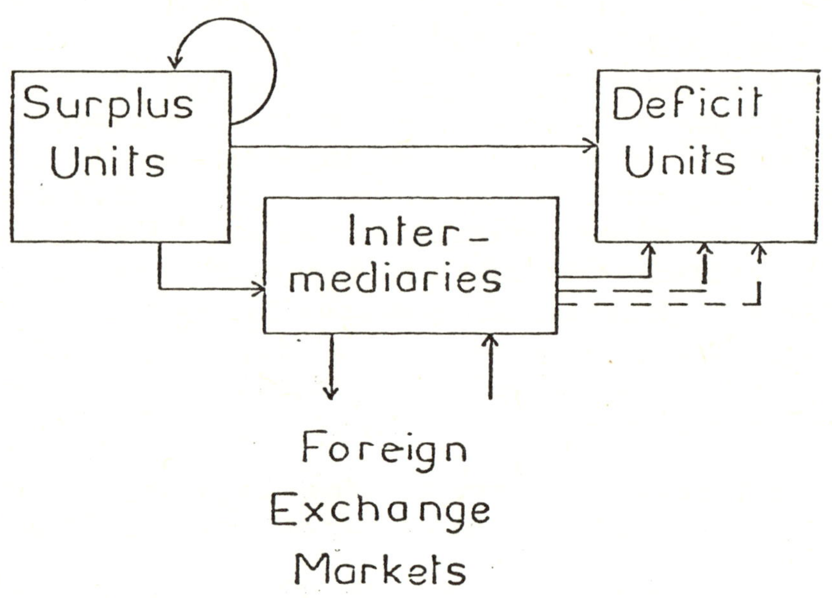

Although there exists a large variety of financial assets, their degree of homogeneity is by far higher than that of commodities: transfer and transformation of financial assets is much faster. So the problem of an adequate composition of the economic area seems to be, at first sight, of a more simple nature.

So far a brief and partial survey has been given about potential fields of activity for regional integration. It is neither complete nor does it take care of the manyfold and important interrelations between the legal, political and economic areas. To go into more details would mean to reach beyond the scope this paper was supposed to cover.

Another deficiency, though, will be made up for: The understanding of integration as a static phenomenon. A proper evaluation of financial integration in particular can be achieved only when dynamic effects are taken into consideration. This supports the view of modern theory and empirical evidence alike maintaining that integration is not a mere process of "institution-building by declaration".

4. The Importance of Monetary Integration

The economic impact of monetary integration, again, should be measured in terms of costs and benefits. It now becomes clear, why there is a widespread scepticism about economic and particularly financial integration as far as South-Asia is concerned: The following summary of the effects of monetary or financial integration shows that additional costs will arise for the official sector (loss of sovereignity) and that the private sector will benefit from higher efficiency in its above mentioned meaning.

In the first place monetary integration implies the reduction or elimination of exchange rate variations. This substracts exchange risk from the total value of risk in international transaction.

Exchange risk can take considerable proportions especially for the foreign trader as it is neither foreseeable nor related to the risk connected with the (better known?) foreign partner.

As the patterns of foreign trade are to a large extent determined by historical factors, a positive influx of financial integration is to be expected only

- when there exist preconditions in the form of comparative advantages
- when additional measures in the field of trade integration have been taken
- in the long run

Besides potential effects on trade the elimination of intra-regional exchange risk represents an increased incentive for investors to finance projects in this region. Among other things this increases the efficiency of the money markets and can consequently lead to repatriating capital into this country; capital which up to then had been invested outside the area.[11]

Since this form of integration requires supra-national administration (in the case of one single currency for the region, otherwise some looser form of cooperation is needed), one can expect that monetary policy is less influenced by one-sided measures of the countries concerned. Thus more stability can be expected in this sector, which would probably intensify the above mentioned tendencies and support the process of mobilizing national financial capital. This would in turn result in the development of a stronger and more active monetary market, which then again inhances efficiency both in this sector and in the whole economy.

These positive aspects stand in contrast to the restraints a closer monetary cooperation imposes on national governments. The more different the level of development in the participating countries, the more different the policy solutions will be. In concordance with traditional development theory this means that a set of multiple interest rates, not to speak of credit rationing, will be applied in order to reallocate funds. Increased mobility of capital can have detrimental effects on these strategies. An analogous experience was made in India when an enlarged network of banking facilities led to an outflow of savings funds from less developed/low productivity regions to metropolitan areas offering a higher return on investment. This problem can easily be avoided if fiscal instead of monetary instruments were used in order to reallocate funds. Or, as Tyabji puts it, "The optimal solution calls for the abandonment of such policies and, where necessary, the substitution of explicit for implicit subsidies to increase the efficiency of the system".[12]

This not only increases efficiency in the use of instruments by the official authorities but, in addition, frees the financial markets from excessive government intervention (the Korean experience with financial repression gives sufficient evidence).

Governments of developing countries rely heavily on central bank credits in order to balance their budgets because neither domestic capital markets nor a domestic tax structure are available to take over this function. A coordination of budget-discipline then is needed in order to avoid unproportional increases in the national money supply.

5. Theories of Monetary Integration

The development of the analytical framework for the discussion of monetary integration coincided with various international currency-crises and the setting-up of plans for a monetary union within the EEC at the end of the sixties (finally resulting in the ambitious but ill-fated 'Werner-Plan`).

The theories were based on the prevailing Keynesian understanding of economic policy. In order to evaluate the economic advantages of a currency union, they focused on the following criteria:

1. Mobility of the factors of production
2. the economy`s level of diversification
3. Fiscal integration
4. The economy`s level of openness

A brief explanation of what these criteria mean to monetary integration shall be given:

ad 1.: The higher the mobility of the factors of production, the easier the adjustment to disparities between the regions with different productivity. Changes in demand have less regional consequences on prices and employment. At the same time, adjustment measures in the foreign trade sector (i.e. a change in nominal exchange rates) become less necessary. As a result, increased stability of real exchange rates can be expected.

ad 2.: The greater the variety of goods traded with foreign countries (those of the future currency-area), the smaller the probability and the extent of changes in the terms of trade caused externally. Accordingly, a high level of diversification has a stabilizing influence on real exchange rates.

ad 3.: The main aspect of fiscal integration is a supra-national budget, being capable of setting off differences in income (caused, for example by, a shift in demand) by progressive taxation and compensation transfers.

ad 4.: The higher the economy`s level of openness, the smaller the necessary changes of foreign trade measures to overcome disturbances. For example, the changes in the exchange rate to increase demand have to be lower when the percentage of exports in GDP is high.

Difficulties in the measuring of these criteria, as well as the fact that they do not exist independently from each other, resulted in the notion, that the question of monetary union is a 'dead-end-problem`.[13]

Vaubel[14] , however, pointed out, that at least the problem of measuring these criteria can be solved by reducing the large number of variants to the one of the real exchange rate.[15]

The real exchange rate can be computed by eliminating inflation in any two countries involved. In practice, constant real exchange rates mean

- the same degree of inflation in both countries and no change of nominal exchange rates

- differing inflation and offsetting exchange rate movements

- no inflation and constant nominal exchange rates

Thus, the question whether a monetary union (in its above stated meaning and being an ultimate goal of closer monetary cooperation) is viable and should be aimed at can be answered by the real exchange rates of the countries concerned: The more uniform their movements, the higher the probability of a positive answer.

Tables 1 and 2 (at the end of this contribution) show the real exchange rates of the 'SAARC`and 'ASEAN` region. It is achieved by taking the U.S.-Dollar as a common basis. "The simplest and most useful measure of real exchange rate variations within a group of countries is the variance of their rates of change vis-a-vis a numeraire".[16]

An analysis of the data leads to the following results:

ASEAN-exchange rates (in terms of variance) show the highest degree of stability (low. 3.93 in

1981; peak: 213.38 in 1983). The 1983 value is caused by a revaluation of the Malaysian currency when all other currencies devalued heavily against the U.S.-Dollar.

Opposite to ASEAN-exchange-rate movements, SAARC-currencies did not revalue or devalue as uniformly via-a-vis the U.S.Dollar: A low of 13.63 in 1983 and a peak of 77.21 in 1982 do not seem to compare very unfavourably to the ASEAN data. Still, the average level of the variance is significantly higher with SAARC than with ASEAN.

For the purpose of judging the viability of monetary integration in both Asian regional groupings, a comparison with corresponding data of a more advanced region in terms of economic integration is most useful. The five major EEC-countries ('major` in an economic meaning), between 1981 and 1984, experienced a variance in their real exchange rate variations of 3.16 (low in 1984) and 41.71 (peak in 1981). Although no erratic movements have occured, there seems to be less real exchange rate stability within the EEC than within ASEAN.

The working of the European Monetary System (EMS) which fixes most of the member countries` currencies to the European Currency Unit (ECU, a common basket-unit of account) may have been of a dominant role here.[17]

This view is supported when the United Kingdom, as it is not participating in the EMS, is excluded from the sample. Then, the variance of the remaining four European currencies ranges from 3.63 in 1985 to 32.48 in 1981.

The following conclusion may be drawn from these results: Closer monetary cooperation by means of narrowing the bands for intraregional exchange rates is viable for ASEAN, rather than for SAARC.

The high variance for SAARC indicates that monetary integration in the above mentioned sense would imply high political costs: keeping fixed SAARC exchange rates would force the member countries\` governments to submit domestic policies to external rules: a problem that is supposed to be the reason for the termination of the Bretton-Woods-system in 1973.

The characteristic of the approach to monetary integration dealt with so far is its implication of Keynesian philosophy. That is, a countries\` government is responsible for reaching the economic targets.

For this purpose it has specific rights and instruments, among them the right to issue the national currency. In a complex political-economic system however, monetary policies can not be pursued independently.

This is one reason for the development of a different approach to monetary integration. The other reason is to be found in the assumption, that governments are not even in a position to fulfil their economic tasks to the benefit of the society.[18] The authors of this theory contend that money is a product like any other product and that therefore its production should not be under the monopoly of the government. This recommendation seems hardly to be welcome by most governments. Still, there can be derived specific economic measures serving the purpose of monetary integration without at the same time causing a fundamental change in the economic system. The concept of a parallel-currency, as explained in the following, may show a way out of the dilemma of 'traditional' theories.

6. The Concept of Currency-Competition

The idea of currency-competition has to be seen against the background of liberal economic theory: the role of governments and administrations in economic life should be limited to its absolute minimum. Responsibility for and activity in the economy should be left to the private sector.

The relationship between the approach dealt with above and the parallel-currency-approach can, plainly speaking, be characterized as 'monopoly versus free competition'. Of course, this touches a classical domain of government economic policy (although parallel currencies have existed in several countries since the mid-nineteenth century).[19]

A brief summary of the theory that underlies this second approach has to be given:

- Money is not a collective good but a private good. Because this is so, there is no reason for production and distribution of this good by non-private authorities.

- The production of money (i.e. the creation of liquidity) has decreasing marginal costs, thus limiting the number of producers (i.e. suppliers of liquidity).

- Competing currencies tend to be less inflationary than monopolistic ones (as, under free currency choice, 'consumers` of money can switch from one currency to another whenever they fear a loss of value of the former). They can therefore choose a certain level of monetary stability instead of subordinating to government decisions.

- Currency competition will finally lead to a small number of currencies (if not a single one) and to a set of financial assets reflecting the true need of the population. Monetary integration would be accomplished then.[20]

- In order to enjoy the mentioned benefits of a free market for money and financial assets, the participants have to be free from money-illusion (i.e. individuals have to base their economic decisions upon real instead of nominal economic data).

This last condition can be called 'transparency` or 'perfect information`. As it is rarely met, particularly as far as developing countries are concerned, certain problems arise: a lack of information on the part of specific social groups (notably those who are not accustomed to financial markets) means that arbitrage to the disadvantage of the less informed will come into being. Although arbitrage will lead to a further promotion of finanical acitivities, this can create social and economic imbalances in the beginning.

It can be assumed that people will have less knowledge of monetary markets the less these markets are developed in a country. In the case of region-wide currency-competition this holds for different countries, too.

So the basic condition for applying this approach to developing countries is that there may be as few differences in 'financial skills` (this does not mean that everybody has to be a financial expert, of course!) as possible, both nation-wide and region-wide.

Chapter 2 shows that this condition is not fulfilled. Regional monetary integration is a promising strategy only if the domestic financial markets are further developed in order to make them harmonize. This does not mean, however, that it will be of importance only at a time when the afore mentioned developement has been completed: Modest intra-regional steps have to be accompanied by domestic development.

7. Summary

In the context of South-South Cooperation the shortage of capital in developing countries is of particular importance. From the point of view of the developing countries this problem should be solved by installing new institutions. Their common features are:

- in many cases they intervene on the world markets

- they are controlled by developing countries and financed by industrialized and OPEC-countries.

It becomes clear that the chances to put this kind of South-South Cooperation into practice are low. It is for this reason that a different form of SSC for Asia is discussed in this paper. In order to increase the capital supply to the Asian developing economies, the opportunities of regional financial integration are evaluated here. This includes an analysis of the importance of regional integration for developing countries, because it has been looked upon with a certain skepticism, in the vace of the well known problems within the EEC.

However, regional integration is not a modern concept. It has been accomplished in many cases since the very first emergence of political systems. Still, methods of integration may have changed slightly.

Modern economic theory offers device a well suited to judge the desirability of regional integration by assigning costs and benefits, respectively, to every single consequence.

Within the field of economic integration international trade used to play a dominant role. It was only during the last decade that financial integration meaning the removal of obstacles to all sorts of monetary and financial transactions has been recognized as being of equal importance.

Nevertheless, academic discussion has been concentrated largely on financial integration among industrialized countries, notably the

European Community, thereby neglecting the impact of closer financial ties between developing countries on their economic development. This is especially true for those regions, where political tensions seem to exclude any economic cooperation.

Two principal approaches to regional financial integration can be identified. The first can be associated with a Keynesian view of economic policy, assigning to governments the responsibility for all major areas of economic development. Financial integration, as can be shown by the 'Theory of Optimal Currency Areas`, relies heavily on its compatibility with all economic aggregates that are related to the monetary one. Under these conditions it is hard to decide on the viability of monetary unions (those being the ultimate goal of financial integration). This problem can be overcome by taking the real exchange rates of the countries concerned as a measure of compatibility: real exchange rates are influenced by all factors determining the viability of a monetary union.

Statistical data show that there is a much stronger coherence of economic development within ASEAN than within SAARC. Prospects for traditional ("Keynesian") monetary cooperation thus are not bad for ASEAN. On the other hand this way of monetary integration conveys high (political) costs for the SAARC-countries, leading to even higher intraregional tensions.

The second approach to financial integration is based on a completely different assumption: reforming the present system of government monopoly of issuing one national money would create competition on financial markets. According to the theory of currency competition, this would lead to a very limited number of, if not one single, currency of high stability. Monetary integration would then be accomplished, bringing forth all the advantages enlarged financial markets grant for economic development.

An important prerequisite for introducing competition to developing countries markets is a minimum level of domestic financial development. This would prevent the less advanced sectors or regions from being 'exploited` (by arbitrage) by those more advanced. Indicators of "Financial Deepening" (as defined by Shaw) for both groups of countries show, that

- the level of financial deepening is higher in ASEAN. For this reason the economies seem to be more ready for free financial markets.

- the disparities in financial development are higher in ASEAN. This gives an edge in competition to the offshore centers Singapore and Malaysia with their sophisticated financial institutions.

There may be concluded that closer financial ties within SAARC and ASEAN are not out of question, especially not as far as the latter is concerned. Yet, provided the political stituation permits the adoption of the free market-approach, special care will have to be taken about the financially less developed sectors in the beginning. Before regional monetary integration can be accomplished, further steps in financial integration of the domestic economy are necessary.

This strategy should not be refuted on other than economic grounds, as the repercussions from closer economic ties on politicaal integration are quite promising. This, again, is prooved frequently by history.

Table 1:

SAARC-U.S. REAL EXCHANGE RATE CHANGES
1981-1985
(%)

	1981	1982	1983	1984	1985 1)
BANGLADESH	-13.59	-19.87	-6.49	4.88	-4.82
INDIA	-7.52	-7.49	1.89	-8.52	-7.15
NEPAL	-2.18	-1.86	-8.62	-14.66	-9.65
PAKISTAN	1.58	-19.97	-6.52	-4.28	-18.58
SRI LANKA	-8.98	-3.58	-2.21	4.19	-8.88
AVERAGE	-6.12	-18.55	-2.79	-3.69	-8.84
VARIANCE	34.94	77.21	13.63	69.51	5.58

1) except for Sri Lanka all 1985 data are estimates

Source: Inernational Financial Statistics, March 1986, IMF

Table 2:

ASEAN-U.S. REAL EXCHANGE RATE CHANGES
1981-1985
(%)

	1981	1982	1983	1984	1985
INDONESIA	1.03	-1.39	-28.89	-6.61	-7.16
MALAYSIA 1)	-6.54	-1.76	1.10	-1.36	-9.29
PHILIPPINES	-2.48	-4.10	-23.33	-4.27	8.07
SINGAPORE	-0.77	-3.59	-0.74	-2.65	-6.25
THAILAND 1)	-4.26	-6.31	0.50	-6.18	-16.10
AVERAGE	-2.60	-3.43	-10.27	-4.21	-6.15
VARIANCE	8.72	3.93	213.38	5.05	78.03

1) 1985 data of Malaysia and Thailand are estimates

Source: Inernational Financial Statistics, March 1986, IMF

Table 3:

EUROPEAN-U.S. REAL EXCHANGE RATE CHANGES
1981-1985
(%)

	1981	1982	1983	1984	1985
FRANCE	-25.61	-15.33	-9.56	-11.57	-8.62
GERMANY	-28.43	-8.27	-5.12	-13.36	-4.85
ITALY 1)	-25.34	-8.67	-8.88	-9.18	-3.87
NETHERLANDS	-29.21	-7.31	-7.29	-13.42	-4.91
UNITED KINGDOM	-13.21	-13.45	-13.99	-12.82	-.18
AVERAGE					
(all)	-24.36	-10.61	-7.35	-12.07	-2.73
(exclusive U.K.)	-27.15	-9.98	-5.69	-11.88	-3.36
VARIANCE					
(all)	41.71	12.60	24.24	3.16	5.88
(exclusive U.K.)	32.48	14.14	9.80	16.10	3.63

1) 1985 data for Italy are estimates

Source: International Financial Statistics, March 1986, IMF

Indicators of Financial Deepening
in Asia, 1983

	M1 per cap. (US-$)	M1/GDP	Q.-Money per cap. (US-$)	Q.-Money /GDP	CPS/GDP	GDP(FS) /GDP
BRUNEI 1)	-	-	-	-	-	0.02
INDONESIA	53.57	0.11	50.94	0.10	0.21	0.05
MALAYSIA	388.35	0.20	801.77	0.41	0.52	0.08
PHILIPPINES	56.12	0.08	109.45	0.16	0.36	0.08
SINGAPORE	1629.27	0.24	3202.50	0.48	0.93	0.22
THAILAND	72.30	0.09	323.06	0.40	0.40	0.09
BANGLADESH	14.24	0.12	17.80	0.15	0.13	0.10
INDIA	42.04	0.16	69.09	0.26	0.26	0.06
NEPAL	19.12	0.13	22.90	0.16	0.08	-
PAKISTAN	85.47	0.28	50.41	0.16	0.27	0.05
SRI LANKA	40.26	0.12	66.57	0.20	0.26	0.05
BURMA 7)	37.47	0.22	15.59	0.09	0.05	0.01
CHINA 2)	68.34	0.29	48.07	0.21	0.73	-
FIJI 3)	287.46	0.12	443.28	0.27	0.24	0.12
HONG KONG 1)	865.39	0.17	651.43	0.13	-	0.26
KOREA	218.85	0.11	521.28	0.27	0.50	0.08

Indicators of Finanoial Deepening
in Asia, 1983

	M1 per cap. (US-$)	M1/GDP	Q.-Money per cap. (US-$)	Q.-Money /GDP	CPS/GDP	GDP(FS) /GDP
MALDIVES	74.12	0.19	41.18	0.11	0.27	-
PAPUA N.GUINEA 4)	77.43	0.18	167.02	0.22	0.22	-
SOLOMON ISLANDS 4)	65.36	0.11	96.72	0.16	0.15	-
TAIWAN 4)	415.65	0.26	871.06	0.54	0.66	-
TONGA 5)	150.10	0.24	-	-	-	0.07
VANUATU	190.58	-	549.50	-	-	-
WESTERN SAMOA	74.60	-	95.80	-	-	-
JAPAN 6)	2834.53	0.29	5812.26	0.59	0.94	0.14
Average ASEAN	368.97	0.14	750.92	0.28	0.43	0.10
Average SAARC	40.23	0.16	45.35	0.18	0.20	0.07
Average other	486.14	0.19	776.03	0.26	0.42	0.11
Average other excl. Japan	283.78	0.18	318.19	0.22	0.35	0.11
Average all	333.94	0.17	637.58	0.25	0.38	0.09

1) Data available for 1982 only
2) Instead of GDP, National Income data are used
3) GDP(FS) consists of 1982 data
4) Data available for 1979 only; GDP is an estimate
5) Data in national currency of Tonga
6) The GDP(FS)/GDP-ratio is computed from 1982 data
7) The GDP(FS)/GDP-ratio is computed from 1981 data

Sources: World Development Report, World Bank 1985
International Financial Statistics, IMF, May 1980 and March 1986
Statistical Yearbook for Asia and the Pacific 1983, United Nations
The Taiwan Economy in Transition, S.Kuo, Boulder 1983
Key Indicators of Developing Member Countries of ADB
April 1983, Asian Development Bank

Sources of Gross Fixed Capital Formation (GFCF)
in Asia, 1984

	GFCF/ capita	National GFCF/ Regional GFCF	GFCF/ GDP	Direct Investment/ GFCF	Portfolio Investment/ GFCF	Other Long Term Capital/ GFCF	Quasi-Money/ GFCF
BRUNEI	-	-	-	-	-	-	-
INDONESIA 1)	152.31	0.05	0.29	0.01	0.02	0.20	0.33
MALAYSIA	653.03	0.02	0.30	0.09	0.10	0.12	1.40
PHILIPPINES 1)	164.68	0.02	0.17	0.01	0.00	0.12	0.67
SINGAPORE 1)	3151.20	0.02	0.23	0.18	-0.01	0.00	1.02
THAILAND	187.58	0.02	0.23	0.04	0.02	0.13	2.01
BANGLADESH 1)	10.43	0.00	0.08	0.00	0.00	0.45	1.74
INDIA 1)	55.01	0.08	0.21	-	-	0.04	1.25
NEPAL 5)	19.13	0.00	0.14	-	-	0.15	0.83
PAKISTAN	50.15	0.01	0.15	0.01	-	0.08	0.96
SRI LANKA	96.73	0.00	0.25	0.02	-	0.22	0.73

Sources of Gross Fixed Capital Formation (GFCF) in Asia, 1984

	GFCF/ capita	National GFCF/ Regional GFCF	GFCF/ GDP	Direct Investment/ GFCF	Portfolio Investment/ GFCF	Other Long Term Capital/ GFCF	Quasi-Money/ GFCF
BURMA	31.91	0.00	0.19	-	-	0.16	0.56
CHINA 2)	25.17	0.05	0.11	0.04	0.00	0.02	1.90
FIJI 1)	34.78	0.00	0.02	1.33	-	-	12.38
Hong Kong 3)	1369.02	-	0.28	-	-	-	0.48
KOREA	616.86	0.05	0.30	0.00	0.01	0.10	0.89
MALDIVES	137.65	0.00	0.31	-	-	0.11	0.42
PAPUA N.GUINEA 3)	135.24	0.00	0.33	0.19	-	0.92	0.62
SOLOMON ISL. 3)	-	-	-	-	-	-	-
TAIWAN 4)	359.53	0.01	0.25	0.02	0.00	0.03	2.15
TONGA 1)	-	-	0.27	-	-	-	-
VANUATU	-	-	-	-	-	-	-
WESTERN SAMOA	-	-	-	-	-	-	-
JAPAN	2958.25	0.72	0.29	-0.02	-0.07	-0.06	0.02

1) 1983 data
2) China GFCF is an estimate
3) 1982 data
4) 1978 data
5) 1980 data

Sources:
International Financial Statistics, IMF, May 1988 and March 1986
Statistical Yearbook for Asia and the Pacific 1983, United Nations
Key Indicators of Developing Member Countries of ADB, April 1983, Asian Development Bank, 1983

Table 6: Restrictions and Regulations Concerning Foreign Investment in selected Asian Countries

Country	Regulations on Entry of Foreign Direct Investment	Regulations on Entry of Foreign Portfolio Investment	Regulations on Degree of Foreign Ownership	Regulations on Repatriation of Profits and Capital	Other Restrictions or Regulations
India	Reserve Bank permission is required for any business activity conducted by nonresidents, noncitizens, and Indian companies with over 40 percent nonresident interest.	Prior approval of the Reserve Bank is required for all transfers of shares of Indian companies by or to nonresidents.	Nonresident participation is normally limited to 40 percent, but participation up to 74 percent is allowed (on a sliding scale) depending on the extent to which a company is engaged in "core" industry or export-oriented production, or in manufacturing industries that require sophisticated technology. Full nonresident ownership is allowed for companies that export their entire production. In addition, all companies are subject to "dilution" formulas which require minimum percentages of the estimated cost of any expansion to be raised through additional equity capital issued to Indians.	Profit remittances by branches of foreign firms require the prior approval of the Reserve Bank. Remittances of dividends to nonresident shareholders do not require prior approval, provided certain conditions are met. Capital invested in approved projects after January 1950 may be repatriated, but Reserve Bank approval must be obtained before effecting a sale which involves repatriation of assets. Proceeds of approved sales are allowed to be remitted in suitable installments, not exceeding four.	Without Reserve Bank permission, residents are prohibited from lending to companies in which the nonresident interest exceeds 40 percent.

Country	Regulations on Entry of Foreign Direct Investment	Regulations on Entry of Foreign Portfolio Investment	Regulations on Degree of Foreign Ownership	Regulations on Repatriation of Profits and Capital	Other Restrictions or Regulations
Indonesia	All investments require the approval of the President on the recommendation of the Investment Coordinating Board. The operating permit for foreign investment is usually valid for a maximum of 30 years.		In principle, investments may be undertaken only through a joint venture with an Indonesian partner.	No restrictions on profit remittances. The law provides that no transfer permit shall be issued for capital repatriation as long as investments benefit from tax relief; at present, however, foreign payments do not require a transfer permit.	A debt/investment conversion scheme exists, allowing foreign creditors holding nonguaranteed claims against Indonesia to use these claims to make investments under the Foreign Capital Investment Law.

Country	Regulations on Entry of Foreign Direct Investment	Regulations on Entry of Foreign Portfolio Investment	Regulations on Degree of Foreign Ownership	Regulations on Repatriation of Profits and Capital	Other Restrictions or Regulations
Korea	All foreign investment requires approval. A list of eligible projects and activities open to foreign investment is maintained; this list has been expanded in recent years.	Korea has announced a program of gradual liberalization of the domestic securities market. At present, local investment trusts can sell unit certificates to foreign investors, and international investment trusts are permitted on a limited basis, but direct foreign acquisition of equity in local companies normally not permitted	Lists of activities are maintained in which full, and 50 percent, foreign participation is permissible.	No restrictions, but proposed remittances must be notified to the Ministry of Finance 90 days prior to the end of the fiscal year.	Foreign-controlled firms in certain industries are subject to limits on the proportion of their output which can be sold domestically.

Country	Regulations on Entry of Foreign Direct Investment	Regulations on Entry of Foreign Portfolio Investment	Regulations on Degree of Foreign Ownership	Regulations on Repatriation of Profits and Capital	Other Restrictions or Regulations
Malaysia	Foreign investment requires prior approval, but most industries are open to such investment.		Under the New Economic Policy (NEP), targets have been set for minimum percentage of local ethnic (bumiputra and non ethnic Malay ownership of total corporate assets by 1990, but these percentages do not necessarily apply to each individual company. Guidelines set targets for local ownership in manufacturing industry, on a sliding scale based on exports and new technological inputs.	No restrictions	The Industrial Coorporation Act of 1975 requires all firms (whether domestic- or foreign-owned) to obtain a license for each product manufactured. Granting of the license may be subject to various performance criteria, including dilution of foreign ownership.

Country	Regulations on Entry of Foreign Direct Investment	Regulations on Entry of Foreign Portfolio Investment	Regulations on Degree of Foreign Ownership	Regulations on Repatriation of Profits and Capital	Other Restrictions or Regulations
Pakistan	Investments by nonresidents are subject to approval, but the Government has announced a liberal policy toward foreign investors, to encourage industrial development.	Nonresident investments in shares of Pakistani companies is permitted, provided the investment is made on the basis of nonrepatriation of capital and dividends. Repatriation is not granted unless the share purchases are an integral part of an approved investment project.	There are no conditions laid down regarding local capital participation, but it is expected that local currency expenditures will ordinarily be met from local equity capital.	Profit remittances are allowed freely where the investment was made with Government's approval. Foreign capital invested in approved industries after September 1954, including reinvested earnings and capital gains, may be transferred without restriction.	

Philippines	All investment is subject to the prior approval of the Central Bank. Preference is given to projects approved by the Board of Investments (BOI), to export-oriented industries, and to other industries not utilizing domestic credit resources.		New enterprises where investment by non-Filipinos exceeds 30 percent, and which are not covered by the Investment Incentives Act, require prior approval by the BOI. If purchases of shares by foreign nationals would reduce Philippine ownership in a firm to less than 70 percent, then permission from BOI is required. There are different arrangements for "pioneer" and "preferred" investments. Normally, enterprises owned or controlled by foreigners are allowed only in "pioneer areas of investment," and at least 60 percent of outstanding voting capital stock of enterprises in "preferred areas of investment" must be owned by Philippine nationals.	Profit remittances are permitted in full, provided they are not financed from domestic borrowing. Full repatriation is guaranteed by law for cash investments made after March 1973 in export-oriented industries, enterprises approved by the BOI, and in securities certified by the Central Bank and traded on the Manila and Makati stock exchanges. Securities must be held for a minimum of 90 days. Noncash investments and cash investments made before March 1973 can be repatriated in a number of annual installments, according to the category of the investment and its net foreign exchange earnings.	Foreign companies can borrow locally provided they have a debt-equity ratio of no more than 60:40 in high priority sectors, 55:45 in medium priority sectors, and 50:50 in low priority sectors. Rules specifying a minimum local content have been established in various industries.

Country	Regulations on Entry of Foreign Direct Investment	Regulations on Entry of Foreign Portfolio Investment	Regulations on Degree of Foreign Ownership	Regulations on Repatriation of Profits and Capital	Other Restrictions or Regulations
Thailand	Certain economic activities are reserved for Thai nationals.			No restrictions on profit remittances. Foreign investments under the Investment Promotion Act are given a guarantee of capital repatriation. The repatriation of other capital is considered on the merits of each case, but approval is normally granted if it can be shown that the funds originated abroad.	There are also limits on the degree of foreign equity participation allowed in various activities eligible for incentives under the Investment Promotion Act. Local-content requirements exist in the automobile industry.

Source: Foreign Private Investment in Developing Countries, A Study by the Research Department, IMF, Washington 1986

References

[1] The nucleus of this article is a paper with the title "Prospects of Financial Cooperation in SAARC and ASEAN", presented to the 9th European Conference on Modern South Asian Studies held at Heidelberg in July 1986.

[2] Zhan Peiji and Cheng Yugui, On the promotion of South-South Cooperation and its Measures, in A. Gauhar (ed.), The Rich and the Poor, London 1983.

[3] cif: Financial Flows to Developing Countries, Asian Development Bank.

[4] For an account of the proceedings of these conferences see: D. Avramovic, Financial Cooperation in Developing Countries: Issues and Opportunities, in A. Gauhar, op.cit.

[5] North-South: A Programme for Survival, London 1980, p. 236.

[6] Avramovic, op.cit.

[7] Lee/Jao, Financial Structures and Monetary Policies in Southeast Asia, London 1982, p. 21.

[8] Hang-Sheng Cheng, Financial deepening in Pacific Basin Countries, in: Economic Review, Federal Reserve Bank of San Francisko, August 1980, p. 43.

[9] The reliability of the figures given there, may, however, be of less significance, as they include the data for the real estate and business

service sectors. Where they are important relative to banking and insurances, a wrong impression may be obtained.

[10] in: Fragen an die Deutsche Geschichte, Deutscher Bundestag, Bonn 1981, p. 51.

[11] Finance and Development, December 1981.

[12] A. Tyabji, Monetary Policies and Financial Structures in ASEAN,

in Contemporary Southeast Asia, Dec. 1985.

[13] Hankel, Währungsordnung bei weltweit ungeregelten Kreditmärkten, in Schäfer, Weltfinanzen, Bonn 1980, p. 39.

[14] Vaubel, Strategies for Currency Unification. Tübingen 1978, pp. 3-4, p. 67, p. 139.

[15] Of course monetary integration is not limited to the outline presented here: The monetary integration of a nationl economy may as well mean the evolution of a more sophisticated use of monetary assets and of monetary instruments, respectively (as counted for by the theory of financial deepening).

[16] Vaubel, op.cit., p. 199.

[17] In this context an earlier collection of data may be taken as a reference: From 1971 to 1976, that is during a period of fundamental monetary reforms world-wide and diverging economic politicies and economic development in the European countries, ASEAN- and EEC-countries experienced a variance of real exchange rates vis-a-vis the U.S.-Dollar of 3.13 (ASEAN-low in 1978)

/ 157.36 (ASEAN-peak in 1979) and 5.9 (EEC-low in 1971) and 61.96 (EEC-peak in 1973).

[18] This idea, originated by von Hayek, is further specified in Salin, Currency Competition and Monetary Union, Den Haag 1984, pp. 2-3.

[19] How anxious indeed authorities are not to loose control of monetary affairs can, again, be illustrated by the European example: Whether or not European citizens should have access to funds denominated in ECU has been a much debated subject in recent years.

[20] In the context of regional integration this means to issue a common currency which is brought into circulation parallel to the existing national currencies.

Bibliography

Agraa, A.M., International Economic Integration. London 1982

Avramovic, D., Financial Cooperation in Developing Countries: Issues and Opportunities, in Gauhar, A, The Rich and the Poor, London 1983

Brandt Commission, North-South: A Programme for Survival London 1980

Cheng, H.S., Financial Deepening in Pacific? Basin Countries, in Federal Reserve Bank of San Francisco, Economic Review, August 1980

Claassen, E.-M., Kompendium der Währungstheorie. München 1977

Contemporary Southeast Asia, Vol. 7, No. 3. Institute of Southeast Asian Studies. Singapore 1985

Deutscher Bundestag (ed.), Fragen an die Deutsche Geschichte. Bonn 1981

Federal Reserve Bank of San Francisko, Economic Review, August 1980

Foreign Private Investment in Developing Countries, A Study by the Research Department, International Monetary Fund. Washington D.C. 1986

Gauhar, A., The Rich and the Poor. London 1983

Glismann/Horn/Nehring/Vaubel,Weltwirtschaftslehre. München 1982

Go, E.M., Patterns of External Financing of DMCs, Asian Development Bank Staff Paper No. 26.Manila 1985

Hankel, W., Währungsordnung bei weltweit ungeregelten Kreditmärkten, in Schäfer, Gefährdete Weltfinanzen. Währungspolitik. Stuttgart 1972

International Financial Statistics, May 1980, Mach 1986, Yearbook 1983, International Monetary Fund

Johnson, H.G./Swoboda, A.K., The Economics of Common Currencies. London 1973

Key Indicators of Developing Member Countries of ADB, Asian Development Bank, April 1983

Krämer, H.-R., Formen und Methoden der Internationalen wirtschaftlichen Integration, Tübingen 1969

Kuo, S., The Taiwan Economy in Transition. Boulder 1983

Lee, S.Y./Jao, Y.C., Financial Structures and Monetary Policies in South-East Asia. London 1982

Marjolin, R., Europe and the United States in the World Economy. Durham 1953

Nsouli, S.M., Monetary Integration in Developing Countries , in Finance and Development, December 1981

Salin, P., Currency Competition and Monetary Union. Den Haag 1984

Schäfer, H.-B., Gefährdete Weltfinanzen, Bonn 1980

Statistical Yearbook for Asia and the Pacific

1983. United Nations 1983

Stützel, W., Über unsere Währungsverhältnisse, Tübingen 1983

Tyabji, A., Monetary olicies and Financial Structures in ASEAN, in Contemporary Southeast Asia, Vol. 7, No. 3, Institute of Southeast Asian Studies. Singapore 1985

Vaubel, R., Strategies for Currency Unification. Tübingen 1978

Wagner, N., Regionale ökonomische Integration in Entwicklungsländern - das Beispiel Süd- und Südostasien. Heidelberg 1983

World Development Report, World Bank, Washington D.C. 1985

Zhang Peiji/Cheng Yugui, On the Promotion of South-South Cooperation and its Measures, in Gauhar, The Rich and the Poor. London 1983

Politics and Economic Development: The Case of Nepal

by Narayan Khadka

The main purpose of this paper is to analyze development/underdevelopment in the political-economic framework. If development/under-development is examined in purely economic terms, the analysis becomes mechanistic and it is difficult to get the right perspective on problems of development. In this case the policy suggestions offered become either ineffective or bear no significance. Politics plays a crucial role in the development of the less developed countries. But in many of these countries there is tremendous political instability or there exists political confrontation between or among various political forces or pressure groups. There is still debate or sometimes even political agitation about the form of government. This has been the major constraint in the development process of the less developed countries. But no sufficient attention is paid to this problem by both political scientists and development economists. This paper is an attempt to examine this issue by taking the case of Nepal.

INTRODUCTION

Nepal is a small country situated on the northern rim of South Asia. It is a mountainous, landlocked kingdom strategically located between two vast, most populous, developing South-Asian powers, China and India. This specific location has dwarfed Nepal`s size and it is generally referred to as a very small country (comparatively there are many countries smaller than Nepal). Viewed in this way Nepal is some 23 times smaller than India and 67 times smaller than China in terms of size of the country. And in terms of population it is 47 times smaller than India and 66 times smaller than China according to the 1982 population data. From a geographical point of view Nepal borders on the Tibet region of China in the north and on India in the east, west and south. The entire northern border of Nepal is sealed off naturally by the Himalayan range which indeed marks off the limits of South Asia as a geographical unit. The border with India is open and extends over 1400 km. This geographical location places Nepal in a landlocked position.

The landlocked position has been a big political and economic problem for Nepal. To be a physical bridge between the two emerging powers of Asia (contemporary writers on Nepal use the term 'sandwitched` or buffer state position) reflects Nepal`s sensitive and delicate geopolitical situation. It also symbolizes a 'living-case-history` between the two nations having diametrically opposed political, economic, and socio-cultural systems. Refering to Nepal`s situation some writers on Nepal maintained that "Kathmandu has frequently expressed its determination to avoid the paths charted by either of its giant neighbour, but it is still to be proved that an alternative system is feasible under such stressful conditions. The natural reactions might well be for Nepal to retreat to the protective shell long provided by its isolation from the harsh realities and ambiguities of international politics. But withdrawal has been specifically and repeatedly rejected by the Nepali political leadership in favour of a policy aimed at carving out a separate and unique international personality distinguishing Nepal from both communist China and democratic India".[1]

Physical location and geopolitical constraint provide Nepal with enough flexibility to maintain her separate identity in many respects. This unique geographical location of Nepal helped to serve the political interest of a type of despotic government called the Ranas from 1846 to 1951 which isolated Nepal by confining it to British India from the rest of the world. During this period Nepal was ruled by the autocratic Rana prime ministers who were chosen from a family hereditary line. The interest of this family rule was to isolate Nepal from western political and economic influences in order to perpetuate their family oligarchy. And this policy was as a matter of fact, in tacit conformity with the political and economic interests of British India. "The political consideration was to preserve peace in the region and maintain along the southern slopes of the Himalayas a chain of friendly states which enjoyed internal autonomy but whose foreign policy was subordinated to the Imperial interest of Great Britain...The economic consideration opening the British policy was to use those states as a channel of trade with trans-Himalayan areas".[2] Along with India`s independence in 1947 and Nepal`s success in overthrowing the Rana government in 1951 Nepal extended on foreign relations to a number of countries.[3] Though Nepal and India have many things in common the political relations between the two countries has passed through different phases. A number of factors such as geography, landlocked position, Nepal`s zone of Peace proposal, the open border and both immigration and emigration have influenced the relations between the two countries.

Nepal`s relations with the Peoples Republic of China witnessed several swings manifested in both war and peace from the time Nepal emerged as a nation state in 1768 to the early sixties. After the introduction of the present form of government the relations between the two countries have been friendly.

After 1951 the internal political situation of Nepal went through different experiments. The period between 1951 and 1960 was a short experiment with a multi-party system of government. After some initial instability and political chaos the late king announced a parliamentary form of government. The Nepali Congress, the largest party instrumental in revolting against the Rana government, obtained the overwhelming mandate. But after a short period of one and a half year the power conflict between the parliamentary government and the king became strong and volatile. And eventually, the king decided to dissolve the democratically elected government and put all the political leaders in jail. Political parties were banned and the fundamental rights were seized. After a brief period of direct rule by the king, an unique political system called the Panchayat system was introduced in 1962. The characteristic features of this system are discussed at length in order to understand the problems of underdevelopment of Nepal.

Socio-Economic Condition:

Geographical location and agriculture have been the main factors to determine the socio-economic political pattern and the cultural moorings of the Nepalese society. Geographically Nepal could conveniently be divided into three regions, the flat land (a narrow strip of territory which extends all along Nepal`s border with India) which occupies about 17 percent of the total area of the country, the hills which are situated between the Himalayan region in the north and the Mahabharat range in the south and which occupy about 68 percent of the total area, and the Himalayan region which lies 80 km north of the Mahabharat mountains, and occupies 15 per cent of the total area. The ethnic composition, religion, political power structure, and socio-economic pattern of the Nepalese society have a tremendous bearing on these regions. Historically and anthropologically, these geographical regions together have been the meeting ground of two civilization, the Mongoloid, and the Indo-Aryan strains who migrated to Nepal from south east, Tibet, and the Indian plains, several hundred years ago.

The geography and the land have formed the social structure of the Nepalese society. These factors have divided the people into different ethnic and cultural groups. People living in the intermontane (central and midwestern) region who were the descendants of the high caste people, migrated from India centuries ago, acquired sufficient land and then dominated the political and economic life of the country. To the present day Hinduism and the caste structure have their genesis in the acquisition of political control through land-ownership. Gradually, the other ethnic groups, who were low caste people and untouchables occupying a position below the high caste people, the Brahmins, and the Chhetries, were socially assimilated. The cast structure based on the ethnic division of labour was used to serve the interest of the ruling high caste people. The process of assimilation of different ethnic groups and the determination of their definite social relation have been made possible through agriculture. It has not only been the mainstay of the people but the main factor in shaping the life style of the Nepalese society. It has also been the source of accumulation of wealth, power, prestige and status, which have given birth to feudalism (according to marxist interpretation it would be called a prefeudal tenet). This has been the source of exploitation of the peasants of Nepal.

Social structure and socio-economic relations determined by agriculture are subject to gradual change emanating from political awakening, spread of education and communication media that have enlarged over a period of time and more particularly after liquidation of the Rana government in 1951. Historically the diverse ethnic groups were living in a symbiotic manner which has been the main basis of Nepal`s national integration - an unique phenomenon in a plural society. But with social interaction among different strata of population, made possible by modern communication, the social processes and relations are becoming complicated. Growing population and deteriorating economy also have a hand in this complication. The economic power structure is moving slowly in favour of the political elites, bureaucrats, the military elites, and the rising business community. The static and composite features of a rural society structured by land and agriculture are being eroded by population growth. This has permitted social mobility and greater interaction among different ethnic groups. But the highest price for this social integration is to be paid by the peasantry. Since poverty could not be attacked, the process of social mobilization and modernization has promoted regionalism and ethnocism in the country. Now the social caste structure and feudal exploitation have acquired new patterns of social relationship.

As mentioned above agriculture has been the core of the socio-economic relation of the Nepalese society. The century old isolation policy of the Rana government was the main factory responsible for the stagnating and traditional agriculture. Although land had been the major source of income and wealth and political power for the Rana government and their feudal chieftains and civil servants, no serious attention was paid to the modernization and improvement of this sector. There was not much done for the improvement of other sectors of the economy either. The demonstration effect from the British rule in India gave a certain impetus to create very insignificant infrastructural facilities and establish some industries. All these were to serve the interest of the ruling family. Lack of any deliberate interest and policy to protect the 'limited self-dependent` economy (because the limited consumption of a few basic needs items were locally produced) the cottage industry base was destroyed and the export of the unemployed to foreign armies and emigration became the general socio-economic phenomena.

After the overthrow of the Rana government the primary task for the people in the government was to start the process of development from scratch. This was a herculian task in a country which lacked everything except land and people. It was therefore, essential to plan modernization and development of the country in a systematic manner.

Planning and Development:

In an underdeveloped and shortage economy like that of Nepal, planning implies the creation of certain basic economic forces for long term development. Planning in Nepal is an attempt to create an ideal combination of both public and private initiatives in development. It tries to combine the features of planning and of market forces. However, to bring the economy on the right track, that is to prevent maldevelopment or lopsided development, the full load of national development lies with the state sector. Certain constraints are also prevalent which obstruct the role of private initiative. Seen from this perspective, the objectives of economic planning in Nepal are mainly to increase production in agriculture not only to meet the national demand for subsistence but as an important vechile for increasing income and employment, and to create an environment for industrialization. This was very essential for absorbing growing unemployment and regulating the supply of consumer goods. Other objectives have been the creation of a basic infrastructural network and the delivery of social goods essential for moral, intellectual and physical development of the people. These important sectors need some discussion, as they constitute the backbone of the economy and hence also serve as the basis for evaluating efforts and achievements of the government vis-a-vis the political machinery.

Agricultural Sector:

After the political change in 1952 the succeeding government, which in a way, embodied the spirit of 'revolution of rising expectations` inherited a backward and traditional agricultural sector, a virtually non-existent infrastructural base and a decaying cottage industry sector. Agriculture was backward in many respects. Firstly the methods of cultivation were poor and unscientific. No modern tools and equipments were available or used. Similarly the use of inputs and the supply of irrigated water was little known to the people. Only about 14700 hectare area were under irrigation.[4] Of the total cultivated land of 2.5 million hectares about 0.59 per cent were under irrigation.

Secondly, there were institutional and organizational problems. Land and agriculture were the main source of exploitation of the tenants by the landlords. In many cases rent[5] and interest on agricultural credit were very high.

Agricultural credit was to be supplied by the landlords since there were no credit institutions in the organized sector. The collection of interest was mainly in kinds and was exorbitantly high. There was no security of the tenancy right. Any tenant could be evicted anytime depending on the sweet will of the landlord. Tenants were subject to other forms of exploitation as well such as compulsory extra payments, free labour, supply of gifts and presents etc., all to be given to the landlord in exchange for the tenancy privilege. Thirdly, land was cultivated in small holdings; however, it provided only a slender margin above the subsistence level (of requirements). Very little agricultural products were exported to India to meet some import requirements. And finally, due to the prevalent land tenure[6] system and the then existing unscientific system of revenue collection, very little revenue was collected from the land. Anyway this was not important as before 1951 it was destined to go to the private purse of the Prime Ministers. Institutional efforts to collect data and facts about agricultural production and land distribution were unknown before 1951.

After the introduction of a democratic government in 1951 several steps were taken to reorganize the agricultural sector. One of the immediate measure taken, was the enactment of the Tenancy Rights Acquisition Act (1952). This was followed by a number of other steps[7] like the establishment of a commission and the enactment of acts in order to provide a legal basis for reorganization.

All these aimed at eliminating the most conspicuous problems such as, insecurity of tenancy, charging of exorbitant rent, accumulated debts and eventually transfers of land to the landlords, etc. In other words, strong legal measures were provided to grant tenancy right, and to regulate the rental contract. Besides, attempts were also made to fix ceilings on landholdings and regulate interest, to prohibit extra imposition, and to abolish the Birta and Zamindar land tenure system. With the implementation of the first five year plan in 1956 heavy emphasis was laid on developing the irrigation capacity. Before the implementation of the Panchayat system in 1962 some 17200 h.a. of land were brought under the irrigation commandment. And by the end of 1980 the estimated commandment area for which supplemental water was available was about 240000 h.a.. It covered about 7.7 per cent of the total cultivated land. The various five year plans also took a number of institutional reform measures. For instance the government created a number of corporations in the public sector to deal with the various problems. These corporations were (a) Agricultural Bank, (2) Agricultural Inputs Corporation, (3) Food Corporation, (4) Agricultural Tools Factory etc. In order to collect data and information on the agricultural production and to study the problem of marketing, one agricultural marketing services division was also created within the Ministry of Agriculture. The government also provides subsidies to research institutes and the institute of agricultural science. In all the various five year plans the government has accorded top priority to the agricultural sector. Since not so long ago a number of donor countries are financing the rural development projects with a view to making efforts to develop the rural base of the economy in an integrated manner.

Industrial and Infrastructural Sectors:

The subsistence agricultural sector, a fragmented and limited domestic market, landlocked position with a long open border with India, a country having a comparatively more developed industrial sector, and lack of infrastructural and financial networks have been the major problems of industrialization in Nepal. Paradoxically, the meeting of certain basic needs through locally produced goods (the informal sector) also hindered the development of a modern and organized industrial sector in Nepal.

Like the ancient crafts and small industries, the informal sector was also seriously affected by the penetration of imported goods mainly from India. The lack of innovativeness and risk bearing capacity of the small saving community, the landlords, the scanty and scattered resources were not mobilized for industrial development in the early periods. On the contrary, these savings were hoarded by collecting gold and bullions or were invested in acquiring more and more land. To a greater extent the indifference of the Rana governments was also responsible for not motivating the saving class. Not only that, the Rana governments also failed to capitalize on the industrial tempo which gained momentum between the mid thirties and mid fourties. The windfall demand created by the Second World War motivated some Indian business men to establish certain consumer goods industries on the Nepal-India border areas. The Terai region had a tremendous potential for cheap labour and an abundance of raw materials for certain industries like textiles, sugar, jute and tobacco industries. Indian businessmen took advantage of the Rana`s policy to promote industries in the early thirties. The then Rana government had announced certain industrial concessions: This was also to promote their family business. The entrepreneurs were able to combine these facilities with the existing raw materials and the transport facilities on the Indian side for meeting the war time needs. But as the war was over the demand also dropped and many industries became the victims of this decline. Consequently the Rana government also withdrew its support. So when the Rana government was liquidated the successor government inherited only a handful of industries which had survived the shock of the war crisis.

In the early years of the democratic period the successor governments could not do anything substantial for industrial development, until 1957 when a new industrial policy was announced. This was partly due to political instability and partly government`s attention on the infrastructural sectoral development. The country`s first five year plan (1956-61) did allocate some financial resources but very little success was attained.

The new industrial policy (1957) expussed the need to promote the industries in the private sector by providing tax relief, land at concessional rates and reasonable tariff protection. This plan also aimed at conducting industrial and economic surveys by obtaining foreign technicians through foreign aid programmes. A number of institutional measures were taken by the Nepali Congress government during its short reign (May 1959 to Dec. 1960). The government had established one industrial development corporation, two industrial estates, and signed a number of agreements with the socialist countries viz. Soviet Union, and China for establishing certain consumer goods industries. These import substituting industries were established after the government had been dissolved. Regarding the promotion of the private sector industries, there was very little progress. From the first to the third five year plan periods, very few industries were set up.

In view of the slow growth in the private sector the government took a pragmatic approach in the Fourth Plan (1970-75). The plan stated, "that the public sector plays an active role in the economic development of countries in the preliminary stage of economic development. Although the policy of creating basic infrastructure is initiated to provide incentives for investment in the private sector, if the provision of such facilities does not result in an increase in the quality of productive investment the government will have to be active in directly establishing industrial projects".[8] The public sector, the plan stated, was to be created for regulating consumer goods and to generate resources for investment. After four years of very marginal success the government revised the policy and announced another industrial policy in 1974 giving more concessions to the private sector. This document emphasized the development of import-substituting industries. This was followed by another policy statement in the Fifth Plan (1975-80). And after one year of slow progress the government again revised the industrial policy and announced another in 1981. A number of concessions and the priority projects for the private sector have been announced in the sixth and the seventh plans; the seventh plan is to be implemented from July 1985.

Through the seventies the government had been emphasizing the development of import substituting, export processing, and basic material producing industries in the private sector. But no major breakthrough was attained. On the contrary the government went on increasing the number of public sector industries set up mainly through external assistance. Some were established accidentally just to dispose of the commodity grants. It cannot be predicted what would have happened in the state sector. The government is now attempting to reduce the number of public sector industries and is also planning to divest its ownership to the private sector. The constraint is that the better off industries, established with the help of two socialist countries, cannot be transferred to the private sector on ideological grounds, and those industries, not running well, have no prospect to sell off to the private sector.

Despite all the attempts of the government to develop the industrial sector, it accounts for only 10 per cent of GDP and even approximately half of this is contributed by the decaying cottage industries sector and the other half by the public enterprises and some 4000 small scale-private firms.[9] The formal sector (public and private sector industries) employs about 1 per cent of the total labour force.

Satisfactory progress has been achieved in the infrastructural sector mainly due to generous financial and technical support from the donor countries. The country had a very limited infrastructural network before the implementation of the five year plan (1956-61)[10] inherited from the Rana government. But now if one looks of the quantitative progress in this field without bothering about the cost-benefit and cost of production factors, it looks impressive. For instance, before the government launched the First Five Year Plan in 1956, the production of electricity in the country was only 6280 KW of which 2077 was hydel power. After twenty years of continuous exploitation of the power potential (the total is estimated to be 83000 KW) the installed capacity of existing power facilities in the country is now estimated to be 149149 KW of which 112543 KW is hydro; 32056 KW diesel and 4550 KW steam generated. With regard to the road transport the country had a total of little more than 240 KM of roads of which only about 100 KM were metalled. The population/road ratio was .050 KM of road per 1000 population. According to the Economic Survey report the total stock of roads in 1983-84 was 5608 KM, of which black topped roads cover only 2509 KM. With respect to railways, the extension of this facility was increased very marginally. It covered around 32 KM of length, and according to the latest report the total length of railway line in 1982 was 43 KM. In 1956 the country had only 335 telephone lines with 25 automatic but as of 1983 the total lines numbered 14743 of which 10297 lines are automatic. Telephone lines are distributed in 23 towns but automatic lines serve only 4 towns. Similarly the country had only 124 post offices or 1 per 85000 people in 1956 but at the end of the fifth plan it was estimated that the number reached a level of 1358 representing a post office population ratio of 1 to 10530. In the same manner the number of air connections has increased from 6 airfields in 1956 to 49 airfields in 1982 of which 26 are in the hill region.

Social Services Sector:

There has been some progress in the field of social services as well. Comparative statistics show that there were only 50 doctors in 1956 i.e., 1 doctor for nearly 180000 population. The number of hospital beds available at that time was 650. But according to the Economic Survey the number of medical doctors up to 1983-84 was 571 and the numbers of hospital beds reached 3048 in the same period. According to the 1981 population estimate, the population/doctor and population/hospital beds ratios would have been 28556 and 5008 respectively. In the field of education literacy rate has gone up from 2 per cent in 1956 to 24 per cent in 1983. The enrollment in primary education was only 9 per cent of the primary school in 1956. In 1983 this has reached 70 per cent. There has been similar progress in the number of schools, higher education centres and the number of students within this period. Some progress has been attained in the field of drinking water and irrigation. About 5 per cent of the rural population and 81 per cent of the urban population have access to piped drinking water. In the field of irrigation quite a noticeable progress has been attained.

Public Sector Investment:

In the course of 25 years of planning and development efforts, the total development expenditures increased from Rs. 214.4 million in the first plan to Rs. 8831 million at the end of the Fifth Plan (1975-80). The total public sector expenditures up to the Fifth Five Year Plan plus the total expenditures of the first three years of the Sixth Plan (1980-85) result in a total public investment (from 1956 to 1983) of Rs. 26044.29 million. If the development expenditures are compared plan after plan they show that the government has tremendously expanded the expenditure capacity particularly after the Fifth Plan. The total expenditure of the first three years of the Sixth Plan is 76.24 per cent of the entire expenditure of all the five year plans taken together. This can be seen from the total development expenditure Table 1. This is partly due to an increase in internal resource mobilization and to a greater extent to the uninterrupted inflow of foreign aid money. For instance the ratio of foreign aid to the GDP increased from about 1 per cent in the first of the first five year plan to about 5.75 per cent in 1982-83.

The massive increase in public expenditure financed from the continuous flow of aid which increased from Rs. 28 million in 1956-57 to Rs. 1934.2 million 1982-83 (excluding technical and manpower training and the administrative costs of the projects run by the donor agencies themselves). The government had planned that nearly 61 percent of the development expenditure were to be financed from the external resources in the sixth plan. But 46 per cent of the total expenditure of the first three years of this plan were financed from foreign resources.

Over this period of time the government was able to raise the share of domestic resources in financing development expenditure. The ratio of the domestic resources to GDP was increased from about 2 per cent to about 8 per cent. But when viewed against the stagnation in GDP this ratio will be a little confusing. And if this ratio is compared with other developing country`s efforts and actual mobilization, Nepal`s progress is very low. According to one study on the international comparison of taxation of a group of 47 countries it was found out that the ratio of tax to GDP during 1972-76 was 16 per cent and the ratio for Nepal was only 5 per cent.[11] The government`s statement that the dependence on internal resources has been increased is also misleading in the sense that a relatively large percentage of printed money is being injected in the economy (about 50.4 per cent of the first three years of the sixth plan).

One important aspect of the ever increasing public sector development spending is, that nearly two-thirds of this investment are channelled into the development of basic infrastructure which is highly capital intensive and has long gestation lags. Of this investment around 80 percent are spent for capital formation (expenditure on imported machinery, inputs such as steel, cement and other equipments). A typical phenomenon of the investment in these sectors is that normally the actual expenditure increases more than the planned ore estimated expenditure. This has hindered the realization of the physical targets. A low physical target achievement with higher actual production costs produce malaise in the economy. Additionally, slow project implementation which has a retarding effect on capital formation, and lack of adequate complementary investment activities such as high investment will be less productive in the stagnating economy.

The Problems:

The huge amount of development expenditure (by Nepalese standards) and the government efforts to develop the traditional economy of Nepal have not produced any tangible for the majority of the population. The economic condition on the other hand is deteriorating due to an unprecedented growth in population, low performance of the agricultural sector, environmental degradation and failure of political institutions and administrative machinery to transmit development efforts to the majority of the people who live in rural areas. In addition there are certain environmental and topographical constraints as well.

But the fact that the economic condition is deteriorating is very obvious. The World Bank report estimated that Nepal`s per capita income in 1983 was 170 U.S. Dollars. The average growth rate between 1960 to 1982 was -0.1 per cent. When seen against the background of growing population the prospect of future growth looks more gloomy. Another crucial problem faced by the Nepalese economy is he declining agricultural production. The magnitude of the problem can be felt when an agricultural country like Nepal is in the grip of a food shortage, as it is now ratio of. The population and food production between 1961-62 (period before the introduction of the Panchayat system) and 1981-82 shows that the per capita food production has declined from 0.30 metric tons in 1961-62 to 0.21 metric tons in 1981-82. This can be seen from Table 2. The GDP at current prices has increased some eight times between these periods but the per capita income has gone up only three times i.e., from 50 U.S. Dollar in 1961-62 to 151 U.S. Dollar in 1981-82. Another dimension of the economic problems of Nepal is the structural stagnation. Before the introduction of the Panchayat system in 1962 the contribution of the agricultural sector was 64 per cent in 1961-62. This has increased to 68 per cent of GDP at current prices in 1981-82. Similarly, there is no change in the structure of employment. For more than three decades the share of the agricultural sector in the total national employment has been 94 per cent. This can be seen from Table 2.

Table 2
Some Indicators of Economic Performance

(Between 1961-62 and 1981-82) (In Million of Rs.)

Indicators/Years	1961/62	1971/72	1981/82
GDP (At Current Price)	3682	8938	30265
Share of Agriculture	2338	6034	16792
(% Contribution of Agriculture to GDP)	64	67	68
Population (Million)	9.7	11.56	15.02
Per Capita GDP (In U.S. Dollar)	50	76	151
Food Production (000 Metric Ton)	3151	3468	3982
Per Capita Food Available	0.32	0.30	0.27

Source: Nepal Rastra Bank Report of the Board of Directors to HMG/N for the Fiscal Years 1961-62-1964-65, and Central Bureau of Statistics and National Planning Commission

The agricultural sector which is the mainstay of the Nepalese people is beset with manifold problems. Some problems will be mentioned here:

a) The production method is largely traditional and depends mainly on the vagaries of the Monsoon.

b) Land available for cultivation is limited by topography and in terms of man-land ratio Nepal is considered as one of the most land scarce countries.

c) The inequality in the distribution of landholdings is quite high and due to the absence of institutional measures to check the present economic problem, this is going to be a big problem. The various land reform measures "constitutes an effort to widen the political base of the panchayat regime".[12] Another problem associated with this issue is the intensive regional inequality in terms of both landholding and agricultural production.[13]

d) The agricultural sector has certain topographical constrainst as well. The hills and mountains constitute about 68 and 15 per cent of the total land in the country but these two regions have very little cultivated land (the hills contain about 0,6 million hectares or less than one-third of the total cultivated land. On top of that agriculture in these two regions is confined mainly to valleys and rainfed upland terraces.

e) The agricultural sector is also suffering from environmental damage which is a reinforcing syndrome to the deteriorating situation of foodgrain production.

Another most crucial problem of Nepal is the unprecedented growth in population particulary after 1971. Although government people and planners attribute this growth to the success of health care, which may be partly true, the nature of the problem is somewhat different. Heavy migration from India after 1979 could be one of the important reasons. It is also likely that the population growth in the previous census was not correctly represented due to statistical discrepancies. This population growth is a sign of faulty planning. In a country of scarcity, mounting population growth means chaos and if sufficient attention is not paid to this issue, the country will face not only economic but political and social problems as well.

As mentioned earlier the industrial sector is now stagnating. Industrial production fell short off target every year. Interestingly the Economic Survey report criticized the policy of the government for the slow industrial development. It reported "some of the important factors for the slow rate industrial growth in Nepal are: lack of sound and organized market, lack of natural resources, inadequate skill, landlocked position of the country and lack of consistency in government policy".[14] Many public sector industries are operating at a high rate of accumulated deficit and the private sector is not fully motivated despite the fact that the government promised to provide all necessary facilities.

The crippling foreign trade situation is another problem. Previously due to Nepal`s landlocked position and open border with India, the trade of Nepal was largely with India. Since a couple of years this situation has changed and the dependence of Nepal`s trade on India is largely reduced. But the main problem now is the shrinking export sector and expanding import requirements. This has resulted in a huge current account deficit. The available data show that during the past five years the trade deficit has increased by 260 per cent from Rs. 1423.4 million in 1977-78 to Rs. 5181.9 million in 1982-83. On the other hand the imports have increased by 150 per cent over the same five years period when valued at current prices. Total imports were Rs. 2469.6 million in the fiscal year 1977-78, went up to Rs. 6313.9 million in 1982-83.[15] This reflects the poor performance of the agricultural and the industrial sectors.

With these problems the question of disparity between regions and population within regions is intermingled. Those with power education and wealth are the major beneficiaries of investment and government efforts; and the poor majority is suffering. The economic realities explained here indicate, that after nearly three decades of development efforts the economy is facing a critical situation. The relatively high amount of investment has served the interest of people who are at the helm of national affairs. This has cast aspersion on the very idea of the 'trickle down' theory. On the contrary, these development efforts of the government have produced dilemma, contradictions and disappointment for the majority of the population. The traditional values and socio-cultural patterns of the majority of the people is being continuously eroded by the process of modernization, creating thus more conflicts and contradictions. This specific situation of Nepal poses a question: how do development economists explain this phenomenon?

Economists Concern:

Since the 1940s there has been a resurgence of the neo-classical and Keynesian paradigm on development of the underdeveloped countries. These theories have no definite answers to the growing impoverishment of the underdeveloped countries. Major analysis of factor endowments or constraints examined in a certain production function framework do not convincingly answer for low or high output; these might even be an aftermath output. The investment-output relation should be seen not in its mechanistic process but in its systemic structure. This systemic analysis of production relation (since national income has been considered by development economists as an universal indicatior of development) provides a perspective as to why a given saving-investment-output transformation is not matched by 'effective demand` or why a targeted growth rate calculated with a given savings-investment level and with an assumed capital output ratio does not produce that target growth rate. Or, why the Rostowian economy cannot take off even after fulfilling the assumed GNP/investment ratio?

Similarly, why are the automatic forces of the leading economic sectors not creating backward and forward investment linkages for self-sustained growth? Other development theories, dualism, unbalanced vs. balanced growth or even structuralism are all static and observe a certain ex post economic phenomenon of the underdeveloped countries. Experience to date shows that the deluge of literature on development economics is concerned with certain purely economic phenomena in an ex post situation. Hence these theories can not provide the right solution to the problems of underdevelopment. As mentioned earlier the systemic composition and the interaction of the various sub systems within the macro system have a profound impact on the organic and mechanistic operation of the savings-investment growth relationship. For a given rate of savings and investments, economic efficiency implies that the social and political institutions and forces are perfectly compatible. Otherwise, the development process becomes indefinite and the effects produce a growing inequality between the stronger and the weaker section of the society.

This important element of development is not given adequate consideration by development economists. As Nafziger pointed out, "in much of the mainstream literature in economic development, the social and political system is taken as given or constant. The analysis of fundamental shifts in socio political variables and non-quantitative economic ones are frequently conveniently excluded with the phrase 'ceteris paribus`. For analytical purposes development economists generally view the economic sphere as a closed system...Only a few of the major interrelationships which affect the economic realm are analyzed".[16] Economists have touched only slightly on the problem of relating economic development with the political and social factors. Some like Dudley Seers have pointed out the consequences of neglecting these variables in the discussion. He stated, that "in fact it looks as if economic growth not merely fails to solve social and political difficulties, certain types of growth can actually cause them".[17] Others like Singer[18], Prebisch[19], Kindleberger[20], Myrdal[21], Rostow and Milikan[22], Silvert[23], Hagen[24], Knight[25], and Owen and Morris[26] belong to a group of authors who have mentioned casually the role of politics in economic development. With the current trend in analyzing the development process in a more interdisciplinary way this interrelationship is receiving some attention.[27]

From the view point of institutional perspective certain issues seem to be very important. They are:

a) how are economic decisions made,

b) how and by whom are these implemented,

c) how are the needs and expectations of the majority of the population reflected or represented in the political-economic decision making process,

d) what are the institutions within which the national economy is to operate, and

e) what makes the people in the government or in the decision making authority honest, efficient, and fully committed.

These crucial agenda and the institutional framework are the sine qua non for development. But these factors are either ignored or given only a passing reference by economists. To explain the interrelationship between development and political process and institutions, the case of Nepal is analyzed in this section.

Panchayat System and Development:

In the introductory section it has been mentioned briefly that an unique system of government called Panchayat was introduced by the late king in 1962. It is specific in that sense that it was (is) a combination of a number of irreconcilable tenets borrowed from different political systems.[28] Political parties were banned right from the beginning and with the dissolution of the elected government, the fundamental rights were seized. All these restrictions were later incorporated in the constitution of 1962.

One of the features of this system of government is that the king has made the attempt to provide a substitute for the multi party system by creating different class organizations. Apparently this was like theoretically indoctrinating the Marxian line by creating the feeling of 'class consciousness' and the need to protect class interest. These class organizations were also designed under the same vertical power structure parallel to the Panchayat system because the system was originally a four tier structured system where power and responsibilities ascend in a vertically hierarchically order i.e., from village to district, district to zone and zone to national assembly. Time and again prolific statements were issued to warn these organizations not to assume any political character. Paradoxically, class organizations were created deliberately to avoid class conflict. To mobilize the politically colorless class interest to the national assembly, the National Panchayat, the supreme organ of the Panchayat system, about 19 seats was given to the various class organizations.[29]

Other features of the partyless Panchayat system are:

a) the constitutional acceptance of the absolute position and power of the king in the system. The king is above constitution and the sovereignty of the nation is vested in ihm.[30] Until recently ministers were nominated by the king and were solely responsible to him. Since the council of ministers was to be nominated by the king, the National Panchayat could not, at least, on pragmatic grounds, dismiss the ministers. The behaviour of the ministers with regard to discharging their duty, has nothing to do with the national legislature.

b) The session of the National Panchayat was to be held (until recently) in camera. The press and other communication media were fully controlled by the government. The public was completely in the dark about national and international aspects.

c) And frequent assessments and evaluations were made in one party system line to judge whether a person was doing or behaving as a Pancha or not. Some top ranking Panchas had this privilege to observe and evaluate the political behaviour of the junior or the new Panchas.

Politics and Development: The Missing Links

Politics plays an important role in speeding up the process of development. In a democratic regime this is done by creating the necessary institutions and processes and through motivation and popular participation of the people. Politics establishes links between these institutions and processes and the needs and expectations of the people. This link is missing in the Panchayat system of government in Nepal.

The economic philosophy of the Panchayat system is full of contradictions and dilemmas. As states in the Directive Principle of the Constitution of the Panchayat system 'the economic objective shall be to establish a system for the setting up of a society by ensuring maximum possible participation of the people in the economic uplift of the country and by providing appropriate protection to private enterprise which would eliminate any undue economic pressure from any class or individual upon any class or individual and to establish a system of cooperative societies...`

The development goals laid down by the directive principle of the constitution are to meet the basic needs of rural people of Nepal by

a) equitable mobilization of natural resources and wealth, and

b) balanced development of all regions.

The foreign policy is specified to make Nepal a zone of peace by adhering to the basic values of the United Nations and the principle of non-alignment.

But the mode of functioning of this system has not been conducive to the development of the country. There are some reasons why politics within the system became inherently unsuitable and ineffective for establishing a link with the development of Nepal. The most important reason is that the very first political action after the institution of the Panchayat system was to denounce the party system of the oppositional forces. The late king himself was entirely against the party system of government which he feared would reduce the role of the King to that of a constitutional head. This provided an immense opportunity for the reactionary and the politically non-entity personalities to join the Panchayat system. All other prominent leaders were either in jail or in exile. Statements or speeches denouncing the party politics or the former government would suffice to grant them entry into the government.

Many times it so happened that quite a few strong critics of the opposition forces got nominated into the National Panchayat of into other key positions. The strategic position of Nepal between India and China also offered a positive prospect for the continuation of this system. So the initial efforts were to suppress the supporters of the multi party system and just continue the system. Thus very little political fervour and consideration were given to develop the country. Another reason why politics under the Panchayat system were not promoting development in Nepal was that the 'election base`of the various decision making bodies was very weak and narrow. Candidates seeking election did not have to make promises or commitment. Hence they were not to be hold accountable for their actions. As elections were indirect and under the constructions of the Panchayat code there had been no mobilization. No public meeting was allowed and therefore no consciousness was awakened. Economic policies and programmes were commonly announced and imposed from above and decision making. Through political process was not encouraged. Not only the people outside the government but even the Panchas were not allowed to criticize the economic policies or programmes of the government. If they did so they would be labeled immediately as anti-nationals. The planning authorities were all nominated on a sociemetric relation basis. Since planning and politics were considered to be two different incongruous activities, some old-fashioned theories were accepted as the manifesto of Nepal`s development. The planners also lacked and are lacking the national perspective and vision.

The narrow and indirect election base (until 1981) gave a virtual monopoly to the feudals and landlords. In a village Panchayat only the landlord could become member of the village assembly. As stated by Shaha, "because of the absence of an adequate communication network the masses of the people at the village level are not aware of even the rudimentary features of either the constitutional and legal framework or the goals and working of the partyless panchayat democracy".[31] This legitimized feudal exploitation because for them any political system would be welcome as long as their supremacy and exploitation was unharmed. Others who are directly or indirectly involved in the task of development cling to the king and his family, which means both power and wealth. As described by Shaha "no wonder that in such a social milieu political processes operate through informal groups and cliques. Formal and rigid associations and institutions do not provide the setting for political decision making and bargaining; factions, cliques, coteries, and ad hoc gatherings of all sorts are the groups that actually matter. Thus cutthroat competition for personal power and self-aggrandizement is often shrouded in a stylized code of polite expressions and respectful and well-meaning pretensions of behaviour".[32]

When we study the political goals and strategies followed in the Panchayat system more deeply the missing linkages between the development process and politics become more obvious. As mentioned above, the oppositional forces were quite active in restoring the multi-party system of government in Nepal. The continuous and unfettered struggle of the dismissed political party members, mainly the Nepali Congress, which was in the government as the first elected government in 1959-60, for reinstituting a democratic system in the country provided the most advantageous opportunity for the reactionary and vested interest groups in the Panchayat system. Loyalty to the king and suppression of the oppositional forces became synonymous for them. Between 1960 and 1979 hundreds of political workers of the oppositional forces were arrested on several occasions. There were various mass agitation movements where the elites, intellectuals, students were involved. This provided to be an immense opportunity for the Panchas to fulfill their personal interest. The whole political machinery energy, and resources were used to check the political agitations. A part of the foreign aid money was said to have been used for this purpose. Since no public criticism was allowed and no public accountability required, there was no moral obligation on the part of the political workers of the Panchayat system. It is so surprising to see that those who

Figure 1

Forward and Come-Back Access to Power.

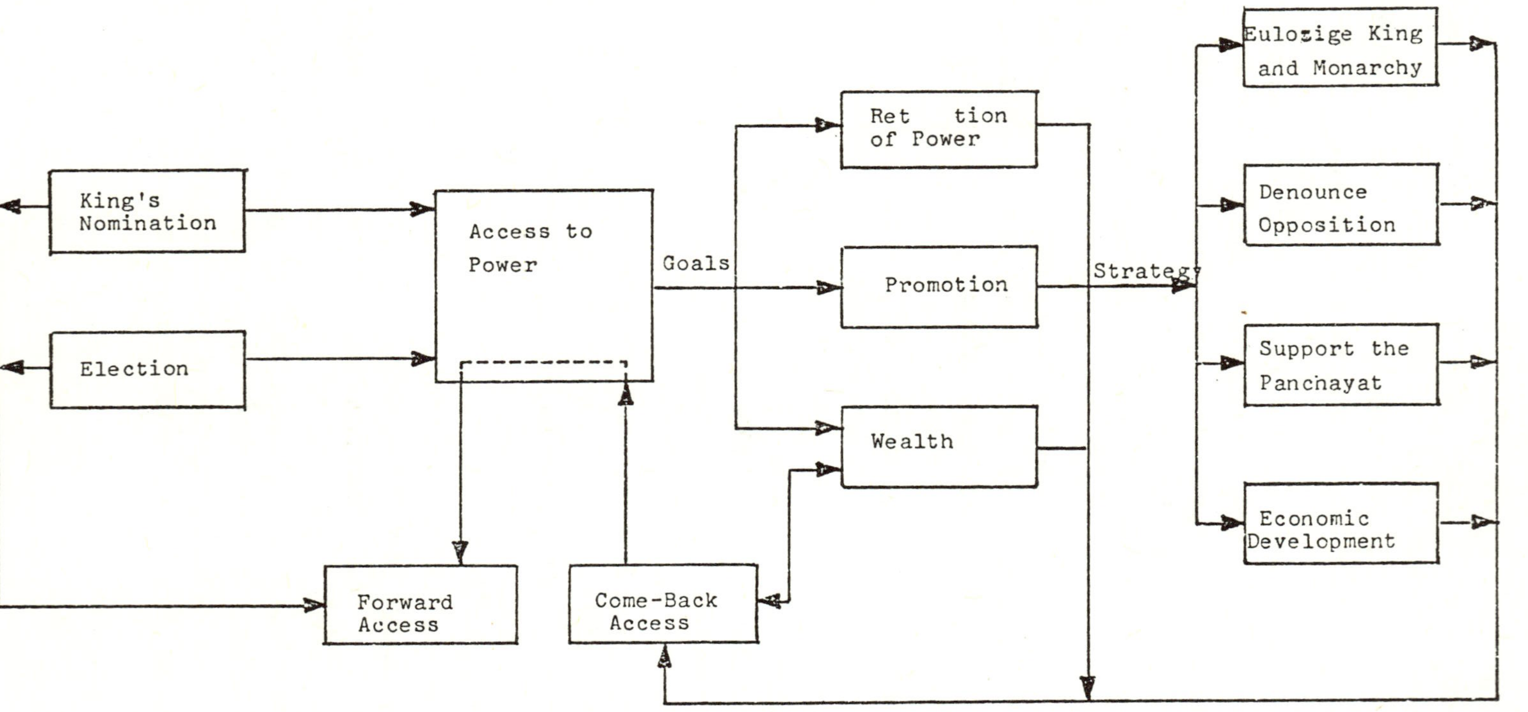

were in power were able to build houses for themselves in the capital city and enjoy all privileges. Rumours of corruption were wide-spread but again nothing could be done. Sometimes commissions were instituted, some innocents were removed from their posts but after some times these activities were discontinued. Corruption and fulfillment of personal interest was institutionalized as an in-built mechanism of the system and continued most apparently until 1979.

This in-built and institutionalized mechanism of power and wealth can be explained very well with the help of the Figure 1. This figure shows that there is a complete chain of political movement from forward access to come-back access of political power i.e., from power to wealth and wealth to power. As shown in the figure access to political power can be acquired either through election (until 1979 indirect) or through nomination by the king. The objectives of being in power are to retain power and accumulate wealth. The strategies adopted were eulogy of the king and the monarchical institution, confrontation with oppositional forces support of the Panchayat system, and casual talk about the development of the country. Thus the task of development is ignored by the political mechanism of the Panchayat system. If we assign a hypothetical value to the percentage of effort in each category of strategies, development efforts would be given only about 15 to 20 per cent of the total priority.

The Dilemma:

The cumulative effect of almost two decades of struggle for the democratic system of government shock the Panchayat system in 1979. When the students movement flared up into mass political agitation like a wild fire, the king made a historical announcement on 24 May 1979. This announcement was to hold a national referendum on adult franchise to decide whether to retain the Panchayat system with suitable reforms or to set up a parliamentary form of government. Before the actual enactment of the referendum the king announced on 16 December that irrespective of which system would be chosen certain fundamental provisions would be incorporated into the constitution. They were:

a) election to the national legislation would be held on the basis of adult franchise,

b) the Prime Minister would be appointed upon recommendation of the national legislative, and

c) the council of ministers would be collectively responsible to the legislature. The national referendum was held on 2 May 1980 and like other referenda in other countries the supporters of the multi-party system lost by a thin margin. After the national referendum the Panchayat system has not produced any desirable result as far as the development of the country is concerned. The election base is widened and a little freedom is now given to the people. But the main problem is that there is polarization among the Panchas. Up to the Prime Minister has been to be chosen by the House`s informal groupings and toppling of the government is becoming a normal political process in the reformed Panchayat system. And since there is also the absence of party-line binding or a common ideology, the relationship or Pancha unity is very informal. It can normally be seen that if a minister is removed from his post, the following day he will become the most vocal critic of the government. Now the Panchayat system is suffering from internal conflicts and contradictions as they have no common ground to criticize the oppositional forces.

Another problem is that the oppositional force, mainly the Nepali Congress, is threatening to organize a civil obedience movement. If this really happens the king has to face a political problem and it is difficult to see which turn politics in Nepal will take. The real dilemma is that the opposition forces are demanding the suspension of the Panchayat system and the nomination of an independent government whose main task would be to conduct the general election fairly and impartially. This force is also demanding amendments to the constitution which will ensure certain fundamental rights, freedom of speech and freedom of movement. On the Panchayat front the Panchas are fighting among themselves for power. The king is not well prepared to accomodate the Nepali Congress people for fear of conflict of interest. He is also not able to find a solution to the internal conflicts within the Panchayat system which he would like to continue. This dilemma is a new political phenomenon. This is slowing down the process of development because so long as the debate on the form of government remains unresolved, development will be simply unattainable.

Conclusion:

Despite two and a half decades of development efforts in Nepal the economic condition of the poor majority is pushed back to an abysmally rock-bottom level. Those already having fallen below the poverty line have disappeared from the economic horizon and those falling on the marginal case have been pushed down to the poverty level. The main cause of this underdevelopment is not factor endowment and its organic composition and mechanistic production as envisioned constraint by development economists, although, it is one but not the root cause. The cause is lack of an efficient political and institutional base on which this mechanistic and non-humanistic economy is to operate. Nepal`s experience shows that a sound economy requires a structure, a system and an efficient political mechanism to produce a "target growth rate". This unique political system and the existing politico-economic environment are such that the growth oriented development paradigm is only a myth. After the dismissal of a democratic government in Nepal in 1960 the late king made an experiment with an unique system of government called Panchayat which was until recently a three-tier structure. This three-tier structure consisted of village, district and the national Panchayat. But this system has failed to serve the interests of the majority of population due to disharmony of interest between political forces and the king. This offered an opportunity for the yested interest groups to work for the Panchayat system in order to fulfil their personal interests. As has been explained in the earlier section, neither ideological commitment nor development programmes were required to acquire political power. So the needs and expectations of the people were never given priority in the Panchayat system. Hence, the institutional process of development has been blocked which is an inherent feature of the system because this system has no moral obligation and no legal framework for mass mobilization. This system has no political ideology nor any sound economic philosophy and therefore, no sense of commitment. All the economic decisions are implemented lackadiasically; the impact aspect of development is completely neglected. The intellectuals and elites were against the system from the very beginning and do not contribute to the developmental task. Similarly the bureaucracy is a political sub-ordinate of the system and over a period of time has developed laxity, inflexibility and inefficiently.

The cumulative and combined effects of all these inherent flaws of the system have made the people undynamic, more traditional, inertialess and indolent. This is perhaps the greatest negative impact of any political system.

The internal conflict and contradictions in the Panchayat system are due to the three elements introduced in the third amendment to the constitution in 1981. Another important reason is that after the referendum the panchas could no longer benefit by criticizing the oppositional forces, mainly the Nepali Congress as its leader Mr. B.P. Koirala had accepted the verdict of the referendum. Workers of the Panchayat system had, thus to loose, a major issue which had been the core element in unifying them. The dilemma is not only that the reformed Panchayat system suffers from contradictions, but it has failed to solve the main economic problems. The political situation has also become more explosive. This is amply proved by the growing dissatisfaction of the people. The civil disobedience movement organized by the Nepali congress in 1985 and the support it obtained from the people shows the urgent need for change. The political volatility of the country is also demonstrated in the mid 1985 by the series of bomb explosions in different parts of the country. The real dilemma lies in accommodating the oppositional forces by liberalizing the Panchayat system. This means a question of shariang of political powers between the King and the elected representatives. But failure to accommodate the political forces has already proved to be a big challenge as the 1985 events have shown.

There were some possibilities of resolving the conflict regarding the participation of some sections of the oppositional forces in the national Panchayat election held in 1986, had the King introduced certain reform measures[33] in the Panchayat. But the King responded only one demand of the oppositional forces i.e., formation of an interim government (but largely from among the old panchas). So the oppositional forces did not participate in the election held in May 1986. Hence the deadlock continued further. But the recent election shows that it has created another dilemma before the King. It has been reported that "the results of the general election held on 12 May (1986) to elect 112 members of the country`s legislature indicate peoples dissatisfaction with the existing non-party Panchayat system. More than half of the newly elected members who unseated old members including some Panchayat stalwarts are comparatively young and want radical changes to the system".[34] This means that if the system continues in its present form and the distance between the King and the democratic force becomes further widened, it will pose a serious challenge to the monarchical institution and the Panchayat system. It is in the long-run interest of the King and the democratic forces that some rapprochement is to be forged. It is quite opportune for the King to accommodate the democratic and other forces, who believe in the democratic process, to accommodate by making certain reforms. It is opportune because these forces are demanding only a marginal change in the system and not its substitution. Failure to do so make the political-economic situation of the country more problematic.

References

[1] B.L. Joshi and L.E. Rose, Democratic Innovation in Nepal, University of California, Berkeley 1966, p. IX.

[2] Ramakant, Nepal-China and India. New Delhi 1976, p. 12.

[3] Some attempts were made in the late fourties to establish diplomatic relation with other countries. For instance, on 26 April 1947 Nepal and U.S. signed an agreement in Kathmandufor the exchange of diplomatic and consular

representatives between the two countries. In July 1947 the British Legation in Kathmandu and the Nepalese Legation in London were raised to Embassy level. Diplomatic relations were also established with France, Netherlands, Tibet, Brazil, and Belgium in the year 1949.

[4] These old canals and their capacity were as follows:

Name of the Canal	Year of Construction	Area Command (in H.a.)
1.Chandra Canal	1928	13000
2.Jagadish Canal	1942	400
3.Juddha Canal	1946	810
4.Others	----	490
		14700

Source: B.P. Chresthes, An Introduction to Nepalese Economy, Ratna Pustak

[5] One study found that "peasants in southern Nepal paid as much as 80 per cent of the crop to the landlord". See E.B. Mihaly,Foreign Aid and Politics in Nepal, Oxford University Press,1965, p. 10.

[6] The land tenure system prevailing at that time could be classified into three types: 1) Birta, 2) Raiker, and 3) Kipat. Birtaland is a rent free land given away to the relatives and officers of the Rana government. Raiker land belonged to thestate but was given to the tenants for cultivation and was subject to revenue payment. The land tenure system prevalent in the eastern hilly regions was called Kipat. This was a community land and the state had no control over this land. Therewas a Zamindari system of

collecting revenue on a commissio basis. See Bhandaz, Kathmandu, 1974 (4th ed.) and The Rising Nepal (Official Daily) and Gorkhapatra February 9 and 17, 1985.

[7] These were Land Reform Commission (1952), Royal Announcement of Comprehensive Land Reform Measures (1955), Land Acts (1957), Birta Abolition Act (1959), Agricultural Reorganization Act (1963) and Land Acts (1964).

[8] See HMG/N National Planning Commission, The Fourth Plan (1970-75), Kathmandu 1974, p. 5.

[9] The composition of industrial output shows that about 70 per cent of production is derived from processing agricultural commodities like rice, wheat, sugar, tobacco, jute etc. About 25 per cent constitute textiles and wood industries. These have a secure market, low risk, high turnover and quick returns.

[10] HMG/N National Planning Council, The Second Three Year Plan (1962-65), Kathmandu, p. 48.

[11] See A.A. Tait, W.L.M. Grätz and B.J. Eichengreen, 'International Comparison of Taxation for Selected Countries` IMB Staff Papers 26 (1) March 1979.

[12] See M.C. Regmi, Landownership in Nepal, Berkeley 1976, p. 227.

[13] The three geographical regions have a lot of variation with respect to population, arable land and production. For instance the Terai area which occupies about 22 per cent of the total area has 44 per cent of the population. It has thus a

population density of 193 per square KM. The extensive highland occupies 44 per cent of the area and has a population of 48 per cent. And the mountain region occupies about 34 per cent of the total area and accounts for only 8 per cent of the population.

[14] HMG/N Ministry of Finance, Economic Survey 1980-81, Kathmandu 1980.

[15] HMG/N Ministry of Finance, Economic Survey 1983-84, Kathmandu 1984, pp. 63-64.

[16] E.W. Nafziger, A Critique of Development Economics in the U.S., in David Lehmann (ed.), Development Theory, Frank Cass and Company 1979, p. 33.

[17] D. Seers, The Meaning of Development, in David Lehmann (ed.), Development Theory, Frank Cass and Company 1979, p. 9.

[18] H.W. Singer, The Distribution of Gains between Investing and Borrowing Countries, in American Economic Review, May 1950.

[19] R. Prebisch, Towards a Dynamic Development Policy for Latin America. UN Commission for Latin America, Santiago, Chile.

[20] C.P. Kindleberger, Economic Development, New York, Mc Graw Hill 1965.

[21] G. Myrdal, The Challenge of World Poverty, Penguin Books 1971.

[22] W.W. Rostow and M.F. Milikan, A Proposal Key to Effective Foreign Policy, Greenwood Press Publications 1976.

[23] K.H. Silvert, The Cost of Anti-Nationalism: Argentina, in K.H. Silvert (ed.), Expectant People: Nationalism and Development, New York, Random House 1963.

[24] E.E. Hagen, On the Theory of Social Change, Homewood, Dorsey Press 1962.

[25] J.B. Knight, Explaining Income Distribution in Less Developed Countries: A Framework and Agenda, in Oxford Bulletin of Economics and Statistics, Vol. 38, No. 3, August.

[26] O. Edgar and R. Shaw, Development Reconsidered, Lexington, D.C. 1972.

[27] See I. Adelman and C.T. Morris, Society, Politics and Economic Development, John Hobkins University Press 1967.

[28] See B. Joshi, and L.E. Rose, Democratic Innovations in Nepal, University of California Press 1966, p. 398. Also see L.E. Pose and M. Fischer, The Politics of Nepal: Persistence and Change in an Asian Monarchy, Cornell University Press 1970, p. 52.

[29] To check and to protect the class interest of the people one Ministry of Guidance was established in 1961. A few weeks after its creation, it intended to establish six class organizations e.g. peasants, labourers, women, students, youth and children. The students and children organizations were withdrawn on the ground of immaturity. Later two others were added to the list, the Graduates, and the Ex-Service men.

[30] As specified in the Directive Principles of the Constitution "the sovereignty of Nepal is vested in His Majesty and all powers, executive, legislative and judicial emanate from Him. These powers are exercised by His Majesty through the organs established by or under the constitution and other laws for the time being in force", see Constitution of Nepal, 1981, HMG/N,Kathmandu, Nepal.

31 R.K. Shaha, Nepali Politics: Retrospect and Prospect, Delhi, Oxford University Press 1975, p. 93.

[32] R.K. Shaha, Essays in the Practice of Government in Nepal, New Delhi, Manohar Publications 1982, p. 113.

[33] The oppositional forces (mainly the Nepali Congress) demanded that there should be an independent government representing the interests of all sections and whose function would be mainly to conduct the election fairly and impartially other demands were taken place. They should be allowed to exercise freedom of movement and speech and that its candidates should be allowed to contest the election under one election symbol. These demands were not met by the government and hence the major political parties decided to boycott the May 1986 general elections.

[34] See Far Eastern Economic Review 29 May 1986, p. 27.

Bibliography

Adelman, I. and Morris C.T., Society, Politics and Economic Development.John Hopkins University Press 1967

Edgar, O. and Shaw, R., Development Reconsidered. Lexington, D.C. 1972

Hagen, E.E., On the Theory of Social Change. Homewood, Dorsey Press 1962

Joshi, B.L. and Rose, L.E., Democratic Innovation in Nepal. Berkeley 1966

HMG/N, National Planning Commission, The Fourth Plan (1970-75), Kathmandu 1975

HMG/N, National Planning Council, The Second Year Plan (1962-65), Kathmandu 1965

HMG/N, Ministry of Finance, Economic Survey 1980-81. Kathmandu 1981

HMG/N, Ministry of Finance, Economic Survey 1983-84. Kathmandu 1984

Kindleberger, C.P., Economic Development. New York 1965

Knight, J.B., Explaining Income Distribution in Less Development Countries: A Framework and Agenda, in Oxford Bulletin of Economics and Statistics, Vol. 38, No. 3, August

Myrdal, G., The Challenge of World Poverty. Penguin Books 1971

Nafziger, E.W., A Critique of Development Economists in the U.S., in Lehman, David (ed.),

Development Theory. Frank Cass and Company 1979

Prebisch, R., Towards a Dynamic Development Policy for Latin America. UN Commission for Latin America. Santiago, Chile

Regmi, M.C., Landownership in Nepal. Berkeley 1976

Rose, L.E. and Fisher, M., The Politics of Nepal: Persistence and Change in an Asian Monarchy. Cornell University Press 1970

Rostow, W.W. and Milikan, M.F., A Proposal Key to Effective Foreign Policy. Greenwood Press Publications 1976

Seers, D., The Meaning of Development, in Lehman, David (ed.), Development Theory. Frank Cass and Company 1979

Shaha, R.K., Nepali Politics: Retrospect and Prospect. Delhi 1975

Shaha, R.K., Essays in the Practice of Government in Nepal. New Delhi 1982

Silvert, K.H., The Cost of Anti-Nationalism: Argentina, in Silvert, K.H. (ed.), Expectant People: Nationalism and Developmen. New York 1963

Singer, H.W., The Distribution of Gains between Investing and Borrowing Countries, in American Economic Review, May 1950

Sikh Attitude towards Obedience to Political Authority: Some Implications

by Jogishwar Singh

(Note: All opinions expressed in this article are strictly the author`s personal opinions. They do not claim to represent the opinion of any governmental agency or government in India)

Events of the past few years in the Indian Punjab have put the political, religious and economic demands of the Sikhs in sharp focus. In the light of these developments, it is relevant to discuss attitudes of the Sikhs towards obedience to political authority. Such discussion may clarify certain aspects of Sikh behaviour which may otherwise appear rebellious and disorderly. With passions inflamed to such an extent that some responsible people talk of "liquidating Sikh terrorists-kill them all off" [1] or "the only thing the Sikhs understood was force" [2], it is all the more urgent to try and understand the impact of Sikh history and tradition on shaping attitudes towards political authority. A detailed discussion of this aspect being beyond the scope of a limited article such as this one, only certain broad outlines will be traced.

Determinant Factors: Living Historical Heritage;

Inseparability of Religion and Politics; Absence of Personality Cult

"History is important to the Sikh in a way that it is not to the Hindu, Buddhist of Jain. He is conscious and proud of its influence and aware that he is still an active participant in an historical process" [3]. One major reason for such an ever-present historical consciousness shaping attitudes towards obedience is the almost continuous chain of popular struggles for acquiring or defending basic rights denied by oppressive political authorities. From the martyrdom of the fifth Guru, Arjan Dev (Guru, 1581-1606), in 1606 [4] to the imprisonment of the sixth Guru, Hargobind (Guru, 1606-1644), in Gwalior fort by the Emperor Jahangir [5] to the martyrdom of the ninth Guru, Tegh Bahadur (Guru, 1664-1675), in 1675 [6] to the travail filled life of the tenth Guru, Gobind Singh (Guru, 1675-1708) to the brutal genocide inflicted by political authorities on the Sikhs between 1710 and 1768 can be traced this tradition of struggle and sacrifices in defence of the Sikh way of life. Obedience was extended only to such political authority as allowed freedom of conscience and left the Sikhs free to practise their religion. The Sikhs did not believe in giving obedience to a political authority merely because it existed and claimed sovereignty over them by force of arms.The spirit nurtured by the Sikh Gurus, so strikingly crystallised by Guru Gobind Singh in the creation of the Khalsa in 1699, runs counter to such obedience unless the political authority claiming it fulfils certain minimum obligations towards the Sikh Panth. [7] The tenth Guru, while repeatedly emphasizing that rebellion was justified only "when all other avenues of protest, including willing martyrdom, were of no avail" [8], does also emphasize that "power must reside in clean, ethical and just hands" [9]. Again, "threat to political authority would not arise so long as the person concerned exercised it for the betterment of his subjects" [10]. Even Maharaja Ranjit Singh was not given unquestioned obedience, and this in the heyday of Sikh power! "Ranjit Singh had to camouflage his monarchy. He knew that he merely directed into a particular channel a power that he could neither slaves of an equal member of the Khalsa...everything was done for the sake of the Guru, for the advantage of the Khalsa and in the name of the lord" [11]. If this was the state of affairs under a Sikh ruler, it is not realistic to expect unquestioning obedience from Sikhs to later political authorities unless they convince the Sikhs that power is being exercised in a just manner and their religion is not under threat.

This introduces a second major factor conditioning Sikh attitudes towards political authority - the inseparability of politics and religion. The whole historical experience of Sikhism reflects such inseparability and no amount of secular arguments based on principles of political science can convince the average Sikh otherwise. Any expectation that, politics and religion being distinct vocations, the Sikh must determine his obedience regardless of how the State affects his religion ignores History and Sikh historical evolution. Guru Hargobind wore two swords; the "Miri" symbolizing temporal authority and the "Piri" spiritual authority. Across the Durbar

Sahib [12] he built the Akal Takht [13] which became the centre of Sikh political decision-making subsequently. It is not proper to consider this intermingling of politics and religion as something suddenly introduced by Guru Hargobind and sanctified by his grandson Guru Gobind Singh. This development was inherent in the evolution of Sikhism. The earlier Gurus were not a political holy men who turned a blind eye to the political situation around them. Guru Nanak (1469-1538) comments extensively on the prevalent political rot of his age. [14] "As important as the religious and communal aspects of Nanaks`s preaching were the political" [15]. The political aspects came to the fore only when the State oppressed the Sikh religion but it does not mean that they were not always shimmering in the background. Guru Amar Das (Guru, 1552-1574) and Guru Arjan Dev are both said to have been involved in politics by representing the cause of over-burdened or unjustly treated tax payers to Mughal authorities [16]. "Guru Arjan clearly had some of the trappings of a temporal prince" [17]. This view is shared by a well known Muslim historian also [18]. "Henceforward the Guru was looked upon by his disciples not only in the light of a spiritual guide but also as a worldly lord and a ruling sovereign" [19]. Guru Gobind Singh considered God Himself as the fountainhead of all political authority. Human beings exercise such authority only as His mandate. [20] Pure and clean hearted people, fired by the love of God, can distinguish good from evil and, accordingly, accept or reject incumbents in office. [21] Sikhism is a wholistic way of life and conduct, embracing political attitudes as well, and not just a set of theological principles or codes of conduct. "Sikhism took a comprehensive and integrated view of religion...to tackle all the challenges trhown up by the totality of life; because life could not be arbitrarily compartmentalised into religious, social and political segments. As such, the goal of religion was to bring about a change not only in the character of the individual, but also in the socio-political environment which determined his development." [22] Again, "the Sikh Panth was, thus, not organised as just another sect to pursue the traditional Indian approach to religion. It was made the basis for...fighting political domination and for capturing political power for a plebian mission". [23] This view may be labelled anachronistic by proponents of total separation of politics and religion. It can, however, not prevent the Sikhs from conditioning their obedience to political authority on its accomodation of their tradition.

Attempts to weaken the hold of the Sikh religio-political party, the Shiromani Akali Dal, by pointing out that it is mixing up religion and politics have failed to cut much ice in rural areas, where most Sikhs live. A large segment of Sikhs votes for the Akali Dal because it purports to safeguard the interests of the Panth. It is a regular part of Akali election propaganda to exhort voters to vote for the Panth. [24] Sikhs questioning the fundamental religion-politics nexus and aspiring to leadership are "leaders in India but not leaders among the Sikhs". [25] They remain generals without troops. Repeated attempts to break the Akali Dal`s political importance by inducing defections from its ranks; dismissal of governments led by it; or creation of rival Akali Dals have provided only temporary gains, failing to break its hold on rural Sikhs because of this nexus nurtured by Sikh historical tradition. [26] This inherent political strength remains a constant factor of Punjab politics.

Interwoven with the hitherto discussed two factors is another important factor, completing a sort of obedience trinity: obedience to an individual. Sikh tradition shows that two broad epochs can be discerned in the evolution of Sikh attitudes towards obedience to an individual:-

(A). Period of the ten Gurus (1469-1708)

(B). Post-Guru Period (1708-onwards)

In the Guru period, emphasis is laid on unquestioning obedience to the Guru. Obedience was one of the criteria determining succession to the Guruship. Guru Nanak, bypassing his own sons, anointed Bhai Lehna as his successor, partly in view of the latter`s unquestioning obedience and devotion to him. [27] The same process operated when Guru Angad (Guru, 1539-1552) bypassed his own sons to nominate his favourite disciple Amar Das as the third Guru, who, in turn, bypassed his own son to nominate his son-in-law Bhai Jetha as the fourth Guru."What was looked for in a successor was moral courage and devotion to the reigning Guru." [28] Even when the Guruship became hereditary in the family of Guru Ram Das (Guru, 1574-1581), this criterion continued to be valid. He did not nominate his elder sons but the youngest son, Arjan Mall, as his successor. [29] The sacred scripture of the Sikhs, the Siri Guru Granth

Sahib, is full of hymns extolling total obedience and devotion to the Guru. [30] However, the word Guru is synonymous with God Almighty at many places in these verses. As already pointed out, the Gurus were not merely religious heads and played a temporal role as well, overt or covert. In any case, from the time of Guru Arjan onwards, the Guru came to play an increasing temporal role in the lives of his Sikhs and obedience to him had a temporal connotation as well. The Sikhs were thus conditioned to render obedience to an individual incorporating spiritual and temporal authority in himself. [31]

Guru Gobind Singh changed this tradition when he vested the Guruship after him in the Khalsa Panth and not in an individual. He demonstrated by his actions how he himself respected the Khalsa. He is said to have accepted being fined by his Sikhs when he made a gesture of saluting Saint Dadu`s grave with his arrow. [32] In the Guru`s composition can be found the apotheosis of the Khalsa. [33] A new spirit was now infused into the Sikhs, with each believing himself as much a leader as the other. The Sikhs had earned their Guru`s trust in them. "After bringing into being a revolutionary organization, the Guru placed a revolutionary ideal before his men; the objective of the Raj Khalsa or the people`s democracy". [34] Fired with a missionary zeal, the Sikhs not only withstood genocidal repression after the Guru`s death; but also showed in practice how the power of faith produced leadership qualities without blind obedience to any individual. This trait can be illustrated by innumerable examples from those times down to the present day. It is only after

1980 that an ebryonic change can be discerned in this pattern. This is discussed later. As has rightly been pointed out, "mindless obedience and self effacement...is not possible among guerilla units because a guerilla force is essentially a political army organized on democratic lines".[35] This trait, developed during the Sikh guerilla war of 1710-1768, has never disappeared from the Sikh bent-of-mind and obedience attitudes.

Banda Singh Bahadur was sent by the tenth Guru as his personal representative to the Punjab.[36] But even he could not obtain mindless obedience from the Khalsa. There was a split in the Panth because it was felt by many that Banda Singh was exceeding the limits of his mission, prescribed by Guru Gobind Singh. His adherents came to be called "Bandai Khalsa", while those harking back to the principles of the Guru were now called "Tat Khalsa". This split shows how even a charismatic and dynamic leader like Banda Singh could not hope for unquestioning loyalty from the Khalsa. A similar reluctance led to prolonged bickering in 1733 A.D. when Zakarya Khan, the Governor of the Punjab, made the offer of a `jagir`and the title of 'Nawab` to the Sikhs assembled in their general assembly the 'Sarbat Khalsa` at Amritsar.[37] The Sikhs were instinctively against the idea of elevating one of themselves as a temporal superior commanding obedience. Only reluctantly was Kapur Singh given the title of `Nawab`, and he commanded no obedience by its virtue. He obtained it through his selfless service of fellow Sikhs. There is a controversy amongst historians, illustrating Sikh attitudes well.[38] Dr. N.K. Sinha rejects outright the notion that the Sikhs struck coins in

1758 bearing the inscription "Mulk-i-Ahmad grift Jassa Kalal" (In the country of Ahmad, conquered by Jassa Kalal) [39] because it goes against the entire trend of Sikh history till then. The presence of an individual`s name on coins, the traditional mark of sovereignty, has never been attempted by any Sikh ruler. Banda Singh made the first ever assertion of such political sovereignty when he got coins struck in 1710. [40] These coins bore the names of Guru Nanak and Gobind Singh and not his own name. "the inscription on Banda`s seal became a model for future inscriptions on Sikh coins and seals." [41] Coins bearing this inscription were struck in 1765 after the capture of Lahore. [42] "Even Ranjit Singh in the plenitude of his power never left the impress of his name on the coins. The theocratic zeal and the democratic spirit were far to deep-rooted to allow any individual to do such a highly objectionable thing." [43] Modern day Sikh leaders like Master Tara Singh, Sant Fateh Singh, or Sant Harchand Singh Longowal always faced opposition and splits when it was felt that they were becoming predominant. Sikh Chief Ministers of the Punjab [44] have never got unquestioned obedience.

These obedience behaviour parameters having been outlined, their interplay in various phases of Sikh history can now be briefly surveyed. For this purpose the following time-divisions are proposed:

(I). Period of the first nine Gurus (circa 1500-1675 A.D.) and of Guru Gobind Singh Till 1699

(II). Creation of the Khalsa and its Early Years (1699-1708 A.D.)

(III). Period of State Persecution and Sikh Response (1710-1768 A.D.)

(IV). Period of Sikh Misals (1768-c. 1800 A.D.)

(V). Maharaja Ranjit Singh and the Lahore Durbar (c. 1800-1849)

(VI). Period of British Rule (1849-1947 A.D.)

(VII). Post-Independence Period (1947- on)

It will now be seen how the Sikh obedience pattern evolved in each of these time-periods.

(I). (1469-1699): Gurus and Disciples

It has already been pointed out how devotion and obedience to the guru recurs as a leit motif for this period. However, even here, obedience was not just a one-way street with nothing being given by the Guru in return. The "Sangat" or assembly of Sikhs is as important in the hymns composed by Guru Arjan as the Guru himself. [45] The Lord becomes manifest in the Sangat; in its company the world-ocean can be crossed and salvation found. [46] Here lies the kernel of the later apotheosis of the Panth as the Guru. Though the ideal of devotion to the Guru was carried to such an extent that two followers are said to have burnt themselves on the funeral pyre of Guru Hargobind [47] , it was well matched by the Guru`s concern and esteem for his Sikhs. Guru Ram Das compares it to a mother`s care for a new-born baby. [48] The implication is clear: the Gurus were given unquestioned obedience because they, in turn, assiduously devoted themselves to the spiritual and temporal welfare of their Sikhs. They did not proffer the idea of blind obedience merely because they were in a position of authority.

The Guru`s actions consistently evolved a political aspect in the Sikh religion. Guru Nanak himself has even been called "the first popular leader of the Punjab in recorded history". [49] His ideas "gave birth to Punjabi consciousness and to Punjabi nationalism". [50] His practical demonstration through his own life that religion did not mean asceticism and isolation from society meant that his followers would be imbued with a political consciousness arising out of their being firmly grounded in the prevalent social order. Guru Angad not only developed the Gurmukhi script and organized a regular system of collecting offerings to meet the expenses of the `Langar`(community kitchen) [51] , he also "ordered his followers to take part in drill and competitive games after the morning service...He started a tradition which made it easy for his successors to raise troops of able bodied men from among his disciples". [52] He is said to have affirmed that "if ever the necessity to fight arose, it was the duty of a soldier to give battle regardless of the odds against him". [53] These are not the actions of someone trying to ensure raising his followers as obedient sheep before political authority. Guru Amar Das established a system of twenty two 'Manjis` under the direction of heads called 'Sangatias` for systematising the collection and transmission of donations. [54] This is the embryo of a taxation system, an adjunct of a political structure. In Guru Amar Das`s time, Brahmins "began to persecute the Sikhs" [55] and poison the ears of Mughal authorities against them. "This was the beginning of the oppression of the Sikhs, which subsequently compelled them to take up arms." [56] The Guru is said to have made even the Emperor Akbar sit on the floor and share a meal in the `langar` with the 'Sangat` at Goindwal before meeting him [57] , a clear lesson that the supreme political authority of the land had no precedence before religion. Akbar was an enlightened sovereign who did not get provoked by this principle of the Sikh faith. Had he sought to suppress the faith, as his son Jahangir began to do, there should be no doubt that the Sikhs would have offered resistance to his political authority, as they did under his successors. The tortures suffered by the fifth Guru so patiently before his martyrdom in 1606 under the orders of the Emperor Jahangir were a living example of higher principles than mere obedience to sovereign power guiding the Sikh faith. Guru Arjan could have saved his life by conforming to the dictates of political authority, yet he chose to affirm instead the supremacy of higher tenets - freedom of conscience and religion. "Within a century, that intervened between Guru Nanak and Guru Arjan, a comparatively small group of followers became a community with an unfolding power development, self reliance and political significance" [58] is the opinion of a German researcher of Sikhism.

Guru Hargobind merely carried forward the momentum of this evolution under changed circumstances. He is said tohave declared in 1633 A.D. that he would "wrest sovereignty from the Mughals and bestow this all on the downtrodden and the helpless." [59] Militarization of the Sikh movement was an organic growth of the Sikh thesis. The sixth Guru built the `Akal Takht` as the seat of Sikh temporal authority. The first three armed clashes between Sikh and Mughal forces took place during his time [60] in which Imperial troops were worsted without exception. "Fighting in the van of the Sikh forces were Hargobind`s own sons, Gurditta and Tegh Bahadur (who later became the ninth Guru)". [61] Even the pacific seventh Guru, Har Rai (Guru 1644-1661), set aside his elder son, Ram Rai, in favour of his second son, Har Krishan (Guru 1661-1664 A.D.), as his successor because Ram Rai is said to have altered the word "Musalman" to "Beiman" in a verse of the Sikh scripture to please the Emperor Aurangzeb. [62] It was thus again affirmed practically, if such an affirmation were really needed, that cultivation of political authority at the cost of compromise with the tenets of the Sikh faith would not be tolerated. The immutability of the verses in the scripture was such a tenet. Guru Har Rai is said to have offered some assistance to Prince Dara Shikoh in the war of succession among the sons of the Emperor Shahjahan. [63] This earned Aurangzeb`s wrath, just as the Emperor Jahangir, his grandfather, had been similarly aroused by the action of Guru Arjan in having blessed the rebellious Prince Khusrau. One can discern this persistent trend: the Gurus set higher store on their belief than on blind obedience to sovereign authority. The ninth Guru Tegh Bahadur`s martyrdom confirmed this in striking fashion. A Muslim historian writing about Guru Tegh Bahadur says that the latter was "universally acknowledged amongst the Sikhs as "Sacha Badshah", or veritable king, who guided the soul to salvation, while a temporal monarch guided merely man`s worldly actions".[64] The ground had thus been prepared. "Any external interference with the affairs of the Sikh gurus and the Sikh Panth was likely to be resented by them; and a persistent challenge to the Sikhs` allegiance to his Guru could force on him the withdrawel of his allegiance to the State."[65] This should be always borne in mind by those clamouring for the Sikhs to separate politics and religion and obey the State. The Guru now is no more a bodily Guru but the Guru Granth Sahib and the whole Panth.

(II). 1699-1710: The Early Years of the Khalsa

The tenth Guru not only changed the external appearance of the sikhs; he also institutionalized the attitudinal change towards political authority that had been slowly evolving before him. If it had been unrealistic to expect blind obedience to the State by the Sikhs even earlier, it became impossible after the creation of the Khalsa in 1699. Henceforth, the Panth was fired by the slogan "Raj karega Khalsa; aaki rahe na koe".[66] It is wrong to consider the Guru`s transformation as a rebellion against Muslim authority on narrow communal lines. He defied equally the oppressive practices of the Hindu hill rajas. He called for resistance to oppression from any political authority regardless of its communal affiliation. The whole thrust of the Guru`s efforts was to make his Sikhs soldier-saints who would be worthy of carrying the honour of the Guruship that he was going to bestow on them. If political authority came in the way of free practice of their ideals, it was not only to be fought but fought as a matter of duty. Through his poetic compositions, his lifestyle and his actions he embodied this ideal, even to the extent of losing all his four sons in the process. Guru Gobind Singh is not a mythological figure of yore. His spirit still infuses the thinking of many average Sikhs. His deeds are ever-present in Sikh minds and colour their perception of political authority. The Guru`s heroic legacy was an immediate Sikh struggle for political independence because the Sikhs became convinced that their religion would always be in dire straits without political power; they would obey only such political authority as safeguarded their religion. "After the death of Guru Gobind Singh, the Sikhs refused to recognize any authority, be it Mughal or Afghan, which they believed would deny them justice." [67]

The rules of the ball game had changed. "If military courage is democratised, as it was in the Punjab, the government can not afford to flout the opinion of the people. It can ignore the masses only when military courage is the monopoly of a ruling caste or of an aristocracy, as the Spartans ignored the helots, as the feudal nobility ignored the commonalty of Europe in the middle ages." [68] No political authority could henceforth hope to earn obedience from the Sikhs by intimidatory postures. Qazi Noor Mohammad`s description of Sikh character in his `Jangnama`, written about 56 years after the death of Guru Gobind Singh, attest how Sikh society had imbibed a heroic spirit. [69] In one of his writings the Guru says " a king must apply the same laws to himself as he does to others". [70] According to him, "peaceful approach can bear fruit only if the opponent has also some scruples and is influenced by religious and ethical values. If he did not have any regard for such values, the only remedy would be to oppose him tooth and nail". [71] This should always be borne in mind if political authority is tempted to procrastinate and indulge in playing games with the Sikhs with a view to dividing them and conceding no demands. The July 1985 accord between the Indian prime minister, Mr. Rajiv Gandhi, and the Sikh leader, the late Sant Harchand Singh Longowal, shows that when negotiations are carried on in good faith and a spirit of accomodation, the Sikhs are not recalcitrant rebels but law abiding citizens of the land. Existence of a tiny minority not in agreement with the accord can not be used as a brush to tar the whole Panth in black colours.

Based on Guru Gobind Singh`s teachings, the natural political order envisaged by the 'Zeitgeist` of the Sikhs was some sort of democratic polity and not a state based on absolute despotism of the individual, be he a monarch or a dictator. Regimes tending to be dictatorial evoke immediate resistance from the Sikhs. By democratic polity is meant a State where the ruled are regularly consulted on matters pertaining to their welfare, and not necessarily a parliamentary democracy as understood in modern parlance. It has been opined that "the democratic values enunciated and promoted in practice by Guru Gobind Singh" [72] have not been paid enough attention. Government was carried on at Anandpur Sahib according to democratic principles before the Guru was compelled to abandon his headquarters there by besieging political authorities. 'Panchas` and 'Jathedars` , regularly elected at public gatherings, carried on administration. The Guru did not impose autocratic leadership or the principle of blind obedience. He respected the popular will of his followers. His authority was based on voluntary submission rendered by people because of his great sacrifices and superior intellectual and spiritual attainments. The Guru even had to revise course in vace of the pressure of public opinion, as in the case of an offer of safe conduct by besieging hill rajas if he evacuated Anandpur. He wanted to educate his followers in representative government. [73] These pristine ideals were later on misused by feudal forces but Sikh ethos has not allowed obedience to autocrats and autocratic systems, individual-based or otherwise, as an accepted corollary of its religious and political tradition. Guru Gobind Singh adapted the traditional Panchayat system into Sikhism when he instituted the Panj Pyaras (the five beloved); "all matters of vital importance to the community were to be referred to this council for deliberation and formulation of concrete proposals. The entire congregation was expected to participate in the popular voice vote on these proposals, which were carried by `sarab-samiti`(unanimity) or `bahu-samiti`(majority decision). The congregation was the prototype of modern general assembly". [74]

It is easy to notice here some resemblance to the system of direct democracy practised by the Swiss in their Communes. This resemblance extends to more than just procedual similarities. In both cases, the Sikhs and the Swiss, there was a basic resistance to oppressive regimes and a desire to be left alone to practise their way of life. Both peoples fought against far superior Imperial armies through guerilla tactics employed by motivated individuals fired with a spirit of liberty in defence of their way of life. Swiss history has instances like those of Winkelried and others sacrifising their lives for their cause. Sikh history is replete with innumerable such feats in which Sikhs courted martyrdom for the sake of the Panth. Bhai Mani Singh, Bhai Taru Singh, Baba Deep Singh and Bhai Mati Das are just some well known `shaheeds`(martyrs) of the Sikh faith. Both nations won renown as good soldiers and as sought - after mercenaries in the armies of others. It appears that such a strong attachment to liberty and one`s way of life arises partly only when obedience is given voluntarily, believing in the good faith of the State and Government and not extraced by force from unwilling subjects. The changes introduced by the Sikh faith, so strikingly consolidated by Guru Gobind Singh were soon put to the test and found more than equal to it.

(III). 1710-1768: Martyrdom and Victory

This period is marked by no less than an attempted genocide of the Sikh Nation by political authorities, first the Mughals and then the Afghans. If Punjab did not become a part of Afghanistan, in spite of formal cession of all territory west of the Indus and the revenue of four districts of Punjab; namely Sialkot, Aurangabad, Gujarat and Pasrur [75] , to Ahmad Shah

Abdali, it is only because of Sikh resistance which never ceased. Had the Sikhs accepted the principle of complete separation of politics and religion and given unquestioned obedience to Afghan sovereign authority, Punjab may have become a part of Afghanistan and Russian troops might today have been sitting on the Yamuna as well as in Chandigarh and Lahore; and not just west of the Khyber Pass. This period of struggle has deeply marked the Sikh psyche and convinced them never to blindly accept political authority. The State carried out an organized genocide of Sikhs. This genocide can be compared to the genocide of Jews in Nazi Germany; not in numbers but in the sense of political authority deliberately attempting to exterminate a minority through unfettered use of State power. The brutalites that were perpetrated on the Sikhs need no retelling here.[76] They are evoked every day in the Sikh 'ardas` (prayer). No wonder that newspaper reports that rupees one thousand per head were said to have been paid to killers of Sikhs in the November 1984 riots[77] strike an immediate chord in Sikh psyche which at once thinks on the period 1710-1765 when the State had itself legally fixed prices for Sikh heads. The comparison is exaggerated but does work irrationally in practice on these lines. It undermines Sikh obedience to political authority. The Sikhs survived their 18th. century ordeal through their faith in ultimate victory and fortuitous political circumstances. This reinforced their resistance to automatic obedience to the State.

Decision-making was carried on through the 'Sarbat Khalsa` and the 'Gurmatta`. After their experience with Banda Singh Bahadur [78], no individual was allowed to so dominate political activity. The 'Sarbat Khalsa' was the general assembly of the Sikhs, taking place biennially at Amritsar. [79] A resolution passed by such an assembly was the 'Gurmatta'(guru's decree). [80] The Sarbat Khalsa appointed Jathedars (group leaders), chose agents and entrusted them with powers to negotiate on behalf of the Panth. [81] Here was no obedience to a powerful individual. This system has even been described as a "federative republic" [82] by a historian. When deemed necessary, an individual was delegated specific powers by common consent through a majority decision. [83] He was barely allowed the dignity of a primus inter pares. [84] "Among the Khalsa no pre-eminence was allowed except which merit and ability naturally give...Anyone who possessed the strength of arms, determination and organising ability could ride with followers behind him and call himself a Sirdar." [85] Not only this, "the democratic functioning of the Army gave their individual soldier a feeling that he was his own leader and the duties he was carrying out were self-imposed". [86] He was "subordinate to none and was his own leader". [87]

This attitudinal defiance was confined not just to the politico-religious sphere but extended to other spheres of the Sikh way of life as well. Banda Singh Bahadur's efforts have been called a "peasant upsurge in eastern Punjab". [88] He was able to rouse "a down-trodden peasantry to take up arms. In seven stormy years Banda changed the class structure of land holdings in the southern half of the state by liquidating many of the big

Muslim zamindar (land owning) families of Malwa and the Jullundur Doab. Large estates were first broken up into smaller holdings in the hands of Sikh or Hindu peasants. With the rise of Sikh power these holdings were once again grouped together to form large estates, but in the hands of Sikh chieftains".[89]

This process did not, however, take away land from many small peasant proprietors given land by Banda Singh. "Banda confiscated jagirs and distributed them among landless farmers."[90] This tradition of a preponderance of small peasant-proprietors in the Punjab can be traced back to Banda. As peasant-proprietors the Sikhs extended their independence in obedience attitudes to the economic sphere. They were directly affected by whether political authority followed policies safeguarding their economic well-being or functioned only through extortionist tax collectors. Agriculture became the favoured occupation of these peasant-proprietors. From this time on can be traced how political decisions affecting agricultural operations became important factors in determining Sikh attitudes towards obedience to such political authority. It should not surprise people nowadays when rural Sikhs get worked up about river water disputes that directly affect the availability of irrigation water to them, directly touching their agricultural operations. If Sikh farmers have become so renowned in the vanguard of the Green Revolution, one of the reasons for this development is their legacy of ability to take progressive decisions, evolved from their historical experience. Sikh progress in the economic sphere can not be divorced from the traits of the Sikh obedience pattern.

(IV). Misal Period: Leaders Galore

Chronologically, the formation of Sikh confederacies called 'Misals` dates from before 1768. This formation occurred in the 1740s when foundations of this system were laid. The date of 1768 has been adopted here because they became unchallenged masters in the Punjab after Ahmad Shah Abdali`s ninth and last invasion in 1769. Misal chieftains gradually deviated from the pristine idealism that had characterised their founders like Sardar Jassa Singh Ahluwalia and Nawab Sardar Kapur Singh Fyzullpuria.

There were twelve Misals. [91] But even in this system obedience was not granted automatically. Troopers joined chieftains of their own free will and could leave when they wanted to. They were "quite at liberty to abandon the profession of arms or to transfer their military allegiance from one chief to another". [92] The Misal chieftains could not take their followers` obedience for granted. They had to continuously respect the wishes of their adherents. "It was only by such means that they could hope to retain them in their service, the slightest show of indifference exhibited by a chief to the interests of his fighting men, invariably ending in the latter going over to another chief". [93] Transfer of allegiance was not treated as desertion or treachery. It was every Sikh`s inherent right. He had the freedom to choose the recipient of his allegiance. There was no question of accepting regimented discipline as understood in modern military sense. This did not mean that the Sikhs were not good fighters. It meant that they were just not willing to accept discipline like sheep. They considered themselves as good as another person claiming allegiance from them. Obedience was given voluntarily, not coerced.

An English traveller describes the Sikh polity thus in 1783: " Sikh government seemed to be an aristocracy but on closer examination revealed a large vein of popular power branching through many of its parts...No honorary or titualar distinctions were conferred on any member; punishments were rarely inflicted in the Army; equalitiy of rank was maintained in civil society which no class of men however wealthy or powerful were suffered to break down. Meeting a Sikh on one of his travels in the hill areas of Uttar Pradesh (the then North West Provinces) the Englishman asked him who his chief was. "He told me (in a tone of voice, and with an expression of countenance, which seemed to revolt at the idea of servitude) that he disdained an earthly superior and acknowledged no other master than his prophet Govind Singh". [94]

There was no question of accepting any chief as supremo. The practice of Gurmatta and the Sarbat Khalsa were followed as before. There was a confederal polity and no personal despotism or obedience to the sovereignty of a single authority. "A nation was up in arms against its enemies and it is the collective efforts of the masses rather than individual achievements that ultimately made the revolution a success." [95] A current Punjabi proverb reflects this tradition of those times - "Khalsa so jo nit kare jang" (Khalsa is he who daily goes to war). This 'jang' was an unceasing struggle against tyranny and intolerance practised by the ruling authorities.

However, removal of foreign danger saw the outbreak of intense rivalry between various Sikh chieftains, till then held in check by the supreme need of uniting in the face of persecution of the Panth. These rivalries constitute a characteristic that has been continuously affecting Sikh obedience patterns to the present day. As soon as the need to combat oppressive political authority recedes into the background, internecine rivalries come to the fore because of a spirit of refusal to recognise obedience to others, unless gained voluntarily respecting the religious ethos of the giver. George Forster had already foreseen in 1783 that some ambitious chief would display the standard of monarchy. [96] This experiment in monarchy did not last long because, among other reasons, there was no respect in the Sikh psyche for the monarchical ideal and no tradition of obedience to it. Dr. N.K. Sinha's comment is apt, "What might have been the most novel experiment in statecraft, degenerated later, in the nineteenth century, into a military monarchy...which, though it dazzles by early success spells ultimate failure". [97] Ranjit Singh's Empire did not conform to the kind of democratic polity envisaged in the ideals of the Khalsa. Obedience to a centralized political authority had no place in Sikh tradition. Ranjit Singh himself was not unaware that his co-religionists were difficult to command. His rule was tailored accordingly, to take due account of Sikh sensibilities towards obedience to political authority.

(V). Ranjit Singh: Apogee or Aberration?

Ranjit Singh did not allow his name to appear on his coins, a most unusual step for an Indian ruler because striking coins in one`s own name was one of the traditional ways of proclaiming one`s sovereign authority in India. His government styled itself as the 'Sarkar Khalsa Jio` or government of the Khalsa. He always claimed to act in the name of the Khalsa. It has been opined that his deference to the Khalsa Panth was dissimilar from the seeming deference of Julius and Augustus Caeser to the Roman Senate which had become a dead institution by their time. The Khalsa on the other hand was a living reality. [98] It was not a case of "Render unto Caeser, what belongs to Caeser" but an unsaid clear acknowledgement of "Render unto the Panth what belongs to the Panth". Sovereignty belonged to the Panth in Sikh history and ethos and not to an individual. Ranjit Singh could never afford to ignore the existence of the Khalsa Commonwealth to which every individual Sikh belonged as a member.

He was not "the supreme embodiment of all economic and political authority. One great limitation was to be found in the living principle of a commonwealth". [99] He is said to have been even sentenced by the Sangat assembled at the Akal Takht at Amritsar for an offence against Sikh social mores. [100] Knowing how Guru Gobind Singh had held God Almighty to be the source of all legitimate political authority, Ranjit Singh strove to render himself acceptable to the Sikhs and earn their obedience by proclaiming himself as God`s viceregent on earth and His humble servant. [101] He thus tried to win obedience from his Sikhs by posing as an Agent of God, [102] seeking legitimization in the eyes of the Panth. He was certainly aware that many Sikhs looked askance at his lifestyle and the Brahmanical practices introduced during his reign. He was no doubt a secular man who appointed non-Sikhs to some of the most important positions at his Court but his distrust of his co-religionists also played a part in such appointments. He knew that the concept of a Maharaja, an individual sovereign, was not in harmony with the tenth Guru`s ideals or the ideology evolved for a Sikh political order during the war of liberation against oppressive State authority. His kingdom was an aberration in the evolution of Sikh politiy based on religious tenets; regardless of how justified it may have been on circumstantial or logical arguments. It ran counter to the Sikh political ethos.

This character was amply reflected in his delicate relationship with the Akalis led by Akali Phoola Singh and Akali Sadhu Singh. The Akalis considered themselves bound by Sikh tenets and not by Ranjit Singh`s laws. They refused to acknowledge any earthly superior, yet Ranjit Singh "dared not crush them though he had the means to do so...dared not defy the religious susceptibilities of his people and abolish the order of the Akalis". [103] Captain Leopold von Orlich, a European officer, mentions that the Akalis had reportedly pelted visitors with mud at some of Ranjit Singh`s militrary reviews. He himself saw the Akalis shouting scornfully in Majaraja Sher Singh`s presence. [104] The Akalis were a living manifestation of the fact that the highest political authority, the Maharaja himself, was not above the Panth.

The organization of Panchayats in the Army was never eradicated. This goes against modern ideas of military discipline on European lines but was fully in accordance with Sikh tradition. These Panchayats were to play an important role in the politics of the Sikh Durbar after the death of Maharaja Ranjit Singh in 1839. After Ranjit Singh`s demise, elected Army Panchayats gradually took over executive authority under the designation of "Panth Khalsa Jio". [105] A French traveller writes, "A Prussian Officer, Mr. Mévius, was in command of a cavalry regiment since many years. Lately, he tried to introduce German discipline, flogging; his Sikhs revolted at once". [106] The Sikhs fought valiantly on the field of battle. It is just that they would not yield obedience even under a Sikh ruler if the commanding authority`s actions came into conflict with Sikh ethos. Ranjit Singh never became a cult figure in the pantheon of Sikh heroes to the extent that might be expected considering how his rule marks the high tide of Sikh political power. One of the reasons for the quick downfall of his Empire after his death was that the Sikhs had not really accepted it as something of a supreme ideal for the Panth. It was not able to unite them in its defence.

(VI). British Rule: Collaboration and Confrontation

The British did not treat the Sikhs severely after annexing the Punjab in 1849. They reaped immediate rewards when Sikh troops helped them by playing a prominent role in recapturing Delhi from the mutineers on September 20, 1857. [107] Sikh troops took the corpses of Mughal princes, slain by the English officer Hodson, to Chandni Chowk and laid them out for display in front of the Sis Ganj Gurdwara where Guru Tegh Bahadur had been executed by the Mughals in 1675, [108] nearly two centuries previously. This illustrates how the Sikhs nurture feelings of vengeance against oppressive political authorities over generations. If they feel grievously wronged by the State their obedience to it will always be tinged with revanchism and be grudgingly proffered.

The relationship with the British overlords suited the feudal Sikh interests. Princely families of cis-Satluj states and rich Sikh landlords by and large remained loyal to the British Crown. The Namdhari Guru, Baba Ram Singh, failed to capture the imagination of the Sikh masses for his campaign against the British. He was nevertheless one of the pioneers of nationalism against the colonialists, giving the idea of 'Swadeshi` and civil disobedience. Sikh masses did not follow him; partly because they considered him to be violating Guru Gobind Singh`s injunction that the last Guru after him was the Siri Guru Granth Sahib and partly because British political authority had wisely given a fair deal to Sikh economic development without having directly interfered in their religious practices. However, this Anglo-Sikh honeymoon did not last long. After recognizing in 1918 that the Sikhs had made more sacrifices for the British Empire than any other Indian community in proportion to its numbers; the Government gazetted them in 1923 as a community of "outlaws and rebels". [109]

What had caused this rupture? Once again Sikh masses had withheld allegiance to a political authority felt to have been acting against their religious interests and unresponsive to their genuine demands for handing over management of their Gurdwaras to an elected body instead of letting it remain in the hands of Mahants and their agents. Traditional Sikh practices of suffering martyrdom while fighting oppressive political authority were witnessed in the struggle for control of the Gurdwaras. A series of successful non-violent 'morchas`(campaigns) forced the British government to concede Sikh demands and enact the Gurdwara Act of 1925 [110] creating an elected body, the Shiromani Gurdwara Parbandhak Committee (S.G.P.C.), to manage Sikh Gurdwaras. Anyone familiar with the sacrifices of the Sikh masses (not richer Sikhs who were staunch collaboraters of foreign rulers) for winning control of their Gurdwaras should be able to understand why Sikhs react so emotionally against real or perceived attempts by political authority to weaken this hard won control.

The Shiromani Akali Dal came into being on December 14, 1920 at Amritsar. [111] It immediately took a leading role in agitating for emancipation of Sikh Gurdwaras from the control of the Mahants. It became the political foil to the Singh Sabha movement of the late nineteenth and early twentieth centuries for renewal of Sikh society on modern lines, including religious renewal. The Akali Dal helped in weaning away Sikh masses from pro-British lobbies like the Chief Khalsa Diwan, reducing them to minority groupings out of tune with the desires of the majority of their co-religionists. The Akali Dal soon became a vehicle for airing Sikh demands, though it never was able to claim allegiance of all Sikhs. Right from the beginning it was plagued by splits on ideological or, more commonly, personal issues because everybody wanted to assert his claim to predominant leadership. In its evolution can be seen some of theh best and worst features of Sikh attitudes towards political authorities in particular and Sikh ethos in general. Capable of mobilising Sikh masses to heights of sacrifice in defence of their Panth, it has often displayed personal rivalries of the pettiest kind, allowing opponents to take advantage politically. Splits seem to have been dogging its existence from the very beginning.[112] The present situation in Punjab reflects this tradition.

This fact of repeated fission of Sikh political entities is partly a direct consequence of the Sikh tradition of not giving obedience to a single political authority and of a refusal to recognize others as better qualified to lead than one`s own self. Sikhs participated actively in the Indian struggle for national freedom from British rule. Many Sikhs were members of the Indian National Congress or its affiliates in the pursuit of this goal of national independence. They believed promises made to them by the Congress Party and helped in driving the British out of India, suffering mutilation of their own homeland, the Punjab, in 1947 along with others living in this province.

(VII). Post-Independence Phase: Continuity and Change

Immediately after independence Jathedar Udham Singh Nagoke, Swaran Singh, Baldev Singh and Gyani Kartar Singh dissolved the Assembly Akali Party and joined the Congress. They proclaimed that henceforth the Akali Dals`s concern would be to preach Sikh religion [113] , implying that politics was separate from religion. Master Tara Singh vehemently contested this announcement and proclaimed that the Akali Dal would retain its political character to safeguard Sikh interests. [114] Thus Sikh masses still in the trauma of partition of the Punjab and its cataclysmically gory aftermath were confronted anew with the question whether religious considerations were to be an integral part of their obedience to political authority or not. Even earlier, Sikh sensibilities had been rubbed raw just after independence. It is said that the then Governor of Punjab, Sir Chandu Lal Trivedi, declared the Sikhs to be a criminal tribe on October 10, 1947 and directed the Deputy Commissioners under his control to take special precautions against them. [115] This was not exactly calculated to facilitate Sikh obedience to the newly emerged Indian State. It was an inauspicious beginning.

The Sikhs, a historically conscious people, had

made many sacrifices along with others for Indian independence. They now felt insulted and offended at this lack of faith in their loyalty. A new feeling of insecurity and alienation took root slowly that their way of life was not properly appreciated. This in turn generated such a behaviour pattern by the majority community as further aggravated the situation. To this vicious circle was soon added the touchy issue of Punjabi language and the linguistic rights of the Sikhs.

It has been opined that "the chief cause of Sikh uneasiness in free India was the resurgence of Hinduism which threatened to engulf the minorities. Renascent Hinduism manifested itself in a phenomenal increase in Hindu religious organizations, the revival of Sanskrit, and the ardent championing of Hindi". [116] the Sikhs resented the fact that Punjabi-speaking Hindus got Hindi recorded as their mother tongue in the 1951 census. Just as had happened with the slow identification of Urdu with the Muslims, communal feelings gradually led to identification of a language with a religion; Punjabi for the Sikhs and Hindi for the Hindus.

The Akali Dal quickly seized this chance for visibly reasserting itself as the champion of Sikh interests. The acceptance of the demand for a Telugu-speaking Andhra Pradesh state unleashed similar demands for a Punjabi-speaking 'Punjabi Suba`. Rejection of this demand was termed by Master Tara Singh as a "decree of Sikh annihilation". [117] The Akali Dal launched a 'morcha` for obtaining a 'Punjabi Suba`. What had proved successful against the British authorities for winning over control of Sikh Gurdwaras was now to be launched against the new political authority in India. The Sikhs, or at any rate many of them in large numbers, felt that they were being unfairly denied their linguistic rights. This generated a new weakening of their obedience to political authority which was felt not to be safeguarding legitimate rights. Extremist voices began to be raised that only a separate Sikh homeland could ensure such protection. This viewpoint was not, however, shared by a vast majority. Punjabi Suba was finally conceded in 1966 after many agitations but by then the inter-communal divide had needlessly been exacerbated.

To the issue of language was added the problem of sustained attempts to weaken the hold of the Akali Dal on Gurdwara funds because of their control over the Shiromani Gurdwara Parbandhak Committee. Attempts were made to divide the Akalis at many stages in the period 1956-1964, the Chief Ministership of Sardar Partap Singh Kairon in Punjab. It was felt that so long as the Akalis controlled the S.G.P.C. their hold on sizeable chunks of rural Sikh votes could not be broken. This policy did yield temporary gains in the sense of weakening successive Akali agitations but ultimately proved counter-productive. Unfortunately, this policy was later on renewed. It was apparently felt that Akali hold on rural, religious minded Sikh masses could perhaps be weakened by outflanking them through encouragement of religious figures mouthing radical Panthic slogans. This policy led to a new and unsavoury chapter in the history of Punjab where the inter-communal divide was widened for political reasons ignoring the disastrous effects this would generate for the country`s integrity.

Apart from its other consequences, this policy led to a situation allowing a fateful actor to stride upon the Punjab scene - Sant Jarnail Singh Bhindranwale. Terms like 'Khalistan` and Sikh State became current in this phase. Religious terminology and an acute knowledge of Sikh obedience traditions were freely used to exacerbate latent Sikh grievances: exclusion of Punjabi-speaking areas from the re-organized Punjab; refusal to allocate a fair share of river waters to Punjab; attempts to interfere in the Sikhs` control of their Gurdwaras and reduction of Sikh recruitment into the armed forces of the country.

Such grievances had for a decade or more been sublimated by sustained economic betterment through the Green Revolution. By 1980 agricultural production was not rising so fast as before, having reached a high plateau of production. Absence of heafy industries in Punjab, coupled with severe curbing of the number of Sikhs allowed to emigrate abroad by foreign governments that now drastically reduced this quota meant that a large stratum of educated youth could no more be gainfully employed. This angry generation of young Sikhs was further alienated by an Akali Dal dominated by landlord lobbies and hungry for power. This generation found its raison d`etre in Sant Bhindranwale. The chain of events culminating in Operation Bluestar of June 1984 and the assassination of Mrs. Indira Gandhi, followed by gory massacred of innocent Sikhs in the capital of

India and other areas are too recent to need recapitulation.

Bhindranwale had convinced many young Sikhs constituting an economically frustrated class that the Sikh way of life was under attack from secular forces. They became his praetorian guard. He promised them a place in the Sun. This development marks a failure of secular educational system in India to foster nationalist ideals. This system made students very aware of modern political thought and diluted Sikh religious tradition of obedience to a pluralistic political order, without inculcating a nationalist ideal to fill the void thus being created in the minds of young Sikhs. Pre-1947 protagonists of 'Khalistan` had spoken of a State "democratic in constitution...a socialistic economic structure with full protection of the culture and rights of the minorities" [118] as well as that the "economic basis of life in such a state is bound to be socialistic, in accordance with the traditions of the Sikh society". [119]

The idea of Khalistan discernible in the utterances of some young followers seems much more theocratic and fundamentalist. This is not in accordance with Sikh obedience pattern which has generally resisted intolerance in any form. As such, a theocratic Khalistan would not be able to command the loyalty of all Sikhs. Sant Bhindranwale became a cult figure for some Sikhs. This itself is at variance with democratic Sikh practices inherent in Guru Gobind Singh`s ideas, practised during the Sikh war of independence against oppressive rule. Herein lies an extremely significant development.

Young educated and dissatified Sikhs, influenced by political ideas of secular education that weaken the traditional Sikh religious concepts of power being legitimate only in a collective Panth, are ready to embrace the concept of unquestioned devotion to charismatic individuals. Herein lies a portent of times to come. If political authority is not accomodating and does not concede genuine demands of the Sikhs, which benefit all Punjabis in many cases, the older obedience pattern based on religious tradition will yield place to this newly emerging pattern, still in its embryonic stage, of blind obedience to a leader challenging established political authority in the name of Sikh traditions. Massacres of Sikhs, far from cowing down this trend, will only accentuate and exacerbate it.

The next thirty/forty years are going to be a crucial time in this regard. Till now, obedience patterns in Sikhism have been resulting in Akali splits and power struggles between Sikh politicians claiming to represent Sikh interests. This has made it easier to continue the British rulers` game of 'Divide et Impera`. The newly emerging obedience pattern among some sections of young Sikhs will make it harder to play such games, especially if some strong individual manages to claim their unquestioning obedience under the legitimizing garb of Sikh ethos. We may now be witnessing a significant 'Wende` in the Sikh obedience matrix. Repression by armed force and suppression of civil liberties may result in accentuating this change by funneling the growth of alienated, sullen and revanchist Sikh youth power willing to embrace new obedience patterns based on theocratic principles. Lack of adequate economic opportunity further complicates this process. Unless the Punjab is speedily industrialized to provide mass employment for Sikh youths not absorbed in gainful employment by the agricultural boom and sagacious policies followed to convince them that the Sikh way of life is not in danger, the future may bode rather turbulent times in this part of the country.

The contrast between Sant Bhindranwale and Sant Longowal was more than one of just political differences or differences of style. It also represents a crossroads in Sikhism for traditional patterns of obedience trends. Only time will tell whether the recent installation of Sardar Surjeet Singh Barnala as the first Akali Dal Chief Minister of Punjab with an undisputed absolute majority marks a renewal of hitherto prevalant obedience trends of their final flicker of glory before yielding place to the waiting impatient Sikh young men with their new obedience patterns. Sant Bhindranwale may be dead; it remains to be seen whether the obedience trend he personified an propagated died with him.

References

[1] The Guardian. Manchester, London. 13 May 1985, p. 8

[2] Ibid. "Cry rings out to kill extremists"

[3] W. Owen Cole and Piara Singh Sambhi, The Sikhs- Their Religious Beliefs and Practices. London, Boston 1978, p. 7

[4] Khuswant Singh gives May 30, 1606 as the date, in Khuswant Singh, A History of the Sikhs. Vol. I. Third impression, Delhi etc. 1981, p. 61

[5] Ibid, p. 5. Also see Muhammad Latif, History of the Panjab-From the Remotest Antiquity to the Present Time. New Delhi 1964, p. 64

[6] Khuswant Singh, A History of the Sikhs, ibid, p. 74

[7] Roughly translated, means the entire collectivity of the Khalsa. Also see for more details about it Jagjit Singh, The Sikh Revolution-A Perspective View. I edn., New Delhi, Chandigarh 1981

[8] Gopal Singh, Guru Gobind Singh and the Social Ideal, in Sikhism and Indian Society. Indian Institute of Advanced Study Publication. Simla 1967, p. 122

[9] Ibid.

[10] J.S. Bains, Political Ideas of Guru Gobind Singh, in ibid., p. 130

[11] Jagjit Singh, The Sikh Revolution, loc.cit., p. 240

[12] The holiest shrine, at Amritsar.

[13] Throne of the Timeless God. See Khuswant Singh, A History..., loc.cit. p. 63. W. Owen Cole and P.S. Sambhi, The Sikhs...loc.cit.,p. 29

[14] See his "Babar Bani". Also Khuswant Singh, A History of the Sikhs, Vol. I, loc.cit., p. 34, footnote 21

[15] Khuswant Singh, A History...loc.cit., p. 48

[16] W. Owen and P.S. Sambhi, The Sikhs...loc.cit., p. 30

[17] Ibid, p. 30

[18] S.M. Latif, History of the Punjab...loc.cit., p. 253

[19] Ibid.

[20] J.S. Bains, Political Ideas of Guru Gobind Singh, in Sikhism and Indian Society, loc.cit., pp. 128-133

[21] Ibid. P. 131

[22] Jagjit Singh, The Sikh Revolution...loc.cit., p. 101

[23] Ibid. P. 102

[24] Vote Panth Nun Paoji.

[25] The Guardian, Manchester/London, May 13, 1985 "Cry rings out.." p. 8.

[26] The first Akali-led coalition ministry, under Sardar Gurnam Singh, was brought down on 25-11-1967 after 8 months through defections. See Khuswant Singh, A History of the Sikhs, Vol. II, New Delhi etc., second impression 1978 of the Indian edition. The second coalition, again led by Sardar Gurnam Singh, fell after 13 months on 25-03-1970 because of defections.The Akali-led coalition ministry under Sardar Parkash Singh Badal was dismissed in 1980. Even in the Assembly elections of 1972, when the Congress Party was riding the crest of post-1971 war euphoria, the

Akalis won 24 seats in a House of 104. See Khuswant Singh, A History...Vol. II, loc.cit., 318. They won 58 seats to the Congress`s 17 seats in a House of 117 in 1977. See Times of India Directory & Yearbook, Bombay 1978, p. 84o. They got 37 seats to the Congress`s (I) 64 in 1980 elections. See Times of India Yearbook, loc.cit., p. 841. Now in 1985 the Aaklis have won 73 seats out of 115.

[27] Khuswant Singh, A History of the Sikhs, Vol. I, loc.cit., p. 49

[28] S.M. Latif, History of the Punjab...loc.cit., p. 250

[29] Khuswant Singh, A History of the Sikhs, Vol. I., loc.cit.,p. 55

[30] Majh ki Var: Verse "gur data gur hivai, gur dipak teh loe"; Gauri Var: "gur satgur ka jo sikh akhaey", for example.

[31] J.S. Grewal & S.S. Bal, Guru Gobind Singh, Chandigarh 1967, pp. 20-21

[32] S.S. Caveeshar, The Sikh Studies. Lahore 1937, p. 109. Also Gopal Singh, in Sikhism and Indian Society, loc.cit., p. 122

[33] Judh jite inhi ke prasad, inhi ke prasad su dan kare;agh augh tare inhi ke prasad, inhi ki kripa phun dham bhare;inhi ki prasad su vidya lai, inhi ki kripa sabh satru mare;inhi ki kripa se saje ham hain, nahi mo so garib karor pare (Dasam Granth - For translation see Tarlochan Singh, Social Philosophy of Guru Gobind Sing, in Sikhism and Indian Society, loc.cit., p. 199

[34] Arjan Dass Malik, An Indian Guerilla War-The Sikh Peoples War 1699-1768. New Delhi 1975, p. 25

[35] A.D. Malik, An Indian Guerilla War...loc.cit., p. 13

[36] Khuswant Singh, A History..., Vol. 1, loc.cit., pp. 101-102

[37] Ibid, pp. 122-123

[38] Ibid, pp. 152-153, see footnote 32

[39] S.M. Latif, History..., loc.cit., p. 230

[40] Khuswant Singh, A History..., Vol. 1, loc.cit., p. 107

[41] Degh o Tegh o Fateh o Nusrat-i-bedirang;Yaft az Nanak Guru Gobind Singh (for translation see Khuswant Singh, A History..., Vol. 1, p. 107, footnote 12

[42] N.K. Sinha, Rise of the Sikh Power. III. edn., Calcutta 1960, pp. 55-56

[43] Ibid, p. 56, footnote 3

[44] Sardars Partap Singh Kairon, Gurmukh Singh Musafir, Gurnam Singh, Lachhman Singh Gill, Parkash Singh Badal, Zail Singh, Darbara Singh and now Surjeet Singh Barnala

[45] Cole and Sambhi, The Sikhs..., loc.cit., p. 26

[46] Ibid, p. 26

[47] J.S. Grewal & S.S. Bal, Guru Gobind Singh, loc.cit., pp. 20-21

[48] Ibid, p. 21

[49] Khuswant Singh, A History of the Sikhs, Vol. I, loc.cit., p. 48

[50] Ibid

[51] Ibid, pp. 50-52

[52] Ibid, p. 52

[53] Ibid, p. 52, footnote 7

[54] Cole and Sambhi, The Sikhs...loc.cit., pp. 20-21. Khuswant Singh calls the heads of these `Manjis`"Masands". For this see Khuswant Singh, A History..., Vol. I, loc.cit., p. 53. This term `Masand`forms the general usage from the time of Guru Arjan in any case.

[55] Khuswant Singh, A History...Vol. I, loc.cit., p. 54

[56] Ibid.

[57] W. Owen Cole and Piara Singh Sambhi, The Sikhs...loc.cit., p. 21

[58] Christine Effenberg, Die politische Stellung der Sikhs innerhalb der indischen Nationalbewegung 1935-1947. Wiesbaden 1984, p. 10. Translated by the author from the German text which reads: "Innerhalb eines Jahrhunderts, das zwischen Guru Nanak und Guru Arjan lag, wurde aus einer verhältnismäßig kleinen Anhängerschaft eine Gemeinschaft mit Machtentfaltung, Selbständigkeit und politischer Bedeutsamkeit"

[59] Jagjit Singh, The Sikh Revolution..., loc.cit., p. 254

[60] Khuswant Singh, A History..., Vol. I, loc.cit., pp. 65-66. Also see A.D. Malik, An Indian..., loc.cit., p. 19

61 Khuswant Singh, ibid, p. 66

[62] Ibid, p. 69, footnote 17

[63] Ibid, p. 68

[64] Syad Muhammad Latif, History of the Panjab..., loc.cit., p. 260

[65] J.S. Grewal & S.S. Bal, Guru Gobind Singh..., loc.cit., p. 26

[66] The Khalsa shall rule; its enemies shall disappear

[67] J.S. Grewal & S.S. Bal, Guru Gobind Singh..., loc.cit., pp. 160-161

[68] N.K. Sinha, Ranjit Singh. Reprint of the III edn., Calcutta 1960, p. 139

[69] Bhai Jodh Singh, Structure and Character of Sikh Society, in Sikhism and Indian Society, loc.cit., pp. 44-45. See also translation of Jangnama by Dr. Ganda Singh

[70] Gopal Singh, in Sikhism and Indian Society, loc.cit., p. 123

[71] J.S. Bains, in Sikhism and Indian Society, loc.cit., p. 134

[72] Wazir Singh, in Sikhism and Indian Society, loc.cit., p. 211

[73] Sardul Singh Caveeshar, The Sikh Studies. Lahore 1937, p. 108

[74] Wazir Singh, Guru Gobind Singh`s Philosophy of Values, in Sikhism and Indian Society, loc.cit., p. 212

[75] Khuswant Singh, A History..., Vol. I, loc.cit., pp. 135-136

[76] For a description of the brutalities committed on the Sikhs by political authorities, see N.K. Sinha, Rise of the Sikh Power, loc.cit., pp. 3-15. Syad Muhammad Latif, History of the Panjab..., loc.cit., pp. 213-217. Hari Ram Gupta, History of the Sikhs, Vol. II. New Delhi, III revised edn., 1978, pp. 31-34

[77] The Guardian. Manchester, London, January 30, 1985, p. 7. "Civil rights group says ruling Congress Party was behind anti-Sikh rioting"

[78] W.L. M`Gregor, History of the Sikhs, Vol. I. London 1846, pp. 111-112

[79] Khuswant Singh, A History..., Vol. I, loc.cit., p. 121

[80] Ibid

[81] Ibid

[82] S.M. Latif, History of the Panjab..., loc.cit., p. 271

[83] Ibid, p. 290

[84] Arjan Dass Malik, An Indian Guerilla War..., p. 40

[85] Ibid, p. 83

[86] Ibid, p. 84

[87] Ibid, p. 89

[88] Khuswant Singh, A History..., Vol. I, loc.cit., p. 101

[89] Ibid, p. 118

[90] A.D. Malik, An Indian Guerilla War..., loc.cit., p. 28

[91] Khuswant Singh, History of the Sikhs, Vol. I, loc.cit., see p. 132. Also see N.K. Sinha, Rise of the Sikh Power, p. 57

[92] S.M. Latif, History of the Panjab..., loc.cit., p. 290

[93] S.M. Latif, History of the Panjab..., loc.cit., p. 290

[94] George Forster, Origin and Making of a Nation, in Rare Documents on Sikhs and their Rule in the Punjab; edited by H.S. Bhatia, New Delhi 1981, pp. 31-32

[95] N.K. Sinha, Rise of the Sikh Power..., loc.cit., p. 2

[96] George Forster, Origin and Making of a Nation, loc.cit., pp. 36-37

[97] N.K. Sinha, Rise of the Sikh Power, loc.cit., p. 2

[98] N.K. Sinha, Ranjit Singh, p. 137

[99] N.K. Sinha, Rise of..., loc.cit., p. 136

[100] Sardul Singh Caveeshar, The Sikh Studies, loc.cit., p. 111

[101] Dewan Ummer Nath, Memoirs of the Reign of Ranjit Singh, in Rare Documents on Sikhs..., loc.cit., p. 149

[102] Ibid.

[103] N.K. Sinha, Ranjit Singh, loc.cit., p. 138

[104] Captain Leopold von Orlich, Travels in India, Sinde and the Punjab, in Rare Documents on Sikhs..., loc.cit., pp. 232-233

[105] Jagjit Singh, The Sikh Revolution..., loc.cit., p. 240

[106] Victor Jacquemont, Etat Politique et Social de l`Inde du Nord en 1830. Paris 1933, republished, p. 237. The original text reads: "Un officier prussien, M. Mévius, commandait depuis plusieurs années un régiment de cavalerie. Dernièrement, il essaya d`y introduire la discipline allemande, la schlague; ses Sikes se révoltérent aussitot". Translated from the French by the author.

[107] Khuswant Singh, A History of the Sikhs, Vol. II. II. impression of the Indian edition, New Delhi 1978, p. 110

[108] Ibid, pp. 110-111

[109] Sardul Singh Caveeshar, The Sikh Studies, Lahore 1937, p. 186

[110] Khuswant Singh, A History of the Sikhs, Vol. II, loc.cit., p. 212

[111] Harcharan Singh Bajwa, Fifty Years of Punjab Politics (1920-1970). I. edn., Chandigarh 1979, p. 21

[112] For a concise account of such splits, see C. Effenberg, Die politische Stellung der Sikhs..., loc.cit., pp. 36-78

[113] Harcharan Singh Bajwa, Fifty Years of Punjab Politics, loc.cit., p. 18

[114] Ibid.

[115] Ibid, p. 83

[116] Khuswant Singh, A History of the Sikhs, Vol. II, loc.cit., p. 293

[117] The Spokesman, New Delhi, October 19, 1955.

[118] Gurbachan Singh and Lal Singh Gyani, The Idea of the Sikh State, Lahore 1946, p. 3

[119] Ibid, p. 13.

Bibliography

Bains, J.S., Political Ideas of Guru Gobind Singh, in Sikhism and Indian Society. Transactions of the Indian Institute of Advanced Study, Vol. 4. I. ed. Simla 1967

Bajwa, Harcharan Singh, Fifty Years of Punjab Politics (1920-1970). I. edn. Chandigarh 1979

Caveeshar, Sardul Singh, The Sikh Studies. Lahore 1937

Cole, W. Owen and Sambhi, Piara Singh, The Sikhs-Their Religious Beliefs and Practices. I. edn.. London, Boston 1978

Effenberg, Christine, Die politische Stellung der Sikhs innerhalb der indischen Nationalbewegung 1935-1947. Wiesbaden 1984

Forster, George, Origin and Making of a Nation, in Bhatia, H.S. (ed.), Rare Documents on Sikhs and their Rule in the Punjab. New Delhi 1981

Gupta, Hari Ram, History of the Sikhs. Vol. II - Evolution of Sikh Confederacies (1708-1769). III. revised Edition. Delhi 1978

Grewal, J.S. and Bal, S.S., Guru Gobind Singh.(A Biographical Study). Chandigarh 1967

Jacquemont, Victor, Etat Politique et Social de l`Inde du Nord en 1830. Paris 1933

Latif, Syad Muhammad, History of the Panjab from the Remotest Antiquity to the Present Time. New Delhi 1964

M`Gregor, W.L., The History of the Sikhs. Vol. I. London 1846

Malik, Arjan Dass, An Indian Guerilla War-The Sikh Peoples War 1699-1768. New Delhi 1975

Nath, Dewan Ummer, Memoirs of the Reign of Runjeet Singh, in H.S. Bhatia (ed.), Rare Documents on Sikhs and their Rule in the Punjab. New Delhi 1981

Orlich, Captain Leopold von, Travels in India, Sinde and the Punjab, in H.S. Bhatia (ed.), Rare Documents on Sikhs and their Rule in the Punjab. New Delhi 1981

Singh, Bhai Jodh, Structure and Character of Sikh Study, in Sikhism and Indian Society. Simla 1967

Singh, Gopal, Guru Gobind Singh and the Social Ideal, in Sikhism and Indian Society. Simla 1967

Singh, Gurbachan and Gyani, Lal Singh, The Idea of the Sikh State. Lahore 1946

Singh, Jagjit, The Sikh Revolution. A Perspective View. I. edn.. New Delhi/Chandigarh 1981

Singh, Khuswant, A History of the Sikhs. Vol. I: 1469-1839. Third Impression, Delhi, Bombay, Calcutta, Madras 1981. Vol. II: 1839-1974. Second Impression. Delhi, Bombay, Calcutta, Madras 1978

Singh, Tarlochan, Social Philosophy of Guru Gobind Singh, in Sikhism and Indian Society. Simla 1967

Singh, Wazir, Guru Gobind Singh`s Philosophy of Values, in Sikhism and Indian Society. Simla 1967

Sinha, Narendra Krishna, Ranjit Singh. Reprint of III. Edition. Calcutta 1960

Sinha, Narendra Krishna, Rise of the Sikh Power. Calcutta, III Edn., 1960

Sikhs and India: The Tragedy of Khalistan

by Christine Effenberg

Since 1981 extremist Sikhs from the North-Indian Federal State Punjab (see map on the next page) urged the Indian Government for Punjab`s separation from the Indian Union. Their intention is to reach the establishment of an independent Sikh-governed State called Khalistan. Moreover, moderate Sikhs stood up for more autonomy of this Federal State.

Ideas for the Punjab`s territorial re-arrangement:

The efforts undertaken by the Sikhs to reach an own Sikh-State are not at all new but can be traced back to the final stage of the Indians` struggle for independence against the British power in India. Already during the period 1940-1947 a separate Sikh-State had been claimed for by the Sikhs. When in those days the formation of Pakistan and with that the partition of the Punjab, the native country of the Sikh, became evident, the political parties of the Sikhs tried to obtain for their community a maximum of rights and privileges from the British. Sikhs played an important role for the British because they provided the British Indian Army with a large number of soldiers. Therefore, the Sikh Party Shromani Akali Dal demanded an own Sikh-State,

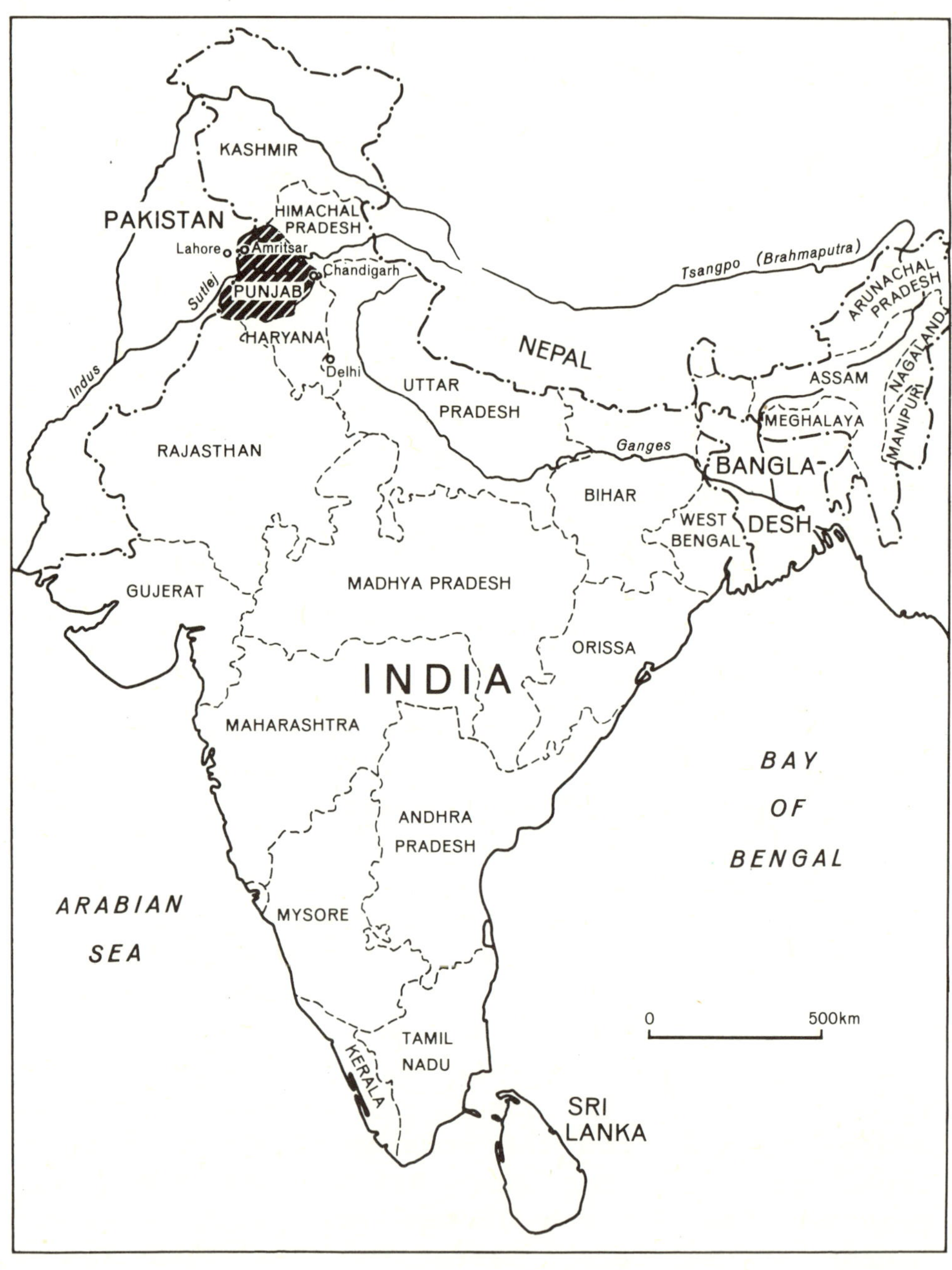
KASHMIR
PAKISTAN
HIMACHAL PRADESH
Lahore
Amritsar
Chandigarh
Sutlej
PUNJAB
HARYANA
Delhi
Indus
Tsangpo (Brahmaputra)
ARUNACHAL PRADESH
NAGALAND
NEPAL
ASSAM
MANIPUR
MEGHALAYA
UTTAR PRADESH
Ganges
RAJASTHAN
BANGLA-DESH
BIHAR
WEST BENGAL
GUJERAT
MADHYA PRADESH
ORISSA
INDIA
MAHARASHTRA
BAY OF BENGAL
ANDHRA PRADESH
ARABIAN SEA
MYSORE
0
500km
TAMIL NADU
KERALA
SRI LANKA

respectively an independent province, in case the British granted an own State - Pakistan - to the Muslims.

The idea of a territorial re-arrangement of the Punjab, however, had come up even in earlier times. Around 1924 Lala Lajpat Rai, who had been leader of the Congress and supporter of the Hindu-Reform Movement Arya Samaj in the Punjab at the beginning of the 20. century[1] made efforts for an East Punjab as independent Hindu-Sikh governed province as well as for a West Punjab as Muslim governed province in order to solve the Hindu-Muslim problem.[2]

"My suggestion is that the Punjab should be partitioned into two provinces, the Western Punjab with a large Muslim majority, to be a Muslim-governed Province; and the Eastern Punjab, with a large Hindu-Sikh majority, to be a non-Muslim-governed Province."[3]

Accordingly, Lala Lajpat Rai demanded part of the Punjab to be an independent Hindu-governed Province as had later been the case by Sikh-leader Tara Singh with regard to Azad Punjab.

The Sikhs, too, refer to the fact that the idea of an independent Sikh-governed State respectively of an independent Sikh-governed Province had not come up as reaction to the claim for Pakistan by Mohammed Ali Jinnah, 1876-1948, in 1940, but considerably earlier in order to protect culture, language and religion of the Sikhs. Because during the "Round Table Conferences" 1930-1932 summoned by Lord Irwin, Vice-King of India, on the occasion of which India`s future under participation of

India was to be decided on, the Sikh-representatives Ujjal Singh and Sardar Sampuran Singh proposed in their memorandum dated November 12, 1931 a territorial re-arranging of the Punjab. It came to it when in the "Second Round Table Conference" the constitutional protection of minorities should be discussed. Point of discussion had not only been the continuation of separate electorates for Muslims, but also the setting of this protection for millions of Parias.[5] Since the Indian representatives had not reached any agreement upon these questions, they had been obliged to accept an award by Prime Minister Ramsay Macdonald. This Communal Award proclaimed on August 16, 1932 granted separate electorates to all minorities including the Sikhs.[6] The Sikhs had been incensed by this concession. Because by that the majority of the Muslims in the Punjab had been politically fixed. Moreover, the claims which had been presented by the Sikh-representatives Ujjal Singh and Sampuṛan Singh in their memorandum dated November 12, 1931, during the "Second Round Table Conference" could not at all be complied with. Because of "their inrivalled position in the Punjab - historical, political and economic - they claim 30 per cent representation in the Provincial Legislature" [7] for the Sikh-community. Moreover, they opposed separate electorates which would strengthen the Muslims, because "the other two communities could not even influence the permanent majority (Muslims), chosen as it would be by constitutents swayed by none but communal motives and aims"..."We cannot accept a constitution which relegates us for all time to the position of an ineffective opposition". In case of the Muslims not deviating from their claim for reserved majority, in this memorandum the Sikh-representatives proposed a territorial re-arranging of the Punjab. The Rawalpindi and Multan Districts without Lyallpur and Montgomery Districts, which have an extreme Muslemic population of seven millions, should either form a separate province or should be fused with the North-West-Frontier. A Punjab with a number of population of approximately 16 millions would have been left behind in which no single community would have possessed the absolute majority. This plan for re-arranging of the Punjab had not been taken into consideration by the British.

The Muslim-League announced on its conference in Lahore in March 1940 the Muslims` claim to an independent Muslim-governed state, which found support by Jinnah with the so-called Two-Nations-Theory.[8] The Two-Nations-Theory tries to justify the independence of Hindus and Muslims as two nations.[9] Based on the Two-Nations-Theory Jinnah called for the right of self-determination for the Mohammedan nation which was to show itself in autonomous Mohammedan states of India`s West and East.[10] Jinnah`s affirmation that Sikhs would not at all have to be afraid of anything in the Muslim-State of Pakistan could not dispel the doubts of the Sikhs, because a great number of them lived in the West of India, the region demanded by Jinnah.[11] The main problem of the Sikhs was now to reach for their independent community a favourable position in order to be able to represent their claims and rights with chance of success - despite the Pakistan-danger in connection with India`s re-arranging. Starting on

May 1940 political representatives of the Sikhs dealt with the so-called Khalistan-scheme - as reaction on the Pakistan-demand - which had been created by Dr. V.S. Bhatti from Ludhiana. Khalistan meant founding a Sikh-governed state which was to serve as buffer state between India and Pakistan.[12] At this time the Khalistan-scheme could not be accounted for by the Sikhs in a convincing way so that the claim for an independent Sikh-governed state was put aside by the Sikhs in favour of the claim for an own Sikh-governed province, Azad Punjab.[13] This claim was the result of Sir Stafford Cripps` proposals dated 1942 to solve the question of India. Since, according to the opinion of the Sikhs, the granting of Pakistan had been fixed in these proposals[14], they triggered the resistance of political Sikh-representations. The claim for Azad Punjab had been stired up by Master Tara Singh, 1885-1967. In those years, Master Tara Singh had been a leader of the extremist Shromani Akali Dal wing and after India becoming independent he had been the most important political leader of the Sikh-community. The proposals made by Sir Stafford Cripps offered Master Tara Singh the chance to show to the Sikh-community the imminent danger caused by Pakistan and the Muslim-government connected with it and to obtain its support. The only solution for the community to get out of this dilemma was, according to Master Tara Singh, to have an independent province for the Sikhs.[15] The Azad Punjab Plan presented comprised Lahore, Jullundur, Ambala as well as part of the Multan-district. In this region the Sikhs would have hold the political balance, since Hindus, Muslims and Sikhs had there been represented in equal parts.[16]

The districts of Rawalpindi and the Multan-districts Attock, Mianwali, Shahapur, Jhelum, Gujrat, Multan, Dehra Ghazi Khan, Muzzafargarh and Jhang were to form a Muslim province, in which the North West Frontier, too,[17] which had a Muslim majority of 90 per cent could be included. According to that, the Azad Punjab Plan also meant the granting of an own Muslim-governed state in India`s North west.

Azad Punjab was expected to include central and Eastern districts of the Punjab with a population which did not only comprise of Sikhs, but also of Punjabi-Hindus.[18] The claim for Azad Punjab, however, lost importance, since in those days not all political Sikh-groups gave support to this demand by Shromani Akali Dal.[19] Moreover: The demand of the Shromani Akali Dal for Azad Punjab was not given great importance by the British, since the political Sikh-groups didn`t show any unity among one another, presented themselves to the public in a quarrelled way and tried to play one off against the other. In addition, the Sikhs did`t possess the majority in the region they laid claim to.[20] If the Shromani Akali Dal succeeded in achieving the support of the other political Sikh-groups concerning the Azad Punjab demand and to approach the British in this demand as united political Sikh-group, there would have been the chance to be regarded by the British concerning this demand in a "more serious" way.

As a step to prepare the Indian independence, the Indian cabinet of war entrusted - in London in 1942 - an Indian Committee with the task to outline a declaration of India. By means of this declaration it was expected to reach the aim of finding a political solution to the question of India in agreement with the Indian parties. The declaration of India had been an offer by the British to the Indians which was to be accepted or to be rejected.

The political Sikh-groups refused the Indian declaration because they were of the opinion that the granting of Pakistan was fixed in it.[21] By it, Master Tara Singh again had the possibility to show the imminent danger caused by Pakistan and the Muslim-government to the Sikh-community. The only solution had been seen by Master Tara Singh in an independent province, Azad Punjab. It is not evident whether Master Tara Singh thought already in those days of an own Sikh-governed state "Sikhistan" when claiming for "Azad Punjab".

In the region of "Azad Punjab" claimed for not only Sikhs but, above all, Punjabi Hindus, too, would have been represented.

On July 10, 1944, C. Rajagopalachari published the so-called Rajagopalacharia plan[22] as reaction on the Indian declaration by the British. The plan granted to the Muslims the separate state Pakistan and was to bring about a compromise with the Muslim League.[23] Almost all political Sikh-groups protested against this plan because of the granting of Pakistan. As reaction on the Rajagopalachara plan followed - in 1944 - the claim of Master Tara Singh for an own Sikh-governed state Khalistan taking the danger of Pakistan as argument and stating that the Sikhs were an independent nation.[24] In the founding of Pakistan the Sikhs saw a danger for their religion, culture and language. According to the

Rajagopalachara plan the native country of the Sikh-community was to be divided into two almost equal parts. One part was to belong to India, the other part to Pakistan. The Sikhs were afraid of disappearing as minority in the Hindu- or Muslim-community, not only in India but also in Pakistan.[25]

Only in 1946 the Sikhs submitted their ideas to the British of which area the future Sikh-governed state should consist. Consequently, the whole Punjab-area with the exception of Multan- and Rawalpindi-districts belonged to it.[26]

It can be summed up that the political Sikh-groups because of their disability to be able to present themselves as a closed political Sikh-representation to the British, were not regarded, like the Muslim League, as a whole as political representation of the Sikhs by the British. Therefore, the demand for a separate province, respectively for a separate Sikh-state in case of the Pakistan-concession, didn`t influence further political decisions by the Britih on the independence of India.

Efforts for separation by the Sikhs in India from independence to the present:

In contrast to the Muslims, India`s independence on August 15, 1947 didn`t mean to the Sikhs the granting of the own state aspired to. On the contrary, the Sikhs - as minority - saw themselves threatened by the founding of the state Pakistan, because many Sikhs lived in the region of the new state. Therefore, it came to a stampede of Sikhs, but also of Hindus,from West Pakistan to India and as countermove Muslims from East Punjab to Pakistan.[27] This move of many Sikhs from West Pakistan to the North-East of the Punjab had the result that the Sikhs could form the majority there. Based on their majority in the North-East of the Punjab the Sikhs now - under the political leadership of Master Tara Singh - called for Punjabi Suba, an independent province within the Indian Union, in which they were enabled to carry on their culture, languagae and religion without hindrance.[28]

Only on November 1, 1966, however, the Sikhs were granted - in the beginning of Indira Gandhi being Prime Minister - Punjabi Suba. According to the resolution by the Federal Government dated May 9, 1966, the former Federal State Punjab was divided into two Federal States with Chandigarh to be the common Federal- and Administration capital: into Punjab where half of the population consists of Sikhs who had, however, thus only indirectly been given self-determination as well as into Haryana with a Hindu-majority.[29]

Granting of an independent Sikh-governed province can be seen as victory of the Sikh-community which has constantly engaged for this demand in the years after independence. In this case the pertinacity and consistency of the political leadership of the Sikhs led to success.

The Federal State Punjab, however, remained only a partial aim with which - up to today - the Sikhs do not want to put up with. Since 1981 the Sikhs again call for an own Sikh-governed State Khalistan, respectively they demand more autonomy.

Their claims are based on "Anandpur Resolution" which had been worked out by the Working Committee of Akali Dal on October 16 and 17, 1973 and which had been presented on August 28, 1977. [30] In the "Anandpur Resolution" among others the Sikhs call not only for the possibility to practise Sikhism in a free religious way, but also for a new "All India Gurdwara Law" and the integration of all regions of the neighbouring states Haryana and Rajasthan, in which Punjabi is spoken. Moreover, they are claiming from the Central Government that Chandigarh becomes the only capital of the Punjab and with that to break away from the Federal State Haryana. In addition to that, they want to get be again preferred with regard to the engagement for the army, as it had been practised under British rulership. Moreover, they call for a regulation to be allowed to hold - without license - knives (= kirpan), revolvers, pistols etc.

This Anandpur Resolution and with that the claim for an own state Khalistan respectively for more autonomy can be traced back to the fact that the Sikhs feel themselves disadvantaged by the Indian Government and hindered in practising their religious tradition. Radical Sikhs talk about an intolerable discrimination of the Sikh-community.

Sant Jarnail Singh Bhindranwale, since 1981 popular religious leader of a part of the Sikh-community acquired status as strongest promoter of the claim for a sovereign and theocratical Sikh-governed state Khalistan. With regard to his efforts to establish this new state he can be compared with the former Sikh-leader Master Tara Singh already mentioned.

Bhindranwale made efforts for a religious revival of Sikhism, since the Sikh-community - as had often been the case in its history - feared to become more and more the minority. He tried to stabilize and to increase the community by forcing the claim for a Sikh-governed state - the "great old dream" of the Sikh-community. Because the latter did not forget that under their King Ranjit Singh they possessed an own independent Kingdom in the 19th century.

Occasionally, Bhindranwale could reckon on the support of the Sikh-party Akali Dal which had been splitted into two rivalling groups in 1980, into the moderate Akali Dal (L) under the leadership of Sant Harchand Singh Longowal and the radical Akali Dal (T) with its leader Jagdev Singh Talwandi.

The riots in the Punjab which had broken out at the end of 1981 in order to liberate Khalistan had mostly been provoked by supporters of the extremist Dal Khalsa existing since 1978 as well as by the academic Sikh-union "All India Sikh Students Federation". Both unions, too, sided with Bhindranwale and executed according to his order the acts of violences. Moreover, it came to carefully directed assassionations of Hindus and Sikhs who served for the Indian Government, or who refused the claim for Khalistan in the public.[31]

On October 6, 1983 the Indian President Zail Singh, a Sikh, too, declared President`s rule in the Punjab as reaction to the bloody riots. Besides that the Indian Government showed its readiness to comply with some claims for autonomy by the moderate Sant Harchand Singh Longowal. For that it urged Longowal that the political body of the Sikhs, Akali Dal, should oppose the riots and should keep distance in public. In return for that it also offered to Longowal participation in government in the Punjab. However, these attempts for agreement by the Indian Government with Longowal, which existed since October 1983, failed.[32]

Meanwhile Bhindranwale succeded - with a great number of supporters - in occupying the Golden Temple in Amritsar, which is the place of highest religious worship of the Sikhs. Ordnance depots had been installed there and supporters should be trained on the field of military for the fight for Khalistan.[33]

In April 1984 the Indian Government prolonged President`s rule in the Punjab by another six months.[34] Because the riots had already spread to the neighbouring states Haryana and Rajasthan. Moreover, the Sikh-leader didn`t show any readiness for agreement with the Indian Government which feared further intensive riots in the Punjab. As reaction to the prolongation of President`s rule the Akali Dal threatened the Indian Government to boycott the export of cereals to other Indian Federal States.[35] This would have meant a disaster since half of the cereals needed in the Indian Union comes from the Federal State Punjab, India`s granary.

Indira Gandhi, Prime Minister of that time, saw herself obliged to take actions:

- because of the acts of violence by Sikh-extremists,

- because of threatening to sabotage cereals supplies, and

- because of attacks by the opposition.

Mrs. Gandhi was said to be to weak as Head of Government and therefore was to resign so that peace could return to the Punjab. Because of the riots Mrs. Gandhi had lost confidence and image with a great part of the Hindu-population.

On June 5, 1984, on the orders of Mrs. Gandhi, Indian troops, the so-called "Operation Blue-Star", assaulted the Golden Temple of Amritsar which was kept occupied by Bhindranwale.[36] The Headquarters were to be phased out and the Khalistan-movement to be smashed. With that Mrs. Gandhi ordered a dramatic blow against Sikh-extremists in order to re-gain the confidence of India`s population also with regard to the forthcoming elections of the House of Commons at the end of 1984. However, consequence of the massacre in the Golden Temple of Amritsar during which hundreds of Sikhs and their leader Bhindranwale had lost their life, was a persistent wave of resentment of the Sikh-community within and outside the Indian Union.[37]

It is the first time in the history of India that the Government - in order to keep the political unity - ordered to attack the sanctuary of the Sikhs highly respected by them. In a country like the Indian Union where the slaughtering of cows in front of temples can still trigger disastrous religious armed conflicts the massacre in the Golden Temple of Amritsar has a high social-political meaning.

With the storming of the Golden Temple Indira Gandhi reached that the Sikh-extremists have to do without their up to that time safe, since sacrosanct, place which served as depot of weapons and military training camp, too. Moreover, since the death of Bhindranwale and his closest fellows, they now belong to a "headless" Khalistan-movement because up to now no qualified successor could enter into the heritage of Bhindranwale. As a result, Mrs. Gandhi incurred the irreconcilable enmity of the Sikhs. They had sworn and called for revenge. Further riots which reach up to the present show that the defiling of the Golden Temple had not been followed by the break of the Khalistan-movement. On the contrary, a great deal of Sikhs, up to this time not interested in Khalistan, now feel themselves as sympathizers and admire Bhindranwale as martyr.

Instead of breaking extremism and separatism the Indian Government reached the violation and further alienation of the majority of the Sikhs as well as a fertile ground for Khalistan.

Already in July 1984 the well-known Sikh-journalist and Sikh-historian Khuswant Singh meant, "I think by this action the government has sown the seeds for Khalistan".[38]

When giving the order to attack the Golden Temple, Mrs. Gandhi made an own goal, for which she had to pay not with the loss of her political past but with her life. On October 31, 1984 she had been killed by two Sikhs. This was the planned act of revenge by Sikh-extremists for storming the Golden Temple of Amritsar on June 5, 1984. The commander-in-chief of the Indian army to storm the Temple also died because of an assassination in Bombay on August 9, 1986.

Mrs. Gandhi`s successor as Prime Minister of the Indian Union, her son Rajiv Gandhi, who had already been sworn in this past on the day his mother was killed has to enter into a difficult political heritage. Because the claim of the Sikhs for an own State Khalistan is not being settled by the successful reprisal against Indira Gandhi. The conflicts between Hindus and Sikhs which have arisen in all parts of India after the assassination of Mrs. Gandhi further on promoted the inimical distance between Hindus and Sikhs and have still been holding on. Within and outside of India the appeal of the Sikhs for a revolt for Khalistan has further on been made.

Abroad the center of the Khalistan-movement is situated in London.

There the National Council of Khalistan (NCK) with its President Jagjit Singh Chauhan is acting. The claims of the National Council of Khalistan for a separate state is based on religious-political, historical and economic arguments.[39] According to the ideas of NCK-leaders Khalistan is expected to include besides the Indian Punjab and the Sikh-majority areas in Haryana, Himachal Pradesh, Rajastan, Jammu also a corridor along the Pakistani frontier, so that the state Khalistan is enabled to dispose of an admittance to the Sea in the Gujarat-region Kutch.[40]

Conclusion:

In this century - for almost 55 years - the Sikhs have engaged themselves in a more or less intensive way for an independent state Khalistan, which is called Sikhistan, too, respectively they called for an independent province, after granting this province more autonomy.

It can be observed that the Khalistan-movement continous periodically flaring up, then stands latently in the background in order to take again action at the next chance. The reason for that is the respective political situation in India and in connection with that the respective degree of enthusiasm for Khalistan of the Sikh-community.

During the final stage of the fight for independence of India 1940-1947 the chance of the Sikhs to get granted by the British a separate Sikh-governed state was given because the Indian Muslims, too, had a chance to get an dependent Muslim-state. Since the Sikhs, however - in contrary to the Muslims under their leader Mohammed Ali Jinnah - did not succeed in contracting and negotiating with the British, as political unity with a Sikh-leader, their claim for an independent state Khalistan lost importance in those days. Because of the disagreement among themselves the Sikhs with their Khalistan-claim had not been taken serious by the British.

After India`s independence the Khalistan-claim had fallen in a latent position. Under the leadership of Master Tara Singh in this time the Khalistan-claim by the Sikh-community had been changed into the claim for an independent province within the

Indian Union. 1966 it led to the division of the old Punjab-region into Sikh-Punjab and Hindu-Haryana with the common Federal capital Chandigarh.

The claim for an independent state Khalistan by a great number of the Sikhs which had taken up again today is the result of a development which has begun in an intensive way around 1980. Starting at this time, Sant Jarnail Singh Bhindranwale succeed by means of his religious Sikhism-revival-strategy which aimed at the political claim for a Sikh-governed state Khalistan, to constantly increase the number of Sikh-supporters. His violent acts led to violent interventions of the Indian government with the result of the massacre in the Golden Temple of Amritsar.

Sant Jarnail Singh Bhindranwale who - as religious Sikh-leader - would have been able to unite a great number of Sikhs under his leadership in the near future was victim of the massacre.

At present the Khalistan-movement is without a leader who finds the interest of the Sikh-crowds. However, the burning situation of the Khalistan-claim continues to exist supported by many violent actions by Sikh-extremists.

However, since the greatest part of the Sikh-community within and outside of India has supported the claim for Khalistan and that since the massacre of Khalistan there are most favourable chances for another massive breaking out of the Khalistan-movement as soon as an adequate leader - comparable with Sant Jarnail

Singh Bhindranwale - can draw the attention of the Sikh-community.

This can only be a question of time, the Indian government will be confronted again with the Khalistan-claim and will have to come to decisions how to maintain the political unity of the Indian Union.

References

[1] For Lala Lajpat Rai and his connections to the Arya Samaj see Norman G. Barrier, The Arya Samaj and Congress Politics in the Punjab 1894-1908, in Journal of Asian Studies, 1966-67, No. 26, p. 363-379

[2] See Lala Lajpat Rai, The Hindu-Muslim Problem, in Lala Lajpat Rai, Writings and Speeches. Vol. II, 1920-28. Edited by Vijaya Chandra Joshi. Delhi 1966, p. 212-213.

[3] Lala Lajpat Raj, Writings and Speeches. Vol. II, 1920-1928. Op.cit., p. 212-213

[5] Dietmar Rothermund, Grundzüge der indischen Geschichte. Darmstadt 1976, p. 105-106.

[6] Khuswant Singh, A History of the Sikhs. Vol. II., Princeton, New Jersey 1966, p. 232; William Roy Smith, Nationalism and Reform in India. Yale University Press 1938, p. 414.

[7] See for that and the following Indian Round Table Conferences Second Session, 7th Sept., 1931-1st. Dec. 1931. Proceedings of Federal Committees and Minorities Committee. Vol. III,

Calcutta 1932, p. 1399-1401.

[8] For the Two-Nations-Theory see Jörg Mittelsten-Scheid, Die Teilung Indiens. Zur Zwei-Nationen-Theorie. Köln 1970.

[9] J. Mittelsten-Scheid, Die Teilung Indiens, op.cit., p. 55. Rama Nanda Aggarwala, National Movement and Constitutional Development in India. 2nd edition., Delhi 1959, p. 261-262. K.K. Aziz, The Making of Pakistan. London 197, p. 163-195.

[10] Dietmar Rothermund, Die politische Willensbildung in Indien 1900-1960. Wiesbaden 1965, p. 184.

[11] Khuswant Singh, A History of the Sikhs. Vol. II, op.cit.,p.241.

[12] Kailash Chander Gulati, The Akalis Past and Present. New Delhi 1974, p. 88. M.S. Sahni, The Sikh Politics 1927-1947 (Diss.). Patiala 1980, p. 282.

[13] For Cripps Mission see Bhim Sen Singh, The Cripps Mission New Delhi 1942, p. 39.

[14] Baldev Raj Nayyar, Minority Politics in the Punjab. Princeton, New Jersey 1966, p. 82-83. K.Ch. Gulati, the Akalis Past and Present, op.cit., p. 93. The Statesman, 2.3.1943.

[15] N.N. Mitra (ed.), Indian Annual Register. Vol. I. Calcutta 1943, p. 299. See also the information of Master Tara Singh about the demand of Azad Punjab in The Statesman, 2.3.1943 and 22.11.1943. Moreover Satya M. Rai, Partition of the Punjab, New Delhi 1965, p. 37-38.

[16] Gurbachan Singh/Lal Singh Gyani, The Idea of the Sikh State, op.cit., p. 9. M.S. Sahni (diss.), The Sikh Politics, op.cit., p. 265. Ajit Singh Sarhadi, Punjabi Suba. Delhi 1970, p. 66-68.

[17] K.Ch. Gulati, The Akalis Past and Present, op.cit., p. 93.

[18] Gurbachan Singh/Lal Singh, The Idea of the Sikh State, op.cit., p. 9. Ajit Singh Sarhadi, Punjabi Suba, op.cit., p. 66-68.

[19] see for that Christine Effenberg, Die politische Stellung der Sikhs innerhalb der indischen Nationalbewegung 1935-1947. Wiesbaden 1984, p. 113-120.

[20] Khuswant Singh, A History of the Sikhs. Vol. II., op.cit., p. 250.

[21] Linlithgow Collection MSS Eur F 25, Number 91 = Correspondence with the Governor of the Punjab and his Secretary 1942, see letter of Bertrand Glancy, Governor of Punjab, to Lord Linlith- gow, Vice-King of India from 1.5.1942, in India Office Library, London. Also in Nicholas Mansergh (ed.), The Transfer of Power. Vol. II, 30.Aug.-21.Sept. 1942, Document Number 7 = Sir B. Glancy to the Marquess of Linlithgow, Extract, Lahore 1 May 1942.

[22] see Mr. C. Rajagopalacharia`s formula, 10 July 1944, in Speeches and Documents on the Indian Constitution 1921-1947. Vol. II. Selected by Sir Maurice Gwyer and A. Appadorai. London 1957, p. 548-549.

[23] B.B. Misra, The Indian Political Parties. Delhi

1976, p. 503.

[24] Tribune, 1. August 1944.

[25] B.B. Nayar, Minority Politics in the Punjab, op.cit., p. 88-98.

[26] N. Mansergh (ed.), The Transfer of Power. Vol. II, London 1977; from that Document Number 56 = Record of a Meeting between Cabinet Delegation, Field Marshal Viscount Wavell and Representatives of the Sikh Community on Friday 5. April 1946.

[27] see for that Leonhard Mosley, The Last Days of the British Raj. London 1961.

[28] For Punjabi Suba see B.R. Nayar, Minority Politics in the Punjab, op.cit., p. 98-118. K.Ch. Gulati, The Akalis Past and Present, op.cit., p. 160-191. Arjit Singh Sarhadi, Punjabi Suba. Delhi 1970. Khuswant Singh, The Punjabi Suba, in The Sikh Review, Jan. 1975. p. 15-23. For the politic in this time see Dalip Singh, Dynamicy of Punjab Politics. New Delhi 1981. For the problem of language and religion see Paul R. Brass, Language, Religion and Politics in North India. Cambridge 1974.

[29] For the separation of Punjab on May 9, 1966 see "Die Teilung des Punjabs, in Indo-Asia No 9, 1967, p. 16-17.

[30] The text of the "Anandpur Resolution is printed in India Today, 15. November 1982, p. 45. Also in Statesman, 14.1.1984.

[31] The Overseas Hindustan Times, 22.10.83 The Hindu, Internat. Edition, 5.11.83.

[32] The Hindu, Internat. Edition, 10.3.84; 17.3.84; 24.3.84; 31.3.84.

[33] The Hindu, Internat. Edition, 31.3.84. The Overseas Hindustan Times, 31.3.84.

[34] The Overseas Hindustan Times, 31.3.83; 24.3.84.

[35] The Overseas Hindustan Times, 31.12.83; 3.3.84; 10.3.84. The Hindu, Internati. Edition, 3.3.84

[36] The Statesman, 11.7.84.

[37] The Statesman, 11.7.84; 22.7.84. Indian Express,13.7.84; 14.7.84; 8.9.84. The Hindu, 14.8.84.

[38] Gentleman, New Delhi, 15.7.84.

[39] India Today, 31.3.82; 15.7.84.

[40] The Khalistan Times, September 1984.

Bibliography

Aggarwala, Rama Nanda, National Movement and Constitutional Development in India. 2nd edition.Delhi 1959

Aziz, K.K., The Making of Pakistan. A Study in Nationalism. London 1967

Brass, Paul R., Language, Religion and Politics in North India. Cambridge 1974

Effenberg, Christine, Die politische Stellung der Sikhs innerhalb der indischen Nationalbewegung 1935-1947. Wiesbaden 1984

Gulati, Kailash Chander, The Akalis Past and Present. Delhi 1974

Indian Round Table Conferences. Second Session, 7th Sept., 1931-1st Dec. 1931. Proceedings of Federal Committees and Minorities Committee. Vol. III. Calcutta 1932

Joshi, Vijaya Chandra (ed.), Lala Lajpat Rai. Writings and Speeches. Vol. II, 19201928. Delhi 1966

Mansergh, Nicholas (ed.), The Transfer of Power 1942-1947.Vol.VII. London 1977

Misra, B.B., The Indian Political Parties. Delhi 1976

Mitra, N.N. (ed.), Indian Annual Register. Vol. I. Calcutta 1943

Mittelsten-Scheid, Jörg, Die Teilung Indiens. Zur Zwei-Nationen-Theorie. Köln 1970

Mosley, Leonhard, The Last Days of the British Raj. London 1961

Nayar, Baldev Raj, Minority Politics in the Punjab. Princeton, New Jersey 1966

Rothermund, Dietmar, Die politische Willensbildung in Indien 1900-1960. Wiesbaden 1965

Rothermund, Dietmar, Grundzüge der indischen Geschichte. Darmstadt 1976

Sahni, M.S., The Sikh Politics 1927-1947. (Diss.) Patiala 1980

Sarhadi, Ajit Singh, Punjabi Suba. Delhi 1970

Singh, Bhim Sen, The Cripps Mission. New Delhi 1970

Singh, Dalip, Dynamicy of Punjab Politics. New Delhi 1981

Singh, Gurbachan/Gyani, Lal Singh, The Idea of the Sikh State. Lahore 1946

Singh, Khuswant, A History of the Sikhs. Vol. II. Princeton, New Jersey 1966

Singh, Khuswant, The Punjabi Suba, in The Sikh Review, Jan. 1975, p. 15-23

Smith, William Roy, Nationalism and Reform in India. Yale University Press 1938

Dravidian Parties in Modern Tamilnadu – Their Strength and Significance

by Dagmar Hellmann-Rajanayagam

Introduction

The political development in the South Indian state of Tamilnadu has for a long time been something of a freak child in Indian politics. Practically nowhere else have regional interests asserted themselves so strongly and over such a long time without, and that is decisive, ever seriously endangering the integrity of the Indian Union. The secessionist demands which were voiced till the early 60s and are coming to the front again at the moment in the wake of the Sri Lanka crisis, were always used more as a kind of 'compromising evidence` to blackmail the government into doing what was desired than as a real threat involving the independence of Tamilnadu. The Tamils knew and know only too well what are the advantages of being part of a bigger whole, though being Tamil is first and foremost in their priorities.

The 'Tamilisation` of state politics over the last two to three decades has contributed a great deal to this state of affairs. This 'Tamilisation` of politics, culminating in the voting to power of regional, 'Dravidian` parties ever since 1967, enabled the Tamils to view the central government with a more detached and kindly eye. This led to both a contraction and expansion of the Tamil ideas which comprised linguistic principles, historical considerations, social and religious efforts and ethnic consciousness. [1] The roots of these Tamil ideas and the Tamil movement can be traced back to the late 19th century and the so-called Tamil renaissance. This renaissance, which primarily took place in the literary and religious fields, initiated such diverse parties and associations as the Justice Party, Cuyamariyatai Iyakkam (Self-Respect Movement) et al. which all claimed to speak for the Tamilians and their rights, but under very different labels. When E.V. Ramacami merged the Justice Party and the Cuyamariyatai Iyakkam to the Tiravita Kalakam (DK) in 1944, he had fused three undercurrents of resentment and protest which had existed in Madras since a long time:

1. Anti-Brahminism;
2. animosity towards the Sanskritic Hindu tradition and
3. resentment against the domination of the South by the North.

The Justice Party provided an important base for the development of the non-Brahmin and social reform movement though the Cuyamariyatai Iyakkam voiced the demands and grievances of the non-Brahmins far more strongly and radically than the Justice Party would have ever dreamt of. The protection and preservation of the Tamil language had been vital points on the programme of the Cuyamariyatai Iyakkam and the early DK, but E.V. Ramacami soon let it be known that the independent Dravidanadu which he envisaged should adopt English as its official language. This was bitterly resented especially by the younger members of the DK who had been brought up on the belief in the sanctity of Tamil language, culture and tradition. Foremost among these was C.N. Annaturai (fondly called Anna = elder brother by his supporters) who formed his own organisation, the DMK (Tiravita Munnerrak Kalakam), in 1949. Insurmountable differences of opinion over social, political and cultural objectives of the movement and its style of leadership contributed to the split. Annaturai wanted the DK to develop into a political party, whereas E.V. Ramacami stressed its character as a social reform movement.

True to its intentions, the DMK took part in the elections from 1957 onwards with growing success and gained the majority of votes in 1967, thus being able to form the state government. After Annaturai`s death, the party could maintain its strength in the elections of 1971, but lost to the AIADMK, founded in 1972, in the elections 1977.

For the DMK the Tamil language, literature and culture are sacred because of their antiquity and ancient glory. The language has to be honoured as the mother tongue of the Tamilians and to be protected from the onslaughts of the North, especially from Hindi. English, though useful as a link language, can on no account replace Tamil on its home ground. The concentration on the language issue led to several bitter Anti-Hindi-campaigns in the state, the most violent among them the language riots in 1965 when Hindi was intended to be made the only national language instead of English. Moreover, the DMK tries to weave history, culture and literature meaningfully into the concept of a better and brighter future in a teleological attempt of creating a golden future on the foundation of a golden past. In religion, too, it finds values not to be cast off so easily. Though conceding the harmful impact of the Brahminic and Aryan tradition which stands in need of reform, it postulates at the same times - in agreement with the purist faction of the Tamil movement - an original Saivite Tamil religion and social order which ought to be acknowledged and revived. The strong anti-Brahmin and anti-religious bias of the early DMK has softened to a demand for social reform, equality and equal chances for all castes and equal rights for all religions as long as their practices are not harmful to any part of the community.

The tide of the Tamil movement very early led to the demand of secession from India and the establishment of an independent Dravidanadu in the late 30s, a demand which survived not only the independence of India but also the split of the DK and lingered on till the early 60s. The justification of secession is claimed to lie primarily in the political, economical and cultural oppression of the South by the North, incompatibility of Northern and Southern cultural and ethnic groups, differential historical development. However, at the same time, the DMK acknowledged that Tamilnadu was part and parcel of a greater Indian culture which should not be discarded, but in which Tamilnadu must have its rightful place. [2]

The question of 'race` further complicated matters: The terms 'Tamilians` and 'Dravidians` were considered to be interchangeable for a long time and nobody bothered about a precise definition. It was, however, implicitly understood that Dravidian and Tamilian were synonymous in the sense that not only were the Tamilians the óriginal people` but that this also gave them a right to claim pride of place in an independent Dravidanadu, a notion bitterly resented by the other Dravidian groups in South India. The Dravidian parties had to come to terms with this fact, and it caused the retreat into Tamilnadu - of the Tamilians, by the Tamilians and for the Tamilians - accompanied by the demand for more state autonomy on the side of the DMK.

Consolidation of the Dravidian Parties

The contraction of these ideals in the present virtual equation of the Tamil language with 'Tamil` or being 'Tamil`.

Language is admittedly the core of identity for the Tamils not only in India, but in other countries as well, but nowhere has this equation been driven so far that it nowadays overrides all other considerations of policy, ethnicity, religion, nationality etc. The present chief minister of Tamilnadu, the movie star M.G. Ramachandran (M.G.R.), is not a Tamil, but a

Malayalee born in Sri Lanka, a fact noted with misgivings by the DMK.

And this is where the expansion comes in: Anybody can nowadays be accepted into the Tamil fold, provided he subscribes to the ideals of the Dravidian parties (the Kalakams) i.e. professes the superiority of the Tamil language over all other languages in the world. [3] Given this, the former enmity against certain castes can be overcome to such an extent, that in 1977 for the first time a Brahmin, Hande, could become a minister in a Kalakam-cabinet. This means, at the same time, that the hostility against religion in general and the Hindu religion in particular as the fount of all social evils is also strongly qualified and that it does not anymore constitute a betrayal of ideology to be seen in temples and performing puja.[4]

This development thus indicates a consolidation of the Tamil ideology and the Dravidian parties in Tamil politics, a conclusion which is borne out not only by the fact that since 20 years, it has been impossible for parties with a national appeal (like Congress and its different split-offs, Janata, CPI etc.) to gain any ground in Tamilnadu, but also by the consideration that even the Congress in its heyday during the 50s and early 60s could only stay in power in Tamilnadu by 'Tamilising`: It exchanged the Brahmin chief minister Rajagopalachari for the Nadar Kamaraj (who was much more 'Tamil`, but therefore also much more parochial, knowing neither Hindi nor English) and it quietly dropped the scheme of 'Kulakkalvi`(education according to the father`s caste occupation for children) introduced by

Rajaji and over which his government toppled. [5] During the language riots in 1965 it was the former protagonist of Hindi, Rajaji, and his newly-founded Swatantra, and Kamaraj, who were in the forefront of the opposition against Hindi. Elsewhere I have shown that the success of Congress during this decade depended to quite an extent on the support by E.V. Ramaca Naicker and his DK. [6]

Yet for the Tamils, the Congress was still too much associated with the 'Hindi Mafia' of the North and they consequently elected the DMK under Annaturai in 1967, and they have continued to vote for Dravidian parties ever since. The Congress, wisely and quietly acknowledging that on its own and as a national party, it cannot gain a foothold in Tamilnadu for the time being, has contented itself with aligning with that Dravidian party that seems destined for success in the respective elections. This policy paid off in so far as the Tamils nearly always voted for the continuation of Congress rule at the centre, whereas in the state, this did not automatically follow. A striking instance for this differential attitude towards the central and the state government was to be seen during the Lok Sabha elections in January 1980, followed by the Legislative Assembly elections five months later in May. [7] The results of these latter elections surprised experts and laymen alike not only because in the eight states which had elections at the same time, the Congress won decisively, but more because of the huge success of the Congress-DMK alliance in the preceding Lok Sabha elections. In spite of this, the AIADMK won 128 seats of 249, while the DMK could only gain 38 seats, 10 less than even in 1977. [8] For people familiar with the political scene in Tamilnadu, however, these results only confirmed a long time trend which could be summed up in the formula: What is right for the central government, need not necessarily be right for Tamilnadu. Centre and state are two different things which it is important to keep apart.

The Victory of the AIADMK

The reasons for the AIADMK`s victory were manifold. Not least the conditions under which these elections were held contributed to its success: M.G.R.`s government had been dissolved after only two and a half years of government without having committed major errors or mismanagement, i.e. without real justification, only to have, as Indira Gandhi expressed it, 'the same party governing the states that governs the centre`. [9] This put M.G.R. nicely into his old star role of the underdog fighting of law and justice against all odds. Relying on this role he managed to put aside doubts about his leadership, especially his attitude towards the farmers` agitation and to win the hearts and votes of the electorate.

Thus, while the voters desired a strong central government after the 'non-government` of the Janata coalition, this meant for them Congress rule in the centre. Already in 1977, Tamilnadu was one of the few states where the Congress could hold its own. This however, did not mean that they likewise desired a Congress government in the State. For Tamilnadu the regional, Dravidian parties are good enough and the Congress should rather be admired from afar. The Tamils are proud of being citizens of the Great Nation India, but never at the expense of their individuality. All attempts by Delhi to 'bring them into line` are strongly rejected. This applies especially to the renewed efforts of Desai`s Janata government to spread Hindi in the South, a factor, which definitely contributed to the Congress` victory in 1980. The Tamils are Tamils first and Indian second. Therefore in May, the DMK was defeated by the ghosts it conjured up, because hitherto, it had been precisely the DMK which argued for more autonomy and more power for the states. The alliance with the archenemy on the regional level thus became untrustworthy.

One of the most astonishing facts of these elections was that an old and shrewd politician like Karunanidhi fell to the same delusions as many other journalists and people in public life. Like the press, the DMK counted on a huge success, and prepared its victory celebrations well in advance. M.G.R. was considered no more than an actor grown old who would not stand any chance against the cunning Karunanidhi.[10] Both DMK and the press overlooked two things:

1) the great role played by the film and movie world precisely for the success of the propaganda and ideology of both DMK and AIADMK, and

2) the structure of the electorate: Political interest and political will and thus political influence have descended from the middle and lower classes to the lower and

> Harijan classes. These were the people who actually voted while middle and upper classes to a great extent abstained from voting altogether.[11] This feature could already be seen during the election campaign which to a great extent was fought and supported by people from the lower classes.

This phenomenon seems to be typical for the election behaviour in Tamilnadu during the last 20 years: the election decision is taken by the lower middle and lower classes. Annaturai won the elections with the votes of the middle class poor, the lower ranks of the intelligentsia, students, teachers, clerks and the lower classes. His propaganda was streamlined for this audience.[12] After Annaturai`s death Karunanidhi managed to keep these classes to the DMK, but not for long: After the split in the DMK, the vote banks also split: While the intelligentsia and the middle classes remained faithful to the DMK, the lower and Harijan classes went over to their idol M.G.R. who had anyway been the main reason for their DMK support. Unskilled labourers, landless peasants, slum dwellers and women are M.G.R.`s main props till today. His appeal is explained when one considers the fact that after the split of the DMK, the 'M.G.R. fan clubs` comprising a huge membership which had hitherto more or less kept aloof from politics, became members of the AIADMK nearly in toto. The factions in the AIADMK of today are mainly constructed along the lines of this differential membership: former DMK members on one side and M.G.R. fan clubs on the other. This leads to the lack of homogeneity in the party today.

During the elections in 1980, the propaganda of both Kalakams was tailored to the needs of the respective electorate: While Karunanidhi demanded help for the educated unemployed and privileges for students, M.G.R. relied on an intensely emotional appeal: During the last days before the elections posters and advertisements appeared all over Tamilnadu in which M.G.R. presses an old woman to his heart saying: "I know what it means to be hungry. I remember how my mother often could not give us one grain of rice for sheer poverty. And I want that no mother in Tamilnadu has to see her children starving again." [13] This propaganda was duly successful. The lower classes consider M.G.R. one of their lot who has 'arrived`, but not forgotten them and will stand up for them wherever he can. [14] Spectacular public gestures like distributing free rice to the victims of the floods in 1978 or huge donations for charitable purposes support this image, and against this, the DMK with its dry ideals of caste reform, abolition of religious superstitions, fight against Hindi and for state autonomy cannot hold out.

The success of the AIADMK can also be attributed to the Tamils` preference for clear situations, i.e. for one-party-government and against coalitions. However, it was quite clear in 1980 that it was not the Congress which lost because of the DMK (as it , at least the Tamilnadu branch, fondly tried to persuade itself), but the DMK which lost because of the Congress. On the other hand, in 1984, the Congress won only because of the alliance with the Congress. The Tamils have made it quite clear, that in regional politics they go their own way, regardless of what the centre might desire or decrete. What is good for India, is not automatically good for Tamilnadu.

The Development of DMK and AIADMK since 1949

This brings us to the Dravidian parties themselves. These start properly with the DK in 1944, though as mentioned, this was not meant to be a political party but a social reform movement, over which question among others, it finally split in 1949 when the DMK came into being. This party has been the most successful in politics among all Dravidian Parties, the AIADMK included.[15] Though only gaining the majority in the LA in 1967, it showed very good results in all elections since 1957, and headed the Madras municipality and other local bodies since 1965 practically without interruption because under the AIADMK, local elections did not take place for nearly ten years, until 1986, and in these again, the DMK defeated the AIADMK decisively.[16] But it lost the municipal elections in Madurai in 1978 and several by-elections since 1973, the most important one that in Dindigul in May 1973,

17 and notably that in Periyakulam, a DMK stronghold in 1982 because shortly before, M.G.R. had announced the populist measure of wiping off the debts of all small farmers (with an income below 4800 Rs.) for loans to the state, a measure, which paid the anticipated dividends.[18] But the disruptive element did not spare the DMK, either. After Annaturai`s untimely death in 1969 the different factions gradually asserted themselves more and more openly, and in 1972, the AIADMK was founded under the leadership of M.G.R. after he

had been suspended as treasurer of the DMK for looking too closely into some shady deals by some party luminaries. This drama seems destined to be reenacted, since in 1984, the treasurer of the AIADMK, Somasundaram, resigned and formed his own Kalakam, also because of alleged corruption of leading party members. [19] Especially after M.G.r.`s illness the fight for succession has openly broken out between the different factions, and again the M.G.R. fan clubs play a crucial role: they support the actress Jayalalitha who joined the AIADMK in 1982 and became propaganda secretary in 1983 as successor, while the former DMK members would vote for Neduncheliyan or Somasundaram and his new Kalakam. [20]

The DMK: Bread- and Butter Politics

It is, however, not the intention of this article to go into the more sordid details of faction-building and splitting resp. floor-crossing of Dravidian parties in Tamilnadu, but here I want to show a certain line of development of the Dravidian ideology and programme which in the end makes these factions and splits unavoidable and almost logical because obviously the mother parties as such are not able to reformulate their programmes and adapt to new circumstances beyond a certain point.

The first instance of this was the breaking off of the DMK itself from the DK in 1949. The sweeping programme of the DK including anti-Brahmanism, caste abolition, hostility towards the North, abolition of religion, linguistic and ethnic priorities all leading to the demand of secession of Dravidanandu, could not be pursued credibly in the newly independent Indian Union. This is essentially the raison d`etre of the DMK. Under the skilfull leadership of Annaturai it adapted itself to the changing conditions of independent India and the Congress politics in Tamilnadu which took up quite some of the earlier programmes and demands of the Dravidian movement. An instance of this was the re-organization of states along linguistic borders in 1955. [21] In a sense this can be understood as a success of Dravidian politics; it forced, however, the DMK to redefine its programme in order to keep up its credibility and its distinctiveness as a Dravidian party. This led to the mentioned contraction and expansion, i.e. the softening of the secessionist demand to one for more state autonomy and most important, the exclusive emphasis on the Tamil component, i.e. Tamil language and to a lesser extent, Tamil culture. Here The DMK was on its home ground, and the Congress in its capacity as an all-Indian party could never hope to challenge it here. This Tamil component, however, touching a cord of Tamil identity and self-perception, was the one that in combination with other factors appealed to people most during the 50s and 60s, and this explains the success of the DMK in 1967, two years after the language riots, in which the Congress under Bhaktavatsalam had rather discredited itself. From hostility towards Brahmins, the DMK went towards opposition of Brahminism as an ideology, from the demand for caste-abolition towards privileges for the lower and backward castes and a programme of progress of castes qua castes, from the rejection of religion towards a qualified acceptance of its valuable components. This was facilitated and made credible by terming these valuable components, the good qualities and customs of Hindu society etc. as 'originally Tamil` and everything considered bad or harmful as 'northern corruption and misrepresentation`. The resentment against the North thus remained, though subdued and modified and it can be detected in Tamilnadu even today. When, for instance, in 1978-79 great propaganda efforts were made by the Janata government to publicize Hindi in the South by several means (special rates for Hindi telegrams, etc.), immediately a virulent Anti-Hindi-campaign was started by the DK, supported by the DMK and the AIADMK.[22] Similarly, in 1983, there were fierce protests when it became known that allegedly a knowledge of Hindi was required proved by an examination for entrance into the railway service which is government-run.[23] Till the present a battle rages between different schools of the Dravidian movement concerning the attitude towards the North: one school, the 'original` DK school, rejects everything northern as bad and degrading, and in the last consequence still clings to separation as the only remedy. Others, and these are to a great extent found in the DMK (and, notably, the Congress) stress the contribution of Tamilnadu and the Tamils towards the development of the Greater Indian, Sanskritic, culture ans religion by softening and reforming the crude early ideas, and by adding new and valuable thoughts and insights to philosophy and ritual, thus moulding Hinduism into something refined and complete, into the 'Great Tradition`. They stress the amalgamation and interrelation of Sanskrit and Tamil culture and literature.[24] This attitude, incidentally, is one especially cherished by tamil

Brahmins, whereas the AIADMK does not give these considerations even a first thought, being quite parochial in this respect. [25] The Brahmins, on the other hand, point out, that it were the Southern Brahmins who wrote the purest Sanskrit and thus the most praised Sanskrit literature.

The Ascent of the AIADMK: Substitution of Reality by the Symbol

With the consolidation of linguistic and ethnic borders and the assertion of the Tamil identity the DMK could have resigned itself to functioning as a normal regional party with an economic and political programme not much different from that of the national parties, albeit with a certain regional flavour: that is what, in fact, it did. Now, however, the astonishing happens: this is obviously not enough for the Tamils who have got used to view politics in terms of North versus South and Tamils against non-Tamils, at least on the regional level and seem to need this polarization to stabilize their identity. The corruption allegations against Karunanidhi by M.G.R. could have been an additional factor to bring people from the DMK to the AIADMK, but given the general 'cleanliness' of Indian politics, one should not overemphasize this factor. Similar accusations have been brought up against M.G.R. without apparent effect to his reputation, on the contrary: For instance, in 1975 it was claimed by the DMK that M.G.R. drew his honorarium as MLA without ever attending the sessions due to his film work. Far from denying this, M.G.R. retorted that from this money he had not used a single paisa for himself, but had given all of it to the poor! [26] As an afterthought he said that during the opening session and during sessions where Karunanidhi was not present, he made it a point to be present! What was important in 1972 was that M.G.R.`s allegation, Karunanidhi had strayed from the narrow path of 'Tamil` politics shown by Annaturai and thus betrayed the Tamil cause found credence among the population. M.G.R.`s image as DMK-hero in all his films certainly helped and now began what elsewhere I have termed the 'substitution of reality by the symbol`. [27] This means that instead of building new roads, the AIADMK renames the existing ones after famous DMK-heroes and obliterates the caste names in others. Instead of disposing of pending bills and departmental affairs, departments are renamed in Tamil and the Hindi or English expressions dropped. Industries which should be drawn into the state are rejected because they are led by non-Tamils; instead noon-meal schemes and a guaranteed dole for unemployed graduates are proclaimed. Irrigation projects initiated by the DMK are dropped because of this fact, instead during water and grain shortages a token fast is celebrated by M.G.R. to make the people`s plight known to the centre and get more grain allotments (the grain shortage occurred because the noon-meal scheme took up all the surplus and because TN did not give rice to the central pool). [28] The examples could be extended ad libitum. The success of these populist politics again indicates the shift of political will and significance away from the middle and lower middle classes and the intelligentsia, the back-bone of DMK-support, towards the lower classes, the real poor, for whom, given their possibilities of influence and achievement, an ambitious programme of industrialisation which bears fruit in 20 years, does not have any meaning in their present plight of feeding the hungry family, whereas a 'noon-meal scheme' which guarantees one square meal a day to at least some of their children even at the cost of sending them to school, has a powerful appeal indeed. This kind of politics has, however, led to a deterioration of the overall situation of Tamilnadu in recent years: From third place among all Indian states it has fallen to 13th place now and it has the highest percentage of poverty in the whole of India: 63%. [29] The unemployment rate is 16%. The Statesman has termed this policy aptly as 'drink for the father, sari for the mother, rice for the child' and attributed its success to the fact that it shows tangible benefits to nearly all components of the poorer classes, besides letting them know that these are given to them as Tamils by another Tamil. [30] Against all his assurances to uphold prohibition in the true Annaturai tradition, M.G.R. virtually abolished it in 1984 and thus enabled the poor classes to have access to cheap liqueur. The huge success of the AIADMK in the elections 1984 in spite of a paralysed and aphasic chief minister and in spite of the indiscipline and lacking cadre work of the party against a well-knit and disciplined DMK probably lies here. For exactly the same reason, it is also improbable that Somasundaram will be successful with his new Kalakam merely because he could prove his allegations of corruption. Unless he finds a dramatic new 'Dravidian' tag for his party which convinces the masses that he is indeed the new 'Dravidian' messias and not M.G.R., his party seems doomed to failure like many other 'split ventures' before, notably the Tamil Teciyak Katci (TTK = Tamil National Party) under Sampath in the 60s which finally had to merge with the Congress. If the rumours that Jayalalitha, the new AIADMK star and M.G.R.'s designated successor, is about to start a new Kalakam, the M.G.R.-AIADMK, to skirt the faction-ridden AIADMK, this party would probably have a far better chance, for apart from the actress and box-office draw Jayalitha, it would have all ingredients already in its name which make it a sure election hit for the masses: Annaturai as well as M.G.R. and the Dravidian ideas are represented. [31]

Programme and Ideology: Impact of the Sri Lanka crisis

It is significant that whereas there existed distinct differences of opinion and programme between the DK and DMK, there exist hardly any of these between DMK and AIADMK. Floor-crossers change from DMK to AIADMK and vice versa without, apparently, being much the worse for it ideologically, whereas party changes from and to the other national parties and the Kalakams practically never occur. However, this should not be mistaken as indicating that the break was merely a 'clash of personalities' resulting from personal enmity between Karunanidhi and M.G.R. The rift has, on the opposite, to do with the mentioned 'substitution of reality by the symbol' which M.G.R. and his movie glamour seem to personify much better than the cool, smooth and a bit pedantic Karunanidhi.

While Annaturai in 1949 claimed to follow the true path of the Tamil movement and to stick to the original ideals of E.V. Ramacami, M.G.R. in 1972 also claimed to uphold the true ideals of Annaturai which Karunanidhi had allegedly betrayed, and consequently named his party Anna-DMK.[32] Differences in ideology and programme have, in the meantime, emerged due to the political developments in the state and due to the fact that one was the ruling, the other the opposition party. However, both parties are still close enough in their programmes and ideals to be practically indistinguishable to an outsider. Thus, the AIADMK has radically denied any desire for separation or secession of Tamilnadu and in 1977 even went so far as to promise close cooperation with the central government (and changed its name to All-India-ADMK[33]). Though M.G.R. in the meantime has also returned to the demand for more state autonomy, it is obvious that he is far more accommodating towards central interests than the DMK has ever been. The demand for secession resp. autonomy which still remains a central point in the DMK programme, has thus nearly completely lost its significance within the framework of AIADMK politics. It has the lowest priority if it is thought about at all. Of course this has also much to do with its becoming irrelevant with the development of Tamilnadu and the growing progress of the state. But it should not be overlooked that it is a sleeping, not a dead issue, as the battle raging about the evaluation of the Sri Lanka crisis between DMK and AIADMK shows clearly. It is not the Sri Lanka Tamils as such, which primarily occupy the minds of the people in this case, but the intrastate and interparty implications it has in Tamilnadu. The demand for secession, vicariously fuelled and fed by the secession efforts of the Tamil guerilla, has been brought to the front again by Karunanidhi with the argument, if the centre is not able to protect Tamils in Sri Lanka, it will not protect us either, therefore we have to propagate secession. [34] The AIADMK has nothing to put up against this argument except the feeble protestation that it strives for a peaceful solution of which nobody can see the outline yet. How dangerous this crisis may prove for Tamilnadu`s policy and thus for the central government, too, may be seen in a remark by some Tamils recently who can by no means be suspected to blindly follow the DMK-propaganda: If the ethnic group persecuted in Sri Lanka had been not Tamils, but a North Indian group, e.g. Sindhis, Marathis, or so, the central government would have long since intervened militarily, so the argument goes. It is clear that the Sri Lanka Tamil crisis concerns Tamils beyond party affiliations, because the different branches of the Congress in Tamilnadu most emphatically demand better protection of the Jaffna Tamils. It is probably no coincidence that recently a new negotiator has been appointed for the talks between India and Sri Lanka: Minister of State for Personnel and Pensions, Chidambaram, a Tamil, a Congress member and a Harvard graduate. It is very likely that this was a move by the centre not only to defuse tensions in Tamilnadu but also pave the way for the Tamilnadu Congress to return to power one day. Besides, completely apolitical organisations like university language associations etc. demand an Indian intervention. [35] The old divide North-

South shows up very clearly here, and if nothing is done to close it, it could have grave consequences for the politics of Tamilnadu, for this remark shows a crisis of confidence for the central government.

Moreover, the AIADMK has not only given up the resentment against Brahmins, but also against 'Brahminism`, and instead professes merely a desire that no caste should impose on the others. [36] Consequently, M.G.R. made the Karnataka Brahmin Hande health minister in his successive cabinets, a move which was bitterly denounced and resented by both DK and DMK. [37] As a sop M.G.R. declared a reservation quota for the Scheduled Castes and 'backward` castes amounting to 68%, something which had been unheard of till then. [38] This was a crucial move because shortly before, M.G.R. had wanted to do away with reservations based on caste and introduce economic criteria for scholarships and preferential admission into educational institutions. [39] This created an outcry all through the state, and M.G.R. retracted from it hastily. The reasons for this can be attributed to two factors peculiar to the Dravidian movement and to the social set-up in Tamilnadu:

1) The Brahmins, though ritually and socially the highest caste, have never been the highest or richest one economically, but were, except for the landowners in Tanjavur, always comparatively poor. They had, however, access to educational institutions and were ready to sacrifice something to enable their children to get a good education. The non-Brahmins, on the other hand, were partly very rich, like the Vellalars and Pillais.

2) The last-named were exactly the castes who founded the JP because of perceived social, ritual and educational discrimination and deprivation.[40] Only E.V. Ramacami extended the scope of the Dravidian movement also to the economically 'backward' and Harijan castes. Even today, the educationally backward castes in Tamilnadu are not in every case the poorest ones. Backward in Tamilnadu thus explicitly means 'educationally backward' and nothing else, and the attempt to base preferential treatment in the educational sector on economic criteria consequently led to bitter resentment and to the final, ridiculously high quota of 68% reserved seats.[41]

The more away from the original Tamil or Dravidian ideas is seen most clearly in the field of religion: The rationalist or atheist DK is treated like a distant cousin who has run away with the silver, and everything smacking of 'rationalism' is quickly denounced and suppressed. Celebrations in honour of E.V. Ramacami are at least frowned upon, and AIADMK members do not take part in these if they can avoid it. M.G.R. himself takes part in pujas, visits temples and consults astrologers about auspicious times and dates. Simultaneously, there is a strong Hindu revivalism to be detected in Tamilnadu which led to the defeat of Christian AIADMK and DMK candidates in favour of a Hindu Munnani (Hindu Front) candidate during by-elections in Padmanabhapuram in the Tirunelveli District in 1983,[42] a very significant development. This development showed its first buds already in the Tamil conference in Madurai in 1981: from a forum for Dravidologists all over the world, they have now degenerated to a forum for self-presentation and self-praise of the Dravidian party in power at the time. 'Rationalist` or attitudes critical towards religion were not accepted in the discussion or in the papers. Delegates from the sister organisation of the DK in Malaysia, the Malaysian Dravidian Association (MDA), were not accepted as delegates at all, in the first place, and the functions began with pujas and a heavy stress on Saivism was to be detected throughout, the emphasis being laid on its being the 'true Tamil religion` uncorrupted by Sanskrit influences.[43] This consideration for the 'Tamil`, Saivite religion shows itself most clearly in the fact, that M.P. Sivananam, a member of the 'purist` faction of the Tamil movement which stresses the linguistic and religious aspects of the Tamil renaissance, and leader of the 'Nam Tamilar` (We Tamils) organisation and the Tamil Aracu Katci (TAK = Tamil Government Party), was elected Speaker of Parliament by the AIADMK in 1977 and retained this post till 1980. The purists have thus finally made their peace with the Dravidian movement.

The last mentioned facet shows the inherent contradictions of the AIADMK ideology which are, however, never recognized, because nobody bothers to think that far. Another instance for these contradictions is the fact that probably never in recent times the knowledge of English in Tamilnadu has descended to such low levels as it has now either because of sinking standards of teaching and learning or because of the opposition to any language other than Tamil in general in the state. No difference is made between learning a language and learning in a language.[44] A Tamil University was opened in 1981 in Tanjavur at the occasion of the World Tamil Sangam, to propagate the greatness of the Tamil language. [45]

CONCLUSION

While thus the contraction of the Tamil programme and identity affected vital components like education, literature, caste, social and religious reform, equal rights for women etc., the expansion worked in the direction of including everything under the language umbrella disregarding all other differences. In this sense, the AIADMK has become truly 'Dravidian', given its Malayalee chief minister and its Kanada health minister! Nevertheless, being Tamil still means a lot to politicians and population alike, because the worst accusation anyone can hurl at another is that of being 'un-Tamil' or not a true Tamil, whatever that may be. [46] Both M.G.R. and Karunanidhi have indulged in mud-slinging of this kind recently. (Incidentally, E.V. Ramacami did not consider himself a Tamil, but a Dravidian, and he spoke Kannada as his first language.) The question of 'race' has turned into the 'importance of being Tamil'.

We have, therefore, to conclude that the Dravidian component in Tamil politics has probably come to stay, but coupled with ever changing economic and social problems, different points of this ideology will be stressed at different times and it will be combined with either populist, capitalist or socialist programmes, as need dictates. In that way, the Dravidian ideology is truly 'unaligned' (as M.G.R. already implicitly acknowledged when he defined 'Annaism` and 'Annaist economics` as a mixture of capitalist, communist and socialist ideas [47]). It seems, however, as if the heyday of the AIADMK might soon be over, if the local elections from April 86 are anything to go by. [48] However, in Tamil politics the only thing that is certain is that nothing is certain, and instead of a reinstallation of the DMK, it is just as possible that we shall shortly see yet another Kalakam coming to the top in Tamilnadu, sounding the deathknell for the AIADMK this time!

References

1 For the programme and development of the DK and DMK see D. Hellmann, Die Cuyamariyatai Iyakkam (Bewegung für Selbstachtung) in der Madras Presidency 1925-1945 - Vorläufer der gegenwärtigen dravidischen Parteien in Tamilnadu, in Internationales Asienforum 9 (1978), p. 243-258

2 D. Hellmann-Rajanayagam, Tamil - Sprache als politisches Symbol, Wiesbaden 1984, p. 143 and passim.

3 Ibid., p. 85

4 Ibid., p. 44 and 103, cf. Indian Express 21.2.85

5 Ibid., p. 37 and 109, see also Robert L. Hardgrave jr., The Dravidian Movement, Bombay 1965, p. 43/44

6 Hellmann-Rajanayagam, loc.cit., p. 33, see also Selig Harrison, India-The Most Dangerous Decades, OUP 1960, p. 86 f.

[7] D. Hellmann, Politische Individualität in Tamilnadu. Ein Bericht über die Wahlen zur Legislative Assembly, in Internationales Asienforum 12 (1981), p. 45-49

[8] Ibid.

[9] Indian Express 6.6.80

[10] Hellmann, loc.cit., p. 47

[11] Indian Express, 31.5. and 1.6.80

[12] Hellmann-Rajanayagam, loc.cit., p. 58

[13] Hellmann, loc.cit., p. 47, cf. Indian Express 31.5.80

[14] Ibid.

[15] Hellmann-Rajanayagam, loc.cit., p. 39, see also Marguerite Ross-Barnett, The Politics of Cultural Nationalism in South India, Princeton UP 1976, p. 91

[16] India Today 15.3.86

[18] The Statesman 18.8.82

[19] The Statesman 5.9.84

[20] Ibid., 12.9.84

[21] Hellmann-Rajanayagam, loc.cit., p. 37, cf. Report of the States Reorganization Commission 1955, New Delhi 1955

[22] The Hindu 30.4.78, the Statesman 8.12.79 and 30.3.80

[23] India Today 28.2.83, the Statesman 26.1. und 6.6.83

[24] Hellmann-Rajanayagam, loc.cit., p. 43

[25] Ibid., p. 84 und 134

[26] The Statesman 13.4.75

[27] Hellmann-Rajanayagam, loc.cit., p. 215

[28] The Statesman 14.2.80 and 11.6.84

[29] The Statesman 9./10.2.83, 11.4.83. However, the gap between very rich and very poor is smaller in Tamilnadu than in other states in India

[30] Ibid., 5.8.85

[31] India Today 15.2.86, cf. The Statesman 21.1.85

[32] Hindustan Times 19.10.72

[33] Times of India 20.6.76

[34] Kumutam 28.11.85

[35] Lanka Guardian 1.5.86, p. 7 and Tamilc Celvi March 1985, p. 247 f.

[36] Indian Express 14.1.81

[37] The Hindu 29.6.80 and The Statesman 19.7.80

[38] Indian Express 6.10.80

[39] Statesman 9.2.80

[40] David Washbrook, The Emergence of Country Politics. The Madras Presidency 1880-1920, London

1976, p. 214 and Eugene F. Irschick, Politics and Conflict in South India. The Non-Brahmin Movement and Tamil Separatism 1919-1929, Berkeley and Los Angeles 1969, p. 98.

[41] The Statesman 9.2.80

[42] Indian Express 21.2.85

[43] Hellmann-Rajanayagam, loc.cit., p. 202/3

[44] Ibid., p. 68

[45] The Hindu 22.3.81

[46] cf. The Statesman 1.10.73 and 26.6.83 and Indian Express 21.8.82

[47] The Statesman 12.9.84

[48] India Today 15.3. and 15.4.86

Bibliography

Hardgrave, Robert L. jr., The Dravidian Movement. Bombay 1965.

Harrison, Selig, India - The Most Dangerous Decades, OUP 1960.

Hellmann, Dagmar, Die Cuyamariyatai Iyakkam (Bewegung für Selbstachtung) in der Madras Presidency 1925-1945 Vorläufer der gegenwärtigen dravidischen Parteien in Tamilnadu, in Internationales Asienforum 9 (1978), pp. 243-258.

Hellmann, Dagmar, Politische Individualität in Tamilnadu. Ein Bericht über die Wahlen zur Legislative Assembly, in Internationales Asienforum 12 (1981), pp.45-49.

Hellmann-Rajanayagam, Dagmar, Tamil - Sprache als politisches Symbol. Wiesbaden 1984.

Irschick, Eugene F., Politics and Conflict in South India. The Non-Brahmin Movement and Tamil Separatism 1919-1929. Berkeley and Los Angeles 1969.

Ross-Barnett, Marguerite, The Politics of cultural Nationalism in South India. Princeton UP 1976.

Washbrook, David, The Emergence of Country Politics. The Madras Presidency 1880-1920. London 1976.

Report of the States Reorganisation Commission 1955. New Delhi 1955

Indonesian Trade Unions and Pancasila

by Eva-Maria Schaarschmidt-Kohl

1. The Development of the Indonesian Trade Union Movement - A Short Outline

The history of the Indonesian trade unions dates back to the beginning of this century, when Dutch rule over the Indonesian archipelago was at its peak. First foundations had been stimulated by activities of Dutch employees. Only with the emerging and spreading of Sarekat Islam (SI) since 1911/1912 [1], the first Indonesian mass organization also active in the field of labour, there arose an indigenous labour movement with a broader scope of influence. Within the rank and file of SI it were especially the socialist inspired cadres being active in the quickly growing labour movement. After having developed into a separate movement, socialism respectively communism were the decisive forces in the labour movement, until 1926/27 when after revolutionary strike movements and communist upheavals it was completely suppressed by the colonial government. Thereafter labour activities had to be restrained to non-political fields. National orientation being string from the very beginning of the Indonesian trade union movement, nationalism now, at the end of the twenties and the early thirties, became the main stream within the labour movement without being able to inspire it as much as socialism could in its early years.

Japanese occupation (February 1942 to August 1945) for Indonesia was as much a casura in her further development as for other countries of SEA: Among others all trade unions were dissolved. The defeat of the Japanese, however, provided the Indonesian leaders with a chance of declaring independence (on 17.8.45) followed by a five year`s independence struggle. Within the first weeks of the Republic Indonesian workers founded fighting organizations out of which the first postwar trade unions emerged. Within the first years the communist orientated (although organizationally independent) SOBSI - Sentral Organisasi Buruh Seluruh Indonesia (Central Labour Organization of All Indonesia) - arose as the strongest trade union central, organizing more than half of all organized workers.[2]

The second strongest was the Central Islamic Trade Union SBII/GASBIINDO [3] and only the third place was occupied by nationalist centrals like KBKI oe KBM. [4] When after the traumatic events of 1965/66 together with the annihilating of the nearly entire communist movement of Indonesia also all what had been left from SOBSI and its members had been banned, it was GASBIINDO being left as the biggest organization. It was this organization which provided the ideological, personal and organizational basis for the government installed FBSI - Federasi Buruh Seluruh Indonesia (All Indonesian Labour Federation) - in 1973. [5] It has since then been the only officially recognized and legal federation of Indonesia. At its congres in November 1985 it changed its name to become SPSI -

Serikat Pekerja Seluruh Indonesia (All Indonesia Federation of Workers). [6] This federation did not only recognize Pancasila as its philosophical basis but developed respectively adopted an analogically drafted theory called HPP - Hubungan Perburuhan Pancasila (Pancasila Industrial Relations). [7]

2. Pancasila - A Short Outline of its Development

The declaration of Independence is anteceded by working out the philosophical principles of the new state: In July 1945 Sukarno introduced his Pancasila [8] - Five Principles, and in August the Constitution of 1945 was passed (being replaced by the one of 1950, but being in force again since 1959). Pancasila has been part of the preamble of Indonesian constitutions since then. In its first version it is as follows:

1. Kebangsaan Indonesia Indonesian Nationalism (in the fullest sense)

2. Internasionalisme - atau Peri-Kemanusiaan -Internationalism (familyhood of nations)

3. Permusyawaratan (Demokrasi Mufakat) - deliberation among representatives

4. Kesejahteraan Sosial - Social Justice

5. Ketuhanan - Belief in One, Supreme God. [9]

After further discussion and elaboration in PPKI - Panitia Persiapan Kemerdekaan Indonesia (Comitee for Preparing Independence of Indonesia) Pancasila - was incorporated into the Preamble of the 1945

Constitution and thus gained status of state philosophy:

1. Ketuhanan Yang Maha Esa - One Deity
2. Kemanusiaan yang adil dan bera dab (just and cililized Humanity)
3. Persatuan Indonesia - Indonesian Unity
4. Kerakyatan yang dipimpin oleh Hikmat Kebijaksanaan dalam Permusyawaratan Perwakilan (People`s rule guided wisely through consultation and representation).
5. Keadilan sosial bagi seluruh rakyat Indonesia (Social Justice for the whole Indonesian People). [10]

This version was to be in force until now notwithstanding minor changes. Its value for Indonesia has always been to give this diversed country, with all its variety of peoples, cultures, religions, languagaes etc. (more variety than can be found in any other country of the world) a unifying philosophical basis: "It has enabled Indonesian society to maintain the rich cultural traditions inherited from the past. It has dealt with some degree of effectiveness with the basic problems in the present. And it provided the Nation a national framework within the common ideals for the future might be pursued together." [11] And it certainly is not by chance that Pancasila has always been invoked in times of crisis. It was. for instance, shield and shelter for Christian minorities against the Muslim majority. And it provided the "orde baru" with the possibility of changing policies without changing its ideological foundation. The history of the Pancasila can be divided into three periods [12] : the first one from 1945 to 1957, the phase of its development, outlining and discussion until the concept of Guided Democracy was prepared, the second one from 1957 to 1965, the period of Guided Democracy (including its preparing phase), and the third one from 1965 to 1978, during the "orde baru", when new stress has been laid on Pancasila. With Parliamental Decree XX/MPRS/1966 has been issued: "The Preamble of the Constitution of 1945 as the Declaration of Independence...containing Pancasila as the State`s Foundation, forms a unity with the Proclamation of Independence on August 17th, 1945, and therefore it may not be changed by anybody, including Parliament..., because, changing the contents of the Preamble means dissolving the State" [13]: This development culminated in the passing of Parliamental Decree (Ketetapan) Nr. II/MPR/1978 [14]. With this Pedoman (P4) Pancasila was made obligatory: "P4 is a life guide and a support to social and public life for each Indonesian citizen, each state functionary as well as each state and social constitution, both central and regional and has to be carried out completely." [15] At the same time stringent courses for all civil servants, having been gradually extended to other functional and political groups of society, were established and made obligatory. [16] For trade union functionaries and even for the industrial working force these courses are obligatory. [17]

3. Pancasila and Trade Unions

Prior to the founding of FBSI Pancasila played a very marginal role in the Indonesian trade union movement: Not even the two bigger nationalist trade union centrals KBKI and KBM referred to Pancasila, at most indirectly, as "kerakyatan" as one of the five silas and Marhaenism having also been invented by Sukarno are ideologically close to Pancasila. Both of the trade union centrals propagated a strategy of social partnership between (national) capital and labour and were against unresponsible strikes. [18] Both trade union centrals were not able of rallying many workers or employees [19]: It is significant that it was a Christian federation, SOB Pancasila - Sentral Organisasi Buruh Pancasila (Pancasila Trade Union Federation), a Catholic one, writing "Pancasila" on its banner. [20] It were the Christians who looked for shelter under this ideological umbrella spread by Sukarno. The Catholic Social Theory, however, had been the basis for its organizational theory and practice (although SOB Pancasila avoided open propagation of this theory).[21] Although it is difficult to quantify the actual strength of former Indonesian trade unions it is possible to state that the communist orientated federation SOBSI had rallied the absolute as well as the relative majority of the Indonesian workers and employees.

Such as military dictatorship has its forerunner in Guided Democracy[22], so there are certain developments within the trade union movement preparing the government installed FBSI: Once the most important Muslim Federation SBII had been based solely on Islam. Socialist ideas, however, had then been recognized in Indonesia so widely that SBII too (as well as the nationalist and Christian trade unions), although strictly anti-communist, had to adopt some socialist principles: "In Indonesia, the influence of socialism has been decisive in shaping the movement and in determining the policies and tactics of the unions...The Moslem unions, too, although denouncing marxism, are often guided by socialist ideas and pursuing socialist aims, to the extent that these ideas and aims are derived fromt he Qu`an." [23] That did not prevent SBII, however, from pursuing a strategy of cooperation between entrepreneurs[24] and workers.[25] SBII`s influence on workers, anyhow not too large, further dwindled when Masjumi had come into miscredit due to its part on the Permesta of 1957 and finally been banned. The leaders of the SBII therefore cut its organizational ties with Masjumi. They did not only restructure it according to industrial branches but gave the federation, now called GASBIINDO a new ideological basis: Now defending the 1945 Constitution and Pancasila got first preference. [26] At the same time relations between GASBIINDO and the military grew tighter. The military, too, derived the legitimacy of its "dwi fungsi" from Pancasila. In this relationship General A.H. Nasution was a leading person. He had "developed the concept of 'dwi fungsi`...which stipulated that the military should be one of the social-political forces, determining the fate of the nation".[27] And it was (among others) Nasution who was invited to deliver speeches at conferences of former SBII and later GASBIINDO. [28] So it came not surprisingly that GASBIINDO took active part in persecuting communists in 1965/1966. After

SOBSI together with the majority of communist groups had been destroyed (and all former members had been banned) GASBIINDO was left as the biggest trade union [29] using this position in getting the base for the all embracing FBSI - Federasi Buruh Seluruh Indonesia, which was to be established (after some preparatory comitees having been founded) on the initiative of "orde baru" government in 1973. [30] FESI had the same organizational structure, i.e. was based on industrial branches, as GASBIINDO had been before, and it had the same chairman, Agus Sudono, and it was based solely on Pancasila. Thus Islam was dropped. To link trade unions` theory and practice more tightly to Pancasila, the HPP - Hubungan Perburuhan Pancasila has been developed.

3. HPP = Hubungan Perburuhan Pancasila (Pancasila Labour Relations)

Such as there had been a preparing the way for FBSI/SPSI through GASBIINDO, so there was a preparing the way for the development of HPP: As early as in the late sixties D. Panggabean for instance gave lectures in North Sumatra about the system of labour management relations called HPP already formulating respective principles. [31] Soetarto (1914-1978), former Director of the Pusat Pembinaan Sumber Daya Manusia, also a leading person of the Dewan Gereja Indonesia, who had written a foreword for the above mentioned book claimed to be the father of this idea of HPP. [32] From this manuscript a very close relationship to Christian ideas of labour management relations is obvious as he states that interests of workers are closely relatied to those of the management, so the workers should always regard the interests of management as well. [33] So, from its very beginning FBSI could make use of this idea and as early as November 1973 Agus Sudono, Chairman of FBSI (former chairman of GASBIINDO) propagated it in his speeches. [34] In a short definition he introduced HPP as follows: "HPP are industrial relations based on just and civilized humanity inspired by the principle of family and aiming at social justice for the entire people of Indonesia." [35] The five principles of labour-management relations as a logical consequence of Pancasila are the following five responsibilities of the workers:

1. Workers bear responsibility for their working place

2. Workers bear responsibility for their family

3. Workers bear responsibility for their trade union

4. Workers bear responsibility for the interests of society and state

5. Workers (as Pancasilaists) bear responsibility in respect to God. [36]

From 4. to 7. December 1974 a seminar was held in Jakarta for "discussion" of this concept. Its participants "agreed" on a text the most essential points of which read as follows: "HPP are relations between workers, employers and government based on values of all silas of Pancasila and the 1945 Constitution having grown and developed out of the ethnic personality and national culture of Indonesia." Founded on this basic understanding, the five principles of HPP are:

1. HPP being based upon the belief of One Almighty God is an industrial relationship estimating labour as a devotion of man to God and his fellow-creatures (pengabdian manusia kepada Tuhan Yang Maha Esa dan sesama manusa).

2. An industrial relation based on humanity regarding workers not as factors of production but as individuals with their own dignity and character.

3. An industrial relation containing a principle enabling Indonesian unity without regarding groupings, different beliefs, ideologies etc.. The entire orientation ought to be aiming at national interests alone.

4. An industrial relation being based on the principle of deliberation (musyawarah) aiming at consensus (mufakat).

5. An industrial relation furthering social justice for the whole Indonesian people, and therefore the whole national income especially in regard to economic development has to be equally shared.
HPP is based on an atmosphere and feeling of harmony between all participants in the process of production, i.e. workers, employers and government as well as society." [37]

Government even more clearly announced its point of view concerning the aims of HPP. In his speech before Parliament on 16.8.1973, Suharto stated:

"Between management and employees there has to be created a good working atmosphere of respect for the respective roles and duties in production process...the only and final aim being rise of production." [38] Here, it were three kinds of partnership being praised: Partner in production, partner in profit, partner in responsibility (in respect to Indonesia, the factory, the nearer society, people and state, God). Again it is the 1945 Constitution, therein especially article 27/p.2 "Each citizen has the right to work and to an existence consonant with human dignity" and article 33/p.1 "Economy is organized as a common effort on the family principle" [39] which is referred to. As means of implementing this, Collective Labour Agreements, tripartite bodies (according to ILO example), arbitrating bodies, strengthening of trade unions are mentioned. [40] Up to the beginning of 1978, these principles have been disseminated in 60 trade union seminars each year [41], Agus Sudono never hesitating to admit that implementation of all these principles is still far away.

4. Workers Reality

The situation of Indonesian workers is characterized by a series of serious problems. Although since "orde baru" when "politics instead of development" has been replaced by "development instead of politics" (like government propaganda announced) industrialization had been furthered from 14% in 1965 to 31% in 1985 [42] of Gross Domestic Product, still the majority of workers (50% in 1985) is employed in the agrarian sector with extremely low level of wages. And it is the most low level incomes which have eroded during the last years. [43] The industrial sector, however, faces similar problems: It is an ever decreasing number of highly paid (and better qualified) workers and an ever increasing number of low paid workers being under high pressure of competition. [44] Closely related to this problem is the one of unemployment and underemployment in all its manifestations. Although in this field, too, exact figures are hardly to be obtained, the following figures might serve to gain a rough view of the dimensions of this problem: "The National Statistical Bureau forecasts a growth in the labour force of 9,3 m. (i.e. 1,86 m. per annum) up to 1989 which added to the 4 m. officially unemployed at the end of the last Plan (it means that some 14 m. jobs have to be found." [45] As economy is not running well since 1984, government is pro-capital [46] and government`s employment policy is full of contradictions, any fundamental changes cannot be expected. FBSI [47] reacting to these problems of which only the most urgent ones have been mentioned (not to talk about working conditions, social insurance and so on) confines itself to the role government has prescribed: The one helping government and entrepreneurs "to achieve an atmosphere of Pancasila labour relations and increase labour productivity".[48] Freedom to strike already being restricted has further been curbed. The legitimating function Pancasila provides is clearly to be seen out of the following statement of Minister Sudomo: "Going on strike is certainly allowed by law, but many people do not read the full text of this law which, by the way, is not yet operational because the measures necessary for its implementation have not been taken. Moreover, one must have permission to strike. And for sure I will not give permission to strike. Because, (in my opinion), going on strike means applying principles of liberal thinking while we are already in the period of Pancasila Industrial Relations." (my emphasis)[49] And "Agus Sudono also told workers that they 'should as far as possible avoid going on strike because the government/Ministry of Manpower so attentively looks after the interests of manpower in Indonesia today." [50] In an interview some years ago Agus Sudono said considering the high level of unemployment going on strike is not a suitable means of furthering the interests of the workers.[51] So, what ought to be fighted against is used as rationalization not to fight - all in accordance with HPP.

5. Conclusion

In theory Pancasila is a very general fundamental philosophy, its strength (among others) lying in the fact that "it provides a national framework within which differences are neither suppressed nor allowed to be completely antagonistic to one another".[52] During the last years, however, Pancasila has been turned into a means of suppression of differences. For Indonesian society in general this might turn out to be dangerous, but that is not our topic. For Indonesian trade union movement in particular, this aspect of conflict suppressing is a disaster. In the first place in making this general theory the basis for all activities in society, thus for workers as well, workers are not given any chance of deliberating or discussing whether this theory is suitable for the particular purposes of their organizations. A look at the history of the Indonesian trade union movement illustrates that - with only very minor exceptions - workers do not regard Pancasila as a suitable theory, although trade union theory and Pancasila have something in common: Both of them have been developed in the context of the National Movement and are an amalgation of modern occidental and traditional oriental values. There are, however, some differences between them: Pancasila has been drafted by a single person (Sukarno) at a certain time (1945) for the whole people, but for one people, the people of Indonesia only, whereas the trade union theory has been developed by so many persons since more than a century, but for a certain group respectively class only, but not only the working class of one nation but of all nations worldwide. So, the character of a trade union is not one of an all embracing harmonizing cooptative organization, but one of fighting for the interests of a particular group, its main weapon being strike. Depriving it of its weapons means depriving it of its function. Throughout the history of trade union movement in general and Indonesian trade union movement in particular the strike problem has not only deserved much attention but also been regarded as an important criteria for the amount of freedom workers have. Indonesian workers cannot and do not accept an organization which is not only not fighting for freedom to strike but does not even use the possibilities provided by law. In the second place, the alleged weakness of Pancasila is that it is a traditional theory[53] , while the Indonesian government adheres to modernization and development especially in regard to industrialization. Trade unions are both: grown out of industrial development and modern institutions, they need an own theory, born out of the particular living and working conditions workers have to face. It is a matter of self-evidence that workers must have the right to develop own theories reflecting their historical, cultural, social and economic experiences. FBSI claims to have developed such a theory, HPP, "And now after all these bitter experiences, we all think that the appropriate industrial relationship between workers and entrepreneurs in Indonesia has to be based on Pancasila".[54] Official statements of FBSI and the Government will suggest that HPP is based on "partnership between workers, entrepreneurs and government" and that they strive for "development from the people, through the people and for the people" [55], but the real character of such "partnership" is clearly revealed in Suharto`s speech on Pancasila Commemmoration Day on June 1st, 1967, in Jakarta, "Social justice means that the weaks have to be protected; that does not mean, however, that the weak don`t have to work anymore only asking for protection, but on the contrary, they have to work according to their ability and knowledge. The protection which is provided is to prevent arbitrariness from the side of the strong to guarantee justice".[56] We see: no partners, but strong and weak without indicating any way of overcoming social inequality, only providing protection against arbitrariness. On the one side government (Suharto) regards "development itself as the very effort for changing one`s fate".[57] On the other side the workers are deprived of their very means of changing their fate, as we have exposed by the statement of Minister Sudomo in respect to striking. So we may state that this kind of theory is by no means an emancipating force. It does not allow the workers to put the question how to change the actual power in society, which gives them no chance to develop the strength necessary to enable them to use the equal position this philosophy of HPP is talking about. But, indeed, asking this question would be a political act, and it is part of HPP ideology that a trade union has to confine itself to non-political activity. Political strength, however, is the only very strength of trade unions in developing countries, economic conditions being characterized by high level of unemployment and poorest working conditions.[58] The third severe problem for Indonesian workers put under the impact of HPP is their alienation from effective international action. Whereas capital in most developing countries, especially in Indonesia, exists both nationally and internationally (through multinational enterprise) HPP binds the workers to national interests alone. Having hardly any possibilities of fighting for their interests facing national capital, it is impossible for them to establish an international front.[59] This example, too, illustrates the contradiction between the theory of Pancasila, of which internationalism is an element, and practice preventing Indonesian workers from seeking international solidartiy.

Indonesian workers today face many problems, instead of having trade unions who fight for their interests, they are forced to accept a government installed trade union[60] based on a government prescribed ideology called Pancasila industrial relations. Of course, we cannot foresee the future, but it is very probable that, if Indonesian workers will be able to create own unions some day, these will not be based on Pancasila.

References

[1] A more detailed analysis of the Indonesian trade union movement until independence I have tried in my dissertation, including a discussion of the influence of Islam: The Political History of the Indonesian Trade Union Movement, Heidelberg 1986.

[2] It is always a great risk giving any figures in respect to Indonesian trade unions, as figures are usually provided by the made unions themselves based on their own estimates. The only way to make use of them is to draw conclusions in respect to relative strength.

[3] Sarekat Buruh Islam Indonesia (Central Islamic Trade Union) has been transformed into Gabungan Sarekat Buruh Islam Indonesia (Association of Indonesian Islamic Labour Unions) in 1962.

[4] Kesatuan Buruh Kerakyatan Indonesia (Indonesian Democratic Workers Federation) and Kesatuan Buruh Marhaen (Marhaen Workers` Federation). Up to 1973 the Indonesian trade union movement has been dispersed into hundreds of unions and union centrals being organized according to industrial basis as well as to ideological basis. See also Garang-Schaarschmidt, Eva-Maria, Indonesian Trade Unions, in Verfassung und Recht ind Übersee,

15/III 1982, p. 333-349.

5 Howfar FBSI is by no means a true labour organization, founded by and for workers, I have also explained in the above mentioned article in: Verfassung und Recht in Übersee, p. 342 f.

6 Government grip on workers` organization tightened, in TAPOL Bulletin No. 73, Jan. 1986, p. 13.

7 See e.g. Sukarno, This is the FBSI - All Indonesian Labour Federation, Jakarta 1974, p. 10.

8 1972 the Ministry of Education and Culture has passed a regulation on the spelling of Bahasa Indonesia: former j, dj, tj, ch became y, j, c, kh.
I`m using this new spelling provided it is not in quotations of elder textes or proper names. Translations from Indonesian texts are by the author.

9 Sukarno, The Pantja sila, 1945, in H. Feith & L. Castles (eds.), Indonesian Political Thinking 1945-1965, Cornell University Press, Ithaca and London, 1970, s. 4o-49.

10 Kansil, Drs. C.S.T., S.H., Pancasila dan Undang-Undang Dasar 1945, Jakarta 1973, p. 46 f.

11 Darmaputera, Eka, Pancasila and the search for Identity and Modernity in Indonesian society. A cultural and ethical analysis, Ann Arbor, Michigan, 1984, p. 385.

12 Following the ones Bonneff, M., Cayrac-Blanchard et al. have suggested in : Pantjasila,

trente annees de debats politiques en Indonesie, etudes insulindiennes/archipel: 2, Paris 1980.

[13] quoted from: Pandangan Presiden Soeharto tentang Pancasila (The views of Presiden Soeharto about Pancasila). Yayasan Proklamasi, CSIS, Jakarta, 1977, 2nd edition, p. 3.

[14] Undang-Undang Dasar - Pedoman Penghayatan dan Pengamalan Pancasila - GBHN Garis Besar Haluan Negara. Ketetapan MPR No. II/MPR/1983, Sekretariat Negara Republik Indonesia (Constitution - Guide for the Realization and Implementation of Pancasila - Guidelines of the State. Decree No. II/MPR/1983, The State Secretary), 1984, p. 25-34.

[15] loc.cit., p. 7.

[16] Morfit, Michael, Pancasila: The Indonesian State Ideology according to the New Order Government, in Asian Survey, 21/8 (Aug. 1981), p. 838-851, p. 847.

[17] Indonesian Workers and their right to organize. INDOC, Leiden, March 1985 Update, p. 7.

[18] Sandra, Sejarah Pergerakan Buruh Indonesia, Jakarta, 1961, p. 175-183.

[19] Although it might seem as if they did - according to a list of the Ministry of Labour 1957-1958. KBKI, however, had been of some importance in some regions only and KBM is not mentioned at all in this list. Hawkins, Everett D., Labour in Transition, in Ruth McVey (ed.), Indonesia, Southeast Asian Studies, Yale University, New Haven, 1967, p. 260.

[20] Moreover Catholics are a minority within the Christian minority of Indonesia (about a ration 1 : 4).

[21] Manuscript of a former official, who has permitted being cited, but doesn`t want his name mentioned. (p. 49 ff.)

[22] See e.g. the elucidating article by Ruth McVey, The Beamtensttat in Indonesia, in Interpreting Indonesian Politics: 13 Contributions to the Debate, ed. by B. Anderson & A. Kahin, Interim Reports Series, Publications No. 62, cornell Modern Indonesia Project, Cornell University, Ithaca, N.Y. 1982, especially p. 86.

[23] Tedjasukmana, Iskandar, The Political Character of the Trade Union Movement, Ithaca, N.Y. 1958, p.. 47.

[24] who ought to be regarded as brothers if they are Muslims and consequently deserve solidarity

[25] Manifest SBII, in Sandra, Anh. VIII, p. 192-206.

[26] GASBIINDO - Soko Guru Revolusi Indonesia, ed. Pengurus Besar GASBIINDO, Jakarta, 1964. (The other principles derived from Koran were kept).

[27] Sundhausen, Ulf, Regime Crisis in Indonesia, in Asian Survey, XXV/8 (August 1981), 795-837, p. 826.

[28] e.g. 1960, 1962, 1964. GASBIINDO - Buku Peringatan Ulang Tahun ke XV, ed. Bagian Penerangan Pengurus Besar GASBIINDO, Jakarta, Juli 1963, p.13.

[29] GASBIINDO at once gave its support to Suharto after he had established his government. FES, p. 219 ff.

[30] A very critical article can be found in INDOC, 1981, p. 78-92.

[31] D. Panggabean, Labour-Management Relations in Indonesia through the ages, Medan 1970.

[32] According to an information given by a former Director of YTKI.

[33] Panggabean, op.cit., p. 27.

[34] e.g. Pokok2 Pikiran Tentang HPP, disampaikan pada Seminar FBSI-AAFLI, pada tgl. 28. November 1973 di Jakarta, in Gerakan Buruh Indonesia dan Kebijaksanaanya. Kumpulan Pidato/Ceramah/Sambutan, oleh: Agus Sudono, Ketua Umum FBSI, 1977.

[35] op.cit. p. 69.

[36] Gerakan Buruh, op.cit., p. 73.

[37] Keputusan Seminar Nasional HPP yang diselenggarakan di Jakarta 4.-7.12.1974, Appendix A of Gerakan Buruh (Decisions of the National HPP Seminar held in Jakarta from Dec. 4th to 7th, 1974), p. 176 f.

[38] cit. according Ali Moertopo, Buruh dan Tani dalam Pembangungan, Rangkuman Ceramah dalam Seminar HPP 4.-7.12.74 dan Sidang MPO-HTKI, 11.-16.3.1975 di Jakarta (Workers and Ramers in Development, Lecture in the HPP Seminar from Dec. 4th to 7th, 1974, 1974 and the MPO-HKTI meeting fromn March 11th to 16th, 1975), 1975, p. 14.

[39] op.loc. 18 f.

[40] op.loc. 125. This must not be mistaken for an encouraging of free trade unions. Legal provisions will prevent growing of any trade unions beside FESI respectively SPSI.

[41] in management and government circles as well. Speech at the Anniversary Celebration and Workers` Day, Jakarta 20. February 1978, in Gerakan Buruh, p. 155-174, p. 169.

[42] including mining, manufacturing, electricity, gas, water and construction.

[43] Hasibuan Nurismansjah, Upah Tenaga Kerja dan konsentrasi pada sektor Industri, in Prisma, 5. Mai 1981, p. 3-19.

[44] Hasibuan, op.cit., p. 19.

[45] INDOC, 1985, p. 24. Estimates of REPELITA III went up to an increase of 1,4 m. job seeking per annum: Iskandar, N., Keadaan dan Arah Perkembangan Angkatan Kerja di Indonesia, in Ekonomi dan Keuangan Indonesia, vol. XXIII, No. 3, Sept. 1975, p. 269-304. See also Simanjuntak, Payaman J., Penganggur dan Setengah Penganggur, in Prisma, 1985, 3, p. 47-53.

[46] Whereas it had been pro-labour during "orde lama".

[47] A change to the better of new SPSI policies cannot be expected as this came about through government`s interference. It should be mentioned that Indonesia`s Minister of Manpower is a military man, who had been Head of the notorious KOPKAMTIE - Operational Command for the

Restauration of Security and order and that the new chairman Imam Soedarwo, appointed by him, is a member of the central board of GOLKAR and an entrepreneur. See "Government`s grip...", op.cit.

[48] Kompas, 12.3.1984; cited according to INDOC, 1985, p. 12.

[49] Berita Buana, 21.12.1983, INDOC 1984, p. 9.

[50] Merdeka, 10.9.1983, cited by INDOC, 1984, p. 16.

[51] Although this interview the author had with Agus Sudono has already taken place in August 1976 (in Jakarta) the statement given is still actual - the situation has even grown worse.

[52] Darmaputera, op.cit., p. 389.

[53] Although, of course, tradition and modernity are not exclusive, the question has been aroused even by a Javanese scholar, whether Pancasila as a very much Javanese orientated philosophy is able to promote modernizing of the whole country. Darmaputera, op.cit., p. 395 f.

[54] Pkokok2 Pikiran, op.cit., p. 389.

[55] Pandangan, p. 73.

[56] Quoted from "Pandangan", p. 70.

[57] Pandangan, p. 73.

[58] See Mitschein, Thomas, Die Dritte Welt als Gegenstand gewerkschaftlicher Theorie und Praxis. Zur Analyse der internationalen Politik metropolitaner Gewerkschaften, Campus Forschung, Frankfurt, New York 1981, p. 80.

[59] Mitschein, op.cit., p. 88.

[60] There are, however, examples of workers who try to build trade unions within the structure of FBSI. They had to realize the existing contradictions between FBSI theory and practice. See e.g. INDOC 1983 Update, p. 16 f. and INDOC Updacte 1985, p. 19 f.

Bibliography

Bonneff, M., Cayrac-Blanchard et al. (eds.), Pantjasila, trente annees de debats politiques en Indonesie, etuedes indonesiennes, archipel: 2, Paris 1980

Darmaputera, Eka, Pancasila and the search for Identity and Modernity in Indonesian society. A cultural and ethical analysis. Ann Arbor, Michigan, 1984

Feith, H. & Castles, L. (eds.), Indonesian Political Thinking 1945-1965, Cornell University Press. Ithaca and London 1970

Garang-Schaarschmidt, Eva-Maria (s.a. Schaarschmidt-Kohl, Eva-Maria), Indonesian Trade Unions, in Verfassung und Recht in Übersee, 15/III 1982, p. 333-349

Gasbiindo - Buku Peringatan Ulang Tahun ke XV, ed. Bagian Penerangan Pengurus Besar GASBIINDO, Jakarta, Juli 1963

Gasbiindo - Soko Guru Revolusi Indonesia, ed. Pengurus Besar GASBIINDO, Jakarta 1964

Government grip on workers` organization tightened, in TAPPL Bulletin No. 73, Jan. 1986, p. 13

Hasibuan Nurismansjah, Upah Tenaga Kerja dan konsentrasi pada sektor Industri, in Prisma, 5, Mai 1981, p. 3-19

Hawkins, Everett D., Labor in Transition, in Ruth

McVey (ed.), Indonesia, Southeast Asian Studies, Yale University, New Haven 1967

Indonesian Workers and their right to organize, INDOC, Leiden, March 1985 Update

Iskandar, N., Keadaan dan Arah Perkembangan Angkatan Kerja di Indonesia, in Ekonomi dan keuangan Indonesia, Vol. XXIII, No. 3, Sept. 1975, p. 269-304

Kansil, Drs. D.S.T., S.H., Pancasila dan Undang-Undang Dasar 1945, Jakarta 1973

Keputusan Seminar Nasional HPP yang diselenggarakan di Jakarta 4.-7.12.1974, Appendix A of Gerakan Buruh, p. 176 f.

Manifest SBII, in Sandra, Anh. VIII, p. 192-206

McVey, Ruth, The Beamtenstaat in Indonesia, in Interpreting Indonesian Politics: 13 Contributions to the Debate, ed., by B. Anderson & A. Kahin, Interim Reports Series, Publications Nt. 62, Cornell Modern Indonesia Project, Cornell University Ithaca, N.Y. 1982

Mitschein, Thomas, Die Dritte Welt als Gegenstand gewerkschaflicher Theorie und Praxis. Zur Analyse der internationalen Politik metropolitaner Gewerkschaften, Campus Forschung, Frankfurt, New York 1981

Moertopo, Ali, Buruh dan Tani dalam Pembangungan, Rangkuman Ceramah dalam Seminar HPP 4.-7.12.74 dan Sidang MPO-HTKI, 11.-16.3.1975 di Jakarta, 1975

Morfit, Michael, Pancasila: The Indoensian State Ideology according to the New Order Government, in Asian Survey, 21/8 (Aug. 1981)

Pandangan Presiden Soeharto tentang Pancasila (The views of President Soeharto about Pancasila). Yayasan Proklamasi, CSIS, Jakarta 1977, second edition, p. 3

Panggabean, D., Labour-Management Relations in Indonesia through the ages, Medan 1970

Pokok2 Pikiran Tentang HPP, disampaikan pada Seminar FBSI-AAFLI, pada tgl, 28 Nopember 1973 di Jakarta, in Gerakan Buruh Indonesia dan Kebijaksanaanya.Kumpulan Pidato/Ceramah/Sambutan, oleh: Agus Sudono, Ketua Umum FBSI, 1977

Sandra, Sejarah Pergerakan Buruh Indonesia, Jakarta 1961

Simanjuntak, Payaman J., Penganggur dan Setengah Penganggur, in Prisma, 1985, 3, p. 47-53

Schaarschmidt-Kohl, Eva-Maria, The Political History of the Indonesian Trade Union Movement before Independence, Heidelberg 1986

Sukarno, The Pantja sila, 1945, in Feith, H. & Castles, L. (eds.), Indonesian Political Thinking 1945-1965, Cornell University Press, Ithaca and London 1970, p. 40-49

Sukarno, This is the FBSI - All Indonesian Labour Federation, Jakarta 1974

Sundhausen, Ulf, Regime Crisis in Indonesia, in Asian Survey, XXV/8 (August 1981), 795-837

Tedjasukmana, Iskandar, The Political Character of the Trade Union Movement, Ithaca, N.Y. 1958

Undang-Undang Dasar - Pedoman Penghayatan dan Pengamalan Pancasila - GBHN Garis Besar Haluan Negara. Ketetapan MPR No. II/MPR/1983, Sekretariat Negara Republik Indonesia, 1984

The History of the Attempt to Establish an Islamic State in Indonesia and its Impact on Indonesian Politics till today

by Holk Harald Dengel

When in Indonesia the efforts come up for discussion to found an Islamic state the name Kartosuwirjo will always be mentioned. Together with the Darul-Islam-Movement founded by him, between 1948-1962 he tried to establish an Islamic state by force and on August 7, 1949 he proclaimed in West Java the "Islamic Indonesian State" (NII).

Being asked in one of his interrogations after his arrest in 1962, when he had elaborated the plan for establishing an Islamic state, he answered that himself as well as the PSII had considered this idea since the Dutch colonial time and that the Masjumi had continued to develop it during Japanese occupation, as well as after having gained independence.

In his pleading in forcent of the military court he explained that in his opinion the proclamation of the Negara Islam Indonesia (NII) had been no rebellion and military units like the Tentara Islam Indonesia (TII), Baris, Polisi etc. had been established before the proclamation. Thus, they are a successor of the Madjlis Islam, which passed the resolution to found these units during the conference of all Islamic Organizations of West Java in Pangwedusan in February 1948.[1]

De facto this is correct; however, Kartosuwirjo withheld the fact that this Madjlis Islam or "Islamic Council" which succeeded the Masjumi in West Java, from the beginning on was thought of, so to speak as an Islamic Government, which was expected to take action in case of the overthrow of the Republic in Yogyakarta after the foundation of an independent state in West Java by the Dutch. So, in Cikoneng and Cihaur the first districts of the Negara Islam Indonesia had been established at the end of March 1948. In May of the same year the Madjlis Islam had been changed into Madjlis Imamah, the "Council of the Imam", which had been headed by Kartosuwirjo as Imam and which practically represented a cabinet.[2]

Kartosuwirjo and his political views during Dutch colonial rule and his activities under Japanese occupation

By the influence of his uncle Marko Kartodikromo, a well-known journalist and literary man who besides Semaun, Alimin, Darsono and Tan Malaka had been one of the prominent members of the Communist Party, Kartosuwirjo was interested very early in politics. The fate of his uncle, who after the communist revolts in 1926/27 had been imprisoned in the Boven Digul concentration camp by the Dutch and who died there, was lamented by Kartosuwirjo in one of his political manifestos he wrote as Imam of the Negara Islam Indonesia.[3]

Already at the beginning of 1923 he entered the youth movement Jong Java and two years later the Jong Islamieten Bond. As was the case with Jong Java, too, he again became chairman of the branch of this movement in Surabaya.

In September 1927 Kartosuwirjo accepted the offer of H.O.S. Tjokroaminoto, the charismatic chairman of PSI and became his private secretary. As was decided by the Congress of the Partai Sarikat Islam Hindia Timoer (PSIHT) in Pekalongan in December 1927 he had been appointed General Secretary of the party. Moreover, it had been decided to transfer the paraty headquarters to Batavia. Here in Batavia Kartosuwirjo worked as a journalist in the party-owned daily newspaper Fadjar Asia, and within only 16 months he was promoted from proof-reader, reporter, editor to deputy chief editor, commissioner and manager of the newspaper.

At this time he always dressed himself by jacket and cravat, a sarong and the traditional Javanese headgear Blangkon. Already some years later as vice-president of the PSII he wears a kind of safari-dress, at this time an unusual clothing for a man in his position; with the first view a big difference to his colleagues. Kartosuwirjo, a taciturn person, intolerant, without compromise and with spartanic style of live, was the exact opposite of the complacent Sukarno.In his articles he attacked the Javanese aristocracy collaborating with the colonial power and he was concerned about the fate of the many small farmers who had farmed out their land to "Western companies and capitalists".[4]

Already in those days Kartosuwirjo had been convinced that independence for his native country could only be reached by means of fighting and that this would demand big sacrifies. By his interpretation of the Jayabaya prophecies he had been encouraged in his conviction. After proclamation of the Negara Islam Indonesia he had translated them from Javanese into Indonesian. Their content was to exert an undeniable influence on him. So, he described the confrontations with the colonial power at the beginning of the national movement as "failed war". As editor of the Fadjar Asia Kartosuwirjo wrote in 1929 "But later, after the outbreak of the Brata Yudha Jaya Binangun, we will be leading our troops.[5]

Moreover, Kartosuwirjo participated in confrontations with the secular nationalists whereby Parada Harahap, chief editor of Bintang Timoer had been the target of his attacks. Kartosuwirjo called his newspaper reactionary and Parada Harahap had been abused by him to be "the rat of Krekot", who sucked up to the secular nationalists and sold his convictions and his soul to others.[6] The most sharp-pointed articles had now no longer been written under his factual name but under the pseudonym "Arjo Djipang". Later, Kartosuwirjo, as Imam of the Negara Islam Indonesia, is said to have held more than 12 assumed names.

An article by Kartosuwirjo concerning national banks triggered exasperation on the part of secular nationalists. In this article he wrote that that what has been described as "national" would be nothing but a bank according to Western pattern which would cause capitalism and would gain its profit by collecting taxes. In Solo the daily newspaper Darmo Kondo wrote, as reaction to Kartosuwirjo`s article, that this article shocked the Indonesian nationalists and made their blood boil.[7]

According to Kartosuwirjo the ideal of an independent Indonesia would not only be the monopoly of secular nationalists; the religious nationalists, too, aimed for this ideal. The difference between both was that for the secular nationalists the independence of their native country was the most important aim, whereas for the religious nationalists this was only a condition and bridge, to reach more highly-minded and true ideals, namely besides independence the establishment of Islam throughout Indonesia. He claimed the unity of the whole Islamic World and he had been convinced that only by this a new world, or "Darul Islam" could be created.[8]

In Kartosuwirjo`s opinion in those days an independent Indonesian State should not be a national state but a state within a Pan-Islamic union. Still in 1940 he wrote in the Hijra-action programme drawn up by him, that the secular nationalists hoped for a Greater Indonesia, the aim of Indonesia`s Muslims, however, was not a Greater Indonesia, but a Darul-Islam where each Muslim could practise the laws of Islam without being limited.[9]

Having become Vice-President of the PSII in 1936 and with that quarrels within the party concerning the party`s attitude towards the colonial government had come up whether the way of co-operation or the way of non-cooperation should be followed, Kartosuwirjo gave his support to an uncompromising application of the Hijra-policy which he described as middle course between co-operation and non-cooperation. By the Party Congress he had been charged to write a brochure concerning the Hijra attitude of the PSII, which had been published in November 1936 approved by Abikusno.

On the 24th Party Congress of the PSII in Surabaya in 1938 it had been decided that under Kartosuwirjo`s leadership a party-owned training centre with the name "Soeffah PSII" should be established, which should be opened in February 1939 for male PSII members only and which was to serve the party as cadre staff training centre.[10]

When Abikusno thought it opportune to join the GAPI and thus turned away from the Hijra-policy, his deputy Kartosuwirjo did not take part in this political about-face and further on pursued in an uncompromising way the refusal of the co-operation with the colonial government. In his opinion the demand of GAPI, the Political Federation of Indonesia, for establishing an Indonesian parliament was only "expression of co-operation by different means".[11] He now consequently carried out his Hijra and moved back to Malangbong in West Java, the native place of his wife, where he founded, together with like-minded persons, among them Jusuf Taudjiri and Kamran, the "Committee of the Defenders of the Truth of the PSII" (KPK-PSII), which had in March 1940 been transformed into an independent party.

Beforehand on the 25th Party Congress which took place in Palembang in January 1940, Kartosuwirjo had been expelled, together with other fellow-members, fromt the party. However, he furtheron followed the establishing of the training centre and the preparation of the Hijra-action-programme even without support and approval by the party. The concept of the Hijra-action-programme comprising 5 points served him as basis for the curriculum of the cadre staff training centre. It had been divided into a political, social, economic, religious part as well as a part regarding Islamic mysticism.

During the Japanese occupation Kartosuwirjo had, for a short period, been Secretary of the Baital-Mail of the MIAI, and after the establishment of the Djawa Hokokai he had worked there in the department Chosaka, which had been responsible for procuring of informations as well as making up monthly economic reports. He had often been sent to the province in order to control the rice levy imposed to the rural population and he had used this chance behind the back of the Japanese above all to maintain the contacts to his old party colleagues in Eastern Priangan. In the eyes of his colleagues in the Djawa Hokokai, all of them well-known PNI-politicians like S.K. Trimurty, Sumanang and Sayuti Melok, Kartosuwirjo had been a correct but very serious and extremely reserved man, who had never talked about his political ideas during this time, but preferred to act behind the screen.

Early in 1944 Kartosuwirjo had gone, together with members of the Djawa Hokokai and the head of the Propaganda Office to the region of Indramayu in order to calm the rural population who had been angry about the high rice levy. In May 1945 Kartosuwirjo led a group of 16 persons who had to organize and to control the defense exercises of the population.[12] Kartosuwirjo, however, never acted as military trainer, but had only to explain the tactics of the guerilla war. These experiences, gained during the Japanese occupation, should later be of great use for him. So, he later copied that what had perfectly been done by the Japanese, namely the transformation of organizations established by thim into new organizations which should guarantee them a better control of various political forces. Moreover, he copied the mobilization of the masses up to the lowest level executed by the Japanese.

The Islamic state, born out of the disturbances of the Indonesian revolution

After the Masjumi had been re-founded in November 1945 as political party, Kartosuwirjo became Secretary of the Executive Committee and he went to Priangan in order to pave the way for setting up the regional branches and offices of the party. When the first "police-action" by the Dutch took place Kartosuwirjo was in Malangbong and since he could not return to Yogyakarta owing to martial implications, he was appointed as representative for West Java by the leadership of the Party. Together with the Islamic fighting corps of the Hizbullah and Sabilillah he started to organize resistance to the Dutch troops, and, moreover, he opposed the decisions included in the Renville-agreement that all military units had to withdraw to Central Java.

On January 10, 1948, Kartosuwirjo called a conference on which 160 representatives of Islamic organizations of West Java had met. During this conference, Kamran, the old supporter of Kartosuwirjo, demanded that in view of the political situation an Islamic state should be established, and a representative of the GPII made an application to the Party-leadership of the Masjumi in Yogyakarta for unseating Sukarno as President, even by a coup d'état if not possible by an other way.[13] The most important agreement by the conference, however, was the planned transformation of the Masjumi and its organizations adjoined into the Madjilis Islam, since according to the Renville-agreement no party of the Republic could be representend in West Java. Furtheron it had been decided to assemble the Tentara Islam Indonesia, the "Islamic Military Forces of Indonesia",whoch were expected to be composed of the Islamic fighting corps. Oni, who was in command of the first TII-regiment, called his regiment "Sunan Rahmat", which was equivalent to a challenge to the Siliwangi Division. Since, according to tradition, Prabhu Siliwangi, a ruler of the Pajajaran Hindu Kingdom is said to have been overthrown by his own son Sunan Rahmat, who had embraced to Islam. According to Oni, the rulership of the Siliwangi Division had come to an end after the formation of the Sunan Rahmant regiment. February 17, 1948, the day on which the first fights with Dutch troops took place, was declared by Kartosuwirjo as the beginning of the Islamic Revolution in West Java, the day which was celebrated annualy as commemoration day.

The Dutch themselves considered the combat effectiveness of Kartosuwirjo`s army only as "quite mediocre", but they attested him good organizing ability as well as efficient supervision of the institutions established by him. According to reports of the Dutch Secret Service the Dutch had not known exactly how to classify Kartosuwirjo and his movement. So,they thought of the Darul-Islam-Movement to be infiltrated by communism, and in a document by the Dutch military command for West Java, Kartosuwirjo and Oni had even been called prominent communists from Priangan.[14]

The local Islamic leaders who pushed forward to positions kept by the TII on Gunung Cupu received an organizational plan of organizations to be set up in their areas such as PADI (Pahlawan Darul Islam) and BKD (Badan Keamanan Desa). They had been explained that it would be their obligation to use, when the occasion would arise, these units to undertake acts of sabotage against the Dutch and traitors. On March 7, 1948, Oni had given the order to the commanders of these units to start in Priangan with a mopping-up operation and to kill all "traitors to religion, state and people".[15] One month later Oni was informed on the result of these actions which had been regarded to be "satisfying and agreeable". Before, however, from March 1-2, Kartosuwirjo had called again a conference in the region of Cirebon, on which all leaders of the regional party offices of the Masjumi in WestJava, and those from Jakarta and Bogor, too, had to participate. On this meeting it was decided that all preparations should be made in order to found an Islamic State in case the government in Yogyakarta should be overthrown or an independent State of West Java should be set up by the Dutch. The resolution of the preceding conference, too, now was carried out, and all activities by the Masjumi were stopped in West Java startin on March 1, 1948. During the following conference in Cijoho on May 1-5, the Madjlis Islam Pusat, in which Kartosuwirjo concentrated the Masjumi and all its organizations, was transformed into the Madjlis Imamah, which consisted of 5 departments, de facato a cabinet, and was presided over by Kartosuwirjo as Imam.[16]

All political and military statements and decisions of the Madjlis Imamah had to be published in the form of communiqués, and had to be distributed among the population. In another steop it was decided to found a principal region for the Negara Islam Indonesia which was called Daerah I, "I region", and in which the Islamic laws were completely put into force. The region which was ruled only half by the ummat Islam and the region which was controlled by the Dutch were classified as Daerah II and Daerah III. As an immediate step the mobilization of the Daerah I population was announced, and all men between 16 and 40 years of age were called up for military service.[17] So called "praying quarters" were installed for the ulamas where day and night no less than 41 persons had to do their prayers and had to perform other religious exercises like reciting of combative Koran sures and where they were instructed in ideological doctrine. Thus, Kartosuwirjo tried, like the Japanese before, and from 1947-1949 the Dutch, too, to mobilize the population by the ulamas for his targets.

It was the task of the leaders of the I and II region to incorporate the adjoining region into their own region, so that in the end it would become the I. region, the Darul Islam. This system to increase the spheres of influence worked in a simple and effective principle which provided the respective local leaders with the necessary motivation. Because, whenever a local leader increased his region he climbed up a rung in the administrative hierarchy of the Negara Islam Indonesia.

From May 9-10, 1948,the Madjlis Imamah met for a second time with Kartosuwirjo as chairman, who had meanwhile taken the assumed name "Kalipaksi"; it was decided to rename the Madjilis Imamah into Dewan Imamah. However, Kartosuwirjo had still hesitated to proclaim the Negara Islam Indonesia, because, on the one hand, there had been internal discussions about the best time for a proclamation and, on the other hand, he had hoped to be able to proclaim the Negara Islam Indonesia on a legal way. Before he asked the leadership in Yogyakarta to give him a testing region for establishing an Islamic State, and he demanded that all military units which remained in West Java should have to assign to his orders. But the commander in chief Sudirman and Hatta gave only support to him as far as his fight against the Dutch was concerned. On July 8, 1948, Abdul Hadi, Soelaiman and Nanggadisoera, were sent out by Kartosuwirjo as couriers to Yogyakarta. In a letter which had to be handed over by the couriers to several politicians of the Republic, among them, Anwar

Tjokroaminoto, Kartowirjo declared that this fight should not remain a regional fight, but should spread out all over the Indonesian archipelago. And he hoped, according to his words that by this an independent Islamic state could come up as soon as possible. Additionally he requested the Masjumi politicians to meet him in West Java in order to discuss together further steps. The letter addressed to his fellow party members was signed by Kartosuwirjo still in his role as head of the Madjlis Islam Pusat, though it had been renamed into Dewan Imamah several months before. A letter to TII-division commander Kamran two days earlier, however, was signed by him as Imam of the Negara Islam Indonesia.[18]

Thus it becomes evident that Kartosuwirjo had not informed the party leadership of the Masjumi in Yogyakarta in detail about the stepsalready undertaken by him. At the end of July Anwar Tjokroaminoto stated that he received Kartosuwirjo`s letter and that he intended to comply with the requests mentioned in it. However, this letter should remain the only reaction on the message of Kartosuwirjo.

Then, on August 25, 1948, the first Communiqué of the government of the Negara Islam Indonesia was published. It ordered a total mobilization and militarization of the population, and two days later, the working out of the constitution of the Negara Islam Indonesia was finished. At the end of October Kartosuwirjo announced in another Communiqué the complete reshuffling of the Dewan Imamah. However, the whole action was nothing but a great feint, because the only thing, which had really been changed, was the assumed names of the members of Dewan Imamah.

When the Dutch broke the Renville Agreement on December 19, 1948, and invaded the central area of the Republic, Kartosuwirjo announced the "Holy War" and declared his fight until the setting-up of the Negara Islam Indonesia, as continuation of the fight for independence in the spirit of the proclamation of August, 1945. [19]

With the end of the Republic in Yogyakarta the right moment for the proclamation had actually come, since the Negara Islam Indonesia was already formally founded by Kartosuwirjo. But he still tried to maintain on a legal way the supreme command of all military units and in his Communiqué dated December 21, 1948, he declared that he, as leader of the Negara Islam Indonesia, would be in a position to take over "the responsibility of the leadership of this homogeneous command for the fight".[20] At this time it was not clear, indeed, who should carry out the governmental power afater the downfall of the government in Yogyakarta, since the Indonesian emergency government PDRI in West Sumatra was set up only one day later in Halaban near Payakumbuh on December 22, 1948, and this had been the case only because the leaders there had been informed by radio news of the downfall of the government in Yogyakarta.

Kartosuwirjo had also been aware of the existence of this emergency government, because in a Communiqué he had stated that the Madjlis Islam and the Tentara Islam Indonesia (TII) had been able to look behind the screen of the Indonesian emergency government and its irregular units, which had been described by him as "nest of scoundrels".[21] Like Kartosuwirjo, many other Masjumi politicians, too, had been disappointed by Sukarno`s attitude, who had stated before, on the occasion of a meeting of Sudirman and Sultan Hamengkubuwono, that in case Yogyakarta would fall into enemy hand he would leave Yogyakarta and lead the guerrilla fight. On the part of the emergency government PDRI one was, moreover, disappointed because of the vact that Sukarno had entrusted - without approval and without knowledge of the PDRI - Mohammad Roem with the mandate to negotiate with Roijen, although Sukarno was de facto and de jure no longer President at this time. So, the former Masjumi politician Sjafruddin Prawiranegara still today convinced that Sukarno was only prepared to negotiate in order to get immediately released from custody.[22] Even the military was not completely aware of the legal situation, so Sudirman, still in April 1949, had asked, via radiogram, the PDRI in West Sumatra, whether someone imprisoned and under control of the Dutch was allowed to negotiate.

Kartosuwirjo who was always against each kind of negotiations with the Dutch, also refused the Roem-Roijen Agreement, by which "the Indonesian buffalo would be shut in the stable of a modern zoo which was called the United States of Indonesia".[23]

When after the breaking of the Renville Agreement the units of the Siliwangi Division had returned again to West Java, confrontations with the TII had arisen there, because Kartosuwirjo had regarded this area, which had been defended by him

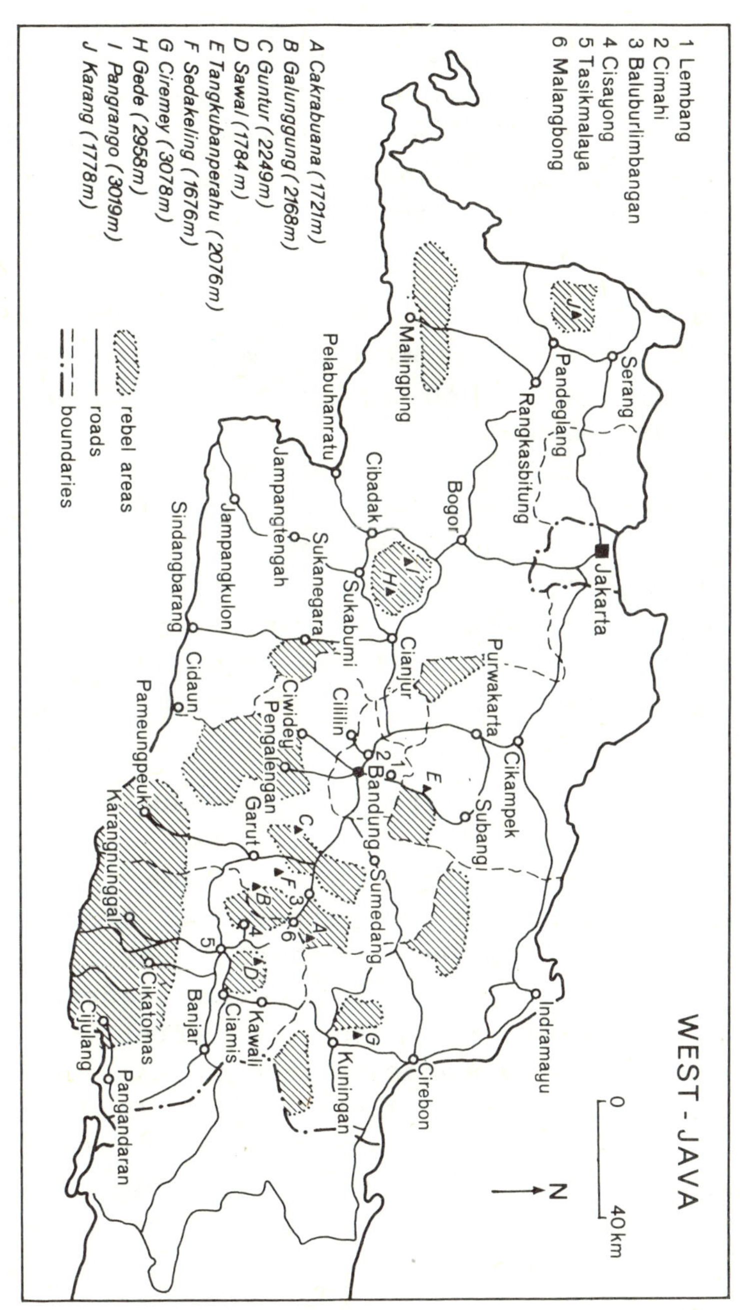
WEST - JAVA
0
40 km
N
1 Lembang
2 Cimahi
3 Baluburlimbangan
4 Cisayong
5 Tasikmalaya
6 Malangbong
A Cakrabuana (1721m)
B Galunggung (2168m)
C Guntur (2249m)
D Sawal (1784 m)
E Tangkubanperahu (2076m)
F Sedakeling (1676m)
G Ciremey (3078m)
H Gede (2958m)
I Pangrango (3019m)
J Karang (1778m)
rebel areas
roads
boundaries
Serang
Pandeglang
Rangkasbitung
Malingping
Pelabuhanratu
Bogor
Jakarta
Cibadak
Jampangtengah
Sukanegara
Sukabumi
Cianjur
Purwakarta
Cikampek
Subang
Jampangkulon
Sindangbarang
Cidaun
Ciwidey
Cililin
Pengalengan
Bandung
Sumedang
Garut
Pameungpeuk
Karangnunggal
Cikatomas
Banjar
Ciamis
Kawali
Kuningan
Cirebon
Indramayu
Cijulang
Pangandaran

against the Dutch, as de facto region of the Negara Islam Indonesia. He had no longer granted the right to the units of the Siliwangi to settle there; "they had not been willing to behave like guests, but they intended to rule the region and the people of the Negara Islam Indonesia", he wrote.[24]

Still on the day of the first battle between the TII and the national armed forces TNI, Kartosuwirjo published a Communiqué in which he called the Republican troops irregulars and obstacles to the Islamic Revolution, that had to be regarded as enemies of the Negara Islam Indonesia.[25] The national armed forces on their part, called the Darul-Islam-Movement the greatest obstacle in the fight for independence, because Kartosuwirjo concentrated his fight mainly on the TNI whereas these were only sporadic combats with the Dutch.

On August 6, Moh. Hatta went to the Round Table Conference to The Hague, which was described by Kartosuwirjo as "shadow play drama or theater drama", "whereby the puppeteer had been in the guise of the damned Dutch colonial power, and the shadow figures had represented the leaders of the Marionette States".[26] One day after Hatta had left for the Netherlands, Kartosuwirjo proclaimed in Cisampah, in the District of Cisayong, on August 7, 1949, under the presence of all members of the Supreme command, the Negara Islam Indonesia. Later on, Kartosuwirjo explained that Hatta`s departure to the Netherlands had been the signal to react, because owing to this a power vacuum had arisen. But certainly he had intenden with the proclamation even before the beginning of the Round Table Conference to confront Hatta with a fait accompli. Still before his departure Muhammad Natsir had been ordered by Hatta to contact Kartosuwirjo in Order to put him off his plans and to make him stop to fight against the TNI. In his reply Kartosuwirjo informed Natsir on thefact that he proclaimed the Negara Islam Indonesia already on August 7, and that the proclamation could not be called off . This had been explained by him in a way which had been typical for him, "I do not want to gulp down my own spittle".[27]

Due to the world political situation of that time, like the cold war between East and West and the events on the Asiatic mainland, Kartosuwirjo hoped that it would not come to the founding of the United States of Indonesia. He expected the outbreak of the Third World War in the near future, and he included the outbreak of this war in the 4 phases which would have to be run through until an Islamic State comprising the whole of Indonesia could be established. According to Kartosuwirjo, Indonesia would appear after this war which would lead to radical changes, as Islamic State on the new world map.

At the beginning of the 50s he had made the offer to Sukarno in two secret notes to dam up, together with the Negara Islam Indonesia the communist influence and to draw back from the previous policy of neutrality and to change over to an anti-communistic course. Because, according to Kartosuwirjo, nationalism had not the power to dam up the influence by communism, because it had not been deeply rooted in the soul of the Indonesian people, which mainly belonged to Islam. He declared that only Islam would have this power, and therefore the government in Jakarta should make Islam the basis of the State.[28] Moreover, Kartosuwirjo predicted that in case the Republic should be in a crisis the nationalists would split up, and a part of them would follow the communists whereas the other part would turn towards Islam.

None of both notes had ever been asnwered by Sukarno. Indeed, Prime Minister Natsir had made several attempts in that time to solve the Darul Islam problem in a peaceful way, however, they had failed, as far as they had been undertaken only half-heartedly already from the beginning on, also because of the fact that on both parts had been forces which had no interest in settling the conflict peacefully. After the end of the Natsir Cabinett in April 1951 Kartosuwirjo had hereafter called the Republic "Communist Republic of Indonesia" (RIK) and its armed forces" Tentara Republik Komunis Indonesia". In a statement by the Negara Islam Indonesia which was published after the Jungschläger-Schmidt affair, Kartosuwirjo wrote that Sukarno would better consult a qualified psychiatrist who should courageous enough "to call the illues of Sukarno and of the RIK by its proper name". And he had continued that "Sukarno would better recover in the lunatic asylum Cikeumeuh in Bogor instead of causing a catastrophe within the Islamic community, and that only in order to satisfy the red greed of Moscow".[29]

Already two months after the proclamation of the Negara Islam Indonesia Kartosuwirjo had simplified the whole administrative system, by putting the civil and military administration together and he reorganized it in a five-graded command system. This administrative system remained effective in an unchanged way for seven years and had been changed in August 1959 only, when a reorganizing of the whole state machinery of the Negara Islam Indonesia had been undertaken. He gave the order to the commanders of the respective administration units to lead the Islamic community "to the place of God`s grace" - if necessary by force.[30]

During his fight, which lasted almost thirteen years, Kartosuwirjo stayed in the mountain region of East Priangan and never went neither to Bandung nor to Jakarta as has often been stated. He also never met captain Westerling or other Dutchmen. However, there have, indeed, been connections during a short period of time between the Darul-Islam-Movement and the APRA and that mainly in the region of Bogor. Probably, Kartosuwirjo knew about those contacts, and he tolerated them worldlessly as long as his movement could profit from them. Moreover, according to the regulations of the Negara Islam Indonesia those connections had not been allowed to be taken up without the approval by the supreme command.

Early in 1950 there had also existed plans by the Dutch to transform the Negara Pasundan into Negara Islam Pasundan. In the Parliament of the Negara Pasundan Affandi Ridhwan who later on tried off his own bat to bring about a peaceful solution of the Darul-Islam problem, had the chance to get hold of a draft of an petition which had been said to have been supported by the Dutch military as well as by the Darul-Islam-Movement and which had foreseen the transformation of the Negara Pasundan into an Islamic State. However, he succeeded, together with Isa Anshary and others to prevent the petition from being brought in. As a consequence, Affandi Ridhwan received threatening letters by the APRA as well as by the Darul-Islam-Movement.[31] According to Kartosuwirjo between 1950-1952 the Negara Islam Indonesia tried to take up contacts to the USA, Pakistan and Saudi-Arabia. These contacts had been said to have been taken up via the embassies of the respective states in Jakarta, whereby the letter for the American Embassy have been addressed to Dean Acheson, Secretary of State in that time.[32]

In one of the last communiqués by the supreme command in October 1952 Kartosuwirjo ordered to accelerate the preparations for the total war in order to be ready for the outbreak of the Third World War. When this war would break out "the command for total warfare" (Perintah Perang Semesta) should then by announced. However, from October 1952 to August 1959, in the course of almost seven years, besides some government statements no communiqué by the supreme command of APNII has been published. Meanwhile it seemed to have become evident for Kartosuwirjo that no Third World War would develop from the Korean War. He firmly reckoned with its outbreak. According to own statements, between 1954 and 1959 Kartosuwirjo retreated to the southern mountain region of East Priangan, whereas Sanusi Partawidjaja acted on behalf of him in the centre of the movement.[33] But exactly in that period, in 1956/57, the Darul-Islam-Movement was it its peak.

When Kartosuwirjo came to hear that his deputy planned a coup against him, he went back to the centre of the movement and performed reorganized the administration and strenghten the administration and commanding structure of the Negara Islam Indonesia, by which Indonesia had been divided into 7 war zones, called "Sapta Palagam".

He seemed to be very much concerned about the condition of his movement. His appeal to the responsibility of each one towards him and the objectives of the movement, to the Islamic solidarity and the adherence to the Islamic laws tolerated this conclusion. Kartosuwirjo again spoke about the meaning of the "command for total warfare". This had been a "Direct command of Allah via the Imam and commander-in-chief of the armed forces of the Negara Islam Indonesia in his function as regent of Allah and representataive of the prophet in the Indonesian archipelago".[34]

Imploringly he declared in a communiqué by the supreme command, "We do know only one Islamic leader, one Imam and one commander-in-chief of the armed forces of the Negara Islam Indonesia". He added that each faith, opinion and action, which would contradict, would be wrong and sinful.[35]

Since it had been part of Kartosuwirjo`s prominent abilities to adapt himself as well as his movement always immediately to new develpments, the reorganizing undertaken by him had certianly been a reaction to the return to the constitution of 1945 accounced by Sukarno in July 1959.

When, because of the military operations initiated against his movement, the defeat baceme evident in June 1961 the "command for total warfare" had been given. However, the motive assigned by

Kartosuwirjo for it had not been given, and the command had not been signed by Kartosuwirjo, but by Taruna, one of his privat secretaries. In this command a "multitude of genocide of the whole traitorous people" as well as the burning down of all buildings had been ordered.[36]

When on June 4, 1962, Kartosuwirjo has been captured by a unit of the Siliwangi Division in the mountain jungle of Gunung Geber, he has been in such a bad healthy condition that he had to be carried off on a stretcher. Even the appeal to his supporters to lay down the weapons had to be dictated by him to his son Darda.

With that Kartosuwirjo`s fight of almost 13 years for an Islamic State had come to an end. In West Java it had caused 11.500 casualities on the side of the civilian population, and had led to a rural exodus of over 1 million people to the cities.[37]

In one of the hearings after his capture Kartosuwirjo stated that he intended to concentrate his Mujahidin in one veteran legion, and he agreed to indoctrinate his supporters in the sense of the Manipol USDEK. However, it had been required that the faith in the sole God would be in the first place. Even Pancasila was now accepted by him as basis for the state, since hr had seen that in the Nasakom communism had been in the third place. Kartosuwirjo now described the conflicts with TNI as "incident".[38]

As reason for the durability of his movement, Kartosuwirjo mentioned the loyalty of his fellows towards him as well as the ability of each one to integrate in the community. He only partially pleaded himself responsible for the crimes by his movement. He could not be made responsible for "each chicken which had been stolen by the Mujahidin"; according to Kartosuwirjo his responsibility had only be restricted to organizational concerns. He admitted to have proclaimed the Negara Islam Indonesia and to have operated with his units against the TNI. However, he denied to have given the command for "total warfare" and for the assassination of President Sukarno.

After the announcement of the death sentence by the military court Kartosuwirjo made a petition for mercy to Sukarno by regretting all his actions undertaken in the past and by stating that he would be in a position to live in the Pancasila as "decent Indonesian citizen".[39]

President Sukarno, however, refused this petition for mercy since ther "had been no reason to comply with the petition". In a will comprising four parts which had been addressed to his family, his supporters as well as to the Indonesian Government, Kartosuwirjo stated that he always acted as Imam and supreme commander of the armed forces of the Negara Islam Indonesia and that all his actions had been based on the orders of Allah and the Sunnah of the prophet. He had been convinced that the ideals of Islam would once be realized in Indonesia, although there would always be forces which would succeed in preventing this.

Early in the morning of September 5, 1962, the death sentence of Kartosuwirjo had been carried out on an island in the Bay of Jakarta - the name of which had been kept secret.

Kartosuwirjo, who used the situation which had arisen by the Renville Agreement to realize his vision of the establishment of an Islamic state, however, never intended to restrict this state on West Java only, he wanted it realized in the whole of Indonesia. So, all statements and communiqués of the Negara Islam Indonesia and even the correspondence of the TII commanders, since most of them mainly belonged to the Sundanese population, were written almost exclusively in Indonesian.

Kartosuwirjo, however, had made the mistake to consider the demand of a minority to establish an Islamic State as desire of the majority of the Indonesian Moslems. Many of the former members of the Darul-Islam-Movement had been affected by the amnesty law in 1963, and after the events of September 30, 1965, some of them had been recruited by the VI Regional Military Command of the Siliwangi as adviser during the suppression of the communist putsch.[40]

Still in October 1970 Danu Mohammad Hasan, Zainoel Abidin, Ateng Djaelani Setiawan and Kartosuwirjo`s son Tachmid Rahmat had signed a common declaration in which they had confirmed their loyalty to the constitution.[41] In 1977, however, had been indications for a reviving of the Darul-Islam-Movement, and in march 1978 members of a "Jihad Command" had to go on trial against whom had been held a hearing because of the attempts in Medan and Padang which had been executed by them at the end of 1976. In the middle of 1978 the security authorities had again searched for Kartosuwirjo`s former fellows in the fight, Adah Djaelani, Ateng, Kurnia, Toha Mahfud and his sons Dodo Muh, Darda and Tachmid Rahmat.[42] At the end of March 1981 a plane of the national airline Garuda had been hijacked. Some weeks before an assault on the Cicendo police station in Bandung, the province Capital of West Java, had taken place. By means of the hijacking the hijackers had intended to get their political friends released who had been imprisoned because of the assault on the police station. In both cases Islamic extremists had been said to have been among the delinquents, whereby a certain Imran had been said to be the ringleader. The trials against the participants had still started before the general elections of 1982 and had lasted until the following year. Early in 1983 another trial had been initiated against 10 members of a successor organization of the Darul-Islam-Movement, among them many who had already fought under Kartosuwirjo. They had been blamed for establishing an underground movement the objective of which had been to found an Islamic state. According to testimonies of witnesses the organizational structure of the movement had been based on the guide book "Pedoman Dharma Bakti" drawn up by Kartosuwirjo.[43] Many Indonesian Moslems however do not want to believe that this extremistic activities had been made in the name of Islam but they assumed that all was staged to discredite political Islam.

With regard to former members of the Darul-Islam-Movement in West Java, South Sulawesi or Aceh, who are still living, obvious differences concerning their personal situation and their authority can be noticed depending on the region. So former Darul-Islam members in West Java who are today respected citizens do not want to get reminded of the past, and they do not want to have their names mentioned in connection with the Darul-Islam-Movement. Others live in poor conditions or are being arrested like Kartosuwirjo`s sons. In contrast to that, members of the family of Kahar Muzakkar, who participated in Kartosuwirjo`s movement at the beginning of the 50s, are now respected citizens in South Sulawesi. Also Daud Beureueh in Aceh, who attained the age of 91[44] and who had been - under Kartosuwirjo - commander of the "war command of the greater region Aceh", and who had surrendered to the authorities only in April 1962, after the Islamic law had come into forde in Aceh, still today enjoys great esteem. So one of his sons had been member of the parliamentary fraction Karya Pembangunan in the Indonesian Parliament, and one of his sons-in-law, a high-rank military, has participated in the election campaign of Golkar for the general elections in 1987. Still in March 1986 Daud Beureueh had submitted a message to President Suharto, in which he called upon President Suharto not to tend to "the left" and to lead state and people in a just way[45] Some of the former heads of the Darul-Islam-Movement have gone abroad like the leader of the Darul-Islam-Movement in Central Java, Amir Fatah, who now lives in South Korea.

Islam and Politics in Contemporary Indonesia:

The restrengthening of Islam, which is most evident in the entire Islamic world today has undoubtedly not stopped aat the frontiers of Indonesia. As the Islamization of Indonesia proceeds further it is beginning to affect also those Muslims who have so far been Muslims in name only but not in religious practice. They adhere now more strictly to the injunctions and customs of Islam. In the younger generation a similar development can be noticed mainly because, since the "old order" religious instruction has been intensified in the schools. This is in accordance with the wishes of the government who, through this development, hopes to build up a bulwork against possible future left-oriented uprisings.

The revival of Islam is most obvious in the capital city of Jakarta, where more and more women and girls wrap themselves up in chaste Islamic clothes which, only a few years ago were a rare sight. The Mosques are no longer able to accomodate the large number of believers during Friday`s prayers and at the bookmarket it has now become commonplace that books with Islamic themes almost automatically become best-sellers.

However, one cannot say with certainly that this new resurgence of Islam will grow stronger or even continue in the future because, if the masses should decide to direct their hopes for a better future through other, more attractive channels and should the government, for reasons of expediency tolerate this, there may be a reversal of the present trend. A well-known Indonesian professor of Psychology termed the religious mania of the past years as "Pseudoreligiosity".

The government supports the demands of the Muslims however, only as long as they concern themselves solely with religious matters. In Indonesia, for example gambling has been forbidden for a number of years; in the province of West Sumatra the sale of alcohol has been disallowed since 1986. In the special region of Jakarta the intermarriage of Muslims with other religious denominations has been made impossible and the latest prohibition affects the advertising of womens underwear.

The greatest fear of the government besides a revival of communism, is the growth of political Islam. It is therefore completely inflexible with regard to political demands, such as the establishment of an Islamic state. Under no circumstances is it willing to compromise and has precluded from the very beginning any development in this direction, which it will resist if necessary by force. The Darul-Islam movement of Kartosuwirjo is still regarded as a dangerous precedent for this kind of development.

However, it has shown itself in the past that whenever the Islamic side is in fear of being suppressed by the government the result may be outbursts of protest actions or even riots. In 1984 in the wake of the forthcoming general elections all political parties and massorganisations were obliged to accept the state philosophy Pancasila as their basic philosophy (asas tunggal). This means that the PPP could not openly claim to be based on Islam.

In September 1984 the bloody riots in the Jakarta suburb of Tanjung Priok took place, followed by burnings and bombings, most spectacular of all the attack on the 1100 years old Buddhist temple of Borobudur. Also during the course of 1984 the tension within the United Development Party PPP increased, the latter being a Muslim political coalition representing four Muslim organisations, the Nahdlatul Ulama (NU), Sarikat Islam (SI),

Perti and Muslimin Indonesia (MI). Around the end of the year the NU, the largest of the four Muslim organisations left the PPP in order to put the aims of the 1926 programme (Khittah 1926) into practice and in the future to dedicate itself only to social, reglious and educational activities.

The withdrawal of the NU from the PPP was the climax of a growing dissatisfaction in the NU since 1981 with the party leadership above all with the chairman J. Naro who had started his political career with the action front of Indonesian scientist KASI and as a parliamentary member of Golkar.

The NU felt betrayed since its representation in parliament underrepresented its actual strength. What increased their anger was the fact that the party leader Naro placed only his close supporters from among the MI in leadership positions, and also dissolved the Majelis Syuro in which the NU had played a major role. In the wake of the forthcoming general election the NU advised its followers to vote, not for the PPP but for Golkar or the Indonesian Democratic Party PDI. The results of the election showed that this advice was heeded since Golkar received 73,16% of the votes and the PDI 10,86%.[46] Together their votes increased by 11,80% as compared to the previous election while the PPP which got 15,96% of the vote suffered a drop of 11,82%. The number of non-voters and voters who cast invalid votes, amounting to 8,1 million was especially high and was interpreted as a sign that the number of "Golput" and "Golka" voters had increased.[47]

A preliminary analysis of the behaviour of voters revealed that approx. 4,7% of the followers of the NU gave their votes to the PDI, while the remaining votes, in equal parts of 31,7% went to the PPP, Golkar and Golput.[48] Most surprising of all was the increase in votes for the PDI - particularly in the slums of big cities which had formerly been a stronghold of the PPP. In this way the PPP in Jakarta and Bandung pushed into third place.

The PDI owes a great deal of its increase in support to the 11 million young voters who went to the polls for the first time and did not disguise their sympathy for the PDI. A new phenomenon at PDI party rallies was the huge amount of Sukarno posters brought along by youngsters - among them sons and daughters of high government officials - and the loud cheers for Sukarno. This could not have been possible without the silent toleration of the authorities. The rediscovery of Sukarno as an idol by the young people however, does not necessarily imply a revival of the teachings of Sukarno, it should rather be interpreted as a protest attitude. However, the bad result for the PPP does necessarily imply a weakening of Islam because the NU, which once knew how to get along with the politics of Sukarno now intends to achieve its goals mainly via Golkar in order to have a greater influence on the political scene and to solve the future clashes of opinion informally, as was the case with the matrimonial laws in 1973. Many former parliamentary members of the NU are now openly declaring their intention to join Golkar or the PDI. For Golkar in the long run this would mean having to deal with the religious demands of the Muslims, especially since the NU was so successfully in their attempt to weaken the PPP, the so-called "aksi pengempisan".

Besides this there is the added danger of an internal struggle within Golkar on one side the forces who wish to see their Islamic aspirations realised and on the other those who wish to block such a development.

Indonesia with over 142 million Muslims, about 88% of the entire population, is the largest Islamic country in the world and the Indonesians on the whole are still considered to be the most tolerant Muslims in the world. However, one should bear in mind that Islam and Politics cannot be separated or as a speaker of the Nahdlatul Ulama at a party rally in Surabaya once put it "if one could separate sugar from its sweetness then one could also separate Islam and Politics".[49]

References

[1] See the author`s thesis, Darul Islam: Kartosuwirjos Kampf um einen islamischen Staat Indonesien. Wiesbaden 1986, p. 168.

[2] Cf. Landjoetan sedjarah goenoeng Tjoepoe. Samboengan Djilid I. (Continuation of Volume I of the history of Gunung Cupu) Cisayong 1948, pp. 38 ff.

[3] Cf. Salinan Pedoman Dharma Bakti. Djilid II. Menggalang Negara Kurniah Allah - Negara Islam Indonesia. (Transcript of the handbook of loyal obligations. Volume II. The establishing of the

State of God`s grace, the Islamic State of Indonesia). Oleh: Karma Yoga. Tjetakan kelima, 25. Mei 1955. Bandung, SUDAM I KODAM SILIWANGI, 1960, p. 278 f.

[4] See Fadjar Asia, 27.4.1929.

[5] See Fadjar Asia, 29.1.1929.

[6] See Fadjar Asia, 17.6.1929.

[7] See Fadjar Asia, 2.7.1929.

[8] Cf. S.M. Kartosuwirjo, Daftar Oesaha Hidjrah PSII (The Hijra action programme of PSII). Bagian Moeqoddimah. Tjetakan pertama. Malanogong: Penerbit Poestaka Da-roel Islam, 1940, p. 21.

[9] Ibid, p. 5 f.

[10] See Soeara PSII II, number 9, 1938, p. 156.

[11] Cf. Komando Daerah Militer VI Siliwangi, Team Pemeriksa. Berita Atjara Interogasi III, Bandung 20.6.1962, p. 2. (Record of inquiry III)

[12] See Indonesia Merdeka I, number 1, 25.4.2605, p. 6.

[13] Cf. Sedjarah goenoeng Tjoepoe. (The story of Gunung Cupu). Djilid I. Cisayong 1948, p. 45.

[14] See Algemene Secretarie te Batavia, September 1952, 2e zending. Kist 1 - 620 Darul Islam en Tan Malaka aanhang.

[15] Cf. Landjoetan sedjarah goenoeng tjoepoe..., p. 14.

[16] Ibid, p. 38 ff. The respective "Ministries" had been: Madjlis Penerangan (Information) under Toha Arsjad, Madjlis Keuangan (Finances) under S. Partawidjaja, Madjlis Kehakiman (Justice) under Gozali Tusi, the former leader of the Masjumi Office in Jakarta, Madjlis Pertahanan (Defence) under S.M. Kartosuwirjo and Madjlis Dalam Negeri (Domestic Politics) under S. Partawidjaja.

[17] Cf. Landjoetan sedjarah goenoeng Tjoepoe..., p. 46.

[18] For the text of Kartosuwirjo`s letter see the author`s thesis Darul Islam: Kartosuwirjos Kampf, ..., p. 190.

[19] Cf. Salinan Pedoman Dharma Bakti..., vol. I, p. 12 ff.

[20] Ibid.

[21] Cf. Salinan Pedoman Dharma Bakti..., vol. II, P. 292.

[22] See Tempo XV, number 43, 21.12.1985, p. 13-14.

[23] Cf. Salinan Pedoman Dharma Bakti..., vol. II, Manifest Politik Negara Islam Indonesia no. I/7, p. 199.

[24] Cf. Salinan Pedoman Dharma Bakti..., vol. I, pp. 178-182.

[25] Ibid.

[26] Cf. Salinan Pedoman Dharma Bakti..., vol. II, p. 292.

[27] Interview with Muh. Natsir, Jakarta, June 1983.

[28] Cf. Salinan Pedoman Dharma Bakti..., vol. II, Nota Rahasia 22.10.1950. (secret note dated October 22, 1950.

[29] Cf. Buku sejarah dokumenter. Buku induk ke I. Jilid II bab V. (A-B-C). Gerakan penumpasan pemberontakan DI-TII S.M. Kartosuwirjo. Disusun oleh Suyono. (Historical documentary book concerning the suppression of S.M. Kartosuwirjo`s DI-TIII revolt)

[30] Cf. Salinan Pedoman Dharma Bakti..., vol. I, pp. 19-22.

[31] A. Ridhwan, Keterangan tertuduh tertulis. (Written statement by the defendant). Bandung: Mei 1953.

[32] Cf. Komando Daerah Militer VI Siliwangi, Team Pemeriksa. Berita Atjara Interogasi I, Bandung 16.6.1962, p. 8. (Record of the hearing)

[33] Cf. Komando Daerah Militer VI Siliwangi, Team Pemeriksa. Berita Atjara Interogasi I, Bandung 16.6.1962, p. 8. (Record of the hearing)

[34] Cf. Salinan Pedoman Dharma Bakti..., vol. I, p. 128.

[35] Ibid, p. 148.

[36] Cf. Departemen Angkatan Darat, Inspektorat Kehakiman, Mahkamah Angkatan Darat Dalam Keadaan Perang Untuk Djawa Da Madura. Berkas Perkara No.X/III/1962 atas nama Sekarmadji Maridjan Kartosuwirjo, p. 23-24. (File of documents of case No. x/III/1962 with the name S.M. Kartosuwirjo)

[37] With regard to the indormation on the losses of the population see the author`s thesis, Darul Islam: Kartosuwirjos Kampf..., p. 121.

[38] Cf. Komando Daerah Militer VI Siliwangi, Team Pemeriksa. Berita Atjara Interogasi V, Bandung 25.6.1962, p. 8. (Record of hearing)

[39] Cf. Mahkamah Angkatan Darat Dalam Keadaan Perang Untuk Djawa Dan Madura. Berkas Perkara No. X/III/8/1962 atas nama tertuduh sekarmadji Maridjan Kartosuwirjo "Imam/Panglima Tertinggi Negara Islam Indonesia", Kepala Pemberontak Gerombolan Kartosu wirjo jang menurut keputusan MAHADPER Djawa dan Madura No.Kpts. X/III/8/1962 telah dihukum dengan HUKUMAN Mati, p. 212. (File of documents of case No. x/III/8/1962 with the name S.M. Kartosuwirjo, "Imam/Supreme Commander of the Negara Islam Indonesia", rebel-leader of the Kartosuwirjo gang, who had according to resolution No. x/III/8/1962 of the army court martial for Java and Madura, been sentenced to death)

[40] See Tempo XII, no. 51, 1983, p. 24. Since April 1985, the VI Regional Military Command became the III Regional Military Command.

[41] Cf. Siliwangi dari masa ke masa. (The Siliwangi in the course of time). Disusun oleh DISJARAHDAM/Siliwangi. 2nd ed. Bandung: Angkasa, 1979, p. 760.

[42] See Tempo VIII, no. 38, 1978, p. 26.

[43] See Kompas 24.2.1983.

[44] Daud Beureueh died on June 17, 1987 and was buried in the grounds of Masjid Baitul A`la lil-Mujahidin in Kota Sigli.

[45] See Tempo XVI, No. 4, 1986, p. 15-16.

[46] Final election results of the Lembaga Pemilihan Umum (LPU) from June 6, 1987.

[47] See Kompas 30.4.1987. Non-voters in Indonesia are called "Golput" (Golongan putih) and those voters who cast invalid votes are called "Golka" (Golongan kabeh). Kabeh in Javanese means "all", thus "Golka" means voters who vote for all contestants.

[48] See Tempo XVII, No. 9, 1987, p. 30.

[49] Cf. Z.A. Achmad, Membentuk negara Islam. (The creation of an Islamic state) Jakarta: Widjaja 1956, p. 6.

Bibliography

Ahmad, Z.A., Membentuk negara Islam (The formation of an Islamic State) Jakarta: Widjaja, 1956

Algemene Secretarie te Batavia, September 1952, 2e zending Kist 1 - 620 Darul Islam en Tan Malaka aanhang.

Buku sejarah dokumenter. Buku induk ke I. Jilid II bab V. (A-B-C) Gerakan penumpasan pemberontakan DI-TII S.M. Kartosuwirjo. Disusun oleh Suyono. (Historical documentary book concerning the suppression of S.M. Kartosuwirjo`s DI-TII revolt) Bandung: Dinas Sejarah Militer, 1975

Dengel, Holk Harald, Darul Islam: Kartosuwirjos Kampf um einen islamischen Staat Indonesien. Wiesbaden, 1986

Departemen Angkatan Darat, Inspektorat Kehakiman, Mahkamah Angkatan Darat Dalam Keadaan Perang Untuk Djawa Dan Madura. Berkas Perkara no. X/III/1962 atas nama Sekarmadji Maridjan Kartosuwirjo. (File of documents of case no. X/III 1962 with the name S.M. Kartosuwirjo)

Kartosuwirjo, S.M., Daftar Oesaha Hidjrah PSII. (The Hijra action programme of the PSII) Bagian Moeqoddimah. Tjetakan pertama. Malangbong: Penerbit Poestaka Da-roel Islam 1940

Komando Daerah Militer VI Siliwangi, Team Pemeriksa.
Berita Atjara Interogasi I, Bandung 16.6.1962
Berita Atjara Interogasi III, Bandung 20.6.1962

Berita Atjara Interogasi IV, Bandung 24.6.1962
Berita Atjara Interogasi V, Bandung 25.6.1962
(Records of the hearing)

Landjoetan Sedjarah Goenoeng Tjoepoe. Samboengan djilid I. (Continuation of volume I of the history of Gunung Cupu) Cisayong, 1948

Mahkamah Angkatan Darat Dalam Keadaan Perang Untuk Djawa Dan Madura. Berkas Perkara No. X/III/8/1962 atas nama tertuduh Sekarmadji Maridjan Kartosuwirjo "Imam/Panglima Tertinggi Negara Islam Indonesia", Kepala Pemberontak Gerombolan Kartosuwirjo jang menurut keputusan MAHADPER Djawa dan Madura No. Kpts. X/III/8/1962 telah dihukum dengan HUKUMAN MATI. (File of documents of case No. x/III/8/1962 with the name S.M. Kartosuwirjo, "Imam/Supreme Commander of the Negar Islam Indonesia", rebel-leader of the Kartosuwirjo gang, who had, according to resolution No. X/III/8/1962 of the army court martial for Java and Madura, been sentenced to death)

Ridhwan, A., Keterangan tertuduh tertulis. (Written Statement by the defendant)

Salinan Pedoman Dharma Bakti. Djilid I-II. Menggalang Negara Kurniah Allah - Negara Islam Indonesia (Transcript of the handbook of loyal obligations. Vol. I-II. The establishing of the State of God`s grace, the Islamic State of Indonesia)
Oleh: Karma Yoaga. Tjetakan kelima, 15. Mei 1955. Bandung: SUDAM I KODAM Siliwangi, 1960.

Sedjarah Goenoeng Tjoepoe. (The history of Gunung Cupu) Djilid I. Cisayong, 1948

Siliwangi dari masa ke masa (The Siliwangi in the course of time) Disusun oleh DISJARAHDAM / Siliwangi. Edisi ke 2 Bandung: Angkasa, 1979

For a Sociology of India: "Tribe" and "Caste" reconsidered

by Margit Urhahn

A critical review of different anthropological approaches to the tribe-caste question and a new perspective on transformations of Indian culture and society.

I. INTRODUCTION

The paper [1] represents a study of tribe-caste relationship in Indian civilization (culture and society) as a contribution to the understanding of its specific configuration, emergence and historical transformations, the latter being determined in their dynamic by this very configuration itself. A methodological prerequisite seems to be - as will be shown - structural understanding before genetical explanation. It gives a review of different views of the tribe-caste relationship, i.e. of different anthropological approaches to the question, and it consists of a short exposition of the ethnographic basis, an outline of the theoretical and methological background of the respective authors and a critical evaluation of these most varied interpretations of almost the same empirical, ethnographic material. Thus, it can be shown how "the choice of a particular field of investigation, the choice of a given range of concepts with which to investigate the field, all express assumptions about the nature of society and about what is theoretically significant and what is not".[1a] Related to this is the general problem of defini-tions in anthropology, the translation of alien terms into the language of the researcher and cross-cultural comparison. "Tribe" and "caste" well illustrate this point in the different approaches reviewed and the respective solutions reached.

The approaches are : historical explanations (hinduization, sanskritization, rajputization); "neo"-evolutionist explanation (M. KLASS on the origins of the caste system from a tribal base); "sociological", structural-functional approach (F.G. BAILEY on change in tribal society and its integration into caste society); an atomistic composition of evolutionary, historical and structural-functional approaches (S.C. SINHA`s different perspectives on "Tribes and Indian Civilization"); structuralist approach (G. PFEFFER on the ideology/collective representations of the tribal societies of Middle India in an overall comparative framework of Indian kinship systems).

A summary of the knowledge of the fragmented research and literature of social anthropologists on this problem (except works on recent, modern developments in Indian tribes and caste society) and the critical insights into the adequacy of the respective explanations could be the starting-point for future inquiry and for new reflections in the light of recent theoretical discussions in Social Anthropology (e.g. a new practice approach) and help to transcend the older approaches in order to arrive at a new level of understanding. Thus, this review should make it possible:

- to embark on further, more substantial explorations into the ethnography of Indian tribes - a postulate that SINHA already made long ago - and its re-interpretation.[2] Here I would like to stress that, in spite of a strong emphasis on theory in this review, the indispensable basis for interpretation and understanding of an alien world is detailed empirical material, i.e ethnography

- to synthesize different theoretical approaches into an integrated framework, an "ecology of explanations", recognizing a hierarchy of analytical levels instead of a shapeless exlecticism or an atomistic composition of the most diverse approaches. It seems more likely to reach a deeper understanding of questions of social evolution and history, of social and cultural change, of the interrelation between ideological-religious and techno-economic spheres of different societies and cultures and the respective ideological transformation of this interrelation.

In sum, the task ahead for social anthropologists and historians of India is to distinguish the levels of continuity and discontinuity in the emergence and development of Indian civilization and to analyze the interplay of systems of ideas and systems of action, of structure and historical process. And here the tribe-caste question, the comparison of their respective social order and the analysis of their interaction, is of central importance. It is part and parcel of the theoretical debate on a "sociology of India", focus of the journal "Contributions to Indian sociology".

From the theoretical and methological point of view my paper wants to emphasize the necessity of fundamental research in Social Anthropology, based on detailed, culture-specific ethnography, by clearing the ground for a generally accepted corpus of definitions and concepts, for an consensus on the conceptual apparatus of the discipline. This - and the building of an integrated framework - is without doubt a difficult and complex task which cannot be carried out without communication with and cooperation of all scholars concerned. But for the time being that seems to be utopia considering the present situation of the scientific community, based as it is on competition and narrow egoistic and egotistic interests of the scholars and the disciplines, the "Schools" or political affiliations with their often destructive polemics against each other. I would like to hope to inspire and motivate at least some scholars to embark on this cooperative interdisciplinary task. It is my belief that within such a framework in which single and very specific questions and problems could be analyzed in a division of labour, individual interests, personal predilections and inclinations would be not al all ruled out, nor are mutual criticism, controversies and openess towards modification, correction and even revision as we go on learning. And such a work would also require self-criticism and self-relativization, reflecting one`s own theoretical bias and social and cultural situation.

II. THE ANTHROPOLOGICAL STUDY OF INDIAN CIVILIZATION

"The distinction in Indian society between tribal people and caste people has been a problem not only - or indeed, not primarily - for sociologists, but it has rather been the concern of the administrators and the politicians. ...Most recently the editors of CONTRIBUTIONS TO INDIA SOCIOLOGY have given notice, so to speak, that they will raise the question again, since the distinction is of relevance to their postulate that "India is one" (Bailey 1961:7). This quotation touches upon a general controversy of fundamental relevance, namely a dichotomy between pure and applied sociological/anthropological research, the first serving the theoretical interests of the academics and the second the political and administrative interests of governments and other political organs. That especially the Indian research in Social Anthropology is and was ever since colonial times orientated towards the pragmatic, administrative and political side and that the corresponding theoretical and methological strategies were directed towards this goal - "Anglo-American empiricism, structural functionalism, pragmatism" and "historicism" - is pointed out by KHARE (1978) and UBEROI (1974) who therefore advocate structuralist studies as a more satisfactory alternative with a deeper explanatory power.

The study of tribe-caste relationship in Indian society is part of the trend among anthropologists to turn to more complex social and cultural systems, in contrast to the concentration on isolated, "homogeneous" tribal societies or villages which was a feature of anthropological studies in India, too, during the first half of the 20th century. It seems appropriate here to recapitulate briefly some of the main views on the structure of Indian civilization and to hint at certain problems of methodology.[3]

The initiative for the comparative study of civilizations (India, China, Islamic world etc.) and the anthropological study of the "cultural pattern of Indian Civilization", in particular, with the methodologically relevant problem of "unity" and "diversity" came from American Cultural Anthropology at the University of Chicago in the fifties under the guidance of REDFIELD, SINGER and MARRIOTT. They developed for India their influential concepts of "primary or indigenous civilization", "Great and Little Tradition" and "universalization and parochialization" (as the process of interaction of both traditions). Later, SRINIVAS added the concept of "Sanskritization" which gave an impetus to studies of mobility and social change in Indian caste society. The central problem was to grasp the totality of the civilization intellectually, "in its full historic and geographic sweep" in relation to, or better, based on the phenomena observed in fieldwork in restricted regional and local settings which reflected the manifold variability of the whole subcontinent; these ethnographic data had to be combined with the findings of indologists and historians from textual sources.

Mention should here also be made of the Orissa Research Project and the following current research work of single scholars at the South Asia

Institute with the interdisciplinary approach to a regional tradition of India, namely that of Orissa. The hitherto "dark ages" of Indian medieval history when the emergence of such regional traditions through the mutual influence and interaction of various levels contributed to the cultural diversity and new sociopolitical structures, are an important field of cooperation between anthropologists and historians. And - in the absence of reliable historical sources for the social and political development of the tribal areas in those times - it is to anthropology that the main task accrues of giving some orientation towards deeper understanding by a detailed analysis of tribal social organization and ideology. "A sociological perspective can orientate historical research" (Bouglé) - this is implied in SINHA`s, PFEFFER`s and DUMONT`s views.

Finally, in a unique and illuminating attempt, DUMONT made his contribution to the adaptation of the discipline of Social Anthropology - combining it with Indology - to the study of the Indian civilization in his book "Home Hierarchicus" and worked out a global, unified picture ("India is one") of its traditional organization. His approach is structural, going beyond the empiricist solutions of the above mentioned American cultural anthropologists and providing a framework and inspiration for further studies of more specific and detailed questions. Thus, his methodological answer is the statement of "unity on the level of ideas", diversity on the level of phenomena". This view emerges from his basic global and comparative approach contrasting India against the Western, modern civilization as the background of the researcher, consideration of the latter being a fundamental epistemological postulate in his understanding of the task of social anthropology or comparative sociology. As will be shown later, his insights - together with PFEFFER`s work on the tribal side - should be the starting point for further detailed study of the intra-cultural level of Indian society with its differentiations, proceeding from the global ideology of caste society and that of the Adivasi. YALMAN, in judging DUMONT`s interpretation of Indian caste society as "more in the nature of a fresh challenge than a full scale analysis", rightly says: "It is true that he has alerted us to the issue but has not given us a treatise on it. The basic problem in the analysis of society remains the interplay between systems of ideas and systems of actions" (Yalman, 1969:124). Rethinking the historical process and human practice as embedded in specific and diverse cultural contexts and admitting the all-pervasive significance of culture are its implications, and a central concern of anthropology. The starting-point - methodologically - for the understanding of the specific development of a civilization would be the analysis of its fundamental ideological structure (structural understanding) before looking at and explaining its actualization with all concomitant inconsistencies and contradictions in historical movements (genetical explanation) and the differentiation of ideology itself.

Finally, MAX WEBER`s comparative study of the sociology of religions, in particular his work on Hinduism and Buddhism, should not be left unmentioned. In the course of a Weber renaissance today, his ideas are being reflected upon once more and newly applied, where necessary in a modified form, within the discipline of South Asian studies.[4]

III. THE PROBLEM OF DEFINITION: "TRIBE" AND "CASTE"

What is a tribe? What is caste? At the very beginning of a scientific work it is usual to give definitions of terms that are central to the analysis. As RADCLIFFE-BROWN rightly said, "there is very little agreement among anthropologists in the concepts and terms they use"; thus, his, as of most anthropologists`, set of definitions is "an exposition of one particular theory, not of a commonly accepted theory". The problem of definitions in anthropology is a specific one since the discipline deals with social and cultural phenomena in different societies and cultures which are not simply facts as in the natural sciences but also "consciousness of things", i.e. there must be a mediation between subjective and objective view. Even if nowadays "the need is recognized at least to distinguish clearly between the categories of thought at the level of ethnography...and the analytical concepts of the discipline" (Pitt-Rivers), the "science" anthropology is still in its infancy as regards its fundamental conceptual apparatus. DUMONT criticizes a superficial sociology that, for instance, presumes the term "caste" to be clear and well-known without coming to a real understanding of the phenomenon by analyzing the total social context in its particularity and applying instead our preconceived and sociocentric categories. Terms cannot be defined as substances in themselves, they are part and parcel of a total structure of an ideology or an scientific theory.

In the attempt to define "tribe" and "caste" in India we can pursue the etymological and semantic history of these terms and see how they are, for the most part, used in the popular, common-sense connotations. The first and fundamental task of anthropology as a comparative discipline is therefore - as postulated by MAUSS for the first time - to make an inventory of all categories and modes of thought of all cultures so as to be able ultimately to define them in terms of their structure and ideological context.

The discussion of the concept of "tribe" among anthropologists[5] was the expression of a crisis in the fundamental orientation of the discipline, namely its empiricism (Godelier). Used as a common-sense term or simply avoided, "tribe" was considered the most meaningless word in the anthropological vocabulary from the point of analytical value (Fried). The only solution of the definition problem for the iridescent and variable social phenomena is to use a term as a mere provisional label for establishing the initial framework of communication and discussion before reaching more precise and unequivocal categories of analysis (Southall).

Such an agreement is necessary in the Indian context, too, since the term tribe has never been defined precisely or satisfactorily, nor, it should be added, can it be on empiricist criteria. There are two problems: first, on the one hand, the attempt at an anthropological definition, and on the other, the designation of "Scheduled Tribes" by the Government of India for administrative and political purposes (protective discrimination) according to ever changing criteria; secondly, there are the castes and the question is how to distinguish one from the other. What today is by some people called "caste", was yesterday by other people called "tribe" or vice versa. The relativity of defining the phenonemon is thus obvious. Two different ways of classification collide here. According to the tribes` own designation of themselves - as everywhere in the world - they as a group are "men, human beings" while the others are aliens, even "non-men", outside the own social universe. The Santal, Munda or Gond of Central India, for instance, call themselves hor, kol or koitor, respectively. On the other hand, the designations given to the tribes by outsiders, the neighbouring groups, administrators or ethnographers vary enormously and the consequence in the Central Indian tribal belt is an almost impenetrable confusion of designations for tribes or tribal segments. The problem of classification and designation had posed itself to the administrators for the Census of India during British colonial rule. But they, just like the first ethnographers and professional ethnologists later on, had difficulties to make out definite criteria for their distinction of tribes and castes: criteria of geographical isolation, animistic religion, own language, economic backwardness, segmentary political organization would hold for tribes as well as for castes.

Likewise, the definition of caste is problematic, and its changeableness is nicely seen to correspond to the respective historical and theoretical standpoint of the one defining.[6] From atomistic descriptions of single castes - sometimes collected together alphabetically as in the columns of a dictionary - with their specific cultural traits to insight into the general characteristics of the caste system and their systematic interrelatedness (endogamy, separation, professional specialization, concept of purity/pollution) the way leads to DUMONT`s structuralist interpretation of traditional caste society from a theoretical comparative view. Essential are his general proposals for a sociology of India, hereby touching on fundamental questions of method and epistemology and giving an impetus to a new direction of basic anthropological research. As DUMONT`s work and the controversies around it are doubtless well known to the specialists on India, only a few points should be mentioned which are of relevance here.

First, concentrating on the caste system, he excluded the tribal population since for him "the most so-called 'primitives` of India are only people who lost contact", and postulated the fundamental homogeneity of Indian civilization - "India is one" - without analyzing this assertion with regard to the tribal groups. This omission is rightly criticized, and the task was taken over by PFEFFER in his analysis of tribal societies of Central India from the same point of view of their ideology (fundamental ideas and values) as compared with Hindu caste society.

Secondly, DUMONT`s global orientation as "a first step", "singling out the all-embracing or predominant ideology as essential to the sociologist" (Dumont) and his central epistemological perspective of mediation between us and the other in which the observer along with his sociocultural background is not excluded from consideration, but on the contrary, is maintained at its core will be accepted as the starting-point for the intra-cultural analysis of Indian society with its internal differentiations in space and time and the corresponding question of interplay between ideology and empirical, "hard facts" and of history. Modifications and corrections may be necessitated by the data and, as DUMONT himself admitted, "the subject is still in its infancy. ...No development is ruled out, ...other themes might be introduced in course of time".

According to DUMONT religion is the central value of caste society and the politico-economic domain is "encompassed", i.e. the economic is not the paramount ideology as in modern western societies. Herein, we can make out a continuity between the Adivasi world view and Hindu caste ideology, an archaic tribal society and a traditional civilization.

IV. HISTORICAL EXPLANATIONS

Anthropologists coined and elaborated the concepts of "Hinduization", "Sanskritization" and "Rajputization" (or "Kshatriyaization") to describe and explain the cultural and social dynamics of Indian caste society and the acculturation and integration of tribal groups into the caste system. In the 1950s and 1960s Sanskritization and Rajputization became prominent in anthropological discussion and also among some indologists and historians of India, while the term "Hinduization" had already appeared in the writings of the early administrators (e.g. H. Risley) and ethnographers (S.C. Roy, N.K. Bose) who by this term designated the process of acculturation, of cultural and social changes among tribes or segments of tribes through their contact with caste Hindus. The process of "gradual elevation from a despised aboriginal tribe to a respectable Hindu caste" was seen as a familiar phenomenon in India, differing according to region or historical time. The division of tribes into a Hinduized section (the prefix "Raj" is added to the tribal name, e.g. Raj Gond, Raj Bhuiya etc.), living predominantly in the plains and in closer contact with the caste Hindus from whom they adopted religious rites, beliefs and social customs and a tribal section living in the more remote hills and forests and retaining their original religion, culture and social customs, seemingly accounts for the uneven acculturative process.

RISLEY (1915) and ROY (1937, 1938) described in detail changes in the tribal groups with respect to their social organization, religion, customs and economy in all their multiplicity throughout time and space. Three aspects were considered as crucial: a religious aspect, i.e. the role of brahmins and Hindu sects in the transmission of new religious contents and symbols; a political and economic aspect of the ascent of tribal chiefs and Hindu rajas emerging from tribal aristocracy and a social organization aspect, i.e. changes in marriage regulations and alliances - the "adoption" of endogamy, attributed as a fundamental characteristic to caste.

A systematic conceptualization of these aspects in their interrelation was not undertaken by these early ethnographers; they remained almost completely at the level of empirical description, only occasionally attempting some explanations ethnocentrically biased and coloured by the spirit of their time. But their ethnographic material remained an important basis for later studies. Especially ROY`s work on the Bhuiyas (1937) and the Kharias (1938) is full of valuable detailed ethnography which could be used for a re-interpretation. All the above-mentioned aspects were taken up again and again in descriptions by SINHA (1962), for instance, but functionally related to the state formation process in tribal areas and the emergence of a regional cultural synthesis of Great and Little Traditions and of feudal political structures.

A more specialized investigation into the phenomenon of the dual dissection of most Middle Indian tribes into a Hinduized and a tribal section - and departing from a general anthropological question of primitive social organization, namely the "ethnological dual classification system" and its presence in India - was made by W. KOPPERS (1944), a representative of a certain cultural history theory (diffusionism) of the Vienna School of Ethnology. The central concern of this School were diffusionist explanations of cross-cultural similarities or parallels. Its essential assumptions were that cultural parallels, i.e. similarities or cultural traits, social institutional forms, customs and beliefs point to and are caused by historical contacts and influences of neighbouring or even widely separated cultures. Thus, for KOPPERS, the distinction of tribal segments into big/small, superior/inferior, greater/lesser etc. halves (Bhil/Bhilala, Little Munda/Great Munda etc.) with respective higher or lower, pure or impure status is due to the unequal contact with Hinduism and Hindu caste society and consequently an unequal acculturative process. And he rejects the presence of an ethnological dual classification system or "dual organization" (a term of the Vienna School and one of its central concerns) as an explanation for this phenomenon. Besides, endogamy which he found characteristic of the superior, pure, more hinduized half of the tribe, is taken over from caste society according to him.

It is PFEFFER (1982c) who vehemently rejects KOPPER`s diffusionist, historical explanation demonstrating a dual classification system in the tribal social order and basing his argumentation on almost the same ethnographic data, but on a structural understanding of "dual organization" instead of an empirical one.

KOPPERS himself had pointed to the problem of the diffusion concept, that there are no fixed laws, neither of transmission nor in acceptance or rejection of cultural traits and that the "apparently arbitrary way in which these (selection, modification, rejection) occur frequently have puzzled ethnologists" (Koppers). PFEFFER interprets Hinduization - against KOPPER`s Hinduization thesis - as the taking over of another "idiom", another expression for saying the same thing; there is a continuity in the ideological structure. Thus, one of the most central of all anthropological problems, namely the explanation of cultural resemblances, is tackled in different ways. But even today it is not yet completely solved to what extent similarities in customs, institutions and collective representations are the product of "spontaneous proclivities of human beings, of their minds" (Needham) and to what extent they are results of historical transmission. A systematic integration of diffusionist explanation and structuralist insight into the development of cognitive categories and the interaction of different modes of thought and value systems together with concomitant politico-economic power aspects seems to me necessary for understanding processes of social and cultural change. Besides, the levels on which changes occur and also the functional interrelation of these levels must be taken into consideration.

Coming to the concepts of Sanskritization and Rajputization or Kshatriyaization - also called the Brahmanical model or Ksahtriya model of imitation -, the first introduced by SRINIVAS (1952) and the latter by SINHA (1962) (Ksahtriyaization is coined by H. KULKE, 1976), only a few essential points with regard to methodology and theoretical approach to the tribe-caste question should be made here. Both concepts relate to cultural and social change, in the first case to mobility within the caste system and in the other - Rajputization - to the integration and assimilation of tribal groups into the caste system. The point of departure is a dichotomous view of "Hochkultur", the all-Indian Sanskritic culture of Great Tradition and the local, folk culture, the Little Tradition. By adoption of "Sanskritic" Hindu rites, beliefs, ideas and customs by the tribals or by low caste Hindus, they become integrated into the caste system or can achieve a higher status in the system, respectively. The terms themselves already indicate restriction to particularistic aspects of a more complex process.

The central questions of the described processes relate to the understanding of hierarchy in the caste system, the relation of secular and ritual status, the relationship between Brahman/Kshatriya, i.e. priest and king and to the general interrelation of the politico-economic and religious-ideological domain in traditional Indian caste society, and - in a comparative framework - in archaic tribal societies of India. A comparative approach to the structural configuration of both types of society related to the historical background may be able to provide a deeper understanding of "state" formation processes on which SINHA and KULKE, for instance, focus their attention and also cast new light on the old controversy of "Indian feudalism". The phenomenon of dual authority, in tribal and caste society, would play a central role for investigation into "political" developments.

Hinduization, Sanskritization and Rajputization are designated as "historical" explanations here because they "explain" the phenomena by reference to the historical origin or historical background of these phenomena ignoring the structural interrelation and thereby failing to reach a systematic understanding. Thus, in the description and analysis of the Hinduization process by SRINIVAS, SINHA and their followers[7] a problematic interrelation between ideological-religious, cultural and politico-economic domains becomes obvious, but it is not systematically explored, or, if so, in an atomistic and particularistic way. A central point pursued by KULKE, following Max WEBER, is hat of legitimation or legitimacy in the establishment of political power structures. Again, for understanding of what happens in tribal societies, the question of traditional authority has to be investigated ethnographically. A thorough analysis of kinship organization or, rather, the total configuration of the archaic tribal social order as PFEFFER has attempted, calls in question the concept of "lineage-based chieftaincies" - following "African models" of British Social Anthropology - as the basis for transition to early tribal states. Likewise, the theory of "segmentary state" - again an "African model" -, adopted by B. STEIN for South India and elaborated by KULKE for Orissa and the orientation of some historians at neoevolutionist theories of state formation must be critically thought over again.

To understand the nature of these complex social and cultural processes it is necessary to go beyond mere empirical descriptions or "sociocentric" functional explanations. The total conceptualization ("totalization" in the Maussian sense) of the relational aspects (political, economic, religious, cultural) of the process still remains to be done. In theoretical terms, the focus must be on the interrelation of cultural-ideological, social and historical facts in a combination of cultural and sociological analysis transcending the dichotomous materialist and idealist (or mentalist) ways of explaining culture and society. There is no one-way and linear causal determination between material and cultural/social factors; matters are much more complicated. The religious, political and economic dimensions cannot be disaggregated; and DUMONT and other anthropologists have shown for archaic and traditional societies that what Western analytical tradition separates and identifies as religion, economy, politics, may either have been combined differently, i.e. differently valued, ideologically, or, more likely, constituted a single interpreting totality. This approach of a "totalization", aimed at giving an integrated account or a more adequate representation of an alien social and cultural reality, requires a different analytical strategy than that of the aforementioned historical or functional explanations and is not at all easy, especially the translation of indigenous concepts and their elucidation in terms of the analyst`s concepts and vocabulary.

DUMONT`s general outline of the relational structure of traditional Indian caste order with all concomitant implications for understanding traditional "economy" and "politics" and PFEFFER`s investigation into the ethnography and interpretation of archaic tribal ideology and exchange structures are only a beginning and it is necessary to go beyond their approach with regard to "history" and "praxis". "History" must be tackled in a new way, in "a more ethnographic sort of historical investigation which pays greater attention to the internal development dynamics of particular societies over time" (Ortner 1984), to culture-specific history. Research into the oral traditions of Indian tribes - a hitherto neglected area - could reveal indigenous interpretations of their own society and "historical" events as a concept of history which restricts itself to objective facts will not do justice to the tribals` own understanding of history.

V. "NEO"-EVOLUTIONIST EXPLANATION

The early studies on the caste system of India were studies in search of its origins (Nesfield, Risley, Hutton, Ibbetson). The question of origins was ignored, however, since the middle of this century and synchronic analyses of regional caste organizations in the village studies and DUMONT`s structural interpretation stood in the foreground.

The problem of the "coming into existence of that South Asian behavioral complex known as the 'caste system`" was taken up again by Morton KLASS in his book "Caste: the emergence of the South Asian social system" (1980). In the tradition of the evolutionist anthropology of White, Service, Sahlins, Fried between the 40s and the 60s he sees the necessity of looking for origins and stages in the socio-cultural evolution, filling the gap which, according to him, the representatives of this approach left behind, namely to apply their theoretical concepts to a locally and historically concrete and specific evolution, the origin and development of Indian caste society. KLASS criticizes the current anthropological research on South Asia as mainly orientated to synchronic studies, "for South Asian anthropology...the apostles of synchrony or even achrony still rule supreme" (Klass 1980:188). What he himself tries to do is to present a reasonable explanation of the emergence of the caste system in terms of contemporary anthropological knowledge and theories. Avowedly an eclectic, he grounds his argumentation on different anthropolotical theories from which he extracts the most useful and adequate for his preconceived hypothesis, ultimately determined by his neoevolutionist[8] standpoint. He uses "whatever methodological or ideological approach - or combination of them - (that) allows me the best grasp of the problem at hand" (1980:3). In a whole chapter he explains his argument for eclecticism (against its critics) and his plea is for a "synthesis of different theoretical approaches which encompasses the knowledge of all theories in an overarching system of explanation and prediction" (1980:187-192).

He draws upon such diverse sources as LEVI-STRAUSS` disquisition on the transformation of totem and caste (Lévi-Strauss 1963), KIRCHHOFF`s ideas on different types of clan organization and their evolutionary potential (Kirchhoff 1955), Marvin HARRIS` and Harry PEARSON`s debate on the role of productive surplus in evolutionary processes, FRIED`s, SAHLIN`s and SERVICE`s discussions of unilineal descent systems for his hypothetical reconstruction of "a scenario of events for a time period for which no records, historical or archaeological, can presently be identified".[9] His approach is largely neoevolutionary, a consequence of which is the restriction to materialist, i.e. ecological, technological and economic factors. An economical view determines also his initial definition of the caste system as a particular system of social stratification based on agricultural production and a redistributive economy and constituted socially of endogamous castes - "marriage circles" - which form a network of economic, political and ritual relationships. Economic interdependence, differential access to basic resources, redistributive exchange and exchange of services and endogamy of the social units are thus the main characteristics of the caste system as seen by KLASS. He arrives at this view by using arbitrarily selected ethnographic sources from works in economic anthropology (substantivist approach) on India combining it with general findings of ecological anthropology (e.g. of Julian Steward).

One can clearly distinguish a cultural materialist and economical standpoint and orientation towards a natural science paradigm.

Culture - ideas and values, religion, symbolism - is secondary and an epiphenomenon and has no causal meaning for the evolutionary process; ecological and techno-economic conditions have priority and determine the "superstructure" and are the prime movers for socio-cultural evolution, too. On the whole, such a concept of evolution completely neglects the question of meaning and symbolism. This theoretical approach for which causal explanations and the acknowledgment of general laws in socio-cultural evolution are central, thus contrasts with "ideational theories of culture", in which interpretation and understanding are central.

KLASS poses two questions: "what kind of socio-economic system" preceded caste society and secondly, what were the causes and conditions for the "transformation" from pre-caste to caste? The main line of his argumentation runs as follows: South Asia was originally inhabited by hunters and gatherers, organized in "endogamous clusters of exogamous, unstratified, stipulated-descent, equalitarian clans" as corporate groups, or "autocephalous 'verband` ", a Weberian term he uses. These single clan societies of the pre-caste period lived in different ecological environments from different modes of subsistence; consequently they showed differences in social organization and ideology and existed in social and economic independence of each other ("societal endogamy"); only within these single clan societies was there a "reciprocal exchange of marriage partners" ("exogamy of sub-units").

Contrary to KIRCHHOFF`s hypothesis, namely that egalitarian clans of common descent have no evolutionary potential and are a "blind alley" for evolutionary progress, KLASS wants to show that in India the caste system in fact emerged from a previous "common-descent corporate kin group structure" of a totemic kind. The totality of this social and economic milieu of clan societies ("galaxy of societies and social groups") developed into the stratified, socio-economic system known as the caste system of South Asia. "I cannot prove any of the forgoing propositions, but I see them as reasonable and conservative conclusions to be drawn from such evidence as we have and from our present understanding of the nature of human society...and in line with all contemporary theory, including both structuralism and neoevolutionism" (Klass 1980:158,159).

For the reconstruction of the "how" of the structural transformation - a term he sometimes uses for the sequence of pre-caste totemic clan society to caste society, borrowed from LEVI-STRAUSS` "Bear and barber" - KLASS concentrates on the decisive factors of stratification, the implications of absolute surplus as a necessary pre-condition for the emergence of complex stratified societies, population growth and pressure following technological advances, all of which are seen by the neoevolutionists as prime movers in the process of socio-cultural evolution. No attention is given to ideology and to cultural, symbolic aspects as these are not crucial for evolution. The cause of social differentiation and stratification is found in ecological, technological and economic conditions and is seen as a linear cause-effect sequence. Concretely, the discovery and spread of rice cultivation (intensive irrigation agriculture), providing an initial impetus, led in time to population growth and pressure on cultivable land resources. The shift to a redistributive economy became necessary in order to handle the relationships between groups with access to land and those without. The exchange of services of non-food producing corporate groups for shares of crops or access to land controlled by the "dominant castes" who were the "allocative centres" for production and distribution as well as for supervision of the specialist service castes, resulted, according to

KLASS, in the "full emergence of what - in all its social, economic and ideological manifestations - we know as the South Asian caste system" (Klass 1980:188).

"This exercise in pseudohistory, or, more kindly, in neoevolutionary anthropological theory building...is fairly certain to be regarded by most of his Indianist colleagues as an intellectual blind alley" - this critique by Silvia VATUK in a review of the book can fully be underlined das KLASS does not bring anything new and illuminating based on new ethnographic, archaeological or historical sources about the complex origin of the Indian caste system, a complexity which HUTTON had already emphasized. For the metholodogical and theoretical discussion it nevertheless seemed to me justified to include this unsuccessful attempt at an evolutionary approach in this review, pointing to the decisive weakness, one-sidedness and reductionism of the neoevolutionist "paradigm" and giving reasons for the necessity to reformulate a theory of socio-cultural evolution or even to find new formulations for structural transformations limited first to restricted, but culturally and historically connected areas before arriving at universally valid statements.

Two main points of criticism may be emphasized: first, too great a generalization abstracted from diverse cultures and societies studied and lack of detailed ethnographic data of the specific society and culture, namely the Indian. And secondly, KLASS` theoretical "atomistic" eclecticism. A general characteristic of the evolutionary approach of this neoevolutionist type is its concern for generalizing on a very selective ethnographic basis. Its representatives show a disparaging attitude towards ethnography and extensive fieldwork as a pre-condition for generalizations and hypotheses; ethnographic examples are only used as an illustration of their preconceived theory. Besides, they overstress the universal and general significance of techno-economic, materialist factors as universally valid causal determinants in the evolutionary process and neglect completely the inner dynamics of the different social and cultural systems due to their specific ideological configuration. The interrelation between the two factors is certainly more subtle and not easily to explain as "vulgar" materialists suppose. KLASS` explanation or, rather, hypothetical reconstruction of a conjectured historical development is crude and not at all documented either ethnographically, historically or archaeologically. His handling of "history" and "evolution" is confused and misleading.

What he does is offer a common-sense, cliché view of caste and tribal society with an ethnocentric bias; he nowhere substantiates for instance the analysis of social organization and its respective social units,be it endogamous marriage-circles or equalitarian totemic clans with Indian ethnographic material. A small selection of ethnographic examples - even from other societies - separated from the total context of the cultural whole is used as illustration of a preconceived, deductive evolutionary hypothesis.

As for his eclecticism, it is a sterile and mechanical mixture of most diverse, often contradictory anthropological theories. Even his acceptance of the evolutionary concepts of White and other neoevolutionist representatives who, among themselves, advocate different lines is often questionable and inaccurate, not to speak of his muddled interpretation of LEVI-STRAUSS` view of structural transformation and his complete distortion of the structuralist`s aim.

This criticism of KLASS` eclecticism does not mean a general criticism of eclecticism, as it is part and parcel of the progress of scientific understanding. "We are all kidnappers of ideas" (Leach), but to arrive at a synthesis of concepts from different theories it is necessary to integrate them into a new order in a systematic way. Questioning the neoevolutionist conceptions of socio-cultural evolution, likewise, does not mean a complete rejection of evolutionary perspectives. "Structuralist" authors like PFEFFER and NEEDHAM, for instance, are interested in such aspects, too. It is no longer considered the task to establish typologies of universal evolutionary stages as in 19th century evolutionism or neoevolutionism, but to analyze systematically the processes of transformations, specific processes and transitions in different historical epochs, cultural regions and societies.[10]

VI. "SOCIOLOGICAL" (STRUCTURAL-FUNCTIONAL) APPROACH

BAILEY is, besides S.C. Sinha, with his continuum concept the author the most cited with regard to the tribe-caste question and a direct opponent of DUMONT in the discussion "For a sociology of

India". However, as will be shown, this continuum concept turns out in the last analysis to be merely an empty formula.

In an article " 'Tribe` and 'caste` in India" (1961) and in his book "Tribe, caste and nation" (1960) he is explicitly concerned with the tribe-caste relationship under the main aspect of social change in a "modern situation" [11], i.e. the economic and political changes produced by the clash of tribal and caste society, their influence on tribal social organization and the simultaneous integration of the latter into the colonial and later the national state of India. BAILEY`s prevalent interest in politics and social change in India determines the focus on the political and economic sphere of society and influences his definition of tribe as an egalitarian, segmentary political system, not an "all-purpose" definition as he admits, in opposition to the "organic", hierarchic caste system.

The distinction between "tribe" and "caste" is for him "a rudimentary exercise in comparative sociology". Rejecting a definition of tribe on historical, geographical, religious, cultural or linguistic criteria as unsatisfactory and without sufficient sociological precision, he wishes to offer a sociological analysis of tribal and caste society and a comparison of their respective social and politico-economic organization; finally, however, he will restrict his analysis to the "subsystem" politics/economics and even here to only one aspect.

He starts from the assumption that tribal and caste society are not utterly and in every respect different from each other, contrasted as whole societies, but that there are similarities, for instance, in kinship organization and in religious beliefs and life though there are striking differences in the politico-economic organization. Consequently, BAILEY restricts the analysis because of his interest (i.e. explaining change from tribe to caste) to one aspect and compares in an atomistic way the politico-economic sphere of both societies, severed from society as a whole.

Methodologically, he proceeds as follows: first, he works out at a theoretical level the difference between tribal and caste society, i.e. he describes the ideal type of both at a high level of abstraction as he puts it, ignoring the question of change or of classification of concrete social groups (static analysis). This leads him to the problem of applying "neat, mutually exclusive concepts to a complex reality" of human behaviour, and to the realization that the distinction cannot be absolutely maintained in reality since both societies show features of the other, and consequently to the formulation of a continuum between the two.

The author exemplifies his approach by the study of Kond tribal society and Oriya caste society, or, more precisely, a local section of a regional caste system, both existing together in the Kondmals - "a particular tribe and its Hindu environment" - and sharing a common historical past. By restricting his analysis to the politico-economic domain which for him plays the main role in ordering social life, he comes to the definition of tribal society as egalitarian and segmentary and of caste society as organic and hierarchic, both as ideal types and as the two poles of his postulated continuum. Ignoring the reality of contact, he describes separately the social relations of both groups in a structural analysis, in an equilibrium state, before proceeding to a dynamic analysis of the process of change from one to the other. The two ideal poles are thus first established in order to "plot the course of change", i.e. the starting point of change (tribal society) and its final point (caste society), in a linear way.

Secondly, to describe the process, the interaction of both is analyzed, and for BAILEY the decisive point is the individual choice of the members of the tribal structure of a new, different structure. Here, the author introduce a historical perspective relying on conjectural historical reconstruction for the tribal situation before the advent of the British.

The main criterion for defining a segmentary and an organic structure respectively, is the access to land and basic resources: with the tribal Konds, the segmentary political system, the access to these is egalitarian; membership of clan is the precondition for the right of holding and exploiting land in the clan territory, "it is not achieved by subordination to anyone else, but by equality as kinsmen" (Bailey 1961:12/13). The Oriya caste society, on the other hand, is hierarchically organized and the castes are related to each other through economic specialization and interdependence; there is differential control over the productive resources of the village which is made up of a land-owning dominant caste and other service castes.

But difficulties arose - as already said - when applying the abstract dichotomy to the reality and classifying concrete social groups as tribe or caste: both societies exhibit features of the other, e.g. with the Kond are associated the Pan, "a dependent caste of Pan untouchable field labourers"; here exactly the same organic link exists that for BAILEY is typical of the caste organization. And in the caste organization, segmentary features are to be found just as in tribal organization. The solution BAILEY gives to this problem is his formulation of a continuum between tribe and caste, and particular groups should be located along the continuum line, with the ideal type of tribe and caste at the respective ends, and with intermediate types either closer to the one end or to the other. But the question arises where does tribe end and caste begin? There is no absolute point of separation. To classify concrete social groups and to locate them on the continuum line BAILEY again takes recourse to the criterion of access to land. "The larger is the proportion of a given society which has direct access to land, the closer is that society to the tribal end of the continuum; conversely, the larger is the proportion of people whose right to land is achieved through a dependent relationship, the nearer does that society come to the caste pole" (Bailey 1961:14).

The whole argument is circular and does not explain anything; it only describes a complex and at first sight incoherent empirical reality. The author constantly confuses levels of abstraction and the empirical phenomena, and does not realize, that the dichotomy lies in the thought process of abstraction and not in the concrete reality.

The process of absorption of the tribals into the Hindu caste system is understood by BAILEY as political and social change, seeing both structures, tribal and caste, as "alternate ways of acting", "as institutional complexes which are there as choices for the individuals in particular societies". This process started, after an earlier differential coexistence of both tribal and caste structures, with the establishment of colonial power and administration, was altered again in modern times with the Indian national state and led to the breakdown of the tribal segmentary political system. The Kond got into a relationship of economic dependence, "typical of the caste system" and their right to land and resources was thence mediated by others. In this way they were integrated into the caste system and their behaviour changed according to the Oriya model. Under this political aspect BAILEY understands "Sanskritization" as the taking over of the Hindu behavioural complex by the tribals and as a political strategy to gain respectability by adhering to Sanskritic culture as the culture of the nation and the Indian-wide hallmark of respectability. He however, points several times to the "modern" system which he differentiates into the "bureaucratic system of colonial times" and the "representative democracy system" of the modern Indian state, only mentioning them as impetus for changes but not analyzing them in detail for he as a social anthropologist is interested in "primitive" and "traditional" types of society. Seeing tribe and caste as alternative ways of acting in the situation of change reintroduces discontinuity again: they are disjunct opposites for individual choices. It is here at the latest that the continuum appears completely questionable.

The continuum concept of BAILEY was adopted by some Indian anthropologists for other areas and tribes (e.g. Sachchidananda); but they finally come to the equivalent of the usual Hinduization thesis: a tribe becomes a caste by taking over the cultural traits of the Hindu castes. No additional insight is gained. And in his attempt to apply the continuum perspective of BAILEY to the Kharia and Pahira tribes in Bihar SINHA fails and rejects access to land as an applicable criterion. Against an economic reductionism SINHA wants to set a multi-dimensional continuum considering also the cultural, religious and ideological spheres of the social totality and seeing "tribe as a system of social relations as well as a state of mind and a cultural tradition" (Sinha 1965:61).

In a direct answer to BAILEY`s article on "tribe" and "caste" DUMONT criticizes his approach as too narrow because restricted to politics-cum-economics, and therefore as "sociocentric", too. A brief quotation from DUMONT summarizes the theoretical approach of an author who followed the structural-functional tradition of Radcliffe-Brown supplemented by the influence of the Manchester School (he was a student of GLUCKMAN): "According to it society lies in the interaction of individuals. The study is therefore empirical or materialistic, and atomistic. Ideas are epiphenonema, and just as society revolves itself anatomically into a collection of individuals, so phenomena fall into individual categories (e.g. political, economic etc.)...The main explanatory scheme is causal, or, what is not too different, diachronic or 'dialectical`. ...this is a sociology of the individual" (Dumont 1970:134).

BAILEY outlines his own conception in a repudiation (1959) of DUMONT`s understanding of comparative sociology. "A valid sociological understanding can be achieved...by making abstractions immediately from behaviour or from other non-verbal information, and by using only our own concepts and evading the ideas of the people" (Bailey 1959:60). A fundamental difference in the epistemological approach to alien cultures and societies is here seen in the opposition between BAILEY`s "sociological" and DUMONT`s "culturoelogical" explanations - as BAILEY calls them -, and also the old controversy about the relationship of society and culture emerges which Parsons and Kroeber decided to solve by allocating culture to the anthropologists and society to the sociologists with unhappy consequences of this separation for a better understanding of the nature of this relationship. Central for British Social Anthropology - and for BAILEY - is society, assuming that society is a higher level of abstraction than culture which is secondary and only one aspect of the social system and the total process of social life. Culture is not observable, has no concrete reality and is but an abstraction (Radcliffe-Brown). Social structure is understood at the level of observed behaviour, it is abstracted from the regularities of interaction between persons or groups. The total structure of a society can be dissected into different substructures - religion, economics, politics, kinship - which are interdependent and related in a systematic way. This relationship is nowhere analyzed in BAILEY`s work, and the rubrics and their evaluation is taken from the society of the observer in a socio-centric way as DUMONT criticizes. Politics-cum-economics, i.e. political activity of individuals with the aim of manipulating the social system for their own ends and profit and achieving control over resources and power over men, is the foundation of society. In this sense, BAILEY postulates another variety of man, "the political man" (1960:256). His "interest theory" of human practice (Praxis) is one of an essentially individualistic and aggressive actor, self-interested, pragmatic and with a maximizing orientation. Against this, newer practice approaches in the eighties (Ortner 1984:144 f.) stand out as a future perspective; yet they could not have been possible without the achievements of structuralist thought. A more differentiated view of the relationship between individual and society is necessary as it is differently construed and valued in different cultures.

In NEEDHAM`s words, one could rank BAILEY - though in a polemic way - among the "pragmatist (bluff, common-sensical) characters, who need not be versed in epistemological, symbolic and related matters to make effective studies of social action" (Needham 1967:50). It should not at all be denied that different interests are legitimate, but a methodological prerequisite must be a clear handling of the different levels of abstraction, not a constant confusion of them as is the case with BAILEY. The boundaries of his definitions and underlying theoretical assumptions keep changing to suit his convenience. The scientific value of BAILEY`s continuum concept - it is often used as jargon in anthropological works on India - for understanding and analysis is to my mind absolutely nil.

VII. S.C. SINHA`S DIFFERENT PERSPECTIVES ON "TRIBES AND INDIAN CIVILIZATION"

In a series of articles[12] Surajit C. SINHA published his study on the "position of the tribes of Peninsular India in the general context of Indian Civilization". It led him to different attempts to conceptualize the complex interrelationship between tribes and caste peasant society in the course of history, concentrating - as a social anthropologist - on the tribal side. "A comprehensive understanding of the development of the primary civilization of India will thus inevitably involve a clear understanding of the primitive level of manifestation of core traditions and their supporting organization, as they are still partially preserved among contemporary tribes" (Sinha 1957a:117). It is through the structural-functional analysis of contemporary tribal groups and their cultures, seen as remnants or untransformed sections of the primitive cultures being arrested in their development through ecological factors of isolation or due to historical accidents, that he wants to arrive at an understanding of their role in the emergence of India`s primary civilization; his aim is a "comprehensive formulation of those structural characteristics and transformative processes which link the tribal cultures of

Peninsular India to the Hindu peasant culture and society and to the Great Tradition". His ethnographic material and comparative analysis relates to the tribal belt of Middle India (Bihar, Orissa, West Bengal mainly) where he finds different tribes in various stages of cultural and economic development and with different degrees of acculturation to the Hindu caste society. It should be emphasized that SINHA`s concern is not the modern, latest phase of cultural and social transformation through modernization and Westernization, but the position of tribes vis-à-vis traditional caste society and Indian civilization.

SINHA developed his ideas in three successive perspectives: an evolutionist perspective, a continuum approach and the view of tribes "as dependent historic structures", the latter being inspired by A.L. KROEBER. At a time (in the 50s and 60s) when three major paradigms were en vogue - British structural functionalism, American cultural anthropology and American "neo-"evolutionist anthropology - SINHA attempted to synthesize them for his project casting some light on specific questions concerning the anthropology of Indian civilization (Sinha 1955).

SINHA proposes to formulate the tribe-caste relationship as follows:

1. given an essential difference between both socio-cultural systems, the relationship consists of acculturation processes, i.e. the tribes are Hinduized,

2. given a continuity between both systems, the tribal cultures represent the original, evolutionary basis for the development of Indian civilization with core cultural patterns common to both (a long-range historical perspective), and

3. the tribal cultures are a backward branch or dependent historic structures of the traditional Indian civilization (a middle-range historical perspective from civilization down to the primitive isolates).

In all three perspectives tribal society is seen by SINHA as "a quality of socio-cultural integration",[13] i.e. a total social and cultural whole, "a system of social relations as well as a state of mind and a cultural tradition" (Sinha 1965:61). He thus does not separate culture and ideological system (religion, value system, world view) from social structure, but stresses the importance of the former which play an equal part in the development of a civilization or sociocultural evolution. Transformation of both the moral and technical order takes place in an interrelated way.

SINHA`s evolutionist perspective is the modified adaptation of a few issues of neoevolutionism (uni- and multilinear lines), a "clarified version of evolutionism" (Sinha 1955) in which he seeks to find out "to what extent are the overall directions of cultural evolution observable in the culture history of the particular people under investigation". And he accepts three generalizations from the evolutionists (White,

Childe) and exemplifies them with his Middle Indian ethnographic material analyzing the transformation of tribal into peasant caste society: first, progressive evolution in technology, secondly, progressive evolution in the direction of enlarging the range of social relationships (ethnic heterogeneity) and third, technology determines the range of social ties. The author also considers the role of individuals or groups in the process, actively striving for and creating technological and social innovations (Sinha 1957b).

Thus, the tribal cultures are seen as the initial primitive level of cultural raw materials with a "core cultural and social pattern" which develop into the local, small peasant communities (Little Tradition) and these into the urban dimensions of Indian tradition (Great Tradition), the latter being a product of elaboration and systematization of this core cultural pattern. The "evolution" is a transformation from one qualitative level of integration to another. For lack of historical and archaeological sources for the prehistoric period and being only able to speculate on the probability that "the basic orientation of India`s primary civilization was laid before the Aryan intrusion, through prolonged interaction of the Little Tradition of the Munda and Dravidian little communities" (SINHA 1957:101), the author compares ethnographic material in a synchronic, structural analysis of the total sociocultural system of the tribes at different levels of integration in order to ascertain the similarities and differences, or the continuities and discontinuities. His conclusion is that "leaving aside the problem of specific historicity, at least, on a formal level of abstraction, the folk (or tribal), peasant and urban dimensions of Indian tradition and culture-community represent a series of increasingly complex levels of sociocultural integration with evidence of continuity in core pattern" (Sinha 1957:117).

Methodologically, he compares the two kinds of systems, tribal and peasant caste, in the totality of their culture pattern, for analytical purposes separated into the functionally integrated elements of habitat, economy, social structure, ideological system, the latter comprising religion, value system and world view with regard to man-nature and man-man relationship.

His ideal type of tribal society comprises a wide spectrum of groups from hunters and gatherers (Hill Kharia, Birhor etc.) to shifting cultivators (Hill Bhuiya, Kond, Juang etc.) and settled agriculturists (Munda, Ho, Santal); that of the caste society is abstracted from peasant communities, i.e. regional or local caste organizations, of West Bengal, Bihar and Orissa. In a summary and tabular comparison of the two he distinguished the significant elements of continuity between the non-Hindu tribal and Hindu peasant sociocultural system and also the emergent aspects or discontinuities.

Confronted with the same problem as BAILEY, namely that the ideal type does not fit the complex reality, he comes to the same solution of a continuum between tribes and Hindu peasantry, partly also under the influence of REDFIELD`s concept of the "folk-urban" continuum which he redefines to fit the Indian scene, namely tribal/Hindu caste continuum. SINHA then specifies both poles and confronts in a more detailed example the tribal Hill Maria Gond near the tribal pole and the Bhumij of Barabhum, a Munda tribe, near the caste/peasant pole. In a rough and general way he enumerates the elements of continuity or common denominators as well as the new emergent aspects of discontinuities in the domains of economy, social structure and ideological system. The decisive changes are found in the move towards social and economic stratification, stressing super- and subordination, specialization of roles, feudalization, ethnic heterogeneity in social interaction, wider communication networks, surplus economy based on settled agriculture, ethical religion and a "puritanical" value system. The changes thus relate to social structure as well as to culture, and in this respect, the concept of "level of sociocultural integration" is the basis for ascertaining them, although the comparison is not one of whole cultures but in fact of atomistic domains. Nowhere does SINHA analyzes the interrelation between these two societal domains - structure and culture - which he only characterizes as functionally interdependent in a generalized way. As for the determinants of this transformative process, SINHA doubts whether technological and economic factors may be considered causal, unlike the neo-evolutionists who regard them as crucial. Obviously, an adequate technological/economic base is needed to support the increased level of complexity, as SINHA assumes, but he denies that technological progress, population growth and increase of settlement size could generate a caste system in a tribal area (1965:78). He admits that the difficult question of the relation between religion/ideology and technology/economy with regard to their role in sociocultural evolution is not yet adequately answered.

In his third perspective of seeing "tribes as dependent historic structures" SINHA`s main aim is to show adaptive processes on the part of the tribals through acculturation and interaction between the two sociocultural systems against the background of the emergence of states. The latter is seen as the structural and cultural medium of integration of the tribals into a wider, centralized, hierarchic and territorially organized political system, a "feudalistic superstructure". He describes and analyses the case of the Bhumij tribe and its kingdom of Barabhum with shorter comparative notes on the Munda Raj of Chotanagpur and the medieval kingdoms dating from the 13th to the 16th century and therefore with little or no reliable documented historical or archaeological sources. SINHA understands the state formation process - he nowhere defines his "state" concept, it must be said - as twofold: an endogenous, internal development "from below", i.e. from the tribal base, and a process of influence or stimulus from outside, but rejecting the "conquest theory" of state formation and speaking instead of "stimulus diffusion" of a Rajut model of state (1962:71). He does not describe the conditions of the developmental process from the tribal base in detail because according to him, the traditional, pre-British tribal organization can only be assumed speculatively. He therefore concentrates on the consequences of the emergence of "feudal" state structures as they are the same whether they emerged as the result of external or internal cause. "The final forms of the political structure of these chieftaincies in central India look more or less alike in essential features, namely a feudalistic superstructure on a tribal base" and a concomitant mutual social and cultural adaptation process. Concretely, the consequences as shown by the author are: the cultural process of Rajputization, dissemination of Brahmanical standards (Sanskritization, though he does not uses the word), a syntheses of Hindu and tribal cults ("upgrading or universalization of regional culture") and the social structural process of stratification in social classes based on differential land-holding and political dominance. The much discussed interrelation between ritual and secular (political and economic) status is only briefly touched on, and the conclusion of the author is, that in spite of the significance of political power and economic wealth, "however, the final validation of a status is in terms of kinship (fictitious or real), marriage alliance and ritual symbols" (Sinha 1962:74).

Apart from the state mediated process of Hinduization SINHA points to the influence of spontaneous interaction of Hindu craftsmen, peasants and priestly castes with the tribal people on the local level of villages (Sinha 1957b). But this is a separation of two factors which in reality are part of a total process.

Of interest for the anthropologist is his ethnographic material on the Bhumij; he gives a brief outline of the traditional pattern of their social organization and culture, a picture which is, however, characterized by the Hindu influence due to these very consequences of state formation. Issues of traditional organization should be studied in detail, in a deeper analysis and with comparison of different tribal groups, issues some of which we meet in PFEFFER`s work again: the original clan organization and the traditional regulation of access to land (the latter with a strong religious content), i.e. dominance of "first settlers" as holders of khuntkatti land and as the "senior line", later gaining dominance in political organization; the traditional function of village headman (Ghatwal) and village priest (Laya) pointing to the phenomenon of "dual leadership/authority"; the quality of social interactions and social distance between Bhumij and other tribal groups, between Bhumij and associated "castes" (craftsmen, herders) and between Bhumij and higher castes, ranging from reciprocity and equality to super- and subordination but a "spirit" of complementarity and cooperation always being present. All this indicates a different "ideology" than we are accustomed to and take for granted, but to understand it better and unbiasedly a lot of ethnographic work and interpretation remains to be done.

Though emphasizing the positive role of state formation in integrating tribal groups into the Hindu social system SINHA does not fail to mention that, due to at times oppressive and expositive policies, tribal "contra-acculturative" movements against the alienation of the sacred ancestral land and the loss of tribal identity took place. But "withdrawal" and "secondary primitivization" are also mentioned as an adaptive strategy for tribal survival. His cursory glance at these phenomena, also designated as revivalist or messianic movements, agrarian revolts etc. in the literature, may be an inspiration to explore deeper the specific interrelation of political, economic, cultural and religious factors in such counter-movements in India on which purely descriptive, historical works have so far been published, but no structural analysis.

A critical evaluation of SINHA`s expositions should make special mention of the following points: With changing perspectives SINHA tried to cast some light on the different aspects of the complex relationship between tribal societies and cultures and Hindu caste society. His study is mainly based on ethnographic data from his own fieldwork or other published ethnographic material and on the synchronic structural-functional analysis of different tribal sociocultural systems at different levels of integration and their comparison. Although he works mainly ethnographically, the dimension of history is always present. It is the main task of social anthropologists - and precisely their task if there are not any historical sources at all or only fragmented or unreliable historical data available - to "orientate historical research" through structural insights and to develop sensitivity among historians for a different ideology or world-view in archaic and traditional societies, one which devaluates chronology thereby posing a limit to a "chronological" reconstruction of their "history". Though SINHA explicitly stated that he was leaving aside the question of specific historicity and demonstrating only the formal logical possibility of the tribal cultures being the evolutionary basis for transformation to Hindu peasant caste society, he, on the other hand, brings in historical data. Evolution or history? - a much discussed question and controversy among social scientists trying to grasp the nature of development of societies - SINHA mixes them up.

As for his comparison of whole sociocultural systems it turns out to be an atomistic confrontation of different domains of the total society (habitat, economy, etc.). Just as BAILEY does not specify the nature of interrelation between the whole and its subsystems, SINHA merely refers to this difficult question without answering it. But unlike BAILEY, he does consider the ideological system, i.e. religion, world-view, values, and points to a qualitative transformation of these; he only fails to account for the context of meaning of the total whole.

SINHA stresses the importance of ethnography and with regard to his analysis of state formation - "a somewhat cursory essay" according to him - says that it was an attempt by him "to attract the attention of the colleagues in the field of tribal ethnography to fill in the major gaps in my representation...". On the whole, the study of this Indian anthropologist offers valuable ethnographic observations and insights, but more or less fragmented; thus, besides filling the "ethnographic gaps", the data should be systematized for re-interpretation and brought into a meaningful order on the basis of an integrated conceptual framework.

VIII. STRUCTURALIST APPROACH

G. PFEFFER`s recent publications[14] can be seen as a continuation and completion of DUMONT`s interpretation of Indian caste society and his studies on the kinship systems of South and North India. PFEFFER brings into focus the importance of tribal societies of India for a complete understanding of Indian Civilization and substantiates DUMONT`s assertion that "India is one". Little detailed anthropological research and no synthetic interpretations of the fragmented ethnographic material on these tribes have been done so far. In the light of published ethnographic data, mainly of early ethnographers, and of his own fieldwork among the tribals of Central India and a structural analysis of the Adivasis world view (Durkheim`s "collective representations") as condensed in their kinship systems he comes to the conclusion that there is an "ideological unity of tribal and caste society", i.e. there is an ideological continuity between them despite the initial impression of complete difference. PFEFFER`s stress is on the tribal side which DUMONT totally neglected in his work on India.

Important are the evolutionary formulations arrived at through comparison of Middle Indian tribal and North and South Indian kinship systems. Discontinuity and ideological differences are seen in the changing relations of production, but this aspect was not actually within the scope of PFEFFER`s work and is not elaborated; it needs further analysis.

With regard to our question of tribe-caste relationship and DUMONT`s statement that the so-called primitives of India are only people who have lost contact, PFEFFER`s analysis of the Adivasi substantiates this statement, too, insofar as he sees an ideological continuity between both tribal and caste society being separated by historical influences; but he ignores the historical dimension, i.e. all that acts as catalyst for the ideological transformation and social differentiation. What SINHA assumed by empirical comparison, namely that the tribes represent "the cultural raw materials" that contributed to the development of Indian civilization - PFEFFER is on the way to proving. His work aims at an intra-cultural comparison within Indian society and culture, a comparison between "non-modern societies" which DUMONT characterized as a "complicated procedure" from the methodological point of view.[15]

But beyond that he views it as a contribution to a general anthropological understanding of elementary forms of exchange and their evolutionary potential.

PFEFFER`s theoretical orientation and methodology marks a departure from the usual diffusionist and historical explanations (Hinduization, Sanskritization, etc.) which merely touch the surface, describing the variability and often inconsistency of these acculturative phenomena. Nevertheless, he shares an interest with previous anthropological studies in questions of the origin of the caste system and its ideological basis, of classification of tribes and of social change. The structuralist approach, however, represents a complete and radical breach with earlier explanatory attempts. It can be seen as a precondition of a deeper and clearer, more systematic understanding of these very questions of origin, evolution and social change.

Before presenting his thesis and some ethnographic aspects and their interpretation in a very summary form, PFEFFER`s theoretical framework should be made explicit as the author himself does so in his publications. The two most important representatives of alliance theory, DUMONT and RODNEY NEEDHAM, have influenced his orientation decisively, and it is their insights and procedure that he adopts for a re-interpretation of Middle Indian ethnographic data. While DUMONT`s study of the caste system and his detailed comparative analysis of kinship systems of South and North India form the background material for PFEFFER`s comparison of the very same systems with the tribal kinship systems of Middle India, he follows NEEDHAM in the "technical" analysis of these prescriptive alliance systems (distinction of three analytical levels: behaviour, norms, categories).

And what NEEDHAM sees as the main concern of social anthropological investigations, namely the discovery of alien systems of social and symbol classification, is also accepted by him.

Relying on the "remnants of the ancient total order ethnographically" PFEFFER analyzes the kinship systems of various tribes of the Middle Indian tribal belt (Munda, Gond, Oraon, Juang, Gadaba, Kond, Bondo etc.), representing today different degrees of assimilation to "Hindu" caste society. The peoples of the hills with their fundamental ideas are seen as a "unified complex beyond the level of the particular tribal entity" (Pfeffer 1982a:1) and as exhibiting two principles common to all: "symmetric alliance and symmetric distance which determine the total concept of the tribal cosmos" (1983a:88). Administrators and early ethnographers had faced problems when trying to name and classify individually the numerous tribes and tribal segments comprising tribes of different language affiliations (Munda, Dravidian, Aryan), different social institutions, and different cultural expressions.

The central thesis of the author is the "structural unity of both types of society", tribal and caste society. Against the superficial impression of the absence of anything like a caste system in the tribal world, he demonstrated marked status differences and social inequalities in a supposedly egalitarian society between tribes or different tribal sections. But these distinctions are of a different type than those of caste society according to him; in the latter the concept of hypergamy, absent in the tribal systems, is introduced by foreign influence, and also characteristic for it is a rigid hierarchical structure. Thus, status differences are present ideologically, but differently symbolized in both types of society. This fact leads him to reject the diffusionist argument (Pfeffer 1982c) that the dual dissection of most Middle Indian tribes into a "tribal section" and a "hinduized section" with different statuses (lower/higher, lesser/greater, inferior/superior, impure/pure) is due to Hindu influence as KOPPERS (1944) in his discussion of an ethnological dual classification system in India maintained.

Status is expressed in the tribal societies as "distance" between close consanguines (as opposition between junior and senior, the basic characteristic of the tribal world view), and characterized by relativity which changes into an absolute hierarchy in the caste system. Interrelated to the concept of distance is the principle of symmetric alliance found in different expressions in the tribal organization, both principles being part and parcel of a "pan-Indian pattern".

It should be made explicit that it is a structural analysis of the kinship systems that reveal the "elementary ideas" and "tribal concepts" pervading the culture and social organization of the tribes in their totality, and through which status is conferred.

In the kinship categories a common mental structure or Durkheimian collective representations are conserved - according to PFEFFER - in spite of modern political and social developments; yet they are no longer manifested in behaviour "on the ground", even sometimes the norms are contradictory or inconsistent. It is the understanding of the "total structure, ideational and social" (Needham) of an archaic social and cosmological order to which the analysis of kinship system and symbolic and social classification leads. All three constitute a totality, separated only for analytical purposes. Ultimately, the comparison of Indian kinship systems should make it possible to arrive at evolutionary formulations. According to PFEFFER, in tribal Middle India the question of social evolution can most easily be traced since here different "formations" sharing a common historical background exist side by side. His decisive question is, however, not "why", but "how" are the material conditions used by the people to develop their social organization (Pfeffer 1984:238). Against a materialist explanation of evolution the author sets the development of cognitive categories or stages of conceptual development. He again follows NEEDHAM`s "formal hypothesis of a typological scale of social evolution" (Needham 1967;45f); but the Indian material induces him to modify it and to suggest an evolutionary alternative which is probably unique to India (Pfeffer 1982a:99). The distinction of categories and social action is central for this evolutionary formulation as contradictions between the two levels point to structural change. "Kinship order of the civilization has evolved out of the tribal order..." (Pfeffer 1982b:51). The patterns of the tribal social organization are yet more sophisticated and complete in comparison to the patterns of the North and the South, which are thus seen by PFEFFER as "simplifications" of the Middle Indian expressions. The Adivasi structures definitely indicate the common relational basis of the phenomena found in the extreme regions. They may even indicate the point of departure (Pfeffer 1982a:39). The reasons for such simplifications are given "a more complicated economic order", "a complex political economy", "external influences from civilization" which all make it impossible to follow complicated and sophisticated rules in practice in tribal organization.

Relativising the fundamental unity in the ideological orientation of both types of society and introducing an evolutionary aspect, the author states, "If, from an original identity, 'Hindu` institutions have been divorced, this was due to the changing relations of production in the plains" (1982b:45).

It is here that further research would be of interest and necessary, inquiring into the relationship between categories and action and following up the statements of NEEDHAM and PFEFFER that innovation comes with social action while the categories remain conservative. Both don`t see any causal relationship between the two at the present stage of investigation and knowledge. That innovation is initiated by social action is testified by the manifold empirical differences in observable behaviour "on the ground" as well as in the variable regional behavioural norms which - according to PFEFFER - mark historical influences; but underlying are common structural principles. Indeed, the very aim of a structural analysis is, first to work out a few common underlying principles behind a complex and confusing variety of phenomena, differences in cultural expressions and in social institutional forms. It is the anthropologist`s task to grasp first the structural order behind, abstracting from the empirical data and building a model for understanding. Once the essentially simple and few principles are found the concrete studies with their data fall into place, i.e. investigation reverts to the manifold empirical data (DUMONT`s "second step"), which can now be better understood in their ideological context.

Technology and environment are - according to this evolutionary conception of PFEFFER and NEEDHAM - not a determinant causal factor for cultural and social evolution but a limiting factor ("Spielraum" as PFEFFER calls it) to the innovative urge of the human mind. "If we focus on technological and pragmatic man, we disguise the richness of ideational worlds and religious experience" (Lévi-Strauss) in archaic cultures, in which one single collective ideological and symbolic orientation integrates the social and cosmological order; individual social behaviour is powerfully constrained by it and there is no place for individualistic choices. It is a classificatory world view in which symbolism and analogical thinking is preeminent in a situation of low technological development which characterizes these cultures. And thus, evolution is seen as a movement from prescriptive systems to non-prescriptive systems, and "systematic and absolute forms of constraint...become superseded by more circumstantial factors" (Needham).

Coming back to the central concern with social and symbolic classification PFEFFER shows how an all-pervading dual classification orders the social life of the tribal societies and how symbolism is a basic integrating factor of the archaic social order. It is an order without an administrative apparatus; "symbolic classification thus subserves the jural purposes of government and legal institutions" (Needham 1979:22).

The "order of the hills" is shown by PFEFFER to be a dichotomous order at all levels of social organization, tribe, clan, village and also in ceremonial life, spatial arrangements etc. Here the author introduces NEEDHAM`s concept of "dual sovereignty" (or "complementary governance" or "diarchy")(Needham 1980), a structural principle expressing formal relations of "bipartition", "opposition" and "complementarity". This dyadic principle underlies the most different archaic social orders, it is an elementary and universal mode of classification in archaic societies. It not only forms the framework of the conceptual order but is also put to use in forms of symbolic action (e.g. rituals and religious ceremonies at marriages, births, funerals etc.). It is symbolically expressed through oppositions like senior/junior, sacred/secular, male/female, East/West etc. The principle of analogy integrates these dyads (binary oppositions) into a system. PFEFFER demonstrates this dual sovereignty for the tribal societies, and he hints at the same dichotomous order in the religious symbolic order of "Hindu" caste society in the plains of Orissa but with different symbols. Thus, just as DUMONT showed that the order of the caste system does not consist in "serial ways of ranking" but in "dichotomies at various levels", PFEFFER reveals the same order in the tribal world. "Dual sovereignty can independently be located in the tribal world and the culture of the plainsmen whom we usually call Hindus" (Pfeffer 1982a:4).

We cannot go into further detail; only a few important aspects of this "new" approach should briefly be mentioned, i.e. elements in the tribal societies which are an integral part or even partly the basis for the caste order.[16] The latter is understood, in a historical light, as the "merger of a bipolar order among those people (the "Aryans"), who in the course of their historical immigrations brought "Vedic" Hinduism from the Northwest and of a similar bipolar order among the indigenous people to whom we can attribute "tribal Hinduism" (Pfeffer 1982a:6/7). These aspects are: status differences, commensality, endogamy, concept of pollution, "dual leadership" (secular/sacred authority). Valued status differences between junior and senior as secular and sacred have consequences for the marriage regulations, - "something like a rule of endogamy emerges" - and for commensality; people of the same status, of the "own group", can eat together, commensality with "the others" is forbidden at ritual occasions. "Clearly commensality (and some ritual consequences) is used here as an idiom through which the basic unit of the "own" group is discriminated from the "others" (Pfeffer 1982b:47). Hinduization of food habits is therefore for him only a different, adopted "cultural expression" or "specific idiom" of the civilization for an idea already pronounced in tribal ideology. Similarly, the status difference junior/senior valued as secular/sacred is attached to the distinction craftsmen/cultivators, the first also associated with the herders and petty traders and designated nowadays as "Scheduled Castes". Its significance is a separation of pure and impure occupations and statuses. And the symbiosis between the two groups, economically and socially interdependent and complementary in their relationship, is interpreted by PFEFFER as originally a religious distinction and not determined by historical influence.

Finally, the phenomenon of "dual leadership" contradicts a superficial impression of the "absence of an influential internal leadership" (Pfeffer). Initially it is not only bound to individuals as office-holders, but it covers all the members of the village and the tribe, i.e. it represents a "Stand". Both are complementary, yet the sacred ritual leader is superior to the secular leader. But no privileged economic position is given to these authorities, they are "primus inter pares" marking the "egalitarian spirit" prevailing in tribal society. There is an obvious continuity between tribal and caste ideology in this separation of authority into sacred and secular; in caste society it is the relationship Brahman/Kshatriya, i.e. the disjunction, and yet complementarity, between priest and king which demonstrates this phenomenon, although some ideological transformation has taken place.

In spite of a fundamental structural unity of ideology in the two types of society PFEFFER points to ideological differences, too. First, there are "superficially, difference of elaboration. Two, three of four status groups in a tribal village oppose many more in a peasant (caste) village. But there are also qualitative differences" (Pfeffer 1982b:54). These qualitative differences lie in the politico-economic sphere. The status definitions are not yet tied to "class privileges" in tribal society and do not mark a permanent discrimination: the status opposition junior/senior in tribal society is never permanently equated with either the "pure" of the "impure" status as is the case in Hindu caste society where pure/impure marks a permanent separation; it is not tied to economic privilege as it is with the latter (Pfeffer). It is discontinuity that comes in with politico-economic change.

The term "ideology" looses here its precision and clarity; its muddled use must be criticized. How is it possible to speak at the same time of ideological unity and of qualitative ideological differences? It seems to me that two meaning of "ideology" are here confused; in DUMONT`s words: the primary level or "Mutter-Ideologie" and the secondary level or "Teil-Ideologien". The transition from tribal to caste society would be a suitable field for the investigation of an ideological transformation of "ideology" itself as a system of ideas and values, a basic collective orientation shared by all members of an archaic society to the use of "ideology" by a dominant group for the legitimation and camouflage of power structures.

RICOEUR (1977) and ORTH (1979) should be mentioned for their excellent articles on ideology and critique of ideology where they show the differentiation of the ideology concept: ideology first as a function of social integration through symbolization and a basic system of meaning, then ideology bound to the function of power and rule. It is from the second meaning that the Marxian sense of false consciousness or mystification is derived. Here the matter cannot be discussed in detail, but it is necessary to "rehabilitate" the concept of ideology for social anthropology, moving away from a one-sided, rigid, pejorative connotation in the Marxian sense, which may well be a final point of analysis, but not an adequate starting point as shown by Ricoeur.

As RÖSEL puts it in his work on the politico-economic aspects of the Jagannath cult in Puri: the social self-understanding of the people as a continuity with the past contradicts the objective social conditions which are those of a class society (Rösel 1980:335). He also points to the continuity from the archaic tribal society to an agrarian "proto-class" caste society being reflected in the religious meritocracy (Verdienstwirtschaft) of the Jagannath temple. It is also PFEFFER who turns to tribal society in his analysis of this archaic merit-economic phenomenon in the tribal world of the Gadaba, thereby demonstrating this continuity ethnographically, and also how the symbolic classificatory tribal world-view is realized in social action (ritual) (Pfeffer 1984).

A critical appreciation of PFEFFER`s analysis and interpretation can here be made only in the context of the methodological and theoretical approach to the tribe-caste question. A detailed review and criticism of the complex and complicated kinship problem cannot be made by me as I am not a specialist in kinship studies. Like DUMONT`s "Homo Hierarchicus" PFEFFER`s work, too, seems to be of "great design", of "ambitious theoretical premiss", an "ouvrage aux grandes ambitions" as two critics have remarked (Lina Fruzetti/Serge Bouez).

While accepting the overall framework of his analysis, yet leaving the critique of detailed kinship questions to other, more competent specialists, my point would be the following:

On the whole I agree with the general orientation of this genuine anthropological approach originating in the French sociological tradition and greatly inspired by MAUSS. In addition one finds some fascinating ideas especially on symbolism and classification of the British structuralist Rodney NEEDHAM whose ambition is "to break free from an academic social anthropology that is increasingly bureaucratic and prudential" and "to achieve something that would be found to possess the humane significance which at present is sought in the imaginative inventions of metaphysics and art" (Needham 1978:76). It is widely agreed that archaic and traditional societies are dominated by symbolism and a classificatory world-view in contradistinction to the "instrumental world-view" of modern industrial societies (Needham 1979:69/70). The ultimate task of the anthropologist is therefore to account for these differences.

It is DUMONT`s interpretation of the ideological structure of caste society and PFEFFER`s comparative study of the kinship systems of South Asia and his presentation of basic ideas and values of Indian tribal societies that constitute the basis for an intra-cultural perspective of Indian civilization, its emergence and historical transformation. It may be objected that the weakness of this anthropological orientation and structural approach lies in its concentration on the ideational domain to the detriment of the empirical variables, of the circumstances "as the complex of biological factors, as the context of economic facts, of historical events and influences, in short, 'reality` which are part and parcel of every communication relationship and cannot be eliminated" (Eco 1972:440).

But due to the complexity of the task of attaining a better understanding of alien cultures and societies as well as of our own, it must be admitted that DUMONT`s and PFEFFER`s approach marks an indispensable "first step" in this direction. At the beginning, the main problem for the anthropologist is the inter-cultural translation of concepts solved by DUMONT through the comparative global confrontation.

And after the analysis of the "primary level that is basic and general" (Dumont) the second step must follow, i.e. consideration of the "secondary levels relative to the primary level", relating to regional patterns, economic phenomena, historical, geographical/ecological and ethnic factors that lead to the empirical manifold diversity of the Indian subcontinent. It is at this secondary level that a variety of ideological schemes come into play which compete with each other in the course of history and are ultimately integrated into a dominant ideology. Thus, BURGHART`s criticism of DUMONT`s "single system model" of Indian culture and society (1983) is only partly valid, since he does not see DUMONT`s global, comparative perspective as a methodological prerequisite for investigation into the intra-cultural differentiation of Indian civilization. One can, at most, reproach DUMONT for having stopped at outlining the global perspective and not following up the second step, the "future outlook of studies" he himself suggested (1980:XXXVI). But he always emphasized that his approach "was a necessary stage, but it was only a stage". It is certainly a more difficult and complex undertaking to analyze the intracultural Indian scene. PFEFFER started with one important part of this intracultural differentiation, the comparison of tribal and caste society. He comes to the conclusion of an ideological continuity between both types of society, but the crucial question of what separates both, their differences, has still to be pursued in detail. Yet this can only be done if sufficient knowledge of the social order of Indian tribal societies is arrived at on the basis of ethnography.

The importance of detailed ethnography, therefore, is again and again stressed - and demonstrated by DUMONT, NEEDHAM and PFEFFER. The structure of the social and cosmic tribal order reveals itself in kinship categories and even in the construction of houses and their arrangement in villages (as "language of space"), in colour combinations and ornaments, in dresses etc. and it is acted out in rituals and ceremonies. In such a world rich in symbols every minute detail has its meaning and is interwoven with the daily life of the members of the social community. And on the basis of this concrete ethnographic evidence and the abstraction of structural principles one comes closer to real understanding than through mere speculation in a general and abstract way. These empirical investigations together with theoretical abstractions and interpretations have hardly begun for the field of anthropological study of Indian tribal societies although more or less ingenious speculations on them are widespread.

Finally, a differentiated "practice approach",[17] not as an antagonistic alternative to a structural approach, but as complementary to it, should be postulated. Here, history comes into play, too.

IX. CONCLUSION

The principal aim of this essay was to review and critically discuss the different anthropological explanations or interpretations of tribe-caste relationship in India and subsequently to formulate questions of priority for further ethnographic investigation and for a theoretical synthesis as a framework for analysis, for an "ecology of explanations" with a hierarchy of analytical levels. The perspective should only be seen as a tentative and global attempt to formulate these issues for further collaborative research; it was not my intention to give a comprehensive and detailed analysis of any of the issues touched upon. Deeper analysis and the use of new ethnographic and historical data and their synthetic interpretation must be left to detailed studies.[18]

The broad perspective under which the question of tribe-caste relationship can be seen is that of the development process of Indian civilization, its specific social and cultural configuration and its sociogenesis which - as indicated - could profit from an integrated framework of approaches. The task of Social Anthropology would be to work out the fundamental ideologies and value orientations of the archaic tribal societies of India and traditional caste society and their respective transformation in the course of history. The structuralist approach with its achievements as regards understanding of alien ideational worlds, contrasted with the background of the researcher, is seen as the basis for further theoretical development focussing on "praxis" and history .

The review should have exposed the perspectivity of any anthropological interpretation or explanation. Criticism of the different pre-structuralist approaches does not mean - it should be explicitly said - that the data and some of the authors` findings are invalid. Their limitations should be seen before the background of their time and the prevailing "paradigms". Besides, many of the controversies arising among researchers apparently dealing with the "same" ethnographic material, are due to the fact that they approach the evidence on different levels of abstraction and analysis without considering this fact. None of the approaches can be accepted as adequate in their claim to exclusiveness. Questions are not answered either by simple materialistic determinism (neo-evolutionism), by pragmatist or utilitarian explanations (Bailey), by historical explanations nor by an approach in which priority given to the cultural order without considering historical and sociological factors looks suspiciously like idealism. In the latter case - the structuralist approach - it sometimes seems difficult to make out clearly whether the analyst attributes a mere methodological priority to ideology and classification or an ontological status. The cultural model and the actual praxis cannot be segregated. Thus, instead of being alternative or competitive, the approaches could be seen as complementary and ordered in a systematic hierarchy of levels, i.e. all aspects - evolutionary, historical, structural, of social change, of individual actors etc. - which the different authors discuss, are valid, yet must be seen in the postulated framework. The perspective of total socio-cultural formations in Social Anthropology with the premise of different emphases and valuations in different cultural configurations and of culturally diverse histories is to my mind fundamental and by no means excludes elements of power struggle, choice, conflicts etc. as exemplified by BOURDIEU`s practice approach (Bourdieu 1979). Methodologically, the symbolic and ideological structures have to be analyzed in their concretization in social institutions, concrete settings and actions, and with the ensuing tensions and contradictions that mark the historical process, mediated by the specific culture.

In order to achieve this totalizing conceptualization and synthetic approach more empirical, ethnographic explorations especially into the tribal societies and cultures of India and a new interpretation of their world view, cosmological schemes, collective representations and respective practice in actions and rituals, their "economic" and "political" organisation is indispensable, supplementing the available material dating from the colonial period and gathered by the administrator-ethnographers and missionaries or subjecting it to a re-interpretation, as the greatest part of their material is with an empiricist intent: analysis is restricted to a single level - to that of observed facts and mere description. Yet "it is the task of anthropology to bring out by careful analysis of each case what are in fact, in an exotic conception of reality, the indigenous criteria by which things are defined and classified" (Needham 1979:15).

I hope to have substantiated the validity of RÖSEL`s statement - already demonstrated by DUMONT and PFEFFER - that it is the necessary, first task of social anthropologists to represent adequately and appropriately and in their ideological and cultural context all social phenomena about which universally generalizing speculations have been going on for some 50 years, i.e. to understand alien symbolic and classification systems. This is the important lesson we could learn from MAUSS and his followers, in the first place. Here, a lot of "basic research" remains to be done, including bringing these classification systems down to the level of praxis. PFEFFER`s article on a ritual of the Gadaba of Middle India (1984) where he describes the social and symbolic classification "in action" in ritual, in the material activity of the people, may be a step towards such an approach. For a "macro-perspective" it seems that mere speculative evolutionary or conjectural historical reconstruction and explanation could be overcome on the basis of structural insights into the cultural configuration of Indian tribal and caste society.

References

1 This paper is an abbreviated version of my doctoral dissertation, Heidelberg 1985/86. After this more theoretical preparatory exercise ethnographic investigations (fieldwork) and interpretation await me in my further anthropological work. I am very grateful to my fried MARGARET RAE for kindly reading and correcting my English manuscript.

1a R. Blackburn (ed.), Ideology in social science. 7. impr. Glasgow 1979, p. 10.

2 There is a lack of detailed ethnographic work and its interpretation on Central Indian tribes dating from recent times. The most detailed descriptions are still to be found in the Census- and Gazetteer-publications of India and in the ethnographies of the colonial administrator-scholars and missionaries, but with out-of-date explanations.

3 See also B.S. Cohn, Notes on the history of the study of Indian society and culture, in Structure and change in Indian society, M.B. Singer, B.S. Cohn (eds.), 1968, pp. 3-27.

4 See e.g. D. Kantowsky (ed.), Recent research on Max Weber`s studies of Hinduism. München 1986.

5 Southall 1970, Fried 1965/66, 1975, Godelier 1978, Helm 1968.

6 Cf. L. Dumont for a short history of ideas concerning "caste", in Homo Hierarchicus. 1980. Rev. Engl. ed. Chicago 1977, pp. 21-32.

[7] Max Weber`s expositions on Hinduization are not dealt with in this review.

[8] "Neo"-evolutionist is used here in spite of a rejection of this term by the leading representative, Leslie White, himself.

[9] Klass dates the origin of the caste system back to pre-Vedic and pre-Aryan time.

[10] See e.g. J. Friedman, M.J. Rowlands (eds.), The evolution of social systems. London 1977.

[11] Cf. Dumont`s critique of social change studies of India and in general (1964).

[12] Sinha 1957a, 1957b, 1962, 1965, 1980.

[13] The concept of "levels of socio-cultural integration" is taken over from Julian Steward.

[14] Pfeffer 1982a, 1982b, 1982c, 1983a, 1983b, 1984

[15] For an intra-cultural view of Indian civilization cf. Burghart, R., For a sociology of Indias: an intracultural approach to the study of "Hindu" society, in CIS. N.S. 17. 1983, pp. 273-299.

[16] See also N.S. Reddy, Caste in a tribal society: the formative process, in CIS. N.S. 7. 1973, pp. 159-167. He argues that the origin of the caste system lay deeper in the indigenous soil rather than in the upper strata of Aryan social organization. Endogamy and commensal relations originated with aboriginal inhabitants and ideas of ritual purity were existent in pre-Aryan India.

[17] Cf. S. Ortner, Theory in anthropology since the sixties, in Comparative studies in society and history. 26. 1984, p. 144 ff

[18] I am preparing a more detailed investigation into "dual leadership" among Central Indian tribes with comparative notes on African and other archaic tribal societies. Stress will be laid on ethnography; theoretically, an atomistic discipline "Political Anthropology" will be called in question, instead a Maussian approach with different enlargements be attempted Besides, a conceptual framework for the cooperation of historians and anthropologists of India should be elaborated.

Bibliography

Bailey, F.G., Correspondence: For a sociology of India?, in CIS. 3. 1959, pp. 88-1o1

Bailey, F.G., Tribe, caste and nation. Manchester 1960

Bailey, F.G., "Tribe" and "caste" in India, in CIS. 5. 1961, pp. 7-19

Bourdieu, P., Entwurf einer Theorie der Praxis. Frankfurt a.M. 1979 (stw; 291)

Burghart, R., For a sociology of Indias: an intracultural approach to the study of "Hindu" society, in CIS. N.S. 17. 1983, pp. 273-299

CIS, Contributions to India sociology. 1. 1957-9. 1966. N.S. 1. 1967 ff.

Dumont, L., For a sociology of India, in CIS. 1. 1957, pp. 7-22

Dumont, L., Change, interaction and comparison, in CIS. 7. 1964, pp. 7-17

Dumont, L., The individual as impediment to sociological comparison and Indian sociology, in Dumont, Religion, politics and history in India. 1970, pp. 133-150

Dumont, L., On the comparative understanding of non-modern civilizations, in Daedalus. 104. 1975, pp. 153-171

Dumont, L., Gesellschaft in Indien. Wien 1976

Dumont, L., From Mandeville to Marx. Chicago 1977

Dumont, L., The anthropological community and ideology, in Social science information. 18. 1979, pp. 785-817

Dumont, L., Homo Hierarchicus. Rev. Engl. ed. Chicago 1977

Eco, U., Einführung in die Semiotik. München 1972

Fried, M.H., On the concept of "tribe" and "tribal society", in Transactions of the New York, Academy of Sciences. Ser. II. 28. 1965/66, pp. 527-540

Fried, M.H., The notion of tribe. Menlo Park, CA 1975

Godelier, M., The concept of "tribe", in Godelier, Perspectives in Marxist anthropology. Repr. London 1978, pp. 70-96

Helm, J. (ed.), Essays on the problem of tribe. Seattle 1968. (Repr. 1971)

Khare, R.S., Structuralism in India: some issues and observations, in CIS. N.S. 12. 1978, pp. 253-278

Klass, M., Caste: the emergence of the South Asian social system. Philadelphia 1980

Koppers, W., India and dual organization, in Acta tropica. 1. 1944, pp. 72-93 a. 97-118

Kulke, H., Kshatriyaization and social change, in Aspects on changing India. Ed., S.D. Pillai Bombay 1976

Needham, R., Terminology and alliance. I. II., in Sociologus. 16. 1966, pp. 141-157 a. 17. 1967, pp. 39-54

Needham, R., Introduction, in Durkheim/Mauss: Primitive classification. 2.ed. London 1969, pp. VII-XLVIII

Needham, R., Primordial characters. Charlottesville 1978

Needham, R., Symbolic classification. Santa Monica 1979

Needham, R., Reconnaissances. Toronto 1980

Orth, E.W., Von der Ideo-logie zur Ideologie-Kritik, in Phänomenologie udn Marxismus. Hrsg. B. Waldenfels (u.a.), Frankfurt a.M., Bd. 4, 1979, pp. 197-234

Ortner, S., Theory in anthropology sine the sixties, in Comparative studies in society and history. 26. 1984, pp. 126-166

Pfeffer, G., Status and affinity in Middle India. Wiesbaden 1982 (1982a)

Pfeffer, G., Tribal social organization and "Hindu" influence, in Internationales Asienforum. 13. 1982, pp. 45-54 (1982b)

Pfeffer, G., Indien und die Dualorganisation: eine Kritik an W. Koppers, in Anthropos. 77. 1982, pp. 134-150 (1982c)

Pfeffer, G., Generation and marriage in Middle India: the evolutionary potential of "restricted exchange", in CIS. N.S. 17. 1983, pp. 87-121 (1983a)

Pfeffer, G., Präskription und Geschichte: Grenzen in pakistanischen Terminologie, in Ethnologie und

Geschichte. Hrsg., P. Snoy. Wiesbaden 1983, pp. 471-485 (1983b)

Pfeffer, G., Mittelindische Megalithen als meritökonomische Kategorien, in Paideuma. 30. 1984, pp. 232-240

Ricouer, P., Ideologie und Ideologiekritik, in Phänomenologie und Marxismus. Hrsg., B. Waldenfels (u.a.), Frankfurt a.M. Bd. 1, 1977, pp. 197-233

Risley, H., The peoples of India. 2.ed. Calcutta 1915. (Orig. 1908)

Rösel, J., Bemerkungen zur interdisziplinären Entwicklungsländerforschung, in Internationales Asienforum. 5. 1974, pp. 243-253

Rösel, J., Der Palast des Herrn der Welt. München 1980

Roy, S.C., The Hill Bhuiyas of Orissa, with comparative notes on the Plains Bhuiyas. Ranchi 1935

Roy, S.C., The Kharias. Vol. 1-2. Ranchi 1937

Sinha, S.C., Evolutionism re-considered, in Man in India. 35. 1955, pp. 1-18

Sinha, S.C., Tribal cultures of Peninsular India as a dimension of Little Tradition in the study of Indian civilization, in Man in India. 37. 1957, pp. 93-118 (1957a)

Sinha, S.C., The media and nature of Hindu-Bhumij interaction, in Journal of the Asiatic Society. Letters & Science. 23. 1957, pp. 23-37 (1957b)

Sinha, S.C., State formation and Rajput myth in tribal Central India, in Man in India. 42. 1962, pp. 35-80

Sinha, S.C., Tribe-caste and tribe-peasant continua in Central India, in Man in India. 45. 1965, pp. 57-83

Sinha, S.C., Tribes and India civilization: a perspective, in Man in India. 60. 1980, pp. 1-15

Southall, A.W., The illusion of tribe, in Journal of Asian and African studies. 5. 1970, pp. 28-50

Srinivas, M.N., Religion and society among the Coorgs of South India. 1952 (2.ed. London 1965)

Tambiah, S.J., Culture, thought and social action: an anthropological perspective. Cambridge, Mass. 1985

Uberoi, J.S., For a sociology of India: outlines of structural sociology 1945-1970, in CIS. N.S. 8. 1974, pp. 135-152

Yalman, N., De Tocqueville in India: an essay on the caste system. (Review article), in Man. N.S. 4. 1969, pp. 123-131

Kinship Categories in two South Asian Societies: Competition and Cooperation in Swat and Kandy[1]

by Inge Rösch-Rhomberg

1. INTRODUCTION

On the face of it perhaps no two kinship organizations could look so different as those of the Islamic Pukhtun in Pakistan and the Buddhist Kandyan Sinhalese in Sri Lanka. The Pukhtun are strongly patrilineal embodying an ideology of egalitarianism with fierce competition between agnates leading to violent and often deadly struggles. The Kandyan Sinhalese have an egalitarian bilateral kinship organization characterized by cooperation and alliance and simultaneously an ideology of caste hierarchy. And yet, the two systems have structural similarities. My aim is to highlight a number of similarities and differences by comparing or rather contrasting them.

There is no question of balancing details against each other, a venture which would unquestionably evoke criticism on methodological grounds.

The opinion of many anthropologists that we could learn something about our own culture through the medium of other cultures and vice versa might be transferable to a comparison of two unfamiliar cultural systems.

"In zones where positivism cannot reach, the testing of system against system is the only hope for advance...As a result new kinds of 'universals` become accessible. This is to move well beyond structuralism of the facile kind, but not I think beyond the programme of Lévi-Strauss himself, frequently contradictory although it is." (ARDENER, 1971:462 f)

Thus, it seems legitimate to confront kinship structures[2], the connective communication principles of which represent antithesis, namely violence and alliance, competition and cooperation.

The analytical concepts used here have been influenced by the work of LINDHOLM, 'Generosity and Jealousy` (1982) and YALMAN`s 'Under the Bo Tree` (1967).

Economic and demographic conditions show some similarities in the villages studied by LINDHOLM and YALMAN. The inhabitants live mainly on irrigated cultivation, supplemented in Kandy by shifting cultivation (chena), in Swat by cattle-breeding. For a population which multiplied rapidly during the last decades, limited land for irrigation purposes imposes severe constraints. Instead of the various traditional share cropping arrangements, land-owners increasingly work on their own fields with the help of additional seasonal workers who are pain in cash.

Both village communities recognize caste-like groupings, variants of the orthodox Hindu prototype (LEACH, 1960:2). As far as Swat is concerned, detailed ethnographic material on the non-Pukhtun is lacking. The ethnographers of Swat concentrated their work on the land-owning Pukhtun. "In Swat, a man without land is no longer reckoned as a Pukhtun, and he loses his place in the family tree" (LINDHOLM, 1982:74). In contrast to the above, YALMAN included all castes when doing research. Kinship categories did not vary within castes.

Following LEACH, "Internally, a caste presents itself to its members as a network of kin relationships, but this network is of no specific type. The kinship systems of caste-ordered societies vary,..." (1960:7), it is considered legitimate, to compare principles of the kinship organization regardless of caste formation.

2. THEORETICAL ASSUMPTIONS

Whereas non-anthropologists usually regard 'kinship` as an uninteresting subject, it is an established convention among anthropologists to consider it to be the very basis of human social structures. NEEDHAM goes so far as to stress that "... the study of these matters conventionally subsumed under the rubric of kinship is part of a search for what can be called primary factors of human experience(...)" and "...it should be the chief and proper task of social anthropology to determine whether there are to be found any absolute features of thought and action..." (1974:36).

Both, LINDHOLM and YALMAN, are inspired by LEVI-STRAUSS` structuralism. Following LEVI-STRAUSS, who suggests that structuralism reflects less a theory, or a clear cut method, but rather a scientific theoretical point of view (1980:224), it is not astonishing that the relationship between the two scientists can only be established over their theoretical points of view:

"The ambition of structural analysis, as stated by LEVI-STRAUSS, is nothing less than the comprehensive exposure of the hidden but fundamental rules of form which lie beneath the surface of the society. Explicitly, such an effort strives to be all encompassing, to bring the entire repertoire of a culture under the aegis of the postulated rules." (LINDHOLM, 1982:XXVI)

"When we speak of social structure what we mean is that a large number of individuals regard the structure of their society in the same way and that they communicate and behave in an appropriate manner." (YALMAN, 1967:4)

Both suppose that categories of thought, manifest in the communication systems of the respective cultures, structure the behaviour of their members. LINDHOLM concentrates mainly on inter-human relationships, i.e. acts of communication in the broadest sense, as exchange patterns, which include for example also violence as a form of communication. For YALMAN communication means language. He sees the paradigmatic structures of Sinhalese thought in their system of kin terms. In this respect YALMAN builds on the work of DUMONT (1953, 1957).

A different viewpoint has been adopted by other anthropologists in their monographs on the Swat Rukhtun (BARTH, 1959) and on the Kandyan Sinhalese (LEACH, 1961) who emphasize a transactionalist or functionalist position respectively.

LINDHOLM and YALMAN do not deny that particular individuals maximize benefits. However, unlike action theorists who underplay constraints or rules, they make it clear that constraints in societies are constants, to which individuals adapt external factors and that manipulations of these rules can only follow the logic of a system of categories.

Problems arise insofar, as LINDHOLM and YALMAN (as also LEVI-STRAUSS) do not systematically distinguish levels of interpretation regarding the realm of categories, the realm of norms and rules and the realm of factual behaviour. How difficult it is to separate the three levels has been emphasized by NEEDHAM, one of the most rigorous advocates of this claim: "...there is no uncategorized social action. Behaviour reflects ideas, and ideas (collective representations) are expressed in categories..."(1967:48).

Whereas the classificatory system of kin terms of the Kandyan Sinhalese enables the isolation of categories in a positivistic sense, this is much more difficult in the case of the Swat Pukhtun, where the kinship terminology has to be classed as a descriptive one containing nonetheless some classificatory elements.

How far it is possible to deduce categories from existing norms in kinship relations is controversial amongst anthropologists, since the analyst has partially to rely on normative statements.

LEVI-STRAUSS combined hypotheses on kin behaviour patterns in elementary societies to a relationship system which he calls

"l'élement de parenté " (1958:56) or "l'atome de parenté " (1973:103 ff).

For LEVI-STRAUSS, the basic building block of a kin system consists of two pairs of correlative oppositions, i.e. on the intragenerational level the relation between 'brother` and 'sister` and between 'husband` and 'wife` and on the intergenerational vertical between 'father` and 'son`, as well as between 'mother`s brother` and 'sister`s son`.

Attitudes are classed positive or negative depending on behaviour patterns between kin or classes of kin which can be institutionalized or non-institutionalized and which are usually sanctioned by taboos or privileges. A positive sign characterizes friendly interaction and mutual generosity, a negative sign hostile, antagonistic or reserved relations.[3]

Although LEVI-STRAUSS` model has some weaknesses, his formal presentation of 'ideal` communication patterns between kin was appealing to me to use for a structural analysis, all the more, as exchange patterns between kin are social phenomena which remain constant over long periods of time. LEVI-STRAUSS regards the relationship between brothers-in-law as the necessary axis around which a kinship structure is built (l'axe inévitable autour duquel se construit la structure de parenté, ...". 1958:57). Taking the above into account, DUMONT`s abstractions in the realm of kin terms regarding the alliance relationship (1953:35) seem to me a pore precise representation for the horizontal part of the LEVI-STRAUSS model. For DUMONT, the crucial relation is not between 'husband` and 'wife` , but between 'brothers-in-law` or between 'sisters-in-law`. It includes a male, as well as a female viewpoint.

When confronting Swat and Kandy, I had to concentrate on male intragenerational relationships because of inadequate data as far as the female sphere is concerned. The same applies to the male intergenerational relationships in the bilateral Kandyan context. Neither of the ethnographers of the Kandyan Sinhalese distinguished systematically between 'binna` and 'deega` context[4] when reporting on kin behaviour patterns. Anyhow, the male intragenerational relation patterns are well and non-controversially documented by all ethnographers of the respective societies and show one elementary difference in the kin systems of Swat and Kandy, competition in Swat and cooperation in Kandy intragenerationally. With respect to the intergenerational relations, I can only allude to another important distinction which could be cooperation in Swat and competition in Kandy as far as intergenerational or external relations are concerned. Yet, details have to be further explored.

Before comparing structural features of two kin systems, some remarks have to be made regarding the kinship organizations of the Swat Pukhtun and the Kandyan Sinhalese in order to give the reader who is unacquainted with the relevant literature an idea.[5]

3. SWAT PUKHTUN

Pukhtun or Pakhtun, often referred to as Pathan, are part of the large Pushtu or Pukhtu (an Iranian language)[6] speaking ethnic group inhabiting adjoining areas of North-West Pakistan and Afghanistan. They all claim to be descendants of an apical ancestor, known as Quais or Abdur-Rashid (AHMED, 1980:128; LINDHOLM, 1982:70). Details of individual genealogies differ, as do genealogies transmitted by historians and ethnographers of the Pukhtun (BARTH, 1959:26 and 1981:59 f; CAROE, 1958:13; GLATZER, 1977:110, et al.).

In Swat, North-West Pakistan, all Pukhtun trace their descent back to Yusuf, one of the descendants of the mythical progenitor. They call themselves Yusufzai. According to LINDHOLM, 'zai` means 'place` and is used to refer to the offspring of very distant ancestors. Genealogical subdivisions relate to regions, villages, sections of villages and subsections of villages. Land rights and social identity are derived from membership in a patrilineage (khel), (LINDHOLM, 1982:XXVI and 74).

According to his patrilineal ideology, a Pukhtun is not only able to classify himself as son of ..., son of ..., son of ..., up to an eponymous male ancestor into the total ethnic group, or into patri-clans on different levels, but, additionally or alternatively, he can see himself in opposition to brothers, to sons of father`s brothers and father`s father`s brothers` sons, etc., who in turn can draw a line to the common ancestor in imagining absent brothers, father`s brothers` sons, etc. Females are missing altogether in this mode of thought (see fig. 3).

Clan names and locality descriptions in Swat often overlap. "Regions are usually made up of three 'brother` clans, two strong and one weak, which are cross-cut by dəla[7] alliances (LINDHOLM, 1982:32). Three village sections (palao) are, according to LINDHOLM, common in Swat villages and even the palao are frequently tripartite. Every subsection of a palao (təl) is dominated by a strong personality, whose name stands for the təl. As speaker of his neighbouring agnates and clients (members of non-Pukhtun groups)[8] the təl leader is expected to assist his neighbours in the village jirga.[9] Within the təl, brothers and father`s brothers` sons (tarbur) constantly fight against each other for leadership and prestige. As a matter of fact, the term 'tarbur` not only designates a patrilateral male parallel cousin, usually of the same generation, it also means enemy and 'tarburwali`, the relationship of enmity and/or agnatic rivalry and alliance prevailing between 'tarbur`, dominated and dominates Pukhtun life (AHMED, 1980; BARTH, 1959; LINDHOLM, 1982). Contrary to other patrilineal segmentary tribal societies, the inherent fission possibilities of the system are already utilized in Swat on the brother-brother level, i.e. not group segments, but mainly individuals confront each other. For LINDHOLM, the underlying pattern in Swati culture is triadic, "...consisting of ego, his temporary allies and his temporary enemies" (LINDHOLM, 1982:32).

Much has been written on the institutions of feud and warfare in Middle Eastern segmentary lineage societies since ROBERTSON-SMITH influential work, 'Kinship and Marriage in Early Arabia` , 1885. Whereas violence against close agnatic kin is disallowed or reduced through taboos in many Middle Eastern Countries (BOURDIEU, 1976; LINDHOLM cites HART, 1970), violence is highly structured in Swat according to LINDHOLM, whose analysis and interpretation of 'tarburwali` follows in part AHMED`s outline regarding the Mohmand, a neighbouring Pukhtun tribe. AHMED sees tarburwali as a "Pukhto paradigm" (1980:181), as the structuring principle of Pukhtun society. In his review of AHMED, CHRISTENSEN argues that AHMED`s concept is miscontrued, insofar as it lacks any allusion to solidarity between close agnates, which really is the Pukhtun 'ideal`. Both positions are encompassed by LINDHOLM`s insightful description of tarburwali, revenge obligations and land rights to illustrate the "...relations of 'complementary opposition` between lineage segments..." (1982:69).

Tarburwali constitutes for LINDHOLM only one form of rivalry. Strained relations prevail not only between agnatic collaterals, but also between fathers and sons and husbands and wives. On a higher lineage level, tarbur ally in a tə l, against another tə l, tə l ally in a palao against another palao, villages against villages, etc. (1982:78 f). LINDHOLM devotes considerable space to an examination of specific rules of violence for hostilities with patrilineal segments of equal scale. He states that violence "...becomes more honorable as genealogical distance increases but...as genealogical scale increases, the obligation to revenge decreases" (1982:87). In Swat, it is expected that a male ego revenges his brothers, his first and second patrilateral parallel cousins (tarbur), his father and father`s brother`s sons, his father`s father and father`s father`s brothers, his sons and brother`s sons and as far as females are concerned, his mother, his sisters and his father`s sisters. Blood revenge has to be executed directly on the murderer and eventually on his father and sons, which is in contrast to many Middle Eastern nomadic tribes, where a killing would threaten all lineage members of the killer over many generations. The obligation to revenge unites tarbur insofar, as "...no man would support the murderer of his tarbur under any circumstances, even if the killer were a long time party ally" (LINDHOLM, 1982:80).

Rights in clan land overlap with revenge obligations, except for females who do not inherit land in Swat. Landed property is owned by individuals, but rules linked to the inheritance and the selling of land show clearly how closely the living agnates of a lineage are connected through mutual obligations. Swat Pukhtun differentiate between clan land (dauftar)[10] which can only be sold to lineage members, and non-clan land (tseri) which is held in shares and can be sold freely. Yet with one restriction: "Share holders in a piece of tseri must be kinsmen" (LINDHOLM, 1982:65). Offences against these unwritten laws would evoke drastic reactions: "An outsider who came to claim land within the village would find his fields burned and his life in danger" (ibid.). Selling land in Swat is, according to LINDHOLM, like selling part on one`s identity. On the other hand, many Pukhtun would go to any extreme to enlarge their plots. Swati inheritance rights favour the descendants of the last surviving brother in case there is one in a group of brothers who has no sons to pass his land on to. Adoption of sons is forbidden. A landsowner is, of course, free to make a testament against the traditional rules, but this would prove fatal for the favoured one, as LINDHOLM emphasizes (1982:62 ff).

In one respect, unity has to be maintained to defend the lineage land against outsiders, and on the other hand, lineage members continually struggle among themselves for power and control of land. (Tarburwali claimed seven killings of tarbur or tarbur`s servants during LINDHOLM`s fieldwork in a village of 2000 inhabitants).

A Pukhtun not only struggles for power and land, but for his honour as well as the honour of the lineage women following the claims of a highly developed code of personal honour (pakhtunwali).[11]

AHMED`s, BARTH`s and LINDHOLM`s reports are identical as far as the antagonistic attitudes between male lineage members are concerned. It is LINDHOLM who gives a brief description of relationship patterns between agnates and affines, between males and females.

According to him, "every male-female relationship has elements of violence in Swat" (1982:127), men look, down on women and try to ignore them altogether (1982:220). Actual and symbolic barriers between the male and female world in Middle Eastern countries are well known. 'Purdah` (seclusion of women) in Swati villages, LINDHOLM observes, "goes far beyond anything enjoined in the Koran". Women are seen as being licentious, morally susceptible, sexually more passionate than men, and, therefore, a constant threat to men`s honour. Women embody in themselves the contradiction of the patrilineal ideology, which on the one hand assigns a central role to their wombs and on the other side ignores them as autonomous lineage members (ibid.).

Women identify themselves with their patriline, their loyalty belong to their fathers and brothers at the expense of their husbands. "Relations between husbands and wives tend to be warlike" (LINDHOLM, 1982:148). Having grown up as a proud member of her patriline, favoured by a socialization process in childhood which forces girls to think and act on their own responsibility, (whereas boys were largely constrained to inactivity)[12], a woman tries constantly to keep her lineage honour in attacking the honour of her husband`s patriline. "Men are encouraged and permitted to beat their wives regularly" LINDHOLM, 1982:61), but, "this is considered perfectly normal, and the wife is even somewhat proud of her battle scars" (LINDHOLM, 1979:16). As LINDHOLM remarks, Pukhtun women are far from the Western image of docile purdah females. Relations between in-laws are generally tense. "...the term of reference for in-laws (skh r) is considered an insult in address (LINDHOLM, 1982:149).

As in many Middle Eastern societies, the brother-sister relationship can also be regarded in Swat as the most powerful bond.[13] "At death, it is expected the sisters will grieve the most for their brother, and vice versa" (LINDHOLM), 1982:126). A Pukhtun would got to his sister first for advice and financial aid, says LINDHOLM. In turn, brothers were responsible for the well-being of their sisters. If problems arise, it is the brother or the mother`s brother (mama) who has to protect the sister or the sister`s daughter and her children.

In contrast to relationships between male lineage members and between brothers-in-law, affection and trust exist between ego and his maternal relatives. "Children who are orphaned are brought up by the mother`s brother, who protects them against the greed of their tarbur" (LINDHOLM, 1982:151). "...Mamagan (people of the mother`s lineage)...are expected to be political allies of their sister`s children" (1982:152). LINDHOLM points out, that a mama is the only person, who has a chance to act as mediator in struggles between tarbur.

Despite a patrilineal ideology, the Swat system of attitudes shows clearly a covert cognatic structure. According to LINDHOLM it is customary in Swat to address all older men, with whom one wishes to be on good terms and who are outsiders, with 'mama` and all younger men with 'mama zway`. A highly idealized friendship pattern, which is interpreted by LINDHOLM to be an emotional necessity in the hostile world of the Pukhtun, could probably be integrated in a relationship system to outbalance the predominantly negative attitudes.

Hierarchical forms can be detected from the 'mushur` and 'kushur` categories, despite an egalitarian ideology founded on the belief that all Pukhtun are descendants of the same mythical progenitor. 'Mushur` is generally used for an elder, but at the same time for a strong and powerful personality. All younger persons are named 'kushur` which means simultaneously follower. When allusion is made to 'mushur` or 'kushur` clans, not junior or senior lines are referred to, but distinction is made between politically powerful and weak clans. The same clan which is 'mushur` in one village, is 'kushur`in another. (LINDHOLM, 1982:213; BARTH, 1959).

To complete this short overview of the Swat kinship organization, some information on marriage rules and practices will be given below:

First marriages are arranged by the parents or close agnates, not by the individuals concerned.

Arranged marriages - even for unborn and younger children - are considered binding for both parties. Divorce is not possible. Widows without sons have to marry a brother of close agnate of the deceased husband. Adult men are allowed to marry additional women corresponding to Koranic law. LINDHOLM writes that due to recent religious propaganda, the Pukhtun became aware that the institution of bride price, i.e. purchasing a girl, is against the Koran; therefore it is nowadays given covertly by the groom`s family to the bride`s father. The bride price is still the largest prestation at marriage.

In addition to the bride price, an important part of a marriage contract is the value of the 'mahar`(jewelry and land rights given to the bride by the groom`s father). However, it is expected that the mahar is returned by the bride to the groom after the wedding night.[14] Yeat, latent rights for the mahar remain. In case of problems, the mahar can be claimed by the wife and her patrilineage. Instead of land, however, cash is transferred. (BARTH, 1959; LINDHOLM, 1982).

No exogamy or endogamy rules exist, at least for Pukhtun men, with the exception of prohibitions laid down in the Koran.[15] Exchange of women (adal badal) is forbidden in Swat. Pukhtun prefer to marry close relatives, which has been verified by LINDHOLM statistically. Classificatory father`s brother`s children[16] marriages score highest (1982:61 and 144). In spite of shortcomings in LINDHOLM`s data, it can be said that about two thirds of the women of a clan analyzed by him married within the same clan; nearly half of the women married a real or classificatory FBS.

LINDHOLM did not find regular alliance patterns: "The only pattern found in the genealogies is that of a lineage segment forming a marriage relationship with another line, marrying intensively with them for a generation or two, and then breaking off the relationship" (1982:144 f).

4. THE KANDYAN SINHALESE

Anthropologists are confronted with an astonishing variety of kinship organizations in Sri Lanka. In addition to his detailed study of the bilateral non-lineal Sinhalese of a Dry Zone village in the Highlands, YALMAN describes variant organizations, such as the patrilocal Kandyan aristocrats, the patrilocal patrilineal hypergamous Sinhalese of the South Coast with a prominent dowry system, the matrilocal Tamil Moors (Muslims) and the matrilineal hypergamous Hindu Tamils of the East Coast. All these forms, including the 'matri-moities` which ROBINSON found in a Highland village (1968), reveal a structural similarity.

Sinhalese, Tamils and Veddha (BROW, 1978) use a classificatory kinship terminology, the meanings of which coincide, i.e. the structure on the level of categories is the same. There is reason to believe that bilateral, patrilineal and matrilineal organizational forms have structural similarities which are still ignored by some anthropologists. In this article, my arguments are confined to the bilateral system which predominates in the Dry Zone of the former Kandyan Kingdom.

YALMAN classifies the Sinhalese kinship terminology[17] as 'Dravidian` which he considers "basically similar to the Kariera terminology of Australia..." (1967:210)[18]. The following criteria stress the clearly symmetrical structure of the Sinhalese system of kin terms, in which independent terms for affines are non-existent: distinction of generation, differentiation of two sexes in each generation, and additional partition of all males and females into two categories in the three central generations (+1, 0, -1), age differentiation[19] within only one male and one female category in G 0.

Kin terms are seen as categories, the system of kinship categories as pattern of thought. YALMAN makes the point that "the main structure is contained in three generations - that is ego`s generation, the first ascending, and the first descending generations" (ibid.). In each generation kin are classified into four categories or two pairs of oppositions: "...two classifications, a socio-biological one into male/female and a cultural one into prescribed/prohibited mating categories, cross-cut each generation into four primary classes" (YALMAN, 1967:212). Terminologically, there is for any individual only one mating category, for a women in G 0 a 'massina`, for a man a 'nena`. The categories 'massina` and 'nena` include the own bilateral cross-cousins (MBCH and FZCH)[20]. In opposition to 'massina` and 'nena`, the categories 'ayya`(eB) and 'malli` (yB) as well as 'akka` (eZ) and 'nangi` (yZ), merge into one category in each sex; these categories include own brothers and sisters, as well as own parallel cousins.[21]

YALMAN deduces from relations between the categories in the three generations (G 0, G+1 and G-1), the following equation: spouse = MBCH or FZCH (1969:609 f).[22] Alliance theorists refer to such a system as a classificatory kinship system with prescriptive alliance (NEEDHAM, 1972/73). YALMAN`s contribution to the study of Dravidian classificatory systems is his finding about the indefinite lateral extension possibility of the system (see fig. 4, horizontal axis in G+1 and G 0).[23]

In ignoring the age distinction on a vertical dimension, however, YALMAN neglects the distance revealing aspect of the nomenclature.[24]

Sinhalese and the ethnographers` definitions of the macro- and micro-groupings on the ground, as jati (caste), variga (sub-caste), pavula (micro-caste or kindred) [25] vary; yet all carry the connotation of kind and category. Groups can be referred to as jati, variga and pavula when contrasting them with others. YALMAN considers for his area of study the 'pavula` as the main intra-caste grouping which he defines as micro-caste or kindred (1967:189 ff).[26] The 'pavula`[27] includes consanguinal and affinal kin who regard themselves to be on a same status level (tatvaya) in a hierarchically ordered system. 'Tatvaya` comprises, according to YALMAN, a balanced status combination of 'wamsa` ("birth status", 1967:176, or intercaste, ritual status", 1967:161 and 173) and acquired status (wealth, profession). "Inside the pavula, discrepancies are magnified and lead to recriminations. The ideal of communal equality is lost when one branch rises far above the others in wealth." ..." ...every pavula is organized on

...two dimensions: it is closed on the basis of putative ritual status, but it is open to wealth." (YALMAN, 1967:203).

Within the 'pavula` , Kandyan Sinhalese use their kin terminology. Within the 'pavula` , marriageable and non-marriageable kin are determined by birth. In the Kandyan case, norms and rules concur with the categorical imperative inherent in the terminology. In contrast to the inhabitants of the maritime provinces, Kandyan Sinhalese are allowed to marry according to 'Kandyan Law` .[28]

With the exception of the arrangement of very formal marriages between rich village members in case of a new or renewed alliance which enclosed registration, most of Kandyan 'marriages`[29] are informal. (In spite of the introduction of marriage registration Kandyan villagers usually do not register marriages. They do register the birth of their children. YALMAN, 1967:160 ff). It is this informality on which YALMAN lays stress. "The underlying assumption is that marriage is nothing new and that it is only a pre-existing relation which is being reaffirmed" (YALMAN, 1967:28).

A mating relation between a man and a woman is according to 'Kandyan Law` legitimate and accepted by relatives and villagers, if the following conditions are met: first, the partners belong to the same caste[30] , second by, the woman is for the man a 'nena`, the man for the woman a 'massina` and third by, man and woman install a 'ge` (smallest consumption unit or household consisting at least of a cooking facility and a granary), or alternatively, a man joins an existing 'ge` as additional husband. The central aspect here is the combination of 'eating and sleeping together`. Commensality is only possible between equals.[31] If the status of the bride and groom is considered incompatible by their relatives, "...a) all visiting is forbidden...and b) all interdining is forbidden... . The wrongdoer and mate are treated, in short, like outcasts." (YALMAN, 1967:185). Couples can separate without formalities.

Post-marital residence among the Kandyan Sinhalese varies according to whether one marries 'binna` (i.e. residence will be established on land owned by the woman or her parents) or 'deega` (the residence alternative on land owned by the man or his parents).

Inheritance regulations are bilateral. Women and men, as YALMAN records, own property (shares on paddy land, gardens, houses and fruit trees) individually and can dispose of it as they please. Leaving out of account a testamentary disposition, all children (sons and daughters) of a man, regardless whom their mothers are, receive an equal share. The same applies to the children of a mother, "...the number of fathers being disregarded" (YALMAN, 1967:130). Claims upon inheritance (urumaya) include, according to YALMAN, the right to a commensal and sexual relationship with a real cross-cousin (1967:133).

Unfortunately, data on 'prescribed attitudes` between kin is not complete in the Kandyan case. LEACH confines the description of kin relations to male relationship patterns (1961:126). TAMBIAH, who supplements the system with a brother-sister behaviour pattern, correctly draws attention to the fact that in a bilateral context "...Lévi-Strauss`s postulate that in 'human society it is the men who exchange the women and not vice versa`..." (1965:163) cannot be accepted for the Kandyan case. Accordingly, a systematic study should be undertaken to compare behaviour patterns in the 'binna` and 'deega` context. However, for the analysis of the intragenerational relationships, a relatively clear picture emerges:

TAMBIAH (1965) and YALMAN (1967) describe that affection between brothers and between elder and younger brothers: "their behaviour toward one another is expected to be one of great reserve. They must pay respect to, and honor one another. I have heard it said that brothers should turn their face away (and indeed turn their backs to each other) when they meet in village paths lest they give offense." (YALMAN, 1967:181).

In contrast to the above, relations between massina (irrespective of age) can be attributed to what anthropologists call 'joking relationship`. "Male cross cousins (machang) are frequently to be seen arm in arm...in the lanes of the village. Even a mere mention of machang will bring smiles to serious faces." (YALMAN, 1967:153). The same applies to the massina-nena (the potential spouses) behaviour pattern. Joking, intimate meeting is allowed. "It is said they may sleep with each other without the permission of anyone." (YALMAN, 1967:27).

As regards the intergenerational attitudes, LEACH reports "extreme respect tending to avoidance" (1961:126) for the father-son relationship, which is confirmed by the other ethnographers.

Contradictory statements have been made as to the behaviour pattern between mother`s brother and sister`s son.

Concluding this chapter with a short reference to factual behaviour of the Kandyan Sinhalese as outlined in the statistics of TAMBIAH (1958) and YALMAN (1967), there is a definite preference towards deega marriage within rich Goyigama kindreds. Yet, couples prefer to live neolocally. Neolocal residence is classified by YALMAN as 'deega` in his statistics. Due to the logic of the system described above, neolocal residence can be either deega or binna. Dowries for daughters were according to TAMBIAH and YALMAN rare and seem to be a recent entry into marriage practices of the influential village members. Real cross-cousin marriages could be quantified (out of 169 relationships of 139 men, 22 were with a real cross-cousin; YALMAN, 1967:213), but classificatory cross-cousin marriages were difficult to assess, as in 'as if` cases, the terminology had to be adjusted (YALMAN, 1967:213 ff and 1962;558 f).

5. COMPARISON

Kinship categories of Swat and Kandy cannot be compared on the level of a terminological kinship system. Unlike Kandyan kin terms, which constitute a classificatory system, the nomenclature of the Swat Pukhtun has to be classed as descriptive. Yet, there are classificatory elements within the Pukhtun nomenclature, as for example the opposition between 'wror` and 'tarbur`. All brothers of an ego are classed as 'wror`, 'wror` are the father`s sisters` sons, as well as the mother`s sisters` and mother`s brother`s sons; whereas the term 'tarbur` embraces the category father`s brothers` sons.

Additionally, however, it is possible to isolate some key terms as binary oppositions, which show a structural similarity for Swat (A) and Kandy (B).

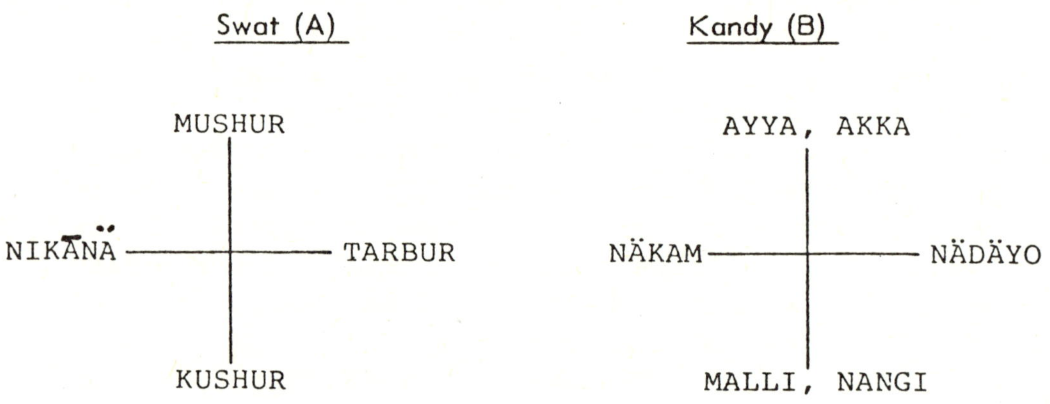

Fig. 1: Hierarchical and egalitarian structural features in Swat and Kandy

Swat Pukhtun (A) and Kandyan Sinhalese (B) differentiate between 'elder` and 'younger` kin (vertical axis, Fig. 1). Whilst the 'mushur-kusher` dichotomy in Swat (A) is not integral to the system of kin terms and only used in connection with clans specified as 'mushur` or 'cushur`, but a symbol of status differences in the macrosphere, the terms 'ayya` (elder brother), 'akka` (elder sister), as well as the complementary terms 'malli` (younger brother) and 'nangi` (younger sister) in Kandy (B) are constituent parts of the micro system. In Kandy (B) 'ayya` and 'malli` are frequently used in the macrosphere to signalize distance and status demarcation - presumably only in intra-caste relationships.

Swat Pukhtun (A) and Kandyan Sinhalese term a 'we-group` , which include cognates, i.e. kin on the father`s and mother's side, with a special expression (nikanä (A) and näkam (B) and oppose it to another category of kin, which are part of the above mentioned 'we-groups` (horizontal axis, fig. 1) - a form of opposition which, according to DUMONT (1976) is frequent in Asiatic cognitive constructions.

Within 'nikanä` in Swat (A) 'purdah` is not requested for females, within 'nikanä` marriages are preferably arranged. In opposition to 'nikanä` the Pukhtun see 'tarbur`, which are the patrilateral male parallel cousins.[32] 'Tarbur` is the paradigm for enemy - 'tarbur`, the enemies and simultaneously potential allies. The father`s brother`s daughter (FBD), the preferred marriage partner in many Islamic countries (MURPHY and KASDAN, 1967), favoured also in Swat (LINDHOLM, 1982:143 f), is theoretically a female 'tarbur`.

In the case of the Sinhalese (B) 'näkam` designates the circle of consanguineous and a final kin, in the realm of which the classificatory kin terms are used by a specific 'ego`, the 'pavula` in the wider sense defined by YALMAN as kindred or micro-caste with typical features of castes, namely demarcation to outsiders by means of endogamy and commensality (1967:189 ff; 202). Within 'näkam' mating possibilities are determined by birth. 'Näkam' enclose the opposing category 'nädäyo', i.e. those who are allowed to mate or marry, the bilateral cross-cousins.[33]

The crucial difference between Swat (A) and Kandy (B) is symbolized through the meaning of the key terms 'tarbur' and 'nädäyo': 'tarbur' (A), the symbol for hereditary enmity, and 'nädäyo' (B), the symbol for hereditary alliance.[34] 'Tarbur' (A), the enemies, are descendants of brothers, 'nädäyo' (B), the allies, descendants of brothers and sisters, as elucidated in the following diagram:

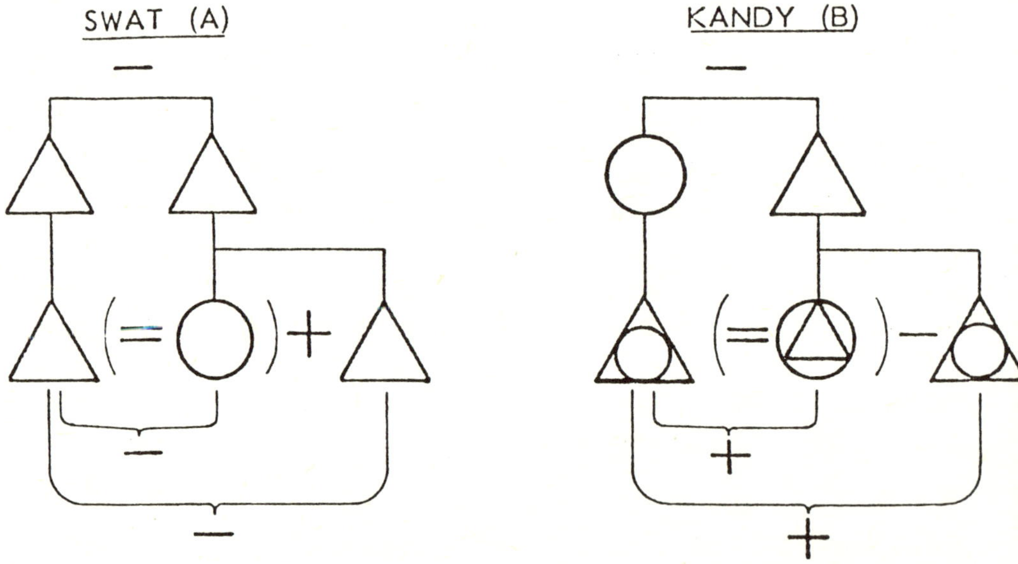

Fig. 2: Graphic representation of intragenerational kinship relation patterns in Swat and Kandy

In Fig. 2, negative signs symbolize antagonistic, reserved of hostile relationship patterns, whereas intimate and friendly interaction, as well as mutual generosity is symbolized through a positive sign.

According to value standards in both societies, marriage should be endogamous. Marriage ratifies in case (A) a separation, in case (B) marriage unites segregated units of the preceding generation. LINDHOLM describes in great detail the capture and separation symbolism of the Pukhtun marriage ritual, of which only a few details will be cited to give the reader an idea: "The wedding is said to be a sad event for the household giving up the girl, and the dolie (bridal palanquin, my comment) is spontaneously likened to the house like coffin used to carry the dead to the graveyard. ... The wedding is not only sad; it has also warlike aspects. The drum which the barber beats to announce engagements and weddings is beaten with the same roll that is used to announce an enemy attack in the days of warfare." (1982:131). Frequently, the role of marriage agent is taken over by the barber (nai), which LINDHOLM interprets as follows: "Giving a woman away is a shameful business, and the nai, as a shameless man, is the logical candidate as marriage arranger" (1982:118). Descriptions of marriages within other Pukhtun tribes by different ethnographers show similarities to LINDHOLM`s comments (GLATZER, 1977; BOESEN, 1979/80). Wife-givers are said to be lower in status than wife-takers. Symmetrical exchange of women is not possible in Swat.

Regarding the aspired marriage to a FBD, bride

price and mahar are said to be higher than in the case of marriages between more distant relatives (LINDHOLM, 1982:143). Incidentally, this fact could be set against one of the functionalist arguments usually brought forward to explain the FBD marriage, namely that in such a case the bride price would be lower. With the aid of the bride price system, a Pukhtun could theoretically acquire as many wives as he pleases from members of the society who are materially worse off. Yet, his family arranges - at least for his first marriage - a liaison with a relative. (Contradictory to Islamic Law there is a stringent prohibition on divorce in Swat (LINDHOLM, 1982:146).

As regards Kandy (B), we are confronted with a prescriptive terminological system, presmises of which have not been altered by conflicting normative rules. As shown in Fig. 4, a Kandyan Sinhalese classifies himself within his endogamous circle (näkam) according to categories which are defined by marriage relations to the preceding generation. All descendants of relatives, who are considered to be in the category 'brother` (ayya, malli) to his own father (as for example category 'C` in G+1), or in case of a female ego in the category 'sister` (akka, nangi) to her own mother (B), are as mating partners for a specific ego taboo. He or she is only allowed to start a 'ge` (commensal and sexual partnership) with the descendants of the category 'sisters of fathers` (nenda; in Fig. 4 'D` when category 'father`, i.e. appa is 'C`) and brothers of mothers (mama; in our example 'A` in fig. 4). That means, the descendants of the 'nädäyo` in G+1 have to keep

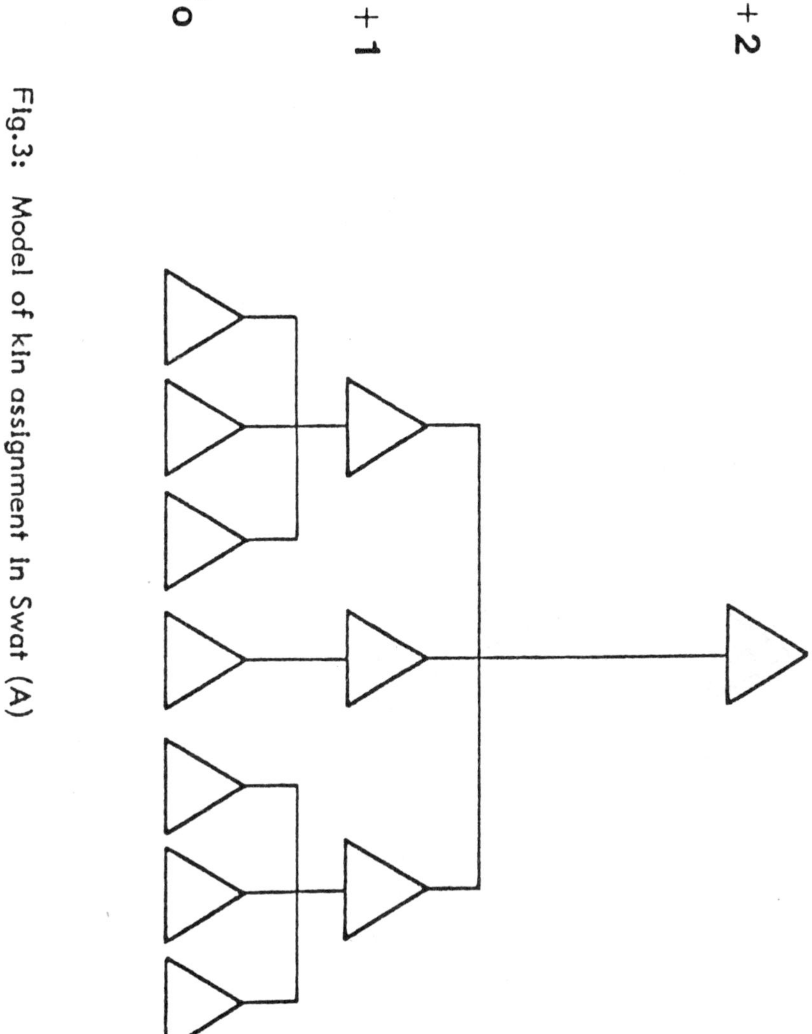

Fig.3: Model of kin assignment in Swat (A)

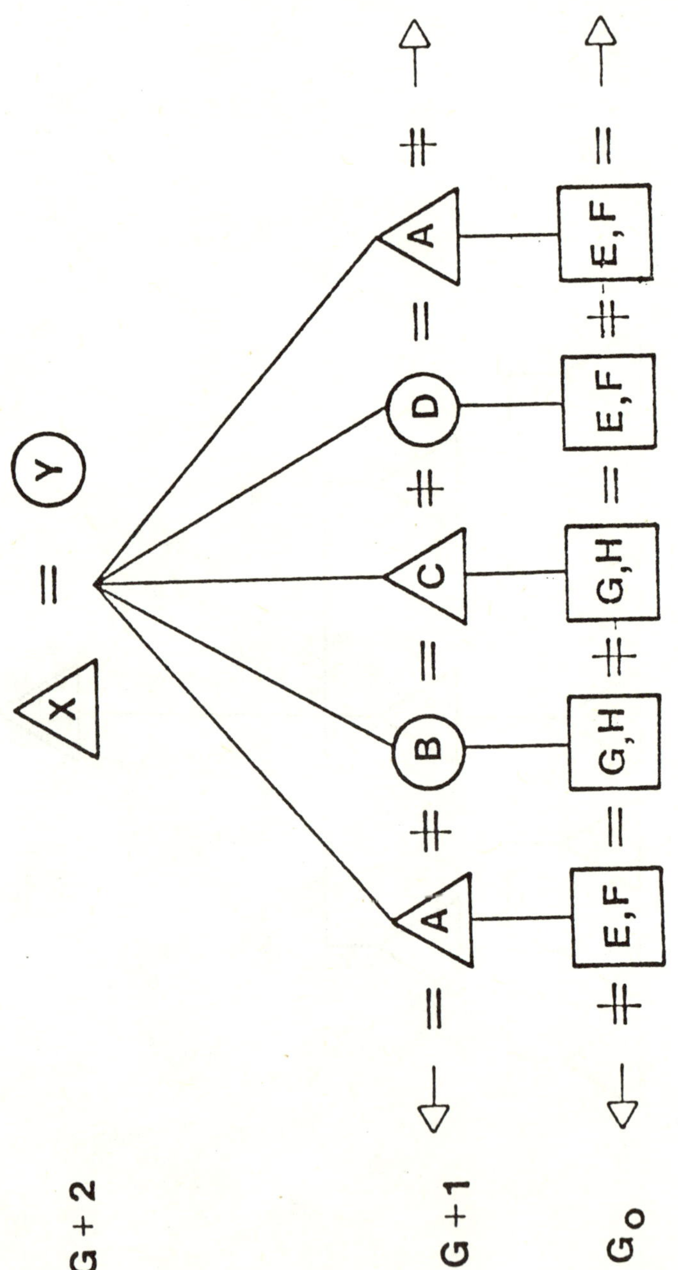

Fig.4: Model of kin assignment in Kandy (B)

distance to each other, whilst the descendants of those who had to keep distance in G+1 are the 'nädäyo` of G 0.

Hence it follows a structural preceptive possibility to fusion and fission in alternating generations, or to formulate it differently, a prefigured pattern for segmentation and fusion processes.

When looking at an official marriage ceremony in Kandy, which according to YALMAN, only takes place in case the exact relationship between potential spouses is not known, i.e. when TAMBIAH`s "fictional, potential and forgotten kin" (1965) have to be re-integrated into the microcaste, involving rituals symbolize unity (tatvaya) of the bride`s and the groom`s 'näkam`, which has to be demonstrated through comensality in public. In Kandy, a bride will be neither bought, nor conquered. Potential mating partners, the 'massina` (in the above example a member of the category 'E` in fig. 4 in case 'F` is female), are asked to express their approval during the marriage ritual. YALMAN stresses the point that the parents of the bride and the groom do not have an official function in the course of the marriage ceremonies. Members of the 'nädäyo` have to attend to the bride and the groom (1967:164 ff). The tying of the couple`s thumbs during the marriage ritual can be regarded as a symbol of unity.

Kin assignment in Swat (A) ensues from a patrilineal ideology which ignores women altogether (fig. 3).[35]

Whilst in Kandy (B) 'brothers` and 'sisters` who have been separated in one generation can be united again by means of their children, respectively by hereditary alliance, (beyond that integration is only possible via an 'as if` alliance), in Swat (A), a common male ancestor can unite brothers and 'tarbur` who have been separated. Integration in Swat (A) is only possible on the basis of common descent. ('As if` descent has been made difficult in Swat through prohibition of adoption of male children).

In the course of history, integration of all Swat Pukhtun to a large social unit has been realized only temporarily to resist invasion and domination. Yet, this could, according to LINDHOLM, only be accomplished with the help of neutral charismatic religious mediators. By analogy with the above, it could be reasoned that integration in Sri Lanka (for example between Tamils and Sinhalese in the course of history) has been achieved through marriage alliances. A mediator (magul kapurala) is necessary in Kandy to reactivate alliances. As YALMAN noted, the magul kapurala is associated with the religious functionary.

Having discussed the horizontal part of a 'system of attitudes`, i.e. intragenerational male behaviour patterns, references has to be made to vertical relationship patterns. As already pointed out, however, data regarding intergenerational attitudes are controversial as far as Kandy (B) is concerned. Nonetheless, data reveal a difference between Swat and Kandy which could be further studied.

In Swat (A) relations between fathers and sons are tense. "Killings of fathers and sons are more frequent than fratricide" (LINDHOLM, 1982.67). In contrast to the father-son relationship, behaviour patterns between mother`s brother and sister`s son show that they can be classed as positive. It is expected that a mother`s brother protects his sister`s children against their tarbur, in case of conflicts. The term 'mama` (mother`s brother) is extended to all older men with whom one wishes to be on good terms, while the term 'mama zway` is extended to all younger men of the same category. It could be that external relations, as for example friendship relations to outsiders which are highly idealized[36], replaced in the course of history a weakened categorical relationship to the mother`s brother.

Internally, imbalanced relationships are in conflict with equality as a central value expressed in the Pukhtun conde of honor (Pakhtunwali), as well as in Islamic thought.

In contrast to the above, Kandyan Sinhalese (B), who maintain intragenerationally, i.e. within the nädäyo, symmetrical or outbalanced and equal relationships, keep distance towards outsiders, which is expressed by the favoured usage of kin terms revealing distance as 'appa` (father) and 'ayya` (elder brother).[37] YALMAN stressed the point, that in case of assumed status differences, Kandyan Sinhalese would never make use of a final terms. In the village he studied violent brawls have arisen only on ceremonial occasions when putative equality is publiclY expressed and individuals presume a faulty assessment of status

(1967:204) and of course when cross-caste unions take place (1967:65 ff).

There is no need to emphasize the fact that an asymmetric hierarchical ideology is inherent in a caste system, which differentiates between higher and lower status. Kandyan Sinhalese minutely specify age differences as far as 'brothers`, 'sisters`, 'fathers` and 'mothers` are concerned. Distance is categorically defined and conforms to the hierarchical ideology. There are no ethnographic reports about conflicts between brothers as in the case of the Pukhtun. On the contrary, descriptions of polyandric households reveal that own brothers, as well as classificatory 'brothers` work together in harmony and share one wife in the same 'ge` (YALMAN, 1967:114).[38]

DAVID speaks of 'hierarchical amity` in the Tamil context regarding kin who are according to DAVID`s translation referred to as 'shares` and 'non-uniters` by the Ceylon Tamils in opposition to the 'uniters` (1973:524)) correspondent to the Sinhalese 'nädäyo`.

If it is possible to deduce classificatory aspects from territorial divisions, in Swat tripartitions cannot be overlooked, as LINDHOLM demonstrated in the case of districts, villages and village sections (1982:78 f) - i.e. asymetrical categories. Institutionalizing the two-bloc system in Swat (dàla) seems to be a necessary reaction to adapt asymetrical categories to the ideal of equality. Kandy`s villages in contrast are traditionally bipartite (YALMAN, 1965). In addition, the residence alternatives 'binna` and 'deega` are characteristically symmetrical.

Another aspect of spacial order could be mentioned. Villages of the Pakhtun in Swat (A) are built as fortresses, individual houses surrounded by high walls, whereas in Kandy (B) houses in Sinhalese villages are scattered around the paddy fields.

6. CONCLUSION

As regards the incorporation of descendants into the respective kinship organizations, it should be clear from the preceding explanations and from Figures 3 and 4, that in case A (Swat) descent on the father`s side is crucial, whereas in case B (Kandy) ego`s position is determined by the place his or her father hold in an alliance network, relations of which are logically ordered.

A male Pukhtun shares land rights with lineage members of his father, who must be his genitor, he shares revenge obligations with brothers and tarbur. He lives patrilocally.

A male Kandyan Sinhalese shares the land rights of all his mothers and fathers with his 'brothers` and 'sisters`. 'Urumaya` claims contain the right to liaise with a 'nena` (MBD, FZD) and therefore latent claims to the land rights of the different sex siblings of the parents. 'Urumaya` claims ensure that his children have the possibility to combine his land with the land of his sisters. So land remains latently in the micro-caste. A Kandyan Sinhalese is able to choose between patri- or matrilocality.

The endogamous groups in both societies keep their land. Some individuals are ruled out, in case A (Swat) eliminated in fights of tarbur, in case B (Kandy) through the disavowal as 'nädäyo`.

Individuals operate within a given cultural framework of values - in Swat (A) by means of 'tarburwali`, the struggle between ideologically equals, who can never be equal; in Kandy (B) by means of marriage between equals, who are equal, but do not necessarily want to remain equal.

Summarizing the arguments, there exists a clearly documented difference between Swat (A) and Kandy (B): unbalanced only negative kin relationships of the male Pukhtun, and balanced (an equilibrium between positive and negative) kin relationships of the Kandyan Sinhalese on the horizontal (intragenerational) level of the kinship structure.

Symbolically, the difference is articulated through the notion of 'tarbur` (those who fight - the enemies) and 'nädäyo` (those who marry - the allies). In case A (Swat) communication takes place over the exchange of enmities and settlement of conflicts, in case B (Kandy) over the exchange of women and men.

As regards the vertical (intergenerational) kin relationships, the ethnographers of Swat (A) conveyed balance. For Kandy (B) the material is inadequate (RÖSCH-RHOMBERG, 1984:100). There is reason to believe that there exists no equilibrium concerning the vertical relations.

It is suggested that the structure inherent in kin behaviour patterns is also visible in other realms of the societies in question. LINDHOLM devoted one chapter of his book to exchange patterns in Swat (1982:114 ff), in which he shows how morality, political action and economic life are all governed by the same set of rules. His description of economic relationships, as for example the relation between employer and employee reveal that Pukhtun are unable to cooperate, that they are neither good bosses, nor good workers. "Pukhtun carry their rivalries into their business life and are unwilling to work for other Pukhtun" (LINDHOLM, 1982:115). "If a Pukhtun works for another Pukhtun he admits the other as his better" (ibid.). "Partnerships are rarely successful due to mistrust among the partners" (ibid.). All cases which might involve transactions between Pukhtun turn out to be unsuccessful, as a Pukhtun avoids relations of dependency to other Pukhtun whilst at the same time trying to press the other into subordination. According to LINDHOLM, these constraints do not apply to relations to non-Pukhtun.

On the other hand, visitors to Sri Lanka will quickly discover that outsiders are confronted to cooperation networks, kinship relations of which cannot be disregarded. Within institutions and business organizations a meticulous arrangement of the hierarchical position of personnel analogously to the age differentiation within kin is striking.

Additionally, concerning categorical constraints, it could be argued that the present bedevilling of Islam as cause for violence in the Western Press should be rejected. Don`t we have to deal rather with 'brother`, who avail themselves of the variant religious controversies to fight for power?

"The Pukhtun have not succeeded in being a great nation because there is an autocrat in each home who would rather burn his own house than see his brother rule it." (Quotation of G. Khan, 1958:46, cited by LINDHOLM, 1982:55)-

References

[1] This article is in part a simplification and generalization of arguments advanced in my unpublished M.A.thesis (Rösch-Rhomberg, 1984) based on data collected by ethnographers of the Swat Pukhtun in North-West Pakistan, i.e. BARTH (1959), FAUTZ (1963) and LINDHOLM (1983), and on the Kandyan Sinhalese in Sri Lanka, i.e. LEACH (1961), TAMBIAH (1958), ROBINSON (1968) and YALMAN (1962, 1967, 1969). Transcriptions of Pukhtun and Sinhalese terms and proper names have been adopted from the work cited. YALMAN, for example used divergent versions in his different article.The following abbreviations and signs have been used in the text and my diagrams: B = brother, Z = sister, F = father, M = mother, H = husband, W = wife, S = son, D = daughter, CH = child, e = elder, y = younger, etc. and combinations of the above symbols, as for example FBD for father`s brother`s daughter, or yZ for younger Sister, etc. Additionally: ms = male speaker, fs = female speaker, G 0 = ego`s generation G-1, -2 = first or second descending generation respectively; G+1, +2 = first or second ascending generation respectively.

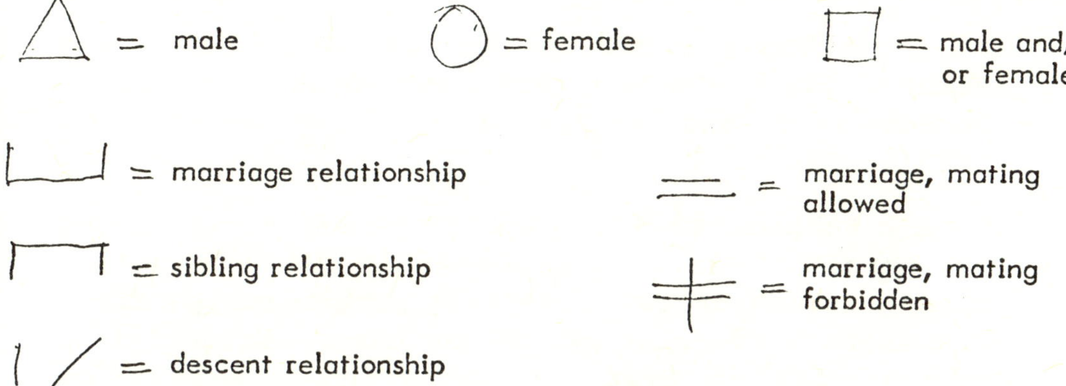

[2] The term 'structure' is used for a confusing variety of concepts which share little with one another except the term itself. In the context of this article, the term 'structure' refers to a system of relations between social relationships.

[3] As LEVI-STRAUSS has already pointed out (1958:83), it is of course unsatisfactory to reduce 'ideal' behaviour patterns to such a simple dichotomy. But for illustrative purposes a 'negative' or 'positive' sign helps to show the point more clearly.

[4] Kandyan Sinhalese classify a marriage or simply the commensal and sexual relationship established between a male and a female either 'binna', or 'deega', according to the ownership of the land a couple chooses to live on. (Binna: residence on land owned by the woman or her parents. Deega: residence on land owned by the man or his parents.)

[5] This rather rough sketch perhaps oversimplifies the picture. Constricted space, however, does not permit a more detailed or differentiated account.

[6] Regarding the distinction between Pushtun and Pukhtun see CAROE, 1958. Pathan is an Anglo-Indian term and not used by Pukhtun speakers (FAUTZ, 1963).

[7] All Pukhtun in Swat attach themselves to one of two oppose political blocs (dàla), irrelevant of clan, lineage or extended family membership. BARTH considers a two-bloc system as the basic political organization in Swat, in which individuals align with a bloc according to their personal objectives. Contrary to BARTH, LINDHOLM stresses the point that the PUKHTUN are organized primarily as an acephalous segmentary patrilineal society with the inherent principle of equality and complementary opposition in EVANS-PRITCHARD`s and SAHLIN`s sense. In spite of all enmity and competition between brothers and cousins, close agnates would ally with each other to fight for grandfather`s land in case of attack through distant agnates (1982:79 ff). BARTH`s own research confirms LINDHOLM`s argument (see for example 1959:126). For LINDHOLM, the dàla system of two opposing blocs constitutes an institution which offers individuals the facility to express constant change of oppositions and alliances.

[8] Clients of the Pukhtun are mainly members of various occupational groups (for a detailed list, see LINDHOLM, 1982:98), servants and workers (fakir), all landless people and according to LINDHOLM "descendants of conquered local people, migrants, or of Pukhtun who have lost their land" (1982:96). Patron-client relationships exist also between Pukhtun and Gujar (a distinct ethnic group of herdsmen, who "...often hold land in the hills as clients of the Pukhtun..." (LINDHOLM, 1982:97).

Apart from the above groups, there are religiously sanctioned landed lineages (BARTH, 1958; AHMED, 1976; LINDHOLM, 1982) which usually live outside villages not considered as Pukhtun clan territory. LINDHOLM reports that there is ranking between the different groups. Yet, commensality would not be affected by ranking. On the contrary, a Pukhtun leader has to impress his clients continually by generous hospitality. According to LINDHOLM, "there are no prohibitions on out-marriage,..." (1982:97), but generally people tend to marry in. As far as the Pukhtun are concerned, they only give wives to the 'holy` lineages, and they sometimes take wives from the occupational groups as additional spouses (BARTH, AHMED, LINDHOLM). Members of the occupational and 'holy` groups often act as mediators between Pukhtun (ibid.).

[9] Jirga: "a council of respected men" (Lindholm, 1982:298) "assembly of Pukhtun elders to decide various inter- or intra-tribal matters" (AHMED, 1980:366).

[10] Until recently 'wesh`, a periodical redistribution of clan land (dauftar) within and between villages, was practiced. (For information regarding the wesh system, see BARTH, 1958; FAUTZ, 1963; JETTMAR, 1983; and LINDHOLM, 1982.

[11] Central claims of 'Pakhtunwali`are 'badal`(blood revenge, revenge of any insult), 'melmastia` (hospitality) and 'nanawatia` (refuge for hosts); see LINDHOLM, 1982:210 ff. Details and emphases of 'Pakhtunwali` differ with the variou Pukhtun tribes (GLATZER, 1977:164 f; STEUL (1981).

[12] LINDHOLM devotes one chapter to illustrate the growing-up process of Pukhtun children (1982:161 ff).

[13] The female-male behaviour patterns reported by LINDHOLM show strong similarities to attitudes experienced by the authoress in Egypt during a six years` stay there.

[14] Regarding mahar, see Sura 4 (4-5) in: Der Koran, translation Rudi Paret, 1980.

[15] According to Sura 4, 22 and 23 the following females are forbidden as marriage and mating partners, FW, M, D, Z, VZ, MZ, BD, WZD, WBD, milkmothers, milksisters, WM, WD, SW; all respected married women.

[16] Differentiating 'parallel` and 'cross` cousins, as is common in anthropological literature, becomes problematic, as soon as it goes beyond first grade cousins. See KAY (1965) and TYLER (1966). In a predominantly endogamous society, where patri- and matrilines mingle in reality, we can only speak of a category of 'FBD`, or 'FBS` in line with a patrilineal ideology.

[17] G_{+2} : Siya = GF = any wife of a 'grandmother`
Achi = GM = any husband of a 'grandfather`

G_{+1} : Appa [7]) = F = FB = MH = MZH
Amma [7]) = M = MZ = FW = FBW
Mama = MB = FZH = F-in-law
Nenda = FZ = MBW = M-in-law

G_0 :	Ayya	[7])= eB = eMBDH = eFZDH
	Malli	[7])= yB = yMBDH = yFZDH
	Akka	[7])= eZ = eMBSW = eFZSW
	Nangi	[7])= yZ = yMBSW = yMBSW
	Massina	= H = ZH = MBS = FZS
	Nena	= W = BS = MBD = FZD
G_{-1} : (ms)	Puta	[7])= S = BS = ZDH
	Duwa	[7])= D = BD = ZDW
	Bena	= ZS = DH
	Yeli	= ZD = SW
G_{-1} : (fs)	Puta	[7])= S = ZS = BDH
	Duwa	[7])= D = ZD = BDW
	Bena	= BS = DH
	Yeli	= BD = SW
G_{-2} :	Munuburu	= GS
	Minibiri	= GD

(YALMAN, 1962:557 and 1967:211)

[18] For a detailed account on the 'Dravidian` kinship terminology, as well as the Kariera kinship Vocabulary see DUMONT, 1983.

[19] For the sake of clarity, additional age differentiation with the help of adjectives which is common in Kandy when refering to appa, amma, ayya, malli, akka, nangi, puta and duwa has been omitted in the above list of kin terms.

[20] See note 16.

[21] See note 16.

[22] When translating kin terms of one cultural system into another, anthropologists are confronted with the problem that they have to use

terms tainted with associations or ideas inherent in the own cultural categories. See also note 16.

[23] In this respect, YALMAN diverges from DUMONT (1953, 1983), who concentrates on the opposition of two categories of kin. Yet, the terminology encompasses both viewpoints. "The manner and extent to which the categorical imperative is given social effect are contingent features, ...they have to be discovered separately by empirical investigation in each individual case" (NEEDHAM, 1972/73:175).

[24] See for example, PFEFFER, 1982, 'Status and affinity` .

[25] For a discussion of the different local concepts see BROW (1978); LEACH (1961:25 and 105 ff); OBEYESEKERE (1967); PERERA (1979); ROBINSON (1968:404) and YALMAN (1967:61 and 189 ff).

[26] Initial critique of YALMAN`s concept of a bilateral 'kindred` using a Dravidian terminology (TAMBIAH, 1965:137, and DUMONT, 1964:77) turned into concurrence (TAMBIAH, 1973) or has been relativised warily (DUMONT, 1983:152).

[27] The expression 'pavula` is also used for the own wife and family. According to information on the spot (the author visited the village studied by YALMAN in 1983), pronounciation differs for the two meanings.

[28] OBEYESEKERE stresses the situational character of the traditional 'Kandyan Law` (1967:48 ff).

29 Defining 'marriage` in the Sinhalese case poses problems. See LEACH, 1961, and YALMAN, 1967:160.

30 Although the traditional caste system has been dissolved by the British, and the modern state does not officially recognize caste, YALMAN found that castes as endogamous groups with own names, own living quarters and special ritual status were still part of a hierarchically ordered system. In the village he studied (1200 inhabitants) about three quarters were Goyigama (Cultivators), 146 Badde (Tom-Tom beaters), 30 Henea (Washermen), 38 Valan Karayo (Potters) and 19 Achari (Blacksmith). Within the Goyigama, who considers themselves as the highest caste, a further subdivision into Aristocrats, Ordinary Goyigama and Low Goyigama was made. (YALMAN, 1967:58 ff).

31 Sexual relationships between different status groups are possible; yet men have to be of higher status than women. See YALMAN, (1967:95).

32 See note 16.

33 See note 16. The categories 'massina`and 'nena` enclose the real bilateral cross-cousins (MBCH and FZCH). It is prohibited to marry an 'ayya`, 'malli`, or 'akka`and 'nangi` (eB, yB, eZ, yZ; bilateral parallel cousins (MZCH and FBCH) are included in these categories).

34 The term 'hereditary alliance` has been used by DUMONT for the first time in connection with the Dravidian terminological system(1953).

35 Due to preferential endogamy in Swat, matri- and patrilines mingle with each other in reality. MURPHY and KASDAN pointed

out that this merger "...produces a latent bilateral structurethat is the very antithesis of the patrilineal ideology." (1967:23)

[36] LINDHOLM`s interpretation of the 'friendship ideal` in Pukhtun society differs from the author`s view expressed here. He contrasts the basic structure (the segmentary lineage system), which led in Swat to 'tarburwali` with an emotional structure of individuals "...that must find expression in every society" (1982:273). He contrasts the reality in which people exist in Swat, "...one of individual egoism, fear of others, jealousy, hostility and contempt" (1982:268) with Pukhtun "hospitality and the pervasive male ideal of friendship..." (ibid.). As LINDHOLM`s notions of this 'emotional structure of the individual` are only vague, and as I am not acquainted with the relevant psychological literature, I omitted the psycho-logical realm of his word, especially as it does not touch upon his analysis of the Pukhtun kinship organization. LINDHOLM kept the two analytical domains clearly separated.

[37] BROW (1978), LEACH (1961) and YALMAN (1967) recorded the use of the terms 'appa` and 'ayya` (father, elder brother) to ex- press distance.

[38] However, the reverse case of 'sisters` sharing a husband in one single 'ge` does not function in Kandy (KEMPER, 1980 and YALMAN, 1967:114).

Bibliography

Ahmed Akbar, S., S., Millenium and Charisma among Pathans. London 1976

Ahmed Akbar, S., Pukhtun Economy and Society. London 1980

Ardener, Edwin, The New Anthropology and its Critics, in MAN 6:449-465, 1971

Barth, Frederik, Political Leadership among Swat Pathans. London 1959

Barth, Frederik, Features of Person and Society in Swat. Collected Essays on Pathans. Vol. II. London 1981

Boesen, Inger W., Women, Honor and Love, in Folk 21-22, 1979/80

Brow, James, Vedda Villages of Anuradhapura. Seattle and London 1978

Bourdieu, Pierre, Entwurf einer Theorie der Praxis. Frankfurt 1976

Caroe, Olaf, The Pathans. 550 B.C. - A.D. 1957. London etc. 1958

Christensen, Asger, Organization, Variation and Transformation in Pukhtun Society. Review article, in Ethnos 46, 1981

David, Kenneth, Until Marriage do us part: A cultural account of Jaffna Tamil Categories for Kinsmen, in MAN 8: 521-535, 1973

Dumont, Louis, The Dravidian Kinship Terminology as an Expression of Marriage, in MAN 54: 34-39, 1953

Dumont, Louis, Marriage in India: The Present State of the Question, in CIS 7: 77-98, 1964

Dumont, Louis, Affinity as a Value. Chicago 1983

Fautz, Bruno, Sozialstruktur und Bodennutzung in der Kulturlandschaft des Swat. Diss., Technische Hochschule Karlsruhe 1963

Glatzer, Bernt, Nomaden von Gharjistan. Wiesbaden 1977

Jettmar, Karl, Indus-Kohistan: Entwurf einer historischen Ethnographie, in Anthropos 78: 501-518, 1983

Kay, Paul, A Generalization of the Cross/Parallel Distinction, in American Anthropologist 67:30-43, 1965

Der Koran, Übersetzung von Rudi Paret. Stuttgart 1980

Leach, E.R., Aspects of Caste in South India, Ceylon and North-West Pakistan. Cambridge 1960

Leach, E.R., Pul Elya. A village in Ceylon. Cambridge 1961

Leach, E.R., Polyandry, Inheritance and the Definition of Marriage: with particular reference to Sinhalese Law, in Rethinking Anthropology, London 1961

Lévi Strauss, Claude, Anthropologie Structurale. Paris 1958

Lévi Strauss, Claude, Anthropologie Structurale II. Paris 1973

Lévi Strauss, Claude, Mythos und Bedeutung. Frankfurt 1980

Lindholm, Ch. and Lindholm, Ch., Marriage as Warfare, in Natural History 88: 11-20, 1979

Lindholm, Ch. and Lindholm, Ch., Generosity and Jealousy. The Swat Pukhtun of Northern Pakistan. New York 1982

Needham, Rodney, Terminology and Alliance II, Mapuche. Conclusions, in Sociologus, NF 17-18: 39-54, 1967

Needham, Rodney, Prescription, in Oceania 43: 166-181, 1972/73

Needham, Rodney, Remarks and Inventions. London 1974

Obeyesekere, Gananath, Land Tenure in Village Ceylon. Cambridge 1967

Perera, U.L. Yayantha, Variga: A Traditional System of Social Organization. University of Ceylon 1979

Pfeffer, Georg, Status and Affinity in Middle India. Wiesbaden 1982

Robinson, Marguerite, Some Observations on the Kandyan Sinhalese Kinship System, in MAN 3: 402-23, 1968

Rösch-Rhomberg, Inge, Kandy and Swat: Variationen in den Verwandtschaftskategorien von zwei südasiatischen Gesellschaften. Unpublished M.A. thesis 1984

Steul, Wille, Paschtunwali. Wiesbaden 1981

Tambiah, S.J., The structure of Kinship and its Relationship to land possession and Residence in Pata Dumbara, Central Ceylon, in JRAI 88/1: 21-44, 1958

Tambiah, S.J., Kinship Fact and Fiction in Relation to the Kandyan Sinhalese, in JRAI 95; 131-173, 1965

Tambiah, S.J., Dowry, Brideprice and the Property Rights of Women in South India, in Bridewealth and Dowry. Ed. J. Goody and S.J. Tambiah. Cambridge Papers in Social Anthropology 7: 59-166, 1973

Tyler, Stephen A., Parallel/Cross: an evaluation of definitions, in SWJA 22: 416-32, 1966

Yalman, Nur, The Structure of the Sinhalese Kindred: A Re-Examination of the Dravidian Terminology, in AA 64: 548-75, 1962

Yalman, Nur, Under the Bo Tree. Berkeley and Los Angeles 1967

Yalman, Nur, The Semantics of Kinship in South India and Ceylon. In Current Trends in Linguistic. Vol. 5, T.A. Sebeok (ed.), The Hague 1969

Sri Lanka and the Maldives - Aspects of Ecological Development in two South-Asian Island Republics

by Wolfgang Werner

Islands from a fascinating part of our planet, each one building its own unique microcosmos. South of the Indian subcontinent, which protrudes as a triangular mass into the Indian ocean, two independent island republics have evolved. Each is closely related to India, both with regard to the origin of nature and man, and to the constant shift of the monsoon-winds, but each forms a world of its own. While Sri Lanka in its geological structure is a sort of appendix of India, a fragment of the old precambrian Gondwana continent, the Maldive islands owe their origin to the life of the sea - to coral reefs, which have developed on a sinking chain of volcanoes, or, according to recent theories of plate tectonics, on a sinking fragment of the Gondwana continent. Sri Lanka and the Maldives thus form two different ecosystems, the one occupying a land mass of 65610 km^2 rising up to 2524 m, the other with only 298 km^2 of land never reaching more than 2 m above sea-level.

Nevertheless, the natural environment of the Maldives resembles that of the coast of Sri Lanka; the human population is from same stock, cultural, economic and political realities correspond. Both are poor developing countries; both have gained independence after Worldwar II; both struggle to improve the quality of life and to overcome poverty while preserving cultural identity. The "development" of recent years sometimes seems to threaten cultural identity and concordance of man and nature while failing to achieve the standards of developed countries. The peoples of Sri Lanka and the Maldives have inhabited their islands for about 2500 years - not always in harmony with nature, but usually with a degree of compromise.

Man of 20th century is threatening this planet and the inhabitants of Sri Lanka and the Maldives are threatening their microcosmos equally quickly. Future development must be in accord with ecological balance, a rule which should be respected equally by the peoples concerned and by foreign consultants. (Plates of this contribution are at the end of the book)

Environmental Facts on Sri Lanka:

The greatest part of Sri Lanka consists of precambrian metalmorphic rocks which were uplifted in several phases. In the northern and north-western coastal belt Miocene and post-Miocene limestones, remnants of marine transgressions, build a different environment. While springs in precambrian rock provide excellent fresh water, those in the limestone belt may be polluted or brackish.

The major soil groups of Sri Lanka are the Red Yellow Podsolic Soils of the wet and cooler mountain region, the laterites of the southwestern wet coastal belt, the Reddish Brown Earths of most parts of the dry lowlands and the Red Yellow Latosols, Solonetz and Solonchak of the limestone area.[1]

The amount of rainfall distributed over the island is very different and depends to a great extend to the luff and lee effects of the central highlands during the monsoon seasons. The convectional rains of the intermonsoon periods bring water to the whole island, and particularly to the sheer precipice of the southwestern mountain wall and the northeast-monsoon brings high rainfall to the north-eastern side of the mountains, but a good amount for the island as a whole. However the southwest monsoon causes the climatical differentiation of the island, as it brings a very high amount of rainfall to the south-west and a serious drought to the rest of the island. The wet zone proper is the zone of the south-west-monsoon rains, the annual amount of rainfall amounting to more than 2000-2500 mm and even more than 5000 mm in some parts. the so-called dry zone is very heterogeneous in its ecological appearance. Precipitation varies between 750 mm/a and 2000-2500 mm/a. In the driest parts in south-east and north-west, sometimes called arid zone, Sri Lanka has its own salterns with low, dry and thorny vegetation.

The greater part of the dry zone was covered until recently by semi-evergreen forest ("jungle", monsoon forest). Dry and wet zone are ecologically divided by an "intermediate zone" as ecotone. The natural vegetation consists of evergreen tropical rain forest with some dry zone trees as component and a certain seasonalty in annual life cycle. The wet zone proper was covered by evergreen rain forest with trees flowering, fruiting and renewing their leaves at any time of the year. The mountains are (or were) covered by evergreen rain forest, as well. Lower montane rain forest replaces lowland rain forest above 900 m with a different species composition, the montane forest of the eastern side being drier and different again. Above 1500 m come evergreen upper montane rain forests, or "mist" forests, covered with moss and lichens, stunted in growth and weathering the heaviest monsoon-gales. Forests reach the top of the highest mountain, Pidurutalagala (2524 m). Thus forests had covered Sri Lanka from the seashore (beach forests, mangrove) up to the mountain peaks.

The rivers of Sri Lanka follow an almost direct course from the central massif to the sea. Only the largest river, Mahaweli Ganga, takes a somewhat irregular course in the mountain area. The other rivers of the dry zone almost dry up during drought season. Of the wet zone rivers only Kalu and Kelani Ganga have some importance for rafting and boat traffic in the lower reaches. Sands or rapids are barriers everywhere else. In the mountain area rafting (with "elephant"-power) is done only on short and suitable stretches. There exist no natural lakes in Sri Lanka, a fact which is very important for the composition of indigenous freshwater fauna. The flora and fauna of Sri Lanka is unique, especially in the wet zone. While the dry zone has close relations to neighbouring South India, the wet zone is a very isolated patch of rain forest environment with close relations to Southeast Asia. Most of the useful plants have been introduced by man, especially the edible ones. It is therefore difficult to imagine what early man could have found to eat besides animal food and the plants he introduced.

LAND-USE AND ECOLOGICAL CONSEQUENCES IN HISTORY

With regard to ecological development, it is important to consider the traditional forms of land use, their success or failure during 2500 years and the natural environment before the arrival of man.

It is an accepted theory that the existing forests of the dry zone are a secondary form of vegetation, which developed after the collapse of agriculture in 13th century. Even in the most remote jungles the bunds of old tanks may still be found. The recently constructed Maduru Oya dam was planned after an old dam had been found accidently in thick jungle about 20 years ago. The question is: did the original forests resemble the forests of today? It must be assumed that they were "wetter" and had a higher proportion of evergreen trees, and that even in the driest parts the forest was more profuse than today.

Also the dry zone rivers were probably perennial and navigable[2] , before the hydrological balance was disturbed.

1. The dry zone civilization (c. 500 B.C. - 1214)

Not much is known about the aboriginal and prehistoric inhabitants of the island, but artefacts prove that they even roamed the high plains at 2100 m and probably affected vegetation there.

In about 500 B.C. the Indo-Aryan Sinhalese immigrated from North India and they must have brought rice cultivation, if it not already existed there, due to South Indian influence. According to old stone inscriptions[3] the early settlers clearly preferred the dry zone, although settlements were tried in the wet zone as well. May be the early settlers were used to a drier climate and tank irrigation and they disliked the constant struggle with the profuse rain forest. The wet and mountain zone remained a stronghold of the aboriginal Weddha population[4]. When the Sinhalese began to settle the wet zone after the collapse of the dry zone civilization, the Weddhas managed to survive in the depopulated dry zone until present.

The dry zone civilization developed the high art of irrigation in a form unique in the world. In the centuries B.C. small village tanks (S.: wewa, T.: kulam) were the centerpieces of the irrigation system (1 village - 1 tank). In the following centuries huge dams were constructed, storing the water in Parakrama Samudra, Kala Wewa etc. These tanks were fed by canals, transporting water from distant rivers (e.g. Elahera canal). While the small village tanks which existed by thousands in the plains, could dry up during the drought periods, the big reservoirs assured a constant water supply. Besides rice cultivation on irrigated land, dry cultivation on the higher land was practised as well, either in garden land, or in form of shifting cultivation (chena). Land was also required for animal husbandry. Thus, in highly populated areas only ribbons of jungle could be left between the villages. These were used as grazing grounds for cattle, a situation comparable to medieval Europe. The villages were fenced against wild animals and the fields were watched by night. Intruding elephants were driven away using drums and fireworks. The strict protection of the elephants by the kings and an affective watching system made coexistence possible, though the herds of elephants were much more numerous than today.[5]

Protection of animals is an old buddhist tradition in Sri Lanka; already in 12th century King Nissanka Malla protected animals around Anuradhapura.[6]

The Sinhalese seemed to practice a successful form of agriculture until 13th century. The central highlands were still forest-covered and relatively uninhabited. The rivers were fed by clear water from the mountains, and the amount of rainfall may have been higher than today.

In 1214 the capital, Polonnaruwa, was finally abandoned.[7] The dry zone civilization collapsed completely in a short time and people migrated to the wet zone. The theories on the causes are numerous,[8] and they should be taken into account when planning the new colonization of the dry zone today. Foreign invasions and civil wars are regarded as a major cause for the collapse of the dry zone civilization, as central authority deteriorated. The complicated irrigation systems were not only destroyed as a warfare tactic, but were also neglected as compulsory labour (rajakariya) was boycotted. The spread of malaria which resulted from this neglect must have been a fatal blow for the civilization. Malaria has been the scourge of the dry zone until 1947 and has revived again during recent years. Was malaria endemic in Sri Lanka before 13th century? If it existed already, it might have been controlled by clean irrigation channels, the avoidance of stagnant pools and high fish population in the reservoirs. But it is possible, that malaria was introduced by foreign soldiers, as happened with other parasitic diseases.[9]

Other civilizations in SE-Asia also collapsed during the same period.[10]

A further reason could have been climatic change, e.g. a general worldwide tendency towards arid conditions since 10th century, which has been indicated by size of annual rings of trees. Salination, erosion, siltation of irrigation systems and decreasing fertility have been discussed, as well.

2. Wet zone civilization and European influence until 1815

After breakdown of the dry zone civilization, the Tamils moved to the extreme north, the Sinhalese populated the southwest. The valley bottoms, coastal swamps and suitable hill slopes were cleared for rice fields. Elaborate canals were not necessary, as the constant water flow of the rain forest streams and rivulets could be used. Only in the drier Uva basin canals were used to bring water across the main divide. The colonization of the highlands must have brought extensive deforestation during the following centuries. Nevertheless, "reserved" forests existed which were not included into the constant cycle of shifting cultivation and vast rain forest areas remained in the southwest. The Sinharaja forest is a small remnant of these. Agriculture seems to have received a more pronounced silvicultural component. Cinnamon bark must be mentioned first. The cinnamon tree (Cinnamomum zeylanicum / C. verum) is indigenous to the rain forests of Sri Lanka. The Sinhalese used to strip the bark of wild growing trees, but in colonial times cinnamon gardens were set up. The cinnamon trade under muslim traders and later Europeans became very important. Cardamom was another spice, collected in the mountain forests, like cinnamon under the rajakariya system.

Foreign influence brought many tropical useful plants to the island. The Arabs introduced coffee, which was planted in village gardens or around temples as ornament. Many plants were imported by the Dutch and British from other colonies (cloves, nutmeg, teak, cocoa, tea, rubber etc.). The Portuguese and Dutch did not much affect the indigenous agriculture. The Dutch started growing cinnamon-bushes in gardens and planted coconut-palms along the southern coast. The interior of the island, the independent Kingdom of Kandy, could preserve its own economy.

3. British plantation industry and traditional agriculture

The defeat of Kandy in 1815 brought a major change to Sri Lanka with respect to land use and ecology. After 1823 the British started their plantation industry in the highlands, with coffee at first, then with cinchona and tea. The planting of tea affected the wet lowlands, too. In this century rubber plantations followed in the low and mid country.

As land which was not under individual ownership was declared "crown land". The vast forest areas which were either untouched as reserved forests, or used for shifting cultivation as common land, were acquired at low prices by Europeans. Thus, the forest cover of the central highlands diminished quickly - and forever. The plantation land was augmented through land sale of indebted peasants. A climatic change was already perceived by TENNENT (1860) who observed that lower rainfall in the mountains probably resulted from the extensive clearing of the surrounding forest.

In 1890 the British started forest plantations in the mountain area to cover the timber and fuelwood demand of the railway and tea estates. The protection of natural forest above 5000 ft

(1524 m) was regarded as a necessity from 1885, to assure the water flow of the river. As the slow-growing tree species of the montane forests seemed unsuitable, trees like Eucalyptus, Pinuns, Acacia were introduced.

The British plantation industry made the highlands of Sri Lanka a prosperous and developed country.

When Sri Lanka gained independence again in 1948, well-maintained tea estates looked like parks, the surface of the tea fields resembling a lawn, overtopped by shade trees. A dense network of roads and railway assured quick transport of goods. The remnant forest had been preserved just before complete disappearance and in 1938-40 several sanctuaries were declared. Too late for the elephant population of the mountains: the big herds which occured even around Pidurutalagala had been slaughtered and the last individuals or small herds moved to the dry zone by that time. Only around Adam`s Peak have some remained. The British plantation economy had left a negative imprint to the landscape, too. Some coffee estates, which had been given up and not replanted with tea, converted to unproductive "patana" grassland. The dry zone and traditional agriculture had been rather neglected until 1850.[11] Rice had to be imported in large quantities. Starting in 1850 and accelerating after 1930, irrigation systems were restored and the resettlement of the dry zone began.

The population, numbering 2.5 million in 1871 and 3.5 million in 1900, reached 7 million at independence. Now it has surpassed 16 million. The quick increase spelled population pressure - pressing back the space for nature. While until 13th century, the wet zone had been nature`s counterweight, and the dry zone thereafter, man is now going to settle and cultivate the whole island.

4. Present development (since 1948)

The plantation sector:

The plantation industry has been inherited from the British. After independence many estates were still owned by Sterling Companies and managed by Europeans. Already between the world wars, the superintendents had more and more assistants from the Burgher community (mainly of Dutch descent), Sinhalese and Tamils. After independence this new planter generation replaced most of the Europeans, adopting their western way of life.

In 1972 the socialist Bandaranaike government passed the land reform act and nationalized all private landholdings comprising more than 50 acres (20.25 ha). In 1975 the estates, owned by foreign companies, were nationalized, too. This policy had catastrophic effects on plantation industry. the European planters and many of the Burgher community left the country. Though a generation of well experienced and capable local planters had evolved meanwhile, the vacancies could not be filled completely, and some men were intrusted with estates, who would have made no more than good field-officers. While in many estate bungalows life is going on as in British times, on other estates one might encounter a 15-room bungalow stripped of its furniture and occupied by one young assistant superintendent and his cook. Lack of experience brought heavy loss to some estates: wrong pruning of tea bushes, bad plucking and manufacturing, theft of manure etc. Long before 1975 companies and managers had seen the end of their lucky days approaching. This led to a reduction in investment in the estates. Old tea fields have to be replanted, gaps of dead bushes to be infilled, factories and machinery modernized. The worst environmental problem of tea estates is soil erosion today, mainly sheet erosion of the topsoil. Some estates or single fields are in a deplorable condition. But even in "well-maintained" tea fields the top soil is removed when oversized tools are used for weeding between the bushes.[12] Another ecological tragedy was the cutting of shade trees. As the tea plant grows as a tree in the undergrowth of subtropical mountain forests, the planters tried to copy the natural conditions with a stratum of trees above the tea bushes. These trees had many effects besides shade. They protected against strong winds and heavy rainfall, helped to loosen the soil and provided green manure, fuelwood for the estate and a habitant for birdlife.[13] The Ceylon Tea Research Institute recommended the removal of shade trees in upcountry for higher yield of tea leaves. Following that advice, after 1964 most of the shade trees were felled. The ecological effects are evident. The parklike landscape turned to a dull, monotonous "green desert". The insect-eating birds disappeared, and application of high pesticide-doses became necessary, what again disturbed ecological equilibrium.[14] Drought periods result in heavy loss of tea bushes. As the estate labourers are short of firewood, they remove fuel from the nearby mountain forests and destroy the last natural refuges of the highlands. Meanwhile, estates have started again to plant shade trees. For the ecological effect, the replanting should be promoted, but that spells again high investment without immediate return. What will be the future of "Ceylon Tea" ?

The production of tea has decreased as a result of mismanagement. Production costs became higher after the 1973 oil-price increase because most factories had switched to diesel engines, and aerial tramways for the transport of leaves to the factory had been replaced by lorries. Prices for fertilization depend on oil-prices, too. New tea estates in East-Africa with yields 3 or 4 time higher than in Sri Lanka enforce competition on the world market.

The situation of tea estates is very heterogeneous today. In some regions the end of tea-growing is imminent, while in others well-maintained and profitable estates exist. While some estates were abandoned (e.g. in eastern Knuckles), others in marginal areas make profit with other cash crops only (cardamom etc.). In the Maskeliya area a crop diversification program was started. From an environmental point of view, it would be a wise decision to use unprofitable tea land for afforestation. Also on profitable estates planting of trees on every spot available would be helpful. The problem of this tree planting policy are the high costs. If the government of Sri Lanka wants to make profit out of the plantation sector, it must invest. A hindrance might be, that the Sinhalese nationalists regard the plantation sector a strange element, and estate managers are said to "ape their white masters".[15] FARMER[15] states, "...that most governments, whatever their colour, have submitted the plantation sector to relative if not absolute neglect." The estate industry might gradually disintegrate into small-holdings and cooperatives. Even on strictly managed estates theft of tea-leaves occurs. The leaves are plucked by labourers at night and sold to another factory as "small-holding" crop.

Another point of view should also be considered. Tea-growing is a monoculture which has been practised in some areas for more than 100 years, often on fields, which were used for coffee and cinchona before. The period of transition in last century and the regular pruning of tea bushes caused a loss of fertile topsoil, the amount depending on regional quantity of rainfall, steepness of terrain and management of estates. With proper management tea-growing could be continued for centuries, but the question arises, whether it could be done in a profitable scale, or whether the cost of production including wages, machinery, fertilizer, pesticides will become too high.

Consideration should be given to the 2 other major plantation industries, rubber and coconut.

Rubber plantations developed mainly this century. They are often prosperous, especially since high oil prices increased demand for rubber. A certain problem of rubber plantations on steep slopes is high soil erosion. Fields with old rubber trees can be used for cocoa-growing with rubber as shade or convert to a secondary rain forest, where the old trees may still be tapped; both forms can be observed in Moneragala.

Coconut products are essential for the local market, as coconuts are a staple food besides rice. No erosion problems exist and intercropping was tested successfully.

Although rubber and coconut are planted in a comparable scale (percentage of surface: tea 3.9; rubber 3.5; coconut 3.8), tea is of greatest influence to environment, as it is grown on steep slopes and in the upper catchment of the rivers.

Forestry:

Forestry is comparable to plantation industry and man-made forests comprise 1.25% of the island surface. Nevertheless a serious shortage of fuelwood and construction timber must be noted. The decline of natural forest cover in course of history has been shown above. Since independence a terrible loss has been observed. Since 1956 the natural forest area declined from 22% to 8% , mainly connected with the resettlement of the dry zone, but also by felling of remaining rain forest areas in the southwest like Sinharaja and Kanneliya.

Forestry in Sri Lanka means planting of introduced, exotic tree species, as indigenous trees are said to be too slow growing, while a species like Pinus caribaea grows successfully even on infertile soil. The administrative report of the Conservator of Forests for the year 1979 [16] gives some information on the activities of the Forest Department.

In 1979 8,248 ha were planted with exotic trees, 638 ha thereof comprised a special project for the afforestation of derelict tea and rubber lands (sic!) and other degraded areas (2/3 pines, 1/3 eucalypts). In the dry zone teak and Eucalyptus camaldulensis are partly planted in the "taungya"-

system by farmers, who can use the interspace for food production (intercropping) in the initial phase. The record of plantations shows, that 54% are stocked with teak (Tectona grandis), 12% with various Eucalyptus-species (mainly in up-country) and 11% with different Pinus-species (50% in up-country again). 15% are planted with mahogany-species. In 1979 the planting of Leucaena leucocephala (ipil-ipil) was commenced on 55 ha. This tree is also recommended in newspaper-advertisements for private land as it improves nitrógen content of the soil, provides green-manure and cattle food and helps to prevent soil erosion. A number of other tree species and bamboo are planted by the Forest Department in very small scale. The jak tree (Artocarpus heterophyllus) introduced in early history, is an important tree in the village gardens, used for its huge fruits and valuable timber. The timber is used for fishing boats and there is a serious shortage of that wood. It is therefore desirable, to plant more jak trees in forest plantations. In Northwestern and Western Province exist 4823 ha of mixed mahogony/jak plantations, the Colombo-Kurunegala road passes through them. Only 4 ha of jak exist in Southern Province.

One kind demand brings them near to extinction in natural forests: ebony! 787 m^3 of ebony logs were sawn in 1980, 218 in 1981. [17]

The various useful species of ebony (Diospyros) disappeared not only by logging of the Timber Corporation, but also by the large scale forest destruction in the dry zone.

Anyway, the planting of indigenous trees, which is done in small or experimental stage (e.g. Dipterocarpus), should be much more inforced, as these are adapted to the environment.

Also exotic trees should be tested, if they are suitable for afforestation. In Sri Lanka no conifers exist by nature. This is remarkable, as the families Araucariaceae and especially Podocarpaceae from southern hemisphere have migrated into most of the mountain forests of tropical Asia. These trees do not have needles like pines or firs, but leaflets, which seem to be better adapted to a humid tropical climate. A small area of 12 ha is planted with Araucaria cunninghamii in Southern Province, but no Podocarpus-trees are planted in up-country. These trees might be more recommendable than Eucalyptus and Pinus. The conifer Callitris had been planted some decades ago, but abolished again, as it did not allow any undergrowth and promoted soil erosion. But these are also negative effects of Eucalyptus and Pinus plantations in the mountains. These "forests" are useless for wildlife and Pinus often sets fire (accidently or deliberately). A big problem for Sri Lanka are illegal activities of the population, concerning forests (illicit felling, gemming and encroachments). More than 6000 offences were reported in 1979.

Food production:

Rice is a staple food in Sri Lanka. As rice growing was neglected during colonial times, imports were necessary. Though rice production has increased from 300,000 t/a around independence to

1,000,000 in recent years, imports are still necessary, due to rapid increase of population. Sri Lanka wants to become self-sufficient in rice production - import of wheat seems to be one "method". In the wet zone food production could be only increased by reducing the present area of rubber and tea.

In the highlands the cultivation of vegetables has increased since independence, either on government farms or by private enterprise. This increased settlement outside tea estates effects the remnant forests, as farmers intrude and cut their firewood.

In the dry zone of Sri Lanka we find the present region of development - and hope for a million of people. The Accelerated Mahaweli Ganga Development Programme, launched by the present government in 1978, has caught the nation like a fever. It is not intended to discuss the feasibility and financial problems of that gigantic project, but the environmental impact and risks.

More than 80,000 ha of undeveloped land will be irrigated - and lost for original flora and fauna. But it must be admitted that areas of comparable size are planned as wildlife and forest reserves in the region, including new national parks like Maduru Oya N.P. Nevertheless it must be doubted if these areas will be sufficient for the elephant population which will not be deterred by the boundaries from visiting rice and vegetable fields of the new settlers. Following old traditions, a watcher system would be sufficient to keep the elephants out of the fields. Today farmers often try to drive them away with guns and many elephants suffer miserable deaths.

Also in the dry lowlands a tree planting campaign should encourage tree growth along roads and channels, in village gardens and even in vegetable fields. It should be noted that in the traditional method of shifting cultivation, the larger trees all remained as a protecting cover.

When resettling the dry zone, the problems of the ancient civilization should be considered. First of all these is malaria, which might rapidly increase with increasing population density. Salination of the soil must be avoided. If the rains of the NE-monsoon are not sufficient to flush the accumulated salts away, this must be done with irrigation water. But will there be water enough? The whole project depends on the water of the Mahaweli river and its tributaries. Victoria reservoir has been filled meanwhile, after the heavy rains of recent years. But drought seasons like 1979/80 and evaporation of the large artificial lakes will make irrigation and generation of electricity difficult.

The heavy rains of the 1985/86 NE-monsoon resulted in disastrous landslides in the highlands, because of the unwise landuse policy of recent years, when agriculture was tried even on steepest slopes. The landslides in January 1986 killed more than 50 people. The Badulla-Nuwara Eliya main road was blocked for two weeks.

Environmental pollution:

This is a problem which also concerns developing countries. In Sri Lanka pollution of the Kelani river and the canal system around Colombo has been reported. Water pollution threatens supply with drinking water, and the situation in Colombo is serious. Also in Kandy, the Mahaweli waterworks are said to be unsufficient, so that water of Kandy lake is added!

Oil combustion creates another serious environmental problem in conurbations. Car traffic has increased rapidly, since the present government released the import restrictions of the Bandaranaike administration. The main roads in the densely populated regions are not only crowded; the dust from lorries and buses is also a real nuisance. Galle Road in Colombo has become a nightmare during rush hour.

Electricity from the new dams in the highlands is now replacing the diesel generators in the Colombo area. New railway lines and modernization of the existing tracks would provide an alternative to road traffic. The narrow gauge Kelani Valley Line from Colombo to Ratnapura-Opanayake (140 km) has been removed, as it was too slow (25.5 km/h instead of 40 km/h on broad gauge).

Plans for a new railway for the Mahaweli area exist (Colombo - Uda Walawe - Gal Oya - Kathiravel; i.e. around the southern escarpment, but it is doubtful if this will ever materialize, as all financial investment is channelled to irrigation works.

The catchword "traffic" leads to "tourism".Foreign visitors in great numbers have ambivalent effects on national economy. While they bring foreign exchange and provide jobs, the demand for "western" food raises market prices for meat, vegetables and fruits. Imported buses and coaches for tourists need imported oil, all consuming valuable foreign currency. Tourism creates a high demand for electricity (lights, refrigerators, air conditioners) and clean water (sanitary purposes and swimming pools) which only aggravate the environmental problems of Sri Lanka. The national parks Yala and Wilpattu were crowded by tourist jeeps which disturb wildlife. Since October 1980 the visit was allowed in big government-vans only.

Natural resources:

Sri Lanka has neither oil nor coal, but it has the richest plumbago (graphite) mines of the world and precious stones. While the plumbago mines in Sabaragamuwa have no adverse effects on the environment, the digging for gems, especially the illegal activities in remote mountain areas promote soil erosion and silting of reservoirs. The water-filled gem pits are dangerous traps for man and ungulates, below 1200 m they can act as breeding grounds of malaria-mosquitoes (Anopheles).[18]

Lime for building material is obtained from limestone bands in the central mountains, miocene limestone in the north - and from coral reefs along the south coast. This destruction of coral reefs is a serious threat to the coast, as the protecting wall against the waves of the SW-monsoon is removed. Though lime burning of corals is prohibited now, it is still practised in public along the roadside, e.g. in Hikkaduwa. The building activities for the tourist ressorts thus help to destroy the very attraction of this area - the coast and the beaches.

Fishery:

Though Sri Lanka is an island, fishery and navigation are rather neglected, and fish has to be imported. The rice cultivating Goygama are the highest Sinhalese caste, a fact which reflects the economic ideals of that race. Fishermen are of low caste because they kill creatures. The shelf around the island is narrow, and deep-sea fishing wight big trawlers is unprofitable, as Sri Lanka does not have the shipbuilding and maintenance facilities like Japan.[19] Sri Lanka has had 6 trawlers since 1979. Traditional fishery is done by beach seine fishing or from outrigger canoes.[20] Beach seine fishing is impossible where coral rocks would tear the nets. Fishing activities are influenced by the monsoon winds and the big waves along the shores. 3.5 t "mechanized" boats (and smaller boats) have been the backbone of the fishery fleet for the last 30 years. Shortage of jak and other suitable timber for building these boats is a serious problem - fibreglass boats are the expensive alternative. These boats are suitable for day-excursions. A 11 t-boat project ("baby-trawlers") was a failure.[21] Prawn and lobster fishing is an important branch of that industry. But overfishing of lobsters in the seventies caused a breakdown of lobster population.

Freshwater fish account for 10,5% of production but they are not appreciated by local consumers. No natural lakes exist in Sri Lanka and the indigenous fauna in the reservoirs is poor. The small rivers harbour an interesting fish fauna, but mainly small species which are hardly suitable as food. The imported Sarotherodon (=Tilapia) mossambicus has become a very important freshwater fish, as it reproduces quickly and feeds on the profuse phytoplancton. One form of "fishery" should be mentioned because of its disastrous effects on the natural environment: the collecting of aquarium fish in sea and freshwater, and water plants for export. Coral fish have permanent territories. When they are caught by scuba-divers, the same method is used for lobster-"fishing", the ecosystem is affected, as immigration through open sea is difficult. The beautiful freshwater fishes, mainly small barbs, of rainforest rivulets are popular among hobby-aquaristics. Also water plants are torn off the river beds. It would be wiser, to breed those plants and fishes in tanks for export, but obviously exploitation of nature is cheaper - for the moment.

ENVIRONMENTAL FACTS ON MALDIVES:

The Maldive islands are a chain of 19 atolls, 764 km long (in N-S direction) and 128 km wide. Addu atoll is situated south of the equator and Suvadiva atoll is the largest in the world. The word "atoll" derives from the Maldives, not only meaning a garland of islands, but also an administrative unit.

The total land area amounts to 298 km2. Only 219 of the 1000 islands are inhabited. The small coral islands ripe up to a maximum of 2 m above sea level. Annual rainfall in the capital Male, Kaafu atoll, is about 2000 mm with a maximum between October and January.

The SW-monsoon produces low precipitation on the flat islands (cf. dry lowlands of Sri Lanka), but strong winds and high waves prevail. Freshwater-lenses in the coral sand of the islands are fed by the rain only. Air temperature varies from 26.3oC to 33.3oC. Vegetation is similar to the coasts of India or Sri Lanka with Cocos, Pandanus (screw pine). Scaevola bushes, mangrove etc. The widespread Calophyllum inophyllum serves as a valuable timber tree.

No mammals exist on the islands. Th Calotes-lizard has probably been imported by man on his boats. The volant fauna includes herons and house-crow (on northern atolls only, but exterminated in Male), seabirds and insects.

Human population of Maldives:

The Maldive people are related to the Sinhalese of Sri Lanka and migrated from Northern India at the same time around 5th cent.B.C. The language Divehi is similar to Sinhala, and the people of the Maldives were Buddhists until 12th century.

Arab merchants brought Islam to the islands, but also linguistic and ethnic influence, mainly to the northern atolls.

Portuguese and French intervention brought no permanent colonial government. From 1887 the Maldives became a British protectorate, in 1965 they gained full independence, again. In 1976 the British abandoned their Air Force base on Gan (Addu).

The Maldives had 143,046 inhabitants in 1978, the capital Male has about 30,000 inhabitants, living on 123 ha.

The shallow and sandy soils allow agriculture in small scale only. No rice cultivation is possible. Millet, maize, maniok, sweet potatoes, sugar cane and bananas are grown. Food comes from different trees: breadfruit, jakfruit, pandanus, mango, papaya, citrus etc. The most important and most suitable tree is the coconut palm, which not only gives food, but also timber, thatching material and fiber. Also on uninhabited islands, the palms are harvested. Copra is an export article of the Maldives.

While poultry and goats add some animal protein to the vegetarian nourishment (pigs are not allowed), fish is the main food of the people. As vegetables and fruits are scarce, deficiency-problems erase. Besides the fruits of Pandanus, even the fruits of the mangroves Bruguiera cylindrica and Sonneratia acida are eaten.[22] The unbalanced fish-nourishment and various infectious diseases like tuberculosis, leprosy, filariasis, malaria etc. result in a life expectance of 40-50 years only, half of the children die before they are 5 years old.[23] Fishery is the most important economy, more than 90% of the population are engaged in it, and around the atolls a 200 miles economic zone has been declared. Fishing is practised outside lagoons only, mainly on thuna, bonito, mackarel etc. Life bait for these predatory fishes is caught around the coral reefs. The best season is during SW-monsoon. As fishing boats the traditional "dhoni" are used, being 13 m long and made of coconut timber. 400 of about 2000 dhonis were mechanized in 1977, 548 in 1978. The fish was normally dried in a process which took 2 - 3 weeks time. "Maldive Fish" was (and is) famous in Sri Lanka, but the import restrictions of the Bandaranaike administration in Sri Lanka since 1972/73 cut that market for the Maldives. Relief came by Japanese refrigerator ships, which bought the total daily catch straight from the fishing boats. This brought foreign exchange for the state and direct income for the fishers, but on local market the prices for fish went up and there is a serious shortage of fish for the poor. Besides fish, black corals, cowrie shells or tortoise shells form other marine products. Cowrie shells were a currency in former times. The export of marine products rose from 8,700 t in 1974 to 13,000 t in 1978.

Today tourism has become almost as important as fishery. Since 1972 37 tourist islands have been reserved, where foreign visitors live an exclusive life. Since November 11, 1981 direct flights from overseas are possible, as the airstrip on Hulule airport has been extended - a disadvantage for Sri Lanka, where many tourists had a stopover holiday or combined travel arrangement. The effects of tourism seem to be favourable on first sight: foreign exchange and jobs for many inhabitants. As spearguns and collecting of corals are prohibited, adverse effects on environment seemed to be avoidable. But these are manifold. On the tourist islands a massive interference to plant community takes place, as most of the undershrub is removed and insecticides are used extensively, to reduce the nuisance of mosquitoes etc.[24] For building material corals are broken from the reefs and coast erosion results. The anchors of diving boats promote this destruction. The most serious problem is water! The foreign visitors need not only drinking water (canned soda water is imported from South Africa or Singapore) but clean water for sanitary purposes, especially after swimming in the salt water. The fresh water lenses of the islands are far from adequate. Thus the fresh water of the tourist islands becomes brackish and contaminated and intestinal diseases must be feared. Waste and sewage of the tourist resorts is another problem, as the coral reefs are polluted (and destroyed by pollution). Strong tidal currents may bring relief - but no solution of the problem. This shows, that for large scale tourism, large scale investments are necessary: waste disposal on boats, sewage treatment plants and rationing of fresh water for the guests. Investments, of course, cut profit, as well as imports of oil, food and tinned beverages for the tourists.

In 1981 60,000 foreigners visited the Maldives, 42 tourist resorts existed by then. The ban of spearguns and export of tortoise shell etc. was a wise decision of the Maldive government, as well as the separation of traditional village life and modern tourist resorts. Thus social problems of tourism in poor developing countries are partly avoided - a contrast to Sri Lanka.

As the people of the Maldives seem to be more marine than the inhabitants of Sri Lanka, shipping is another form of income for the country. More than 35 Maldive cargo ships ply the Indian Ocean. But as no dockyards for modern ships exist in the Maldives, they must be bought and maintained abroad.

CONCLUSION

As Sri Lanka is a much bigger island than the small coral atolls of the Maldives only part of ecological problems are common to both countries. Similarities exist between the coastal belt of Sri Lanka and the Maldives: coconut and other useful plants, besides rice, coral reef ecology and fishery. Fresh water problems of the coral islands are similar to the north of Sri Lanka. Both countries are poor developing countries, but the natural resources of Sri Lanka are much richer than those of the scanty atoll environment of the Maldives.

Development in harmony with nature is a difficult task, but growing environmental problems in poor developing countries show vividly, that it must be attempted. Supply with clean drinking water must be safeguarded; soil, forest cover and wildlife must be protected to maintain stable ecosystems. It must be feared, that western influence, foreign invasion in form of mass-tourism spoil an ecological development. Consequences and alternatives would be "soft" forms of foreign aid, which take in account the traditional knowledge and culture of the receiving part.

Tourism should be limited in number to avoid negative effects (social and environmental). Ecological development means development with empathy.

Acknowledgements

Prof. Percy Silva, Colombo, and Mr. David Robson, Brighton, were so kind to read the manuscript and to give their critical comments. It is very much appreciated, that Mr. Robson took the hard work to improve the English style of the text.

References

[1] Cooray, P.G., Geology, with special reference to the Precambrian. 1984.

[2] Brohier, R.L., Food and the people. Colombo 1975.

[3] Brohier, R.L, 1975

[4] cf. Seligman, C.G./Seligman, B.Z., The Veddas. 1911.

[5] Gooneratne, B.M.W., The Ceylon Elephant: its decimation and fight for survival. Ceyl.Journ. Histor.& Social Stud., 10, 1 & 2: 149-160. 1967.

[6] Gooneratne, B.M.W., 1967:157.

[7] Brohier, R.L., 1975.

[8] cf. Indrapala, K. (edit.), The collapse of the Rajarate civilization and the drift to the south-west. Peradeniya 1971.

[9] cf. Schweinfurth, U., Filariosen auf Ceylon-Versuch einer standörtlichen und historischen Analyse, in Geographische Zeitschrift, 72,2: 113-128, 198

[10] Burma, Siam, Cambodia; cf. Indrapala, K., 1971.

[11] Perera, N.P., Natural resources, settlements and land use. Monographiae Biologicae 57: 453-492. 1984.

[12] Gooneratne, 1980.

[13] Marby, H., Tea in Ceylon. Wiesbaden 1972.

[14] Marby, H., 1972.

[15] Gooneratne, 1980.

[15] Farmer, B.H., An introduction to South Asia. London 1983, p. 225.

[16] Nanayakkara, V.R., Administration report of the Conservator of Forests for the year 1979. Colombo 1980.

[17] Department of Census and Statistics. Sri Lanka 1982.

[18] Schweinfurth, U., The importance of the geoecological approach in the control of diseases in a tropical country - the example of Ceylon (Sri Lanka). Yonsein reports on tropical medicine, 8,1, pp. 85-94, 1977.

[19] Econ Review 1977.

[20] Gläser, T., Fischerei und Fischereiwirtschaft im nördlichen Ceylon. Wiesbaden 1983.

[21] Gläser, T., 1983.

[22] Koechlin, B., Notes d`ethnographie sur l`alimentation aux Maldives, in Asie du Sud-Est et Mone Insulindien, 9, 3-4, pp. 25-48, 1978.

[23] Dupuis,J., Les Maldives, in Cahier d`Outre-Mer, 27, 105, pp. 5-21, 1974.

[24] Eibl-Eibesfeldt, I., Die Malediven. München 1982.

Bibliography

SRI LANKA

Abeywickrama, B.A. (1976), The role of plants in man`s environment. Vidurava, 1,3, pp. 4-7

Brohier, R.L.(1975), Food and the people. Colombo

Cooray, P.G.(1984), Geology, with special reference to the Precambrian. Monographiae Biologicae 57, pp. 1-34

Cramer, L.H.(1983), The undesirability of Pinus plantations in the catchments. Loris, 16,4, pp. 167-171

Department of Census and Statistics, Sri Lanka (1982): Statistical pocket book of the Democratic Socialist Republic of Sri Lanka. Colombo

Deraniyagala, P.E.P. (1958), The Pleistocene of Ceylon. Colombo

Dissanaike, A.S. (1984), Ecological aspects of some parasitic diseases in Sri Lanka. Monographiae Biologicae 57, pp. 353-369

Domrös, M. (1976), Sri Lanka - Die Tropeninsel Ceylon. Wiesbaden

Fernando, C.H. (ed.) (1984), Ecology and biogeography in Sri Lanka. Monographiae Biologicae 57, The Hague

Fernando, I.S. (1978), On the Kelani Valley Line. Econ.Review (SL), 4,6/7, pp. 24-26

Gläser, T. (1983), Fischerei und Fischereiwirtschaft im nördlichen Ceylon. Wiesbaden

Gooneratne, B.M.W. (1967), The Ceylon Elephant: its decimation and fight for survival. Ceyl.Journ.Histor.& Social Stud., 10, 1&2, pp. 149-160

Gunaratna, M.H. (1980), The plantation raj. Colombo

Indrapala, K. (ed.) (1971), The collapse of the Rajarate civilization and the drift to the southwest. Peradeniya

Iriyagolle, G. (1978), The truth about the Mahaweli. Nugegoda

Hoffmann, T.W. (1968), A plea for orderly land use in Ceylon. Loris, 11,4, pp. 176-180

The Mahaweli Ganga Development Project (Special Report). Econ.Review (SL), 4,8/9, pp. 3-22

Marby, H. (1972), Tea in Ceylon. Wiesbaden

Meijer, W. (1979), Plant a tree for posterity. Loris, 15,1-2, pp. 12-15, 106-107, 132

Nanayakkara, V.R. (1980), Administration report of the Conservator of Forests for the year 1979. SL Min. of Lands; Colombo

Perera, N.P. (1984), Natural resources, settlements and land use Monographiae Biologicae 57, pp. 453-492 (Ecol. and biogeography in Sri Lanka)

Schiemer, F.(ed.)(1983), Limnology of Parakrama Samudra-Sri Lanka. Developments in Hydrobiology 12; The Hague

Schweinfurth, U. (1977), The importance of the geoecological approach in the control of diseases in a tropical country - the example of Ceylon (Sri Lanka). Yonsei reports on tripical medicine, 8,1, pp. 85-94

Schweinfurth, U. (1982), Landscape change and geomedical consequences in the highlands of Sri Lanka (Ceylon). Mountain Res.& Developm., 2,2, pp. 195-199

Schweinfurth, U. (1984), Filariosen auf Ceylon - Versuch einer standörtlichen und historischen Analyse. Geographische Zeitschrift, 72,2, pp. 113-128

Schweinfurth-Marby, H. (1979), Die Situation des Ceylon-Tees 1979. Beobachtungen auf Sri Lanka. Kaffee u. Tee Markt, 19,5, pp. 3-7

Seligman, C.G./Seligman, B.Z. (1911), The Veddas. Reprint 1969. Oosterhout

Tennent, J.E. (1860), Ceylon. 2 vols., repr. 1977 (IV), Dehiwala.

Werner, W.L. (1981), Illicit gemming in up-country sanctuaries. Loris, 15,6, pp. 334-335

Werner, W.L. (1983), Save the Doona-forests. Loris, 16,4, pp. 194-197

Werner, W.L. (1984), Die Höhen- und Nebelwälder auf der Insel Ceylon (Sri Lanka). Trop. u. subtrop. Pflanzenwelt 46, Wiesbaden

Werner, W.L. (1984,b), Im Reich des Löwenkönigs - Nationalparks in Sri Lanka. Nationalpark, 43,2, pp. 43-47

Werner, W.L. (1985), The upper montane forests of Sri Lanka. Sri Lanker Forester, 15, 3&4 , 1982 (publ. 1985), pp. 119-135

Wijesinghe, L.C.A. (1978), Why are exotic species used for forestation? Econ.Review (SL), 4,2/3, pp. 24-26

MALDIVES

Department of Information and Broadcasting, Rep. of Maldives (1979 ?), Maldives - Facts and figures

Dupuis, J. (1974), Les Maldives. Cahiers d`Outre-Mer, 27,105, pp. 5-21

Eibl-Eibesfeldt, I. (1982), Die Malediven. München

Fosberg, F.R. (1957), The Maldive Islands, Indian Ocean. Atoll Res.Bull. 58

Hussaini, S.A. (1975) , Profiles of national development - a collection of features on the social and economic conditions in some countries of SE Asia and the Pacific. Colombo (Col.Plan Bureau)

Jacobsen, A. (1982), Wie Inselglück vermarktet wird. Frankfurter Allgemeine Zeitung (FAZ), 148, R2 (1-7-82)

Koechlin, B. (1978), Notes d`ethnographie sur l`alimentation aux Maldives Asie du Sud-Est et Monde. Insulindien, 9, 3-4, pp. 25-48

Malten, T. (1983), Malediven und Lakkadiven - Materialien zur Bibliographie der Atolle im Indischen Ozean. Wiesbaden

Maniku, A. et.al. (1977), Discover Maldives. Male

Maniku, H.A. (1977), The Maldive islands - a profile. Male

Metzner, J. (1978), Malediven. Handbuch der Dritten Welt 4, pp. 451-461. Hamburg

Community Forestry in the Hills of Nepal

by Dietrich Schmidt-Vogt

I. Introduction

A sizeable part of current development activities in the Kingdom of Nepal is directed at what has come to be known as the ecological crisis of the Himalayas. The 1970`s marked a sudden awareness of deforestation in the Himalayan mountains and of the alleged consequences - erosion in the uplands, siltation of rivers, flooding in the Gangetic plain. The problem was commonly seen to have arisen in modern times in response to population growth and subsequently increased demands for agricultural land and fuelwood. There was the spectre of ecological disturbance, even destruction, initiated on a limited regional scale, but growing into a crisis of international dimensions with as yet unperceived repercussions, ecological or political (IVES, 1984).

Due to intensified research, the views held on deforestation in the Himalayas are more complex today. Deforestation is no longer seen as a recent manifestation of modern influences, but as a process, which originated much earlier. [1] The causes are no longer attributed solely to an increase in forest clearing and fuelwood demand, but also the impact of collecting leaf fodder for livestock is now recognized, and more generally the close interrelation of forests and hill agriculture acknowledged. Forest degradation is today seen to have resulted to a considerable degree from the mixed particular type of mixed farming, practised in the hills of nepal.

In Nepal, this recognition of the singular importance of forests for agriculture has run parallel to a growing emphasis on community forestry as a viable approach to the improvement of both hill forests and hill farming. Community forestry as a means to improve the life of rural dwellers in developing countries was advocated in an FAO report, published in 1978. [2] The essential idea is, that forestry in developing countries, where a large part of the population is living by agriculture, should be adapted to the needs of rural communities. Forests should therefore be established in cooperation with local communities and in consideration of the varied requirements of the local economy.

Not only because hill farming in Nepal is so markedly dependent on forests does community forestry appear to be such a suitable concept, but also because of the particular geography of the Nepal hills. They present an immensely complex environment with enormous climatiac, ecological and ethnic diversity in a mountain country of rugged topography, intricate drainage and great altitudinal range. What applies in one place may not hold true for the neighbouring valley and sweeping generalizations are quickly refuted by the reality of regional variation. On such terrain, a concept which derives its rationale from each individual local situation through close cooperation with the local community may prove to be more successful than any large-scale national programme.

Community forestry was started in Nepal in the late 1960`s but it gained momentum with the National Forest Plan of 1976 and with a reform of forest legislation, which signified a shift from the previous policy of centralization and provided the opportunity for greater community involvement and for more practical experience with community forestry.

II. Historical Precedent: Village Forests in British India

The FAO paper "forestry for local community development" has been regarded, from the date of its publication in 1978, as the fundament of community forestry projects in developing countries. The first attempts at introducing community forestry to Nepal were initiated a few years earlier, though. The activities in the Chautara Forestry Division, which will be discussed later, had some influence on the formulation of the FAO paper and in turn were subsequently modified according to FAO proposals (SHEPHERD, 1981).

But both the idea and its application in South Asia are much older and were first tried in British India during the second half of the 19th century.

Sir Dietrich Brandis, head of the British Indian Forest Service from 1864 to 1883, very early drew attention to the receding forests of India and tried to introduce a remedy with the establishment of village forests, a concept which he knew from Europe and wished to adapt to the conditions of British India. As early as 1868 Brandis advocated village forests on an experimental basis in Mysore. Communal land, which had deteriorated under the double pressure of coppicing and grazing, was to be set aside as village forest and managed according to a simple system of rotational grazing with tracts of land temporarily enclosed. In addition he suggested the establishment of forest plantations specifically for agricultural purposes, such as provision of leaf fodder. Village forests were to be owned by the village community with both, responsibility and benefits equally shared among the villagers, and managed by local personnel under government supervision.

The proposal was rejected by the Mysore Government, but the idea was incorporated into the Indian Forest Act of 1878, which enabled regional governments to confer land upon village communities and impose regulations on the management of village forests (HESMER, 1958).

This early initiative contained the essence of community forestry as it is envisaged in Nepal today. In Sir Brandis own words:

...the object must be to constitute village forests for the benefit of village communities, or groups of villages, and to arrange for their protection and management by the community under the control of the state. Not only will these forests yield a permanent supply of wood and fodder to the people without any material expense to the state, but if well managed, they will contribute much towards the healthy development of municipal institutions and of local self government.[3]

Brandis, in this early statement, evinces his ability to look beyond the immediate concerns of forestry. He saw village forests not only as a means to supply an economic need, but also perceived the political and social benefits that could accrue from active community involvement. Moreover, he very early pointed out the importance of forestry for farming, which today is receiving so much attention. He wrote in 1883:

It must now be distinctly recognized that not only does the provision of timber and firewood come within the legitimate scope of forest administration in India, but one of the most important duties will, in future, be to increase the supply of cattle fodder, particularly during seasons of drought in the drier districts.[4]

From these brief remarks, Sir Dietrich Brandis appears as a precursor of ideas, which today, about 100 years later, are seen to open a new perspective for forestry in developing countries.

His efforts to establish village forest in British India during his term of active service failed. His ideas were never completely forgotten, although, during the final period of colonial rule and the early stages of independence, they resulted in little more than recommendations and resolutions. At present, social forestry, as this concept is more commonly named in India, is attracting renewed attention from the National Commission on Agriculture and from Indian foresters (TIWARI, 1983), and social forestry activities have been started throughout the country (CHATTERJEE, 1985).

III. Forests and Farming in the Hills of Nepal

Following the terminology used in English publications on Nepal, the country may be divided into three major landscape units - the main range of the Himalaya, the Middle Hills and, beyond the E-W trending ridges of Mahabharat Lekh and Siwaliks, the Terai lowlands.[5] Only the lower hills, from about 600 - 2000 m, comprising the main agricultural range of Nepal outside the Terai, will be discussed here. The country above 2000 m is more sparsely populated the mixed farming system with stock-grazing in high pastures during the summer season is quite distinct as compared to lower elevations, and the montane forests, beginning at about 2300 m, are in better condition than the forests below. Also the Terai will not be considered here, since the patterns of use in Terai and hill forests are very different. An important component of the Terai forests is the sal tree (Shorea robusta), which is highly rated as quality timber. Both, the relative ease with which sal can be felled and transported on the level Terai plains and the proximity to India, where such timber has been in great demand since the construction of the colonial railway, have been responsible for the large-scale commercial felling of forests, a practice, not yet encountered in the Nepal hills.

The hill region is limited in the south by the 3000 m high Mahabharat Lekh and rises from valley bottoms at about 600 m towards the Himalayan range

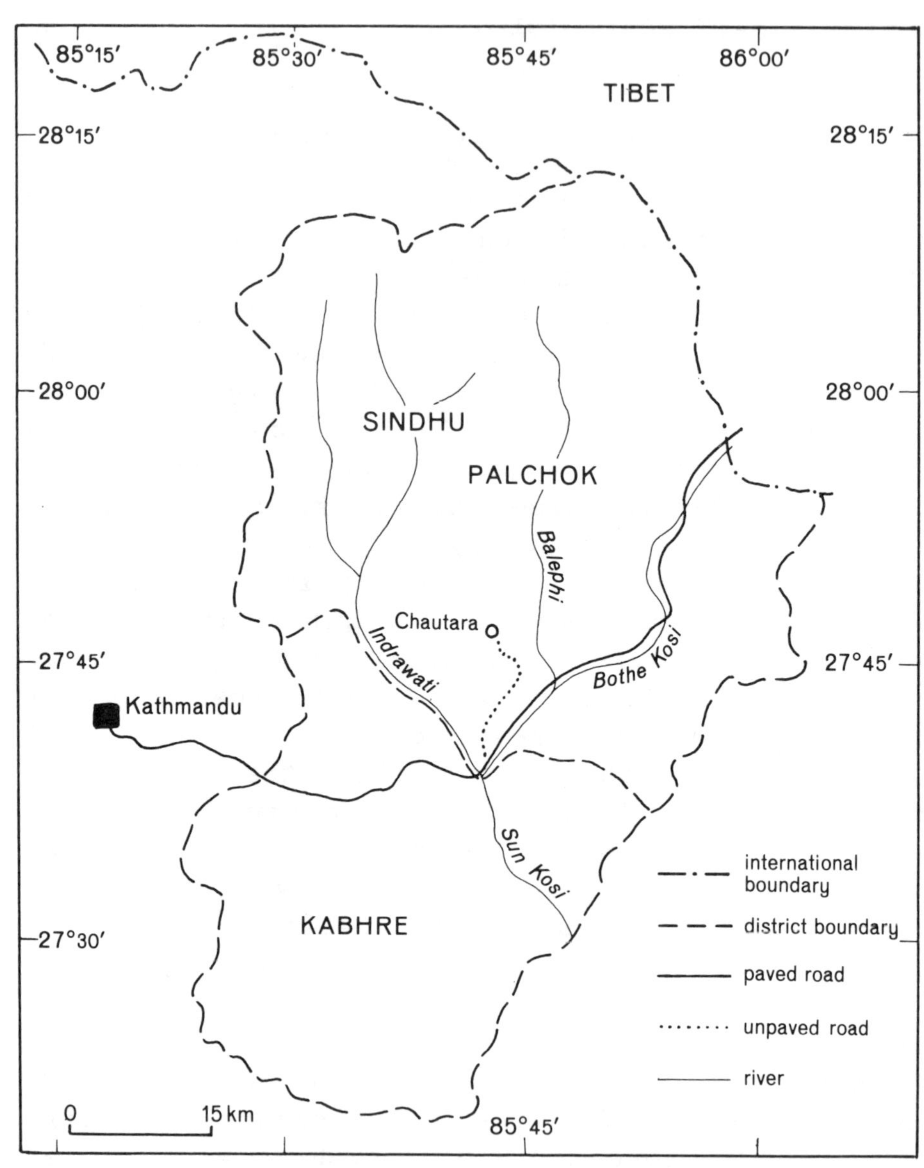

Draft: D. Schmidt-Vogt

Chautara Forest Division

Source: GILMOUR and APPLEGATE (1984)

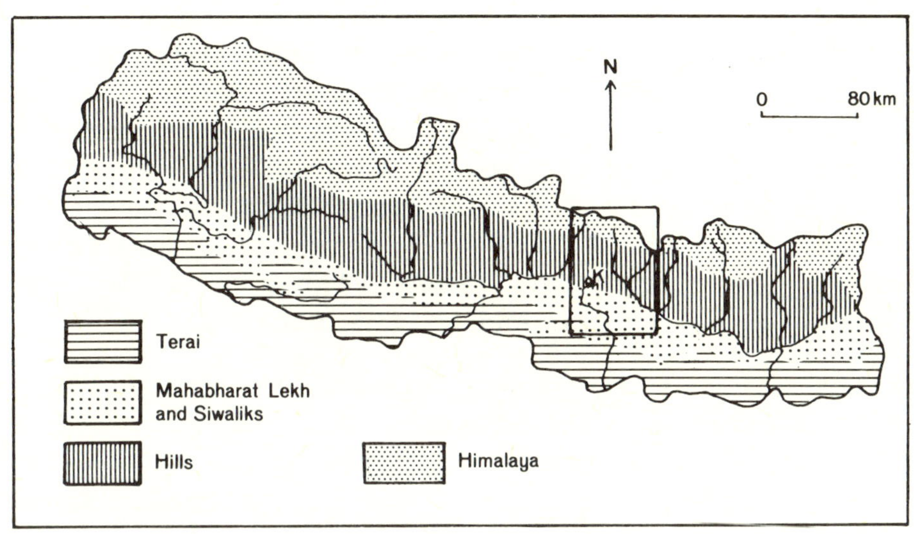

the major landscape units of Nepal Draft: D. Schmidt-Vogt
Source: HAGEN (1980)

in the north. Rivers, draining from the Himalayan mountains have cut the country into numerous N-S trending ridges. The steep and dissected terrain inhibits transport and thus profitable utilization of heavy logs; pressure on the forests therefore results primarily from the immediate needs of the village farmers. Only remnants of the former forest cover are left (see Plates 1 & 2 . The collection is at the end of the book).

Valley bottoms and lower elevations up to 1200 m are occupied by sal forest. Sal is succeded by chir pine (Pinus roxburghii), reaching up to 1800 m. Chir pine dominates on drier slopes, Schima wallichii and Castanopsis indica occur on the wetter sites. At 2000 m, the upper limit of the altitudinal range discussed here overlaps with the lower marges of montane forest, characterized by several species of evergreen oak (SCHWEINFURTH,1957); DOBREMEZ, 1976).

Most rainfall occurs during the monsoon period from June to September. There is more summer rainfall in the eastern than in the western part of the country, but whereas in the east there is only a short period of winter rain in January, winter rains add substantially to the total rainfall in the west. Annual precipitation varies between 1000 and 2000 mm with great local variation due to altitudinal difference and topographic situation. The monsoon months are followed by a dry period with low temperatures in the winter months from December to February and a hot season from March into May.

Despite continuous outmigration, still more than 50% of the total population were living in the hill region in 1981 (GOLDSTEIN et al., 1983). Population density is about 1500 people per km² of cultivable land (PFOFFENBERGER, 1981) with the average size of land holding per household less than 0.5 ha (WYATT-SMITH, 1982). The farmers grow wet rice on irrigated terraces near valley bottom and on the lower slopes, and corn, millet ant wheat as major crops on the dry terraces above. In addition to crop growing, also livestock is kept with an average of 5-6 large animals, buffalo and cattle, and about 5 small animals, usually sheep and goats, per household (WYATT-SMITH, 1982).[6] Animals are mainly kept for draught power and for manuring purposes, since only animal dung is used by the hill farmer as fertilizer. A very distinctive feature of the agricultural landscape in the hills are trees on farm terraces, single or in groups, which are lopped for leaf fodder or firewood (see Plates 2 & 3. The collection is at the end of the book).

Public forests and private trees on farmland are used for diverse purposes. Collecting of firewood as a factor contributing to deforestation has received so much emphasis, that BAJRACHARYA (1983) even speaks of a "fuelwood bias". Estimates of the share of fuelwood in the total energy consumption in Nepal range between 78% and 92% (STEIGER, 1984). Some figures for fuelwood consumption in the hill region, per capita and per year, are given below.[7] From such estimates, extreme pressure on forests was inferred, sometimes rather intuitively. Not all fuel derives from public forests, though. One study provided evidence that trees on private land constitute an important resource and that somewhat less than 50% of fuel requirements are met from other sources than public forests (CAMPBELL, 1983).

Demand for construction timber is a very variable factor due to the multitude of house types in Nepal (KLEINERT, 1983; TOFFIN, 1981), but is generally of less significance than other uses.

The most important link between forests and farming is through livestock. Except for buffalo, animals are rarely stall-fed, but mainly kept on fallow land, pastures or in the forest. Fodder production as such is not practised and feed supply over the years is uneven in amount and composition. A sufficient quantity of green fodder is available during the rainy season, June to September, from fresh growth on pastures, terrace walls and in forests, and from green maize stalks. In the dry season, the animals are mainly fed with crop residues such as rice, wheat and millet straws, and by grazing on fallow land. Green fodder is now available only as leaf fodder from private trees and from forests (WEISE, 1984). It was estimated that 25% of the green fodder during winter come from private trees and 75% from forests, forests supplying altogether 23% of the total feed (SHRESTHA, 1983).[8]

Leafs, grasses and weeds are also collected from the forest in order to provide bedding for the stall-fed animals. Bedding material and dung are composted and carried as fertilizer on to the fields before the onset of monsoon (WEISE, 1984).

There is thus a constant transfer of nutrients from forest to farmland, for animal fodder and for manuring purposes. WYATT-SMITH (1982) estimated, that 2.8 ha of forest land are required to sustain cultivation on 1 ha of farmland. Such quantitative assessments are very difficult to make and subject to uncertainties, but they point towards the undisputable fact, that forests are an integral part of agriculture in the hills of Nepal.

IV. Forest Legislation in Nepal

Before 1957 forest land was practically owned by the crown, but there was little government involvement except to encourage forest clearance and cultivation as a means to increase revenue from land and cultivation as a means to increase revenue from land titles (BAJRACHARYA, 1983). But here is evidence that under the Kipat communal ownership system[9] community control of forest use was practised and there are reported cases of locally developed forms of forest management.[10]

After the overthrow of Rana rule in 1951, the new government enacted the Private Forests Nationalization Act of 1957 which brought all forest land under government control. The Act was intended to provide a framework for the protection of forests, but in reality achieved the opposite result (BAJRACHARYA, 1983). Communal responsibility was suspended and government supervision remained insufficient. This stimulated a mentality to use forests while they were there and before anybody else could use them.[11]

A change of policy came with the National Forestry Plan of 1976. It was acknowledged that the Private Forests Nationalization Act had led into the wrong direction, that government effort alone was not sufficient to safeguard protection and development of forests, and that direct participation of local communities would have to be encouraged (NAFP, 1979). Most important as a legal basis for the development of community forestry were the Panchayat Forest Rules and the Panchayat Protected Forest Rules, enacted in 1978 and amended in 1980. The fundament of these laws was the Panchayat Legislation of 1962, according to which the country had been divided into panchayats - administrative units made up of 9 wards with about 3000 - 4000 people living in several villages. The new rules permitted that government forest could be granted to village panchayats as

- panchayat forest: degraded land, handed over for the purpose of reforestation and maintenance: a maximum of 125 ha could be given to hill panchayats;

- panchayat protected forest: forest land, handed over for improvement, protection and management; hill panchayats would be entitled to 500 ha.

It was calculated that the Forest Department would be authorized to give away a total of 367.000 ha as panchayat forest and 1.467.500 ha as panchayat protected forest. This would amount to ca. 45% of the existing national forest land coming under the responsibility of village panchayats (MANANDHAR, 1982).

V. Community Forestry in Nepal

Community forestry in Nepal is practised both on a regional and on a national level.

The regional approach, based on a natural unit, such as a watershed, or on administrative units, such as forest divisions and districts, is of longer standing and was first tried in Upallo Gerkhu of Nuwakot District in the late 1960's under the Trisuli Integrated Watershed Development Project (MANANDHAR, 1982). This project was terminated in 1970, but in 1973 a fresh start was made in the Chautara Forest Division, first from local initiative and later under the guidance of the Nepal-Australia Forestry Project. The operations of this project will be described in detail in the following chapter as a case study of community forestry in practice. Nepal-Australia Forestry Project is exclusively concerned with forestry programmes but reforestation and improvement of existing forests with people's participation are also practised by the various integrated development projects in Nepal. They are listed below:

Rasuwa-Nuwakot Integrated Rural Development project; World Bank

Kosi-Hill Area Rural Development Project (KHARDEP); United Kingdom

Sagarmatha Integrated Rural Development Project; Asian Development Bank

Nepal-Australia Forestry Project (NAFP); Australia

Resource Conservation and Utilization Project (RCUP); USAID

Tinau Watershed Project;Switzerland/Germany

Rapti Area Development Project; USAID

Karnali-Bheri Integrated Rural Development Project (K-Bird);Canada

Integrated Hill Development Project (IHDP) Switzerland

(Source: WALLACE (1981); MANANDHAR (1982))

In 1980 the Community Forestry Development and Training Project was set up as the first national level project in community forestry. A description will follow in chapter V.2.

V.1. Community Forestry Operations of the Nepal-Australia Forestry Project[12]

At present, the Nepal-Australia Forestry Project (NAFP) has the longest practical experience with community forestry in Nepal. However, it was not designed as a community forestry project from the beginning, but gradually, rather through practical application than by following a preconceived course, it developed a viable and tested concept for reforesting community land and is now taking on the issue of how the newly established forests are to be managed.

V.1.a. Project History and Structure

The involvement of Australia dates back to 1962 when, under the Colombo Plan, the government of Nepal asked for Australian assistance with the establishment of eucalypt plantations. Eucalypts and chir pine (Pinus roxburghii) were planted in the Kathmandu Valley from 1963 to 1971. Activities were restricted to the Kathmandu Valley until 1977, but evolved from mere planting to the establishment and management of nurseries and species trials (GILMOUR, 1982).

In 1978 a new phase was inititated. Among other tasks, NAFP was now responsible for reforestation in the Chautara Forest Division. Community forestry was to become a cornerstone of the reforestation programme. Unique in this process was the fact that community forestry was not imposed as a new concept on a largely unpreprared population, but introduced in response to local initiative. In the early 1970`s the villager`s attitudes in the Chautara Forest Division, as probably anywhere else, were strongly affected by the results of the Nationalization Act. They did not see any point in protecting forests since they had no clear title to forest land and since the District Forest Officer (DFO) was authorized to issue cutting permits to anybody outside the community - and often did so for his personal enrichment. In 1973, two panchayats and the DFO of the Chautara Forest Division, Mr. T.B.S. Mahat decided on a mutual agreement. The panchayats formed committees and took over responsibility for the forests within their domain; in return, the DFO agreed not to harvest trees without consulting the committees (WALLACE, 1981).

A beginning in local self-help had been achieved and after a period of consultations between Mr. Mahat and staff of NAFP, the project leaders decided to concentrate on the Chautara Forest Division and to support a process, which seemed even more promising now, with the new Panchayat Forest Rules furnishing a sound legal basis.

NAFP understood its activities in the Chautara Division as a pilot project in applied community forestry and from the beginning placed much emphasis on research. This was supported by the unique administrative structure of NAFP, which is administered by the Forestry Department of the Australian National University in Canberra, with the head of the Forestry Department at the same time acting as project director.

NAFP is a bi-lateral aid project of His Majesty`s Government of Nepal (HMG) and the Australian Devleopment Assistance Bureau (ADAB). Cooperation between Australian experts and Nepali counterparts follows guidelines, set down the governments of Nepal and Australia in 1979. Operations are decided by members of both governments, meeting in biannual intervals. Practical matters, such as nursery and plantation establishment are jointly decided by the Project Manager and the District Forest Officers (GILMOUR, 1982).

V.1.b. The Chautara Forest Division

The two districts of Sindhu Palchok and Kahbre, which make up the Chautara Forest Division, constitute a land area of about 450,000 ha. Of these, 185.900 ha are covered with forest and shrubland (NAFP, 1982). In the south the division is reaching down into valley bottoms at 500 m, in the north it includes the mountains of the Jugal Himal with attitudes surpassing 7000 m. Project activities concentrated on the most heavily populated zones between the valley floors and elevations up to 2000 m. Population in 1981 was 540.000 and growing at an annual rate of 1.8% (SHEPHERD and GRIFFIN, 1983). This is lower than the 2,6% national growth rate (GOLDSTEIN, et al., 1983) due to outmigration. Population density in Sindhu Palchok is 95/km² (Weise, 1984). In the same district 96% of the landowners own o.5 ha of land or less. The number of livestock is around five animals (SHRESTA, 1982).

The Chautara Forest Division counts among the most deforested parts of Nepal. In estimating the area of forest land necessary to sustain 1 ha of cultivated land, NAFP arrived at a ratio of 3:1, very similar to the result of WYATT-SMITH (1982), quoted above. But when the ratio of existing forest land to cultivated land was calculated, it appeared that the forests were insufficient, both in area and in productivity, to fully sustain cultivation (SHEPHERD, 1985).

The major demands upon forests were for fodder, fuelwood and construction timber, with fodder representing by far the most important forest product. Fuel consumption with 500 kg per capita and per year[13] was remarkably low, when compared with figures for other parts of Nepal and probably indicate a fuel shortage (GRIFFIN et al., 1985). The ultimate goal of project activities is seen in again creating a sound basis for the mixed farming system in the Chautara Forest Division, increasing area and productivity of forests by tree planting on government, panchayat and private land, forested or non-forested. It was recognized that eventually all uncultivated land up to 2000 m will have to be reforested in order to ensure sustained agricultural productivity (SHEPHERD, 1985).

V.1.c. Afforestation Practice

The maximum area to be planted annually was projected at 1000 ha (SHEPHERD and GRIFFIN, 1983). In the beginning, planting proceeded at a relativly slow pace with 100 ha planted in 1979 and 280 ha in 1980 but the performance was stepped up continuously and currently the rate of 1000 ha is exceeded. The quantitative achievements in afforestation from 1979 to 1984 are listed in the following table:

Afforestation activities in the Chautara Forest Division

plan-ting season	no. of Nur-series	annual seedling produc-tion (no.)	annual area of planta-tion (ha)	no. of panchayats partici-pating	cumulative plantation area (ha)
1979	4	765.000	100	5	100
1980	16	825.000	380	18	480
1981	21	1.210.000	452	24	932
1982	29	1.314.000	699	40	1631
1983	38	1.900.000	990	57	2621
1984	52	2.100.000+	1200+	71+	3821+

+ estimated figures only

Source: GILMOUR and APPLEGATE (1984)

In 1985 the total plantation area exceeded 5000 ha (SHEPHERD, 1985). Somewhat more than 50% of plantations were established on government land, the remainder on panchayat land. The size of these plantations is generally less than 30 ha, some are even as small as 1 ha or less (SHEPHERD, 1985).

Since every panchayat is legally entitled to 125 ha of panchayat forest and 500 ha of panchayat protected forest, the total area available to community forestry could amount to 110.000 ha, if all 176 panchayats in the Division are taken together (SHEPHERD and GRIFFIN, 1983).

The guiding principle of reforestation is, that plantations are established only in cooperation with the local community and that participation in the plantation programme is voluntary. The project will therefore act only upon request from a panchayat to the DFO. Community forestry is expected to spread through the division in a process of spontaneous diffusion, with the experience of one successful panchayat acting as a catalyst for many others. As a first step, a nursery site is determined and a nursery built with local labour and with material and expertise provided by the project. After completion, the nursery is maintained by local helpers and run by a foreman who was trained by and receives payment from NAFP. The community then has to agree on the site of the future plantations and which land is to be declared panchayat forest of panchayat protected forest. Trees are planted with voluntary labour and the community is responsible for the protection of plantations from livestock and uncontrolled use. With respect to the last point, NAFP has scored its most important success. Whereas in other parts of Nepal, fences are regarded as indispensable to the establishment of new forests, planting and the protection of established forests in the Chautara Forest Division were achieved without them (see Plate 4 at the end of this book). Consultation and cooperation with the community during plantation establishment was seen to have resulted in a new (or revived) spirit of communal responsibility for forests.

V.1.d. Species Selection

Whether a forest plantation will be successful will depend initially on a careful plantation policy, but, in the long run, to a large extent on the choice of tree species. They must be adapted to the ecological constraints of the available planting site and should be regarded by the village people as useful. Only when the forests are of value to their economy can villagers be expected to keep up interest in maintaining them.

When the plantation programme was started, choice of plantation species was governed by the fact, that only the most degraded land was available for planting, where only hardy species had a chance of survival. These are Shorea robusta for the valleys and lower elevations (up to 1200 m), Pinus roxburghii for the middle elevations (900-1800 m), Pinus patula (an exotic from Mexico) in the higher elevations (1500-2400 m), together with Pinus wallichiana above 1800 m (SHEPHERD and GRIFFIN), 1983). Up to now, mainly pines were planted. The qualities of pine as a pioneer and protective cover on degraded land are obvious, but its value to the village community is limited. Pine trees can be used primarily for construction timber, but the demand for such timber is not very great. Pine does not provide fodder and, compared to other species, only inferior firewood (this applies especially to Pinus roxburghii).

Clearly the hill farmers would prefer braodleaf species which are useful for many purposes, such as firewood, fodder and bedding, but NAFP encountered great difficulties in establishing broadleaves in plantations. Villagers are now encouraged to grow more fodder trees on their private land in some form of agroforestry practice and free seed is provided for that purpose (SHEPHERD, 1985).

But whereas broadleaf plantations on degraded land do not seem to be feasible at the moment, an increase in broadleaves may be achieved through forest management.

V.1.e. Forest Management and Harvesting

To ecological purists, the thought of harvesting forests at a stage, when planting them seems to be the most imminent necessity in the face of ecological degradation, may sound unorthodox, but it must be part of a strategy that seeks to protect forests by making them useful to the village community. So far, little thought has been given to the management of forest plantations in Nepal, but NAFP is currently working out options within its domain.

Forest management applies to species composition and stand structure of forests. The double objective is, to ensure that forests maintain productivity and protective functions under the given ecological conditions and provide products, which are useful to village farmers.

It was demonstrated that the needs of farmers for forest products are very diversified and that accordingly pure pine plantations, although ecologically viable, are of only limited economic use. But over the years, as a consequence of probably both protective cover and reduced grazing pressure, a rich undergrowth with many broadleaves has come up beneath the pines (see Plate 5 at the end of the book). These

could provide the basis for restructuring the pine stands into mixed forests at a later date. The native broadleaf Schima wallichii has proven to be extremely capable of regenerating naturally under pine and its potential is currently under close scrutiny (SHEPHERD and GRIFFIN, 1983). In the light of these findings, the pine plantations are seen as a pioneer stage, which, depending on site constraints and community demands, may be either maintained or diversified into a mixed conifer/broadleaf forest or finally transformed into a pure broadleaf forest.

Harvesting these forests requires other concepts than the standard techniques of classical "temperate zone" forestry, which do not concur with the requirements of hill farmers. The predominant concern of classical forestry is with the sustained production of stemwood. Stemwood is of subordinate interest to hill farmers, who rarely cut a tree, but instead lop off its branches and gather its leaves or, if they cut a tree, prefer small diameters that can be easily transported. This practice of constant, almost daily utilization of standing trees or forests requires a type of forest management for which, as yet, hardly any systematic knowledge is available (SHEPHERD and GRIFFIN, 1983). Some precedence is provided by traditional methods of European forestry, such as the simple coppicing or the coppice with standards systems, but the physiological responses of indigenous Nepalese trees to such treatment are not exactly known. Questions, such as to what intensity a tree can sustain utilization without too much reduction of productivity (MOENCH et al., 1986) and as to whether higher fodder production is attained by just fostering fodder trees or by combined planting of grass and trees, will be of significance and can only be answered by more research into ecological properties and economic demands. NAFP is now carrying out studies of this kind through management trials, where different types and intensities of pruning and thinning are applied to forest plantations.

It is understood that only simple management systems should be used in community forestry since in future not only planting and protection but also management would be within the responsibility of villagers. More sophisticated management systems could be applied to government land and agroforestry methods are considered for private land (SHEPHERD and GRIFFIN, 1983).

V.2. The Community Forestry Development and Training Project

In 1980, after two years of preparatory activity, the Community Forestry and Training Project (CFDP) was set up with a World Bank loan and additional financing from USAID, UNDP and HMG of Nepal. The main aims of the project are the development of community forestry in the hills of Nepal and training of qualified forestry personnel. In contrast to the projects mentioned before, which are working within regional limits, this project is operating on the national level. With respect to the community forestry component of its programme, the objectives are:

- to establish 11.750 ha of panchayat forest

- to improve 39.100 ha of panchayat protected forest

- to establish 0.9 mio trees on private land

- to introduce 15.000 improved stoves

- to establish regional seed stores; a Tree Seed Unit had been established in Kathmandu by the Nepal-Australia Forestry Project in 1981 (MANANDHAR, 1982).

The programme is implemented by the Community Forestry and Afforestation Division (CFAD) of the Department of Forests. The field activities are carried out by Community Forestry Assistants, a new type of field worker who is not assigned to a specific territory, and, on the regional level, by the respective Divisional Forest Officers and panchayat representatives.

Panchayats, which are to be part of the programme, are selected according to criteria such as acute shortages or capability for community action (PELINCK et al., 1984). When a panchayat has been selected, Community Forestry Assistants are sent there to explaing the programme to the villagers. Nursery construction and plantation establishment are achieved in a procedure similar to the one adopted by NAFP, of intense consultation with village leaders and population before decisions are made. In this process the programme is adapted to the specific requirements of the local panchayat. Whereas the routine of setting up nurseries and plantations is well established by now, forest management has not been approached in earnest yet. But consensus with the local population should be considered a priority also with respect to forest management. The practice that forestry field staff prepare their own plans for panchayat forests and panchayat protected forests should be discouraged and the management plan should become "...a contract between the Government and the villagers...signed by the pradhan pancha, the chairman of the local forest committee and the DFO".[14]

VI. Conclusion

Community forestry is a new approach to reforestation and forest management in developing countries. In this paper the current practice of community forestry in the hills of Nepal was briefly outlined. It was also shown, that the idea of a forestry system, adapted to the specific needs of rural communities in South Asia, is not that new and that the introduction of such a type of village-oriented forestry had already been attempted in British India during the second half of the 19th century.

But community forestry is more than just a reforestation programme and belongs as an integral part to the larger issues of rural and communal development. In this respect, the introduction and success of community forestry signify a change both in the rationale of foreign aid projects and in the administrative policy of the government of Nepal.

In recent years, increasing criticism was leveled at the massive aid programmes of the past, which had generally benefitted the urban rather than the rural population (SHEPHERD, 1981). Similar opinions were voiced in Nepal and especially agricultural aid was criticized for having relied too much on technical transfer and financial investment, for a tendency to favour pilot projects which promised quick results, and for its inflexibility in adapting to local conditions and in developing appropriate methods and technologies (PANT, 1983). This generated an atmosphere for greater emphasis on rural development and greater responsiveness to local conditions and local requirements. Accordingly, community forestry as a forest programme for the needs of rural communities and as a component of rural development received attention and was finally advocated by FAO to become a guiding principle for foreign aid projects, concerned with forestry in rural regions.

In the recent past, the administration of Nepal endeavoured to achieve more decentralization and participation. The panchayat legislation of 1962 had been intended to provide some scope for decentralization but, in the face of growing discontent, the shortcomings of the original design and the necessity for further measures were acknowledged (KNALL, 1983).

The National Forest Plan of 1976 and the Panchayat Forest Rules of 1978, which admitted the fact, that government effort alone could not take charge of protection and development of forests and which provided the legal basis for more direct participation by permitting communal forest ownership (BAJRACHARYA, 1983), was part of a general political process towards devolvement of responsibility from the central government to the districts and local panchayat level.

The primising start of community forestry in Nepal may be partly explained by this complementary convergence of a new outlook in foreign aid policy, laying emphasis on rural community development, and of the willingness of the Nepal government to accept greater local autonomy, at least in some matters.

The importance, accorded to community forestry in Nepal, indicates a growing awareness that economic development is feasible only through cooperation with the rural people, not by the application of preconceived development plans and not by the activities of a centralized administration.

References

[1] A recent study in Sindhupalchok and Kahbre Districts has provided evidence that the loss of forest land to agriculture was primarily due to attempts at maximizing land tax, which commenced with the establishment of the Kingdom of Nepal (1768) and lasted into Rana times (1856-1951). This process ceased at least 100 years ago and human pressure has since then resulted rather in degradation of remnant forests than actual forest loss (MAHAT et al., 1984).

[2] FAO Forestry Department, Forestry for local community development, Rome 1978.

[3] Passage from an article for the Journal of the Scottish Arboricultural Society, Vol. X., Part II, 1884; quoted from TIWARI (1986).

[4] Quoted from TIWARI (1983), pp. 2-3.

[5] See lower section of map.

[6] Figures on hill farming and forest use are quoted from the available literature only to provide a rough approximation. It should be kept in mind that knowledge is still imperfect due to regional variation and uncertain quantification. There are generally more data available for the eastern and central regions of Nepal where most aid projects are located. In comparison, very little is known about the west.

[7] MAUCH (1974), 540 kg; LEVENSON (1979), 686.5 kg; WIART (1983), 681 kg; METZ-FOX (1983), 573 kg mean consumption, 633 kg maximum consumption.

[8] These estimates concerning composition of animal feed and quantitative share of the individual components are based on regional studies in Sindhupalchok District and reflect local conditions. Considerable variation due to varying local circumstances must always be taken into account. See e.g. METZ-FOX (1983) for a village situation where crop residues play a more important role throughout the year and where more leaf fodder is fed during monsoon than during the dry season.

[9] See REGMI (1975).

[10] See FÜRER-HAIMENDORF (1964, 1975) for theh Khumbu region where Sherpas had conceived a system of local forest control, with forest guards (shingo naua) appointed by and responsible to the village. See also LEVENSON (1979) for the Pokhara area.

[11] FÜRER-HAIMENDORF (1975), in the sequel to his first book on the Sherpas of the Khumbu (1964) described, how the local system of forest control deteriorated, not immediately as a result of the Nationalization Act, but upon introduction of panchayat administration in 1962. Responsibility for the forests was transferred to the new panchayat office, 4 days walk from the Khumbu, with the practical result, that forests from than on were used without restraint.

[12] The writer of this paper received the support of Nepal-Australia Forestry Project during his stay in Nepal, 1982-1984, and was able to carry out his own field-work from the NAFP Field Head Quarter in Chautara. Utmost gratitude is expressed to Prof. D.M. Griffin, Project Director, for his invitation and to NAFP staff for their help.

[13] 50% of fuel consisted of wood taken from the forests and 12% of wood taken from private trees; the rest came from weeds and residues (GRIFFIN et al., 1985).

[14] PELINCK et al. (1984), p. 10.

Bibliography

Bajracharya, D., Deforestation in the food/fuel context: historical and political perspective from Nepal, in Mountain Research and Development. Vol. 3, No. 3, 1983, pp. 227-240

Campbell, J.G., People and forests in Hill Nepal. Draft Document HMG/UNDP/FAO; Community Forestry Development Project; Kathmandu 1983

Chatterjee, N., Economic aspects of social forestry in India, in Y.S. Rao, N.T. Vergara, G.W. Lovelace (eds.), Community Forestry: socio-economic aspects. FAO Regional Office for Asia and the Pacific. Bangkok 1985, pp. 67-114

Dobremez, J.-F., Le Népal: écologie et biogéographie. Paris 1976

FAO Forestry Dept.: Forestry for local community development. Rome 1978

FAO Forestry Dept.; Forestry for rural communities. Rome 1978

Fürer-Haimendorf, Ch.v., The Sherpas of Nepal: buddhist highlanders. London 1964

Führer-Haimendorf, Ch.v., Himalayan traders: life in highland Nepal. London 1975

Gilmour, D.A. (ed.), Operations of the Nepal-Australia Forestry Project in the Chautara Forest Division. NAFP. Kathmandu 1982

Gilmour, D.A., People, forests and erosion - experiences from the Middle Hills of Nepal. IUFRO-

Symposium on "Effects of Forest Land Use on Erosion and Slope Stability", Honolulu, Hawaii 7-11.5.1984, pp. 15-21

Gilmour, D.A.; Applegate, G.B., Community forestry as an option for containing environmental degradation - a case study from Nepal. IUFRO-Symposium on "Effects of Forest Land Use on Erosion and Slope Stability", Honolulu, Hawaii 7-11.3.1984, pp. 41-46

Goldstein, M.C.; Ross, J.C.; Schuler, S., From a mountain-rural to a plains-urban society: implications of the 1981 Nepal Census, in Mountain Research and Development. Vol. 3, No. 1, 1983, pp. 61-64

Griffin, D.M; Gilmour, D.A.; Shepherd, K.R.; Mahat, T.B.S.; Applegate, G.B., Forestry for the needs of rural populations in Nepal. Paper presented at the Ninth World Forestry Congress, Mexico City, July 1-12, 1985

Hagen, T., Nepal: Königreich am Himalaya. Bern 1980

Hesmer, H., Leben und Werk von Dietrich Brandis 1824-1907. Abhandlungen der Rheinisch-Westfälischen Akademie der Wissenschaften. Vol. 58, Opladen 1958

Ives, J., The Himalayan Ganges problem in the context of peace and resource-use conflict management, in Mountain Research and Development. Vol. 4, No. 4, 1984, pp. 363-365

Kleinert, C., Siedlung und Umwelt im Zentralen Himalaya. Geoecological Research Vol. 4. Wiesbaden 1983

Knall, B., Dezentralisation und Partizipation in Nepal, in Snoy, P. (ed.), Ethnologie und Geschichte: Festschrift für Karl Jettmar. Wiesbaden 1983

Levenson, B., Fuelwood utilization: a study of the demand and available fuelwood resources at six selected villages. Phewa Tal Technical Report No. 9. Kathmandu 1979

Mahat, T.B.S.; Griffin, D.M.; Shepherd, K.R., A historical perspective of the forests of Sindhu Palchok and Kabhre. IUFRO-Symposium "History of Forest Utilization and Forestry in Mountain Regions", ETH Zürich 3.7.9.1984

Manandhar, P.K., Introduction to policy, legislation and programmes of community forestry development in Nepal. HMG/UNDP/FAO Community Forestry Development Project, Field Document No. 1a. Kathmandu 1982

Mauch, S., The long term perspective of the region`s forest resources. IHDAP, SATA. Kathmandu 1974

Metz-Fox, J., Managing public lands in a subsistence economy: the perspective from a Nepali village. PH-D Dissertation, University of Wisconsin. Madison 1983

Moench, M.; Bandyopadhyay, J., People-forest interaction: a neglected parameter in Himalayan forest management, in Mountain Research and Development. Vol. 6, No. 1, 1986, pp. 3-16

NAFP, Nepal`s National Forestry Plan 1976 (2033); an un-official English translation. Kathmandu 1979

NAFP, Land use survey for the Chautara Forest Division. NAFP Occasional Paper. Kathmandu 1982

New Era, Community and forestry development: a study of villager`s attitudes towards forest and forestry development in Sindhupalchok District of Nepal. Kathmandu 1980

Pant, T.N., Foreign aid and agricultural development in Nepal, in Foreign Aid and Development in Nepal; proceedings of a seminar (Oct. 4-5, 1983), Kathmandu, pp. 155-195

Pelinck, E.; Manandhar, P.K.; Gecolea, R.H., Community development in Nepal, in Unasylva. Vol. 36, No. 143, 1984/1, pp. 2-12

Poffenberger, M., Patterns of change in the Nepal Himalaya. New Delhi 1980

Regmi, M.C., Landownership in Nepal. Berkeley, Los Angeles 1976

Schweinfurth, U., Die horizontale und vertikale Verbreitung der Vegetation im Himalaya. Bonner Geogr. Arb. 20, 1957

Shepherd, K., The Nepal-Australia Forestry Project, in Australian Forester. Vol. 44, No. 4, 1981, pp. 210-221

Shepherd, K.; Griffin, D.M., The Nepal-Australia Forestry Project: a case study of research and development; paper to IUFRO Work Conference "Applying Results from Forestry Research". Edingburgh, Scotland, 25 July - 1. Aug., 1983

Shepherd, K., Managing the forest and agricultural systems together for stability and productivity in the Middle Hills of Nepal; paper presented at the International Workshop on Watershed Management in the Hindu Kush - Himalaya Region, Chengchu, Sichuan Province, China 14-19. Oct. 1985

Shresta, R.L., The relationship between the forest and the farming system in Chautara, Nepal, with special reference to livestock production. Master thesis. Australian National University, Canberra 1982

Steiger, J., Energie und wirtschaftliche Entwicklung in Entwicklungsländern: das Beispiel Nepal. Wiesbaden 1983

Tiwari, K.M., Social forestry in India. Dehra Dun 1983

Tiwari, K.M., Sir Dietrich Brandis and social forestry, in Tributes to Sir Dietrich Brandis; Brandis Memorial Prize Centenary, Forest Research Institute and Colleges, Dehra Dun 11th July, 1986, pp. 15-19

Toffin, G. (ed.), L`homme et la maison en Himalaya: écologie du Népal. Paris 1981

Wallace, M.B., Solving common-property resource problems: deforestation in Nepal. PH-D Dissertaion, Harvard, Cambridge, Mass. 1981

Weise, S., The monsoon feeding system for ruminants: a case study of three panchayats in the

Sindhupalchok District of Nepal. IHDP. Kathmandu, Winterthur 1984

Wiart, J., Ecosystème villageois traditionnel en Himalya Népalais: la production forestière suffit-elle aux besoins de la population; Thèse 3ème cycle, Université de Grenoble 1983

Wyatt-Smith, J., The agricultural system in the hills of Nepal: the ratio of agricultural to forest land and the problem of animal fodder. APROSC Occasional Papers 1; Agricultural Projects Services Centre; Kathmandu 1982

List of Contributors (in alphabetical order)

Dengel, Holk Harald, (M.A. Dr.), historian; topic of his doctoral thesis is "Darul-Islam: Kartosuwirjos Kampf um einen islamischen Staat (Darul-Islam: The fight of Kartosuwirjo for an independent islamic State Indonesia). Research in origin and development of the Darul-Islam-Movement in Westjava. Research work in Indonesia. Present research focus: His most recent book is annoted bibliography of new Indonesian literature on the history of Indonesia. Further scientific works are a revised version of his M.A. thesis about Indonesia under the new order. Another book concerning the Darul-Islam-Movement will be published in Indonesia with the title "Timbul dan tenggelamnya Negara Islam ciptaan Kartosuwirjo.

Contact address: South Asia Institute, University of Heidelberg, Department of History, Im Neuenheimer Feld 330, 6900 Heidelberg / FRG

Hellmann-Rajanayagam, Dagmar (M.A. Dr.), historian, topic of her doctoral thesis is "Tamil - Sprache als politisches Symbol (Tamil - language as political symbol). Research in Tamil nationalism in South India, Tamil minorities in South East Asia. Research work in India (Madras), Sri Lanka (Jaffna), Singapore and Malaysia. Present research focus: The Tamil independence movement in Jaffna, Sri Lanka.

Contact address: South Asia Institute, University of Heidelberg, Department of History, Im Neuenheimer Feld 330, 6900 Heidelberg/FRG

Effenberg, Christine (M.A., Dr.), historian, topic of her doctoral thesis is "Die politische Stellung der Sikhs innerhalb der indischen Nationalbewegung 1935-1947 (The political position of the Sikhs within the Indian National Movement 1935 until 1947). Research in historical and political developments of the Sikhs and in history of North India since fifteenth century. Research work in India (Punjab), Pakistan (Lahore) and Great Britain (London). Present research focus: Nationalism in Punjab; The "Khalistan-Demand" of the Sikhs.

Contact address: South Asia Institute, University of Heidelberg, Department of History, Im Neuenheimer Feld 330, 6900 Heidelberg/FRG

Kaiser, Martin (M.A), economist. Research in transfer of resources, methods of planning and evaluation, development policy, computer aided economic and social research. Short-term expert in the field of infrastructure, town planning. Fieldstudies in Africa and Asia.

Contact address: South Asia Institute, University of Heidelberg, Department of Economics, Im Neuenheimer Feld 330, 6900 Heidelberg/FRG

Khadka, Narayan (Dr.), economist; topic of his doctoral thesis is "Public Enterprise in Nepal: It`s Financial Performance in Relation to Government Budgets". Research in foreign aid and development, industrial economics and regional cooperation. Research work in France (Paris, Development Centre of OECD) and Great Britain (Brighton, Institute of Development Studies)

Contact address: South Asia Institute, University of Heidelberg, Department of Economics, Im Neuenheimer Feld 330, 6900 Heidelberg/FRG

Rösch-Rhomberg, Inge (M.A.), anthropologist; she is a doctoral candidate in Social Anthropology. Research in ethnographic research methods. Research work in Egypt, Tanzania and Korea. Present research focus: Cognitive Anthropology, kinship structures, exchange theory and social processes.

Contact address: South Asia Institute, University of Heidelberg, Department of Ethnology, Im Neuenheimer Feld 330, 6900 Heidelberg/FRG

Schaarschmidt-Kohl, Eva-Maria (Dr.), political scientist; her doctoral theses is about the development of the Indonesian trade union movement until independence. Research in social movements of the Philippines, Malaysia and Indonesia.Present research focus: A Study of post-independence development of the Indonesian trade union movement and a handbook for the Indonesian trade union movement.

Contact address: South Asia Institute, University of Heidelberg, Department of Political Science, Im Neuenheimer Feld 330, 6900 Heidelberg/FRG

Schmidt-Vogt, Dietrich, geographer. State exam (geography and english literatue); currently he is writing a doctoral thesis on "High altitude forests in the Jugal Himal, Eastern-Central Nepal". Research work in Nepal. Present research at the Geography Department, South Asia Institute, is concerned with agroforestry in South Asia.

Contact address: South Asia Institute, University of Heidelerg, Department of Geography, Im Neuenheimer Feld 330, 6900 Heidelberg/FRG

Singh, Jogishwar (M.A. in Physics and History, D.E.S.S. degree in Administration of International Organizations and in International Relations) physicist and historian; currently he is writing a doctoral thesis on "Government and Institutional Rural Credit in an Indian District". Research in administration of international organizations and international relations. Research work in France (Paris).

Contact address: South Asia Institute, University of Heidelberg, Department of History, Im Neuenheimer Feld 330, 6900 Heidelberg/FRG

Urhahn, Margit (Dr.), anthropologist and librarian; topic of her doctoral thesis is "Grenzen und Übergänge von Kasten- und Stammesgesellschaft in Indien" (Discontinuities and continuities between caste and tribal society in India). Research interests: Anthropological theory. Epistemology of anthropology. French anthropological tradition (Mauss, Dumont, Bourdieu). South Asia, anthropology & history. Indian tribal societies and cultures, ethnography & "history". Alien systems of thought, symbolic and classification systems & practice. Relevance of anthropology today (e.g. problem of applied anthropology, "development" anthropology etc.).

Contact address: South Asia Institute, University of Heidelberg, Department of Tropical Hygienics and Public Health, Im Neuenheimer Feld 330, 6900 Heidelberg/FRG

Veit, Wolfgang (M.A.), economist; currently he is writing a doctoral thesis in economics. Research in monetary flows of south- and southeast asian states and extra-regional states.

Contact address: South Asia Institute, University of Heidelberg, Department of Economics, Im Neuenheimer Feld 330, 6900 Heidelberg/FRG

Wagner, Norbert (Dr.), economist; Research in international economic relations and development economy. Research work in USA and Asia.

Contact address: South Asia Institute, University of Heidelberg, Department of Economics, Im Neuenheimer Feld 330, 6900 Heidelberg/FRG

Werner, Wolfgang L. (Dr.), geographer; topic of his doctoral thesis is "Die Höhen- und Nebelwälder auf der Insel Ceylon (Sri Lanka). Research in plant-geography, ecology, nature conservation in South Asia. Research work in Sri Lanka, Maldives, India Indonesia, China and Thailand.

Contact address: South Asia Institute, University of Heidelberg, Department of Geography, Im Neuenheimer Feld 330, 6900 Heidelberg/FRG

Appendix 1:

List of plates of the contribution "Sri Lanka and the Maledives - Aspects of Ecological Development in Two South-Asian Islan Republics

by Wolfgang L. Werner

Photographs:

Plate 1. Giritale tank near Polonnaruwa, view towards W (Ritigala): restored irrigation reservoir, semi-evergreen monsoon forest of the dry zone (2-10-80)

Plate 2. Rice terraces in the mountains, near Mulhalkelle, northern slope of central highlands. Traditional agriculture of the wet zone (25-10-80; 1200 m)

Plate 3. Tea estate in Hatton area; typical factory, tea fields up to the hilltop (10-3-79; 1200 m)

Plate 4. Tea fields and Pinus afforestation in miserable condition. St. John`s Hill, Knuckles (4-6-80); 1300 m)

Plate 5. New clearings for vegetable cultivation on steep slopes.Hanguranketa-area (25-10-80;700 m)

Plate 6. Beach seine fishing in Nilaveli (22-3-80)

Plate 7. Coral island in the Maldives (Vilingili). Coconut-palms and Scaevola-shrub. The reef in the background is discerned by the dark water of the deeper sea-floor (24-11-80)

Plate 8. Plants in a Maldive village: Coconut, breadfruit, papaya (26-11-80)

Plate 9. Malé harbour. Handcarts and bicycles instead of motorcars; government buildings and dhonis ("house-boats") in the background (27-11-80)

Plate 10. Traditional sailing boat and modern cargo-vessel of the Maldives (28-11-80)

Plate 1.

Plate 2.

Plate 3.

Plate 4.

Plate 5.

Plate 6.

Plate 7.

Plate 8.

Plate 9.

Plate 10.

Appendix 2:

List of Plates of the contribution "Community Forestry in Nepal"

by Dietrich Schmidt-Vogt

Plate 1. Landscape in Sindhu Palchok District, north of Chautara. On the left, hilltop with plantation established by NAFP (23.2.1984/1570 m).

Plate 2. Agricultural landscape in Sindhu Palchok District, west of Chautara. Note remnant forests and the fodder trees on terraced land (19.7.1984/1400 m).

Plate 3. NE-facing slope with fodder trees on terraces, near Chautara (7.8.1984/1450 m).

Plate 4. Pinus patula plantation. Degraded land adjoining to the left indicates grazing pressure and the effective protection of plantations by the villagers; Padle Pani nursery, north of Chautara (5.12.1984/1550 m).

Plate 5. Pinus roxburghii plantation with natural regrowth of broadleaves, near Chautara (5.12.1984/1500 m).

Plate 1.

Plate 2.

Plate 3.

Plate 4.

Plate 5.

BEITRÄGE ZUR SÜDASIENFORSCHUNG

Stuttgart: Franz-Steiner-Verlag-Wiesbaden
ISSN 0170-3137

1 Cultures of the Hindukush: selected papers from the Hindu-Kush Cultural Conference held at Moesgård 1970 / ed.by Karl Jettmar. In collaboration with Lennart Edelberg. - 1974. XIV,146 p.
ISBN 3-515-01217-6

2 Die Holztempel des oberen Kulutales: in ihren historischen, religiösen und kunstgeschichtlichen Zusammenhängen / von Gabriele Jettmar. - 1974. XI,133 S. ISBN 3-515-01849-2

3 Regionalism in Hindi novels / by Indu Prakash Pandey. - 1974. 179 p. ISBN 3-515-01954-5

4 Community health and health motivation in South-East Asia: proceedings of an international seminar organized by the German Foundation for International Development and the Institute of Tropical Hygiene and Public Health, South Asia Institute, University of Heidelberg, 22 October to 10 November 1973, Berlin / ed.by Hans Jochen Diesfeld and Erich Kröger. - 1974. VIII,199p.
ISBN 3-515-01990-1

5 Die britische Militärpolitik in Indien und ihre Auswirkungen auf den britisch-indischen Finanzhaushalt 1878-1910 / von Werner Simon. - 1974. VI,296 S. ISBN 3-515-01978-2

6 Die wirtschaftliche Situation Pakistans nach der Sezession Bangladeshs / von Winfried von Urff; Heinz Ahrens; Peter Lutz; Bernhard May; Wolfgang-Peter Zingel. - 1974. - XIX,453 S.
ISBN 3-515-01979-0

7 Muslime und Christen in der Republik Indonesia / von Wendelin Wawer. - 1974. 326 S. ISBN 3-515-02042-X

8 The Muslim microcosm: Calcutta, 1918 to 1935 / by Kenneth McPherson. - 1974. VII,162 p. ISBN 3-515-01992-8

9 Adat und Gesellschaft: eine sozio-ethnologische Untersuchung zur Darstellung des Geistes- und Kulturlebens der Dajak in Kalimantan / von Johannes Enos Garang. - 1974. X,193 S.
ISBN 3-515-02048-9

10 The Indo-English novel: the impact of the West on literature in a developing country / by Klaus Steinvorth. - 1975. III, 149 p.
ISBN 3-515-02049-7

11 The position of Indian women in the light of legal reform: a socio-legal study of the legal position of Indian women as interpreted and enforced by the law courts compared and related to their position in the family and at work / by Angeles J. Almenas-Lipowsky. - 1975. IX,217 p. ISBN 3-515-02050-0

12 Zur Mobilisierung ländlicher Arbeitskräfte im anfänglichen Industrialisierungsprozess: ein Vergleich der Berufsstruktur in ausgewählten industrienahen und industriefernen Gemeinden Nordindiens / von Erhard W. Kropp. 2. unveränd. Aufl. - 1975. XVII, 231 S. ISBN 3-515-01976-6

13 Die Sozialisation tibetischer Kinder im soziokulturellen Wandel, dargestellt am Beispiel der Exiltibetersiedlung Dhor Patan (West Nepal) / von Gudrun Ludwar. - 1975. XI,209 S.
ISBN 3-515-02063-2

14 Die Steuerung der Direktinvestitionen im Rahmen einer rationalen Entwicklungspolitik / von Leo Rubinstein. - 1975. XI,260 S.
ISBN 3-515-02064-0

15 Ein erweitertes Harrod-Domar-Modell für die makroökonomische Programmierung in Entwicklungsländern: ein wachstumstheoretischer Beitrag zur Entwicklungsplanung / von Axel W. Seiler. - 1975. VII,230 S. ISBN 3-515-02092-6

16 Islam in Southern Asia: a survey of current research / ed. by Dietmar Rothermund. - 1975. VIII,126 p. ISBN 3-515-02095-0

17 Aspekte sozialer Ungleichheit in Südasien / hrsg. von Heinz Ahrens und Kerrin Gräfin Schwerin. - 1975. VII,215 S.
ISBN 3-515-02096-6

18 Probleme interdisziplinärer Forschung: organisations- und forschungssoziologische Untersuchung der Erfahrungen mit interdisziplinärer Zusammenarbeit im SFB 16 unter besonderer Betonung des Dhanbad-Projektes / von Dieter Blaschke. Unter Mitarbeit von Ingrid Lukatis. - 1976. XI,201 S. ISBN 3-515-02131-0

19 Einfluss des Bergbaus auf die Beschäftigungsstruktur in ländlichen Gemeinden: gezeigt am Beispiel des Dhanbad-Distriktes, Bihar, Indien / von Erhard W. Kropp. - 1976. XII,184 S.
ISBN 3-515-02132-9

20 Drei Jaina-Gedichte in Alt-Gujarâti: Edition, Übersetzung, Grammatik und Glossar / von George Baumann. - 1975.XVIII,176 S.
ISBN 3-515-02177-9

21 Eigentumsbeschränkungen in Indien / von Franz-Josef Vollmer. - 1975. VIII,147 S. ISBN 3-515-02307-0

22 Nomaden von Gharjistân: Aspekte der wirtschaftlichen, sozialen und politischen Organisation nomadischer Durrani-Paschtunen in Nordwestafghanistan / von Bernt Glatzer. - 1977. XII, 234 S.
ISBN 3-515-02137-X

23 Buddhistische Politik in Thailand: mit besonderer Berücksichtigung des heterodoxen Messianismus / von Walter Skrobanek. - 1976. VII,315 S. ISBN 3-515-02390-9

24 Lohnpolitik und wirtschaftliche Entwicklung: ein Beitrag zur Analyse der Verteilungsproblematik unter besonderer Berücksichtigung Indiens / von Gunther Dienemann. - 1977. VII,318 S.
ISBN 3-515-02389-5

25 Der Gleichheitssatz in der Praxis des indischen Zivilverfahrens / von Dierk Helmken. - 1976. XII,286 S. ISBN 3-515-02134-5

26 Der Einfluss von Produktionstechniken auf die Produktion der Hauptfruchtarten im pakistanischen Punjab: methodische Probleme der Erfassung und Quantifizierung / von Berhard May. - 1977.

XVIII,403 S. ISBN 3-515-02580-4

27 Tai-Khamti phonology and vocabulary / by Alfons Weidert. - 1977. 92 p. ISBN 3-515-02582-0

28 Rudras Geburt: systematische Untersuchungen zum Inzest in der Mythologie der Brâhmaṇas / von Joachim Deppert. - 1977. LX, 396 S. ISBN 3-515-02583-9

29 Der Reisanbau im unteren Kirindi Oya-Becken: Analyse einer Reisbaulandschaft im Südosten der Insel Ceylon / von Gisela Zaun-Axler. - 1977. XIX,286 S. ISBN 3-515-02584-7

30 Faktoren des Gesundwerdens in Gruppen und Ethnien: Verhandlungen des 2. Rundgesprächs 'Ethnomedizin' in Heidelberg vom 29. und 30. November 1974 unter Schirmherrschaft des Südasien-Instituts, Institut für Tropenhygiene und Öffentliches Gesundheitswesen und Seminar für Ethnologie / herausgegeben von Ekkehard Schröder. - 1977. XIII,125 S. ISBN 3-515-02585-5

31 Von Armut zu Elend: Kolonialherrschaft und Agrarverfassung in Chota Nagpur, 1858 - 1908 / von Detlef Schwerin. - 1977. XIX, 551 S. ISBN 3-515-02407-7

32 The Nilgiris: weather and climate of a mountain area in South India / by Hans J. von Lengerke. - 1977. XVIII,340 p. ISBN 3-515-02640-1

33 The social setting of Christian conversion in South India: the impact of the Wesleyan methodist missionaries on the Trichy-Tanjore diocese with special reference to the Harijan communities of the mass movement area 1820-1947 / by Sundararaj Manickam. - 1977. VIII,296 p. ISBN 3-515-02639-8

34 Religiöses Volksbrauchtum in Afghanistan: islamische Heiligenverehrung und Wallfahrtswesen im Raum Kabul / von Harald Einzmann. - 1977. IX,346 S. ISBN 3-515-02652-5

35 Untersuchungen des Königswahlmotivs in der indischen Märchenliteratur: Pañcadivyâdhivâsa / von Gabriella Steermann-Imre. - 1977. XII,316 S. ISBN 3-515-02597-9

36 Schichtungsmodelle, Schichtungstheorien und die sozialstrukturelle Rolle von Erziehung: eine theoretische Diskussion und eine empirische Fallstudie aus Indien / von John P. Neelsen. - 1976. XII,240 S. ISBN 3-515-02638-X

37 Innovationsfaktoren in der Landwirtschaft Indiens: gezeigt am Beispiel ausgewählter Dörfer des Dhanbad Distrikts, Bihar, Indien / von Harald Hänsch. - 1977. XII,277,34,4 S. ISBN 3-515-02704-1

38 Der indisch-pakistanische Konflikt und seine wirtschaftlichen und sozialen Kosten für Pakistan in den Jahren 1958-1968 / von Hans Frey. - 1978. XIX,234 S. ISBN 3-515-02716-5

39 Arleng Alam: die Sprache der Mikir; Grammatik und Texte / von Karl-Heinz Grüssner. - 1978. 222 S. ISBN 3-515-02717-3

40 Indian merchants and the decline of Surat, c. 1700-1750 / by

Ashin Das Gupta. - 1978. X,305 p. ISBN 3-515-02718-1

41 Bangladesh: constitutional quest for autonomy, 1950-1971 / by Moudud Ahmed. - 1978. XVI,373 p. ISBN 3-515-02908-7

42 Bestimmungsgründe und Alternativen divergierender regionaler Wachstumsverläufe in Entwicklungsländern: eine theoretische und empirische Analyse unter besonderer Berücksichtigung der Regionalentwicklung in Ost- und Westpakistan 1947-1970 / von Heinz-Dietmar Ahrens. - 1978. XV,392 S. ISBN 3-515-02827-7

43 Das tibetische Handwerkertum vor 1959 / von Veronika Ronge. - 1978. VIII,181 S. ISBN 3-515-02793-9

44 Hunza und China (1761-1891): 130 Jahre einer Beziehung und ihre Bedeutung für die wirtschaftliche und politische Entwicklung Hunzas im 18. und 19. Jahrhundert / von Irmtraud Müller-Stellrecht. - 1978. VII,139 S. 3-515-02799-8

45 Interdependenzen zwischen gesamtwirtschaftlichem Wachstum und regionaler Verteilung in Pakistan / von Heinz Ahrens und Wolfgang-Peter Zingel. - 1978. XXXVI,882 S. ISBN 3-515-02830-7

46 Institutioneller Agrarkredit und traditionelle Schuldverhältnisse: Distrikt Dhanbad, Bihar, Indien / von Hans-Dieter Roth. - 1978. XIX,364 S. ISBN 3-515-02795-5

47 Comparative evaluation of road construction techniques in Nepal / by Hans C. Rieger and Binayak Bhadra. - 1979. XIII,257 p. ISBN 3-515-03120-0

48 Labour utilization and farm income in rural Thailand: results of case studies in rural villages, 1969-70 / by Friedrich W. Fuhs in cooperation with Gregory Capellari and Fred V.Goericke. - 1979. XVI, 371 p. ISBN 3-515-03001-8

49 Aruṇantis Śivajñânasiddhiyâr: die Erlangung des Wissens um Śiva oder um die Erlösung. Unter Beifügung einer Einleitung und Meykaṇṭadevas Śivajñânabodha aus dem Tamil übersetzt und kommentiert von Hilko Wiardo Schomerus. Hrsg. von Hermann Berger, Ayyadurai Dhamotharan und Dieter B.Kapp. 2 Bde. - 1981.XVI,745 S. ISBN 3-515-03874-4

50 Tamil dictionaries: a bibliography / by Ayyadurai Dhamotharan. - 1978. 185 p. ISBN 3-515-03005-0

51 Die Problematik regionaler Entwicklungsunterschiede in Entwicklungsländern: eine theoretische und empirische Analyse, dargestellt am Beispiel Pakistans unter Verwendung der Hauptkomponentenmethode / von Wolfgang-Peter Zingel. - 1979. XIV,554 S. ISBN 3-515-03002-6

52 Viêt-Nam: die nationalistische und marxistische Ideologie im Spätwerk von Phan-Bội-Chau (1867-1940) / von Jörgen Unselt. - 1980. XIII,304 S. ISBN 3-515-03133-2

53 Auswirkungen der Nahrungsmittelhilfe unter P. L. 480 auf den Agrarsektor der Entwicklungsländer: dargestellt am Beispiel Indiens / von Joachim von Plocki. - 1979. 240 S. ISBN 3-515-03144-8

54 Paschtunwali: ein Ehrenkodex und seine rechtliche Relevanz / von Willi Steul. - 1981. XIV,313 S. ISBN 3-515-03167-7

55 The Stûpa: its religious, historical and architectural significance / ed. by Anna Libera Dallapiccola in collaboration with Stephanie Zingel-Avé Lallemant. - 1980. VII, 359, [103] p. ISBN 3-515-02979-6

56 Faktorproportionen, internationale Arbeitsteilung und Aussenhandelspolitik: eine theoretische und empirische Analyse unter besonderer Berücksichtigung von Singapur, Westmalaysia und Pakistan / von Norbert Wagner. - 1980.XV,333 S. ISBN 3-515-03300-9

57 Jyotiṣa: das System der indischen Astrologie / von Hans-Georg Türstig. - 1980. XVIII,343 S. ISBN 3-515-03283-5

58 Naṉṉûl mûlamum kûḻaṅkaittampirâṉ uraiyum / ed.by Ayyadurai Dhamotharan. - 1980. XXVIII,246 p. ISBN 3-515-03284-3

59 Britische Indien-Politik, 1926-1932: Motive, Methoden und Misserfolg imperialer Politik am Vorabend der Dekolonisation / von Horst-Joachim Leue. - 1981. XI,259 S. ISBN 3-515-03395-5

60 Städte in Südasien: Geschichte, Gesellschaft, Gestalt / hrsg. von Hermann Kulke; Hans Christoph Rieger; Lothar Lutze. - 1982. XVIII,376,41 S. ISBN 3-515-03396-3

61 Die Erörterung der Wirksamkeit: Bhartṛharis Kriyâsamuddeśa und Helârâjas Prakâśa zum ersten Male aus dem Sanskrit übersetzt, mit einer Einführung und einem Glossar versehen / von Giovanni Bandini. - 1980. 200 S. ISBN 3-515-03391-2

62 Die landwirtschaftliche Produktion in Indien: Ackerbau-Technologie und traditionale Agrargesellschaft dargestellt nach dem Arthasâstra und Dharmasâstra / von Johannes Laping. - 1982. X, 155 S. ISBN 3-515-03521-4

63 Kânphaṭâ: Untersuchungen zu Kult, Mythologie und Geschichte śivaitischer Tantriker in Nepal / von Günter Unbescheid. - 1980. XXXIII,197,16 S. ISBN 3-515-03478-1

64 Die Kasten-Klassenproblematik im städtisch-industriellen Bereich: historisch-empirische Fallstudie über die Industriestadt Kanpur in Uttar Pradesh, Indien / von Maren Bellwinkel. - 1980. 1980. XII,284 S. ISBN 3-515-03499-4

65 Tamang ritual texts 1: preliminary studies in the folk-religion of an ethnic minority in Nepal / by András Höfer. - 1981. 184p. ISBN 3-515-03585-0

66 Tamang ritual texts 2 / by András Höfer. - (forthcoming) ISBN 3-515-03852-3

67 Towards reducing the dependence on capital imports: a planning model for Pakistan's policy of self-reliance / by Heinz Ahrens and Wolfgang-Peter Zingel. With a contribution by Syed Nawab Haider Naqvi. - 1982. XVI,337 p. ISBN 3-515-03853-1

68 Aspekte der regionalen wirtschaftlichen Integration zwischen

Entwicklungsländern: das Beispiel der ASEAN / von Alfred Kraft. - 1982. X,298 S. ISBN 3-515-03801-9

69 Indien, Nepal, Sri Lanka: Süd-Süd-Beziehungen zwischen Symmetrie und Dependenz / von Citha Doris Maass. - 1982. XXI, 380 S. ISBN 3-515-03802-7

70 Grundbedürfnisse als Gegenstand der Entwicklungspolitik: interdisziplinäre Aspekte der Grundbedarfsstrategie / Norbert Wagner und Hans Christoph Rieger (Hrsg.) - 1982. VIII,220 S. ISBN 3-515-03838-8

71 The vagrant peasant: agrarian distress and desertion in Bengal, 1770 to 1830 / by Aditee Nag Chowdhury-Zilly. - 1982. XV,196 p. ISBN 3-515-03855-8

72 Orissa: a comprehensive and classified bibliography / by Hermann Kulke in collaboration with Gaganendranath Dash and Manmath Nath Das, Karuna Sagar Behera. - 1982. XXIII,416 p. ISBN 3-515-03593-1

73 Adat, Macht und lokale Eliten:eine Studie zur Machtstruktur der Pfarrei Habi in Sikka, Flores, Indonesien anhand der Einführung der Institution Gabungan Kontas 1975/76; eine empirische Untersuchung / von Paul Rudolf Nunheim. - 1982. XVI,345 S. ISBN 3-515-03834-5

74 Tamil: Sprache als politisches Symbol; politische Literatur in der Tamilsprache in den Jahren 1945 bis 1967; mit besonderer Berücksichtigung der Schriften der Führer der dravidischen Bewegung: E. V. Râmacâmi und C. N. Aṇṇâturai / von Dagmar Hellmann-Rajanayagam. - 1984. VII,249 S. ISBN 3-515-03894-9

75 Moderne Gesetzgebung in Indien und ihre Auswirkung auf die Landbevölkerung: eine Dorfstudie aus Uttar Pradesh / von Eva Prochazka. - 1982. XI,133 S. ISBN 3-515-03893-0

76 Status and affinity in middle India / by Georg Pfeffer. - 1982. VII,104 p. ISBN 3-515-03913-9

77 Indology and law: studies in honour of Professor J. Duncan M. Derrett / ed. by Günther-Dietz Sontheimer and Parameswara Kota Aithal. - 1982. XI,463 p. ISBN 3-515-03748-9

78 Über Entstehungsprozesse in der Philosophie des Nyâya-Vaiśeṣika-Systems / von Hans-Georg Türstig. - 1982. XIX,101 S. ISBN 3-515-03951-1

79 Cheap lives and dear limbs: the British transformation of the Bengal criminal law 1769-1817 / by Jörg Fisch. - 1983. VII, 154 p. ISBN 3-515-04012-9

80 Brata und Âlpanâ in Bengalen / von Eva Maria Gupta. - 1983. X, 210 S. ISBN 3-515-04063-3

81 The Moḍî documents from Tanjore in Danish collections / edited, translated and analysed by Elisabeth Strandberg. - 1983. 386 p. ISBN 3-515-04080-3

82 Agrarverfassung und Agrarentwicklung in Thailand / von Fried-

rich W. Fuhs. - 1985. XVIII,311 S. ISBN 3-515-04553-8

83 Mokṣa in Jainism, according to Umâsvâti / by Robert J.Zydenbos. - 1983. IX,81 p. ISBN 3-515-04053-6

84 Fischerei und Fischereiwirtschaft im nördlichen Ceylon: Standort und Lebensraum der Fischer im Norden der Tropeninsel / von Thomas Gläser. - 1983. XV,196 S. ISBN 3-515-04054-4

85 Thailands Lehrer zwischen 'Tradition' und 'Fortschritt': eine empirische Untersuchung politisch-sozialer und pädagogischer Einstellungen thailändischer Lehrerstudenten des Jahres 1974 / von Ingrid Liebig-Hundius. - 1984. XII,342 S. ISBN 3-515-04121-4

86 Ethnologie und Geschichte: Festschrift für Karl Jettmar / hrsg. von Peter Snoy. - 1983. 654 S. ISBN 3-515-04104-4

87 Malediven und Lakkadiven: Materialien zur Bibliographie der Atolle im Indischen Ozean / von Thomas Malten. - 1983. 101 S. ISBN 3-515-04125-7

88 Astor: eine Ethnographie / von Adam Nayyar. - 1986. XIII,120 S. ISBN 3-515-04344-6

89 Zwischen Reform und Rebellion: über die Entwicklung des Islams in Minangkabau (Westsumatra) zwischen den beiden Reformbewegungen der Padri (1837) und der Modernisten (1908); ein Beitrag zur Geschichte der Islamisierung Indonesiens / von Werner Kraus - 1984. X,236 S. ISBN 3-515-04286-5

90 Energie und wirtschaftliche Entwicklung in Entwicklungsländern: das Beispiel Nepal / von Jürgen Steiger. - 1984. XX,329 S. ISBN 3-515-04345-4

91 Kampf um Malakka: eine wirtschaftsgeschichtliche Studie über den portugiesischen und niederländischen Kolonialismus in Südostasien / von Malcolm Dunn. - 1984. XV,275 S. ISBN 3-515-04123-0

92 Portraits in sechs Fürstenstaaten Rajasthans vom 17. bis zum 20. Jahrhundert: Voraussetzungen, Entwicklungen, Veränderungen; mit besonderer Berücksichtigung kulturhistorischer Faktoren / von Juliane Anna Lia Molitor. - 1985. 179 S. ISBN 3-515-04346-2

93 Bangladesh: era of Sheikh Mujibur Rahman / by Moudud Ahmed. - 1984. XI,282 p. ISBN 3-515-04266-0

94 Die politische Stellung der Sikhs innerhalb der indischen Nationalbewegung, 1935-1947 / von Christine Effenberg. - 1984.VI, 232 S. ISBN 3-515-04284-9

95 'Hir': zur strukturellen Deutung des Panjabi-Epos von Waris Shah / von Doris Buddenberg. - 1985. VIII,156 p. ISBN 3-515-04347-0

96 Dialectics and dream: an evaluation of Bishnu Dey's poetry in the light of Neo-Marxian aesthetics / by Subhoranjan Dasgupta. - (forthcoming)

97 Das Tor zur Unterwelt: Mythologie und Kult des Termitenhügels in der schriftlichen und mündlichen Tradition Indiens / von Ditte König. - 1984. XII,389 S. ISBN 3-515-04410-8

98 Religionspolitik in Britisch-Indien 1793 - 1813: christliches Sendungsbewußtsein und Achtung hinduistischer Tradition im Widerstreit / von Cornelia Witz. - 1985. VIII, ISBN 3-515-04527-9

99 Landschenkungen und staatliche Entwicklung im frühmittelalterlichen Bengalen (5. bis 13. Jahrhundert n. Chr.) / von Swapna Bhattacharya. - 1985. XIV,171 S. ISBN 3-515-04534-1

100 Vijayanagara - city and empire:new currents of research / ed. by Anna Libera Dallapiccola in collaboration with Stephanie Zingel-Avé Lallemant. - 1985. ISBN 3-515-04554-6
Vol.1. Texts. - XIII,439 p.
Vol.2. Reference and documentation. - X,221 p.

101 Zur Relevanz mikroökonomischer Theorie für die Analyse des ökonomischen Verhaltens der Wirtschaftssubjekte in Agrarsektoren von Entwicklungsländern / von Rainer Marggraf. - 1985.IX,295 S. ISBN 3-515-04513-9

102 Zur Methodik kosten-nutzen-analytischer Bewertung verteilungsorientierter Preispolitik: mit empirischen Untersuchungen zur Agrarpreispolitik Thailands und der Europäischen Gemeinschaft / von Lothar Oberländer. - 1985. XV,320 p. ISBN 3-515-04490-6

103 Zentrale Gewalt in Nagar (Karakorum): politische Organisationsformen, ideologische Begründungen des Königtums und Veränderungen in der Moderne / von Jürgen Frembgen. - (forthcoming)

104 Regionale Tradition in Südasien / hrsg. von Herrmann Kulke und Dietmar Rothermund. - 1985. XXIV,256 p. ISBN 3-515-04519-8

105 Law and society East and West: dharma, li and nomos, their contribution to thought and to life / by Reinhard May. - 1905. 251 S. ISBN 3-515-04537-6

106 Darul-Islam: Kartosuwirjos Kampf um éinen islamischen Staat Indonesiens / von Holk H. Dengel. - 1986. VIII, 255 S. ISBN 3-515-04784-0

107 Aṅkâḷaparamēcuvari: a goddess of Tamilnadu; her myths and cult / by Eveline Meyer. - 1986. XII,329 p. ISBN 3/515-04702-6

108 Die Vâḍabalija in Andhra Pradesh und in Orissa: Aspekte der wirtschaftlichen und sozialen Organisation einer maritimen Gesellschaft / von Elisabeth Schömbucher. - 1986. IX,253 S. ISBN 3-515-04835-9

109 Guru-Śiṣya-Sambandha: das Meister-Schüler-Verhältnis im traditionellen und modernen Hinduismus / Ralph Mark Steinmann. - 1986. XI,312 S. ISBN 3-515-04851-0

110 Herrschaft und Verwaltung im östlichen Indien unter den späten Gangas, ca.1038-1434 / von Shishir Kumar Panda. - 1986. III,184 S. ISBN 3-515-04861-8

112 Developments in Asia: economic, political and cultural aspects / ed. by. C. H. Effenberg. - (in press)

113 Annotated bibliography of new Indonesian literature on the history of Indonesia / by Holk H. Dengel. - (in press)

114 Die Stadt Badulla: Strukturentwicklung und Zentralität eines Ortes im östlichen zentralen Hochland der Insel Ceylon (Sri Lanka) / von Siegbert Dicke. - (in press)

115 Social accounting matrix und politische Entwicklungsökonomie: zu einem praxisnahen Daten- und Modellsystem für Entwicklungsländer / von Elmar Kleiner. - (in press)

116 The problem of 'Graeter Baluchistan': a study of Baluch nationalism / Inayatullah Baloch. - (in press)